Praise for *Creator, Father, King*

Joshua Cooley has written a terrific devotional for young people! From January 1 to December 31, this is a biblically solid and relevant collection of insights into God's Word, Christ-centered thinking, and Jesus-honoring living. I will buy this book for my grandchildren—I can't think of a stronger endorsement!

Randy Alcorn
Author of Heaven, Does God Want Us to Be Happy?, *and* It's All about Jesus

In a world of uncertainty, today's young people need something they can depend on. They need truth—not the changing waves of cultural opinions. Joshua Cooley's book, *Creator, Father, King: A One Year Journey with God*, is just what teenagers need. In daily bites, this book masterfully gives young readers a thorough foundation in biblical truth—the kind of real information about essential matters of faith that can guide them through their entire lives. It's like having a friendly, gentle mentor providing a complete, exciting education about God and his world—and the importance of having a relationship with him through Jesus Christ.

Dave Branon
Author of Beyond the Valley *and writer for* Our Daily Bread

Joshua has hit another home run with *Creator, Father, King*. As a father of young children, I am always looking for ways to shepherd their hearts to the Lord, and this devotional is perfect. Joshua has presented a great opportunity to begin the discipline of spending time with the Lord on a daily basis. I pray that God's love for you through his Son, Jesus Christ, would be revealed through this devotional!

Brian Roberts
Former fourteen-year major league baseball player and two-time all-star

Creator, Father, King is an insightful and inspiring devotional that gives young people a valuable tool to help them grow in their Christian walk by pointing them to the glory and majesty of God. Joshua Cooley has done youth and their parents a great service by writing this devotional book.

Tim Ellsworth

Director of communications at Union University and author of God in the Whirlwind *and* Pujols: More Than the Game

Popular author and youth leader Joshua Cooley has crafted a collection of daily devotionals for teens that are current and inspiring. Each day's reading is designed to magnify the Lord as Creator, Father, or King by highlighting biblical truth in a voice that connects with twenty-first century teenagers. This will be a great tool for individual discipleship, family devotions, Bible study in a local school, or a study guide for your entire youth group. No matter the setting, teens will grow as they meditate daily on his Word.

Ken Coley

EdD, senior professor of Christian education, Southeastern Baptist Theological Seminary

Joshua Cooley masterfully ties engaging content to a faithful theological foundation, this time creating a devotional for youth. This 365-day journey affords young readers an opportunity to gain a deeper understanding of God as an amazing Creator, a compassionate Father, and a reigning King. Each day delivers effective explanations of the biblical text coupled with relatable stories, answers to honest questions, and engaging fun facts. It is like having a youth pastor walking day-by-day with your child.

Eliza Huie

LCPC and author of Raising Kids in a Screen-Saturated World *and* Raising Teens in a Hyper-Sexualized World

God's character, his power, and his unfathomable love for us are foundational to Christian faith. Joshua does a fantastic job taking readers on a year-long journey into a deeper understanding of their heavenly Father. This is an especially important resource for kids today.

Jesse Florea

Author of The One Year Sports Devotions for Kids, Growing Up Super

Average: The Adventures of Average Boy, The One Year Devotions for Active Boys, *and* The One Year Every Day Devotions

As a high schooler, I was deeply formed in my young faith by reading through Oswald Chambers' devotional classic, *My Utmost for His Highest*. In *Creator, Father, King*, Joshua Cooley offers today's teenagers 365 daily readings that are deeply rooted in Scripture and accessible for adolescents. If your child has questions about God, this book will help them find the answers!

Drew Hill
Pastor and award-winning author of Alongside: Loving Teenagers with the Gospel

Creator, Father, King: A One Year Journey with God is a resource that ministers truth to youth while cultivating an atmosphere where meaningful conversation can happen with their parents. This resource is such a gift, for it leads young hearts to God by rehearsing the gospel of Jesus Christ while providing great potential to strengthen the parent/child relationship. This is a double blessing for the sake of Christ's name in the heart of youth and in their homes.

Bud Burk
Pastor for children and family discipleship, Bethlehem Baptist Church, downtown campus

Joshua Cooley understands the depths of theology and the world of boys of girls! His engaging language will draw kids in and encourage them to grow in their knowledge of God every day. I love the "Now What?" sections that give kids an immediate way to act upon the truths they're learning; it'll help them draw a straight line from doctrine to life.

Jared Kennedy
Co-founder and managing editor of Gospel-Centered Family and author of The Beginner's Gospel Story Bible *and* God Made Me for Worship

In *Creator, Father, King*, Joshua Cooley weaves together a Bible study of God's character, with compelling illustrations and fun facts that will keep you turning the page, looking for more, day by day. Joshua makes important gospel connections to help the reader understand the larger story of the Bible. The gospel message he presents in the pages of this book has the power to transform lives. If you're looking for a Bible study you can easily fit into your day, or for a mealtime devotional to use with your family, get a copy of *Creator, Father, King*. You won't be disappointed.

Marty Machowski
Pastor and author of Long Story Short: Ten-Minute Devotions to Draw Your Family to God, The Ology, The Gospel Story Bible, *and other gospel-rich resources for church and home*

I'm always looking for the best books—Bible resources that I can place with confidence in the hands of my own kids. This book is a perfect fit. With *Creator, Father, King*, Joshua Cooley is fast becoming one of the most trusted voices for teens today. Fusing Bible study, theology, and wisdom for life, with lots of fun and interesting facts, this new 365-day devotional will capture your middle- and high-schoolers' interest and guide them into the riches of God's Word.

Champ Thornton
Pastor and author of several books, including The Radical Book for Kids *and* Why Do We Say Good Night?

How many young people give up reading the Bible because it felt boring, confusing, or irrelevant? This book will not only teach you how to read the Bible, but it will help you meet God in the Bible. And learning to meet God in the Bible will prepare you, more than anything else, for whatever future he brings for you.

Marshall Segal
Managing editor of desiringGod.org and author of Not Yet Married

Creator, Father, King

creator
father
KING

A ONE YEAR® JOURNEY WITH GOD

JOSHUA COOLEY

Tyndale House Publishers
Carol Stream, Illinois

Visit Tyndale online at tyndale.com.

TYNDALE and Tyndale's quill logo are registered trademarks of Tyndale House Publishers. *Wander* and the Wander logo are trademarks of Tyndale House Ministries. Wander is an imprint of Tyndale House Ministries, Carol Stream, Illinois.

Designed by Jacqueline L. Nuñez

Edited by Erin M. Gwynne

Unless otherwise indicated, all Scripture quotations are taken from the *Holy Bible*, New Living Translation, copyright © 1996, 2004, 2015 by Tyndale House Foundation. Used by permission of Tyndale House Publishers, Carol Stream, Illinois 60188. All rights reserved.

Scripture quotations marked ESV are taken from The ESV® Bible (The Holy Bible, English Standard Version®), copyright © 2001 by Crossway, a publishing ministry of Good News Publishers. Used by permission. All rights reserved.

Scripture quotations marked NIV are taken from the Holy Bible, *New International Version*,® *NIV.*® Copyright © 1973, 1978, 1984, 2011 by Biblica, Inc.® Used by permission. All rights reserved worldwide.

For information about special discounts for bulk purchases, please contact Tyndale House Publishers at csresponse@tyndale.com, or call 1-800-323-9400.

ISBN 978-1-4964-3494-4

Printed in the United States of America

26   25   24   23   22   21   20
7   6   5   4   3   2   1

TO EVERY YOUNG READER:
May you grow richly in your faith, in God's amazing grace,
and in the knowledge of his endless love for you in Jesus Christ.

Introduction

GOD.

In the English language, that word is only three letters long. Yet it brings a sense of wonder, reverence, and awe. Few other words in human history carry its weight—or mystery.

Billions of people around the world believe in God—or at least the idea of a supreme deity or higher power that governs the universe. But how many people fully understand who God is, what he is like, and why he created them? How many people know that they can have a close, personal relationship with the Creator of all things? How many people realize that they can bring all their sin and brokenness to him? How many people understand how to worship him? How many people truly grasp that they can *know* God?

These are questions of eternal significance. Yet there seem to be as many mistaken ideas about God in the world as there are fish in the ocean. This is a problem. People are looking in all the wrong places—or not looking at all. While we can't know everything about God—he's far too great for that—he has sufficiently revealed himself to us in his Word, the Bible. The Creator *wants* to be known by his creation!

Everything we need to know about God is found in the Bible, which God himself inspired. Scripture is our only source of inerrant, authoritative, and sufficient truth about God and his plan of salvation for sinful humanity through his Son, Jesus Christ. This devotional book was written to help draw you closer to God by consistently pointing you back to his Word. Our quest will reveal truth about the Lord from all sixty-six books of the Bible—Genesis through Revelation.

So we approach our goal—deepening our understanding, worship, and exaltation of God through faith in Jesus—with great joy and excitement! There is no greater purpose in life than glorifying our Creator. As 1 Corinthians 10:31 says, "Whether you eat or drink, or whatever you do, do it all for the glory of God."

But we also embark on our study of God with great care and humility.

How do you adequately describe the great I Am? How do you communicate all the wonders of the Ancient of Days? How do you perfectly praise the eternal King of the universe who reigns in inexplicable heavenly splendor?

You don't.

At least, you acknowledge there's no way to do it *perfectly*. Any book (outside Scripture) that tries to comprehensively describe God's glory and majesty will fall short. The Lord God Almighty is far too great to be summarized by human words.

Yet he still calls us to worship him and draw near to him. So we take heart, lift our hands toward heaven and cry, "Abba, Father!," desperately longing for more of his presence, peace, power, and love, which he delights in lavishing upon his children.

Wherever you are in your faith journey, I pray that by reading this book, God will conform you more into the image of his Son through faith in Christ and obedience to his Word. As Hosea 6:3 says, "Oh, that we might know the Lord! Let us press on to know him. He will respond to us as surely as the arrival of dawn or the coming of rains in early spring."

So turn the page. Let's press on together to know the Lord. He will faithfully respond.

Joshua Cooley

JANUARY 1

Your word is a lamp to guide my feet and a light for my path.

PSALM 119:105

GET READY.

It's a new year, and we are about to embark on an epic journey. This book will be an exciting, ambitious adventure purely because of its Subject. The theme is not a what, where, or when. It's a Who.

For the next 365 days, we'll be talking about God. We will explore God's perfect character and his eternal plan of redemption to save sinners. This is a monumental task, impossible to accomplish in one devotional book. God is too big to be contained within finite, printed pages. But he calls us to seek him and know him. So we excitedly prepare for our quest.

As we do, we might ask questions. The critical questions on a journey of this magnitude are endless:

- Who is God?
- What is he like?
- Can we know him at all? If so, how much?
- Why can't we see him? Or can we?
- Is he perfectly good?

The list goes on and on. We certainly don't want to get distracted by the questions and swerve off course as many others have.

Like travelers exploring a vast territory, we need a map—something to guide our trek. So we begin this yearlong study of God by turning to the only source of divinely inspired knowledge that God has provided: the Bible.

What's It Mean?

The answers to everything we need to know about God can be found in the Bible. It is the foundation for the Christian faith, the source of our knowledge of God, and the basis for this devotional.

The Lord has graciously chosen to reveal himself to us through

Scripture. We'll go into much greater depth about God's Word later on, but at the outset, it's important to acknowledge that the Bible is the only inerrant, authoritative, and fully sufficient book that was given to us by God himself, written under divine inspiration by holy men (2 Peter 1:20-21).

God cannot be fully known. He is far too great for that. But everything he wants us to know, he has revealed to us in his Word!

Now What?
Commit to reading *Creator, Father, King* this year. Have your Bible with you so you can study the verses mentioned in this book.

Did You Know?
Approximately forty authors, all under the Holy Spirit's inspiration, wrote the Bible over the span of at least 1,300 years.

JANUARY 2

The LORD our God has secrets known to no one. We are not accountable for them, but we and our children are accountable forever for all that he has revealed to us, so that we may obey all the terms of these instructions.

DEUTERONOMY 29:29

HAVE YOU EVER WONDERED about the following subjects?

- the size of the universe and all the wonders in outer space
- the secrets found within the depths of the world's oceans
- the human body
- dinosaurs and how they went extinct
- the opposite sex and why they do what they do

(That last one is a real brainteaser!)

These are fascinating topics in life that we might learn a lot about but never fully understand. We can add another, infinitely greater, entity to the list: God.

What's It Mean?

At the outset of our exciting, wonderfully worthwhile exploration of God's holy nature and righteous acts throughout history, it's important to understand this: we can know a lot about the Lord, but we certainly can't know everything.

Does this concern you? Does it disappoint you? It shouldn't!

God is holy, meaning he is set apart and majestically transcendent above his creation. (We'll dig deeper into God's holiness in the January 10–11 devotions.) His ways are inscrutable—impossible to understand.

This is a good thing! After all, a god who can be fully known by finite humans isn't much of a god at all. But this is not the biblical God. Every time the Bible speaks about this aspect of God, it calls on us to worship him for his inscrutability.

As the apostle Paul says in Romans 11:33-36, "Oh, how great are God's riches and wisdom and knowledge! How impossible it is for us to understand his decisions and his ways! For who can know the LORD's thoughts? Who knows enough to give him advice? And who has given him so much that he needs to pay it back? For everything comes from him and exists by his power and is intended for his glory. All glory to him forever! Amen."

Despite God's incomprehensible majesty, he is not aloof or unknowable. Amazingly, he is a personal God who desires close fellowship with his children. He has made known a great deal about himself to us in Scripture. As today's verse says, we are "accountable forever for all that he has revealed to us."

Now What?

Join Paul in giving glory to the holy God who makes himself known through his Word!

Did You Know?

Today's verse was part of God's covenant given to Israel through Moses before his people entered the Promised Land.

JANUARY 3

Before the mountains were born, before you gave birth to the earth and the world, from beginning to end, you are God.

PSALM 90:2

ETERNITY IS A REALLY LONG TIME.

The concept of eternity stretches the human imagination beyond comprehension. Our finite minds can only process so much, and our earthly experience tells us that everything has a starting and ending point. How, we wonder, can something never have a beginning or an end?

But the Bible clearly states that eternity is real. In fact, Scripture declares that humans are created beings with a clear starting point (conception in our mothers' wombs) who possess souls that will live forever (either in glory or judgment after physical death, depending on whether we have submitted our lives to Jesus Christ in repentance and faith). Like humans, everything else in the universe—rocks, trees, mountains, oceans, all creatures in the animal kingdom—was created.

But there is one Being who wasn't. There is Someone who has neither beginning nor end.

He is God.

What's It Mean?

Perhaps the idea that God is fully eternal—without beginning or end—doesn't surprise you. Maybe you've heard it many times before, and you're wondering what the big deal is.

Well, it's a very big deal.

If God weren't eternal, he'd have a point of origin like everything else. Anything that is created is subservient to something—or someone—else.

But no one created the Lord God Almighty. He is the self-existent Creator of all. He has always existed and always will.

This means that God doesn't play by anyone else's rules. He governs everything that he made and sets all the standards of right and wrong. When you self-exist before time, light, matter, energy, life, and anything else in the universe—and then you create all those things out of your own power, will, and love—you have the authority to rule over everything exactly as you choose.

God—eternal in glory, power, and majesty—deserves all our praise!

Now What?
Take some time to think and pray about what God's eternal nature means for your life.

Did You Know?
In Revelation 1:8, God exclaims, "I am the Alpha and the Omega—the beginning and the end." In ancient Greek, the original New Testament language, *alpha* is the first letter of the ancient Greek alphabet, while *omega* is the last letter. God used a vivid first-century cultural metaphor to describe his nature.

JANUARY 4

God is Spirit, so those who worship him
must worship in spirit and in truth.

JOHN 4:24

AS HUMANS, WE LOVE TO SEE, smell, hear, taste, and touch. That's
why the world around us is so wonderful. There are so many good things
for our senses to enjoy.

Take our sense of sight, for example. With our eyes, we can behold a
gorgeous Maui sunset, or the snowcapped Swiss Alps, or a cloudless night
with a million stars magnificently winking at us. We can see dolphins danc-
ing through the surf, stallions sprinting across the turf, and eagles soaring
through the sky.

But the Being who created and rules the universe is completely invisible
to us. We cannot see God.

What's It Mean?

As today's verse says, God is a spirit. Maybe this surprises you. But God's
spiritual nature is such an important topic to understand that for the next
two days, we're going to discuss this aspect of God's character.

God's invisibility doesn't mean he's not real. Some people don't believe
in God just because they can't see him. But if something's existence is determined merely by human sight, then by that logic, we'd have to conclude
that wind doesn't exist either. This, of course, is absurd. Even though we
can't see wind, we know it exists because we see its effects when it rustles
tree leaves, or fills a yacht's sail, or causes great damage in a hurricane.

Likewise, even though we can't see God, we know he exists because
we see "his effects," so to speak. We see the beautiful world he created. We
marvel at how he keeps the entire universe running in an orderly way. We
rejoice at how he works in human hearts.

The apostle Paul addresses this in Romans 1:18-20 when he talks about
"sinful, wicked people who suppress the truth by their wickedness. They
know the truth about God because he has made it obvious to them. For ever

since the world was created, people have seen the earth and sky. Through everything God made, they can clearly see his invisible qualities—his eternal power and divine nature. So they have no excuse for not knowing God."

In other words, not believing in God just because you can't see him is not a good enough excuse. Likewise, Psalm 14:1 says, "Only fools say in their hearts, 'There is no God.'"

Don't be a fool! Look further than your eyes and believe in the God who is spirit.

Now What?
Pray for the faith to believe in the God you cannot see.

Did You Know?
In John 20:29, Jesus blessed everyone who believes in him without the benefit of seeing him!

JANUARY 5

God is Spirit, so those who worship him must
worship in spirit and in truth.

JOHN 4:24

TODAY IS THE SECOND part of our two-part series on God's spiritual nature. This is of vital importance in understanding God.

Yesterday, we learned that the invisible God calls us to believe in him even though we can't see him. But perhaps you're still scratching your head, not fully understanding God's spiritual nature. You might be wondering, *Okay, so God is a spirit. But what does that mean? What is he like?*

What's It Mean?

First, we must admit God's greatness and our limitations. Any human attempt to fully explain God's character and attributes, including his spiritual nature, is going to fall far short.

To help us understand, let's look at what God is not. He is not "The Man Upstairs." He's also not a white-bearded Father Time, a bolt-throwing Zeus-like character, or a ghost. He is not a spirit that is present in all the things he created (that's called pantheism). All of these notions are unbiblical, man-made ideas that dishonor God and grossly misrepresent his nature, holiness, and majesty.

God does not have a size or shape. He doesn't have a body or consist of physical matter. Whenever Scripture talks about God having human body characteristics (e.g., his "arm" in Exodus 15:16; his "lips" in Isaiah 30:27; his "eyes" in Hebrews 4:13), the biblical author is using metaphorical examples to help his readers understand something about God.

God is also not confined to a particular time or a place, like humans are. And he cannot be seen unless he reveals himself in a form that we can perceive, such as the pillar of cloud and fire (Exodus 13:21-22), Isaiah's vision (Isaiah 6), or the partial revelation of his glory to Moses (Exodus 33:18-23).

There is great mystery to this aspect of God, and that's okay. God never intended us to know him fully; he is far too awesome for that. But we can know him intimately. He is a personal God whom we can call our heavenly Father.

All told, he is more amazing than we can imagine!

Now What?
Praise the God whom you cannot see but you can know deeply and personally through Jesus Christ!

Did You Know?
God's spiritual nature was displayed most beautifully in Jesus' incarnation. God the Son, who did not originally have a physical body in eternity past, took on human flesh (John 1:14) to save God's people from their sins.

JANUARY 6

Hear, O Israel: The LORD our God, the LORD is one.

DEUTERONOMY 6:4, ESV

ANU, MARDUK, AND ASHUR. Osiris, Ra, and Thoth. Zeus, Poseidon, and Athena. Mars, Apollo, and Mercury.

And that's just the tip of the polytheistic iceberg.

The ancient civilizations of Mesopotamia, Egypt, Greece, Rome, and many others fabricated countless false gods in an attempt to explain the origin of the universe and the mysteries of the human experience. Today, most cultures around the world are not polytheistic like ancient times (although Hinduism still teaches the existence of many gods).

But for thousands of years, God has proclaimed the message clearly through his Word: "Hear, O Israel: The LORD our God, the LORD is one" (Deuteronomy 6:4, ESV). In ancient Israel, this famous verse was known as the Shema, which is the old Hebrew word for "hear" or "listen"—the opening command of the verse.

Throughout Scripture, God confirms that he is the one true God and that polytheism is a bunch of baloney:

- I am the LORD; there is no other God. (Isaiah 45:5)
- This is the way to have eternal life—to know you, the only true God, and Jesus Christ, the one you sent to earth. (John 17:3)
- There is one God and one Mediator who can reconcile God and humanity—the man Christ Jesus. (1 Timothy 2:5)

What's It Mean?

Why does it matter that there's one God—and not a pantheon—who created and rules the universe? How should this truth affect our lives?

God answered that in the very next verse following the Shema: "And you must love the LORD your God with all your heart, all your soul, and all your strength" (Deuteronomy 6:5).

As the only true God in the universe, the Lord deserves undivided rights to our hearts. He requires our utmost allegiance and devotion. Our worship in life is not to be distributed among anyone else. God alone reigns over the universe, and because of this, we should exclusively praise and obey him out of hearts overflowing with gratitude and love.

Through the Shema and all of Scripture, the one true God has spoken to you about himself. Have you heard?

Now What?

Prayerfully ask God to reveal where you might not be giving him your entire heart.

Did You Know?

There were more than two thousand gods and goddesses in the ancient Egyptian pantheon.

JANUARY 7

May the grace of the Lord Jesus Christ, the love of God,
and the fellowship of the Holy Spirit be with you all.

2 CORINTHIANS 13:14

WHEN YOU THINK OF Genesis 1, what comes to mind?

If you are like most people with even a basic understanding of the Bible, you probably think of Creation—and rightfully so. The first chapter of Scripture goes into vivid detail about how God made the universe.

Yet look carefully at Genesis 1, and you'll find some fascinating details about God's nature. In fact, only two verses into the Bible, we see an allusion to God's triune nature when we read about God the Father in verse 1 and "the Spirit of God" in verse 2. (A prophetic allusion to Jesus Christ, the eternal Son of God and the second Person of the Trinity, comes a few chapters later in Genesis 3:15.)

In Genesis 1:26, when God was about to create humans, he said, "Let *us* make man in *our* image, after *our* likeness" (ESV, emphasis added). Why didn't God say, "Let me make man in my image"? Why does God refer to himself in the plural?

Because it's an amazing reference to his unique three-in-one nature.

What's It Mean?

There is only one God (Deuteronomy 6:4), but there are three distinct persons that make up the one true God: the Father, the Son (Jesus), and the Holy Spirit. All are equal in their divine natures yet separate in their roles.

Is this confusing to you? If so, don't be discouraged! No human can fully comprehend the awesome wonders of the Trinity. There is beautiful mystery to it. If God could be completely understood by mere mortals like us, he wouldn't be a very great God, would he?

The study of the Trinity fills entire books. We're going to take the next three days to discuss God's glorious triune nature. These are just some initial steps of what should be an awe-filled, lifetime journey in understanding this amazing aspect of God.

Now What?

Ask God to give you a greater love and understanding of his three-in-one nature.

Did You Know?

You won't find the actual word *Trinity* anywhere in the Bible, yet it is one of the most important theological doctrines (or beliefs about God) in Christianity. References to the Trinity are scattered throughout Scripture, including today's verse and Matthew 3:16-17; Matthew 28:19; 1 Peter 1:2; and Jude 1:20-21.

JANUARY 8

*God the Father knew you and chose you long ago, and his
Spirit has made you holy. As a result, you have obeyed him
and have been cleansed by the blood of Jesus Christ.*

1 PETER 1:2

LIFE IS FULL OF great mysteries.

What really goes on at Area 51 in Nevada? What was the original purpose of Stonehenge? What happened to the biblical Ark of the Covenant?
And who ever thought liver and onions sounded good for dinner?

We will never know the answers to all of life's most puzzling questions.
Perhaps the greatest—yet most beautiful—mystery of all is the Trinity. As
we discussed yesterday, there is only one God, yet he exists in three distinct
persons—Father, Son, and Spirit—who are equal in their divine natures yet
separate in their roles.

Even though each person in the triune Godhead is equal and perfect, it's
important to know the distinctions between and various roles of the three.

What's It Mean?

One of the primary roles of God the Father was to speak the universe into
existence. While the Son (Colossians 1:15-16) and the Spirit (Genesis
1:2) were also greatly involved, it was the Father who actually uttered the
powerful words of Creation, starting with, "Let there be light" (Genesis
1:3).

In heaven's eternal plan of salvation, the Father charted the course. He
also sovereignly chose those whom he would save (Ephesians 1:4-5) and
actively sent the Son to earth to pay the redemption price for human sin
(Galatians 4:4-5), extending remarkable mercy and grace to lost sinners.

The Son of God—not the Father or the Spirit—came to die on
the cross for the sins of mankind, accomplishing the work of redemption. And the Spirit applies Jesus' redemptive work in a Christian's life by
regenerating a spiritually dead heart to new life (what we call "being born
again") through faith and by helping believers become more like Christ

(sanctification). Although the Son and Spirit are equal in deity to the Father, they are both willingly subordinate to him in how they function within the Godhead and among humanity.

This is just a brief glimpse into the Trinity and its distinction of roles. Praise God for his glorious three-in-one nature and how it eternally benefits all believers!

Now What?

Do further book study on the Trinity. Ask a parent or another trusted adult for recommendations, if needed.

Did You Know?

The doctrine of the Trinity is revealed progressively through Scripture, being implied in the Old Testament (e.g., "let us" in Genesis 1:26) and explicitly mentioned in the New Testament (e.g., today's verse).

JANUARY 9

The voice from the majestic glory of God said to him, "This is my dearly loved Son, who brings me great joy."

2 PETER 1:17

FATHER, SON, AND HOLY Spirit—this is the Trinity.

But people have been debating the exact relationship between God the Father and God the Son for thousands of years. At the root of this confusion is the phrase "Son of God," which the Bible consistently applies to Jesus. The Bible also clearly presents Jesus as God.

Is there a dilemma here? Can Jesus be both God and the Son of God? It's a valid question—and one that's so important to understand. Entire false religions have been built on misunderstandings about this question.

So which is it? Is Jesus God, or is he the Son of God?

Actually, he's both. To explain, we can look to God's inerrant Word.

What's It Mean?

As we discussed in the January 6 devotion, there is only one God (Deuteronomy 6:4), consisting of three distinct persons—the Father, the Son, and the Spirit (1 Peter 1:2). All are equal in their divine natures yet separate in their roles.

When the Bible refers to Jesus as the "Son of God," it's always a title used to emphasize Jesus' full deity (John 10:22-39; Hebrews 1). It is never meant to imply Jesus is the offspring of God the Father. As fully God, Jesus was never created. He is eternal (John 1:1; Revelation 21:6).

The title "Son of God" also speaks to Jesus' humble obedience to God the Father in the Incarnation. Like a wise human son obeys his earthly father, Jesus willingly submitted to the Father's plan of salvation, came to earth as a man, and paid the indescribably high redemption price—dying on the cross—for sinners like us. The apostle Paul beautifully details this in Philippians 2:5-8:

Have this mind among yourselves, which is yours in Christ Jesus, who, though he was in the form of God, did not count equality with God a thing to be grasped, but emptied himself, by taking the form of a servant, being born in the likeness of men. And being found in human form, he humbled himself by becoming obedient to the point of death, even death on a cross (ESV).

Aren't you glad that the eternal Son obeyed the Father for your sake? The Father was pleased with the Son, and you should be forever grateful!

Now What?
Check out the following passages on Jesus' divinity: John 1:1-18; Colossians 1:15-19; Titus 2:13; and 2 Peter 1:1.

Did You Know?
Jesus' favorite title for himself was "Son of Man," a reference to Daniel's vision of the pre-incarnate Christ in Daniel 7:13-14.

JANUARY 10

Holy, holy, holy is the Lord God, the Almighty—the one
who always was, who is, and who is still to come.

REVELATION 4:8

HAVE YOU EVER CLIMBED to the moon on a ladder? Or calculated the distance from Poughkeepsie to Pluto with a tape measure? Or explored the universe to its farthest limits in a spaceship?

Obviously, these things are impossible. But they hint at the holiness of God.

Wait, you might be wondering, did you say, "Holiness"? Don't you mean God's majesty, greatness, glory, or something? What does all this have to do with his holiness?

I'm glad you asked.

What's It Mean?

When it comes to God's holiness, which we'll be meditating on today and tomorrow, most people focus on his moral purity. And yes, God's holiness undoubtedly means that he is entirely without sin. He cannot sin or do anything contrary to his perfect nature.

But the extent of God's holiness goes even further beyond his sinless nature. When the Bible describes God as holy, it is first and foremost talking about his transcendence.

That's a big word. The dictionary defines it as "exceeding usual limits" or "being beyond comprehension."

This transcendence includes God's separateness from sin, but it's not limited to that. His holiness means there is nothing like him in all creation—not even close. God is so perfectly exalted above anything else—in all of his majesty, power, wisdom, love, etc.—that human language cannot adequately describe him.

Isaiah 55:9 says, "Just as the heavens are higher than the earth, so my ways are higher than your ways and my thoughts higher than your thoughts." In other words, Isaiah was saying, "Just like you can never measure from earth to the end of the universe, so also you cannot measure how much God transcends his creation."

There is simply nothing to compare God to in the universe. He is that excellent! He is that awesome!

He is holy.

Now What?

Spend some time meditating on Psalm 8, a chapter on the Lord's holiness.

Did You Know?

God's holiness is one of the main reasons for the second of the Ten Commandments: "You must not make for yourself an idol of any kind or an image of anything in the heavens or on the earth or in the sea" (Exodus 20:4). Any attempt to worship God with a man-made image fashioned after something in his creation is an abomination to his glory.

JANUARY 11

*Holy, holy, holy is the Lord God, the Almighty—the one
who always was, who is, and who is still to come.*

REVELATION 4:8

YESTERDAY'S AND TODAY'S VERSE come from one of the most beautiful chapters in the Bible.

In the fourth chapter of Revelation, the last book of the Bible, the apostle John receives an incredible vision of heaven's inner chambers, where four mysterious angelic creatures and "twenty-four elders" surround God's throne in constant worship of heaven's eternal King. Three times—signifying emphasis and completeness—they cry out, "Holy, holy, holy is the Lord God, the Almighty!"

Clearly, we need to understand God's holiness.

What's It Mean?

The word *holy* means "separate" or "set apart." As we learned in yesterday's devotion, a primary aspect of God's holiness is his transcendence above all creation—his complete exaltation and glorious majesty far above anything else in the universe. Today, we turn our attention to the other major aspect of his holiness: his separateness from sin.

Not only does God not sin, he cannot sin. He is set apart from it. Sin is not within God's character. To do evil would be to contradict his very nature and the moral laws that he set to govern his creation since the beginning. He is completely pure and righteous in all his ways.

This is great news for us! In a world where sin so often destroys, it is wonderful to know that there is a holy God in heaven who is separate from sin—a God who loves us and offers the chance to be holy in his sight through faith in the redeeming work of his Son, Jesus Christ!

Now What?

Do a word search in a Bible concordance or a website such as BibleGateway.com (with an adult's permission) to see how many times the

Bible uses the word *holy*—both to describe God and to call his people to be holy like him.

Did You Know?

Some of the many biblical examples of God's separateness from human sin can be found in the stories of Moses and the burning bush (Exodus 3), the command to separate the Holy Place from the Most Holy Place in the Tabernacle (and later, Temple) with a veil (Exodus 26), and Uzzah's death for touching the Ark of the Covenant (2 Samuel 6).

JANUARY 12

*He is the God who made the world and everything in it. Since he
is Lord of heaven and earth, he doesn't live in man-made temples,
and human hands can't serve his needs—for he has no needs.*

ACTS 17:24-25

I don't need your help!
I don't need anybody!
I can do this on my own!
I want to be independent!

Have you ever said those words, or have those thoughts crossed your
mind? If you're like most folks, you have.

Deep down, we all crave independence. We want to make decisions
on our own. We want to rule our destinies and be masters of our own
domain. We see this in Scripture as early as Genesis 3—the original fall of
humankind.

Teenagers are especially prone to desire independence as they make the
slow, often painful, metamorphosis from childhood to adulthood with all of
its privileges and responsibilities. This desire for independence isn't all bad.
Every adolescent needs to learn how to grow up, leave their parents' shadow,
and make decisions on their own.

But we must be careful of why we want independence. A prideful desire
for self-sufficiency can lead to disastrous results. God created us to need
others and—more importantly—to need him.

God, however, is different. God is a completely independent Being.
And this is a good thing.

What's It Mean?

Read today's Scripture passage again from Acts 17:24-25. God has no needs.
He doesn't need anything from us. He doesn't need anything from creation.
He is completely independent and self-sufficient.

God was never created, he has always existed, and he doesn't require anything from anyone. He exists perfectly apart from his creation.

Yet don't mistake God's independence for indifference. While God wasn't lonely when he created humans, he very much wanted to create us. He created us for his glory (Isaiah 43:7).

God is not distant or aloof. He is a loving, caring heavenly Father who wants to fellowship with those created in his image (Genesis 1:26-27). He knows the most intimate details about us. He intricately formed us (Psalm 139:13), "delights" in us (Isaiah 62:4), and sacrificed his own Son to reconcile us to him (Romans 5:10).

Is God independent? Yes. Is he also loving? Absolutely!

Now What?

The next time you crave independence, consider asking God and a loved one for help.

Did You Know?

Today's Scripture passage comes from the apostle Paul's time in the city of Athens as he tried to convince the ancient Greeks to abandon their worship of many gods and believe the gospel.

JANUARY 13

You must not forget this one thing, dear friends: A day is like a thousand years to the Lord, and a thousand years is like a day.

2 PETER 3:8

DO YOU EVER WISH you could be in more than one place at once?

Think of everything you could accomplish! You could finish your homework, do your chores, play video games at a friend's house, compete in your soccer team's championship game, and enjoy a European vacation—all at the same time!

Or what if you could see the past, present, and future simultaneously? Imagine the knowledge and the power you'd have! You could see the lives of your entire family tree, stretching back into antiquity. You could potentially stop accidents before they'd happen. You could know who wins every major sporting event from now until the Lord returns!

Alas, this is wishful thinking. Humans are finite creatures, bound by the laws of space and time.

But God isn't.

What's It Mean?

As the eternal Creator, God *made* space and time. They exist because of his will, and he rules over them.

We can only be in one place at one time. But God is not limited in this way. In Jeremiah 23:24, God asks rhetorically, "Can anyone hide from me in a secret place? Am I not everywhere in all the heavens and earth?"

Since God is a spirit (John 4:24), he is also not restricted by spatial constraints. We measure ourselves by height and weight. God doesn't have a size. Second Chronicles 2:6 says, "Who can really build him a worthy home? Not even the highest heavens can contain him!"

Time is also a servant, not a master, of the Lord God Almighty. He doesn't have to squint or crane his neck to see into the future or look at old photos to remember the past. He sees all time—including every moment of human history—at once with perfect clarity (see today's verse) because he created and governs it.

Is your head spinning? That's okay. These are deep, fascinating truths that stretch our understanding and proclaim God's incomparable glory. Praise him!

Now What?

Now is a good time to worship the God who *transcends* space and time! A few good passages to meditate on are Psalm 139:7-10 (God's omnipresence) and Isaiah 46:9-10 (God's unique power over time).

Did You Know?

When Jesus, the eternal Son of God, incarnated into human form, he willingly subjected himself to spatial dimensions—only being able to be in one place at any given time—to become our great High Priest (Hebrews 2:17).

JANUARY 14

*Do you know the balancings of the clouds, the wondrous
works of him who is perfect in knowledge?*

JOB 37:16, ESV

THINK OF HISTORY'S SMARTEST people.

There's Nicolaus Copernicus, the sixteenth-century astronomer whose
ideas about a heliocentric universe were so radical for his era that one of
his related books was banned by the Catholic church for centuries after his
death. There's George Washington Carver, whose inventions and brilliance
in agriculture helped revolutionize the industry in the early 1900s. There's
Katherine Johnson, whose mathematical genius helped NASA achieve
America's first human spaceflight in 1961. And who can forget Albert
Einstein, the eccentric-looking physicist who is most famous for his equa-
tion $E = mc^2$ and his theory of relativity?

Yet, relatively speaking (no pun intended, Big Al), all these braini-
acs look like preschoolers with counting blocks compared to God. That's
because God is omniscient.

What's It Mean?

Omniscient means "all-knowing." God knows everything. Let that sink in
for a moment.

God . . . knows . . . everything.

EVERYTHING.

The Lord God Almighty created the universe, so there's nothing in the
entire cosmos that is beyond his knowledge or understanding. Whatever
knowledge humans have acquired—all the great discoveries of mathemat-
ics, physics, medicine, technology, and so on over the centuries—God has
always known and ordained.

Unlike humans, God doesn't have to attain knowledge. He has eternally
known all things. And his memory doesn't fade over time.

But here's a critical point to understand: God is not simply a repository
of endless facts, like a gigantic computer or an endless encyclopedia. There

are some really smart people out there who are human and make terrible mistakes.

But God—in his infinite, holy knowledge and wisdom—always does what is best according to his perfect will. It's why the apostle Paul exclaims with delight in Romans 11:33, "Oh, how great are God's riches and wisdom and knowledge! How impossible it is for us to understand his decisions and his ways!"

Now What?

The next time you excel in school, praise the omniscient God who owns all knowledge and wisdom!

Did You Know?

No one fully knows God, right? Well, no—except for God himself. Because we are finite, we cannot know everything about ourselves, let alone God. But he possesses an eternal *self*-knowledge. This is what 1 Corinthians 2:10-11 alludes to. Mind-boggling!

JANUARY 15

*O Sovereign LORD! You made the heavens and earth by your
strong hand and powerful arm. Nothing is too hard for you!*

JEREMIAH 32:17

LOOKING BACK, IT'S STRANGE to think that Adolf Hitler was once
an itinerant artist in Austria who painted postcards and advertisements
to make ends meet. Or that Joseph Stalin was the son of a poor cobbler
who attended a theological seminary to become a priest in the Georgian
Orthodox Church. Or that Fidel Castro was the sports-loving son of a
wealthy Cuban sugarcane farmer.

But now, we remember these men as some of the worst dictators in history. Once these men came to power, they wielded authority ruthlessly, and
millions suffered and died for it.

These tyrants are just several examples from the twentieth century of
rulers who inherited great power and then abused it terribly. History is filled
with similar stories.

As we study God's attributes, we turn our attention to God's power.
Throughout Scripture, the biblical authors constantly draw our attention to
God's power over his creation. But here we must make a critical distinction:
God's power is nothing like human power.

And that's a very good thing!

What's It Mean?

God is omnipotent—that's a theological term that simply means God possesses all power. He can do all things according to his perfect will. As today's
verse says, nothing is too hard for him or outside the boundaries of his abilities. Even one of his names—"Lord God, the Almighty" (Revelation 4:8)—
speaks to his infinite supremacy in the universe.

But we need to understand another important—and beautiful—point
about God's omnipotence. He does not wield this incredible authority like
a wicked human ruler. His power is never selfish, spiteful, or shortsighted,
and he never uses it to take advantage of others.

Nahum 1:3 says, "The LORD is slow to get angry, but his power is great." You certainly can't say both of these things about the infamous despots of human history.

The Lord God Almighty's power is holy, flowing from his righteous character. He always exerts his power to glorify himself (which is always for our good) and show love to his children.

This is a God you want to be all-powerful! This is a God you want to worship!

Now What?

Think the kings of the earth have power? If so, read Psalm 2 and Psalm 102:15.

Did You Know?

There are some things God cannot do. He cannot lie (Hebrews 6:18) or be tempted to sin (James 1:13). So while God is all-powerful, it's not entirely accurate to simply say, "God can do anything." It's better to say, "God can do all things according to his perfect will."

JANUARY 16

Anyone who does not love does not know God, for God is love.

1 JOHN 4:8

GOD IS LOVING.

Perhaps you're thinking to yourself, *Thanks for that pearl of wisdom, Captain Obvious. Of course God is loving! Doesn't everyone know that?*

Well, no, they don't. For many people, their life experiences cause them to question God's goodness and love.

That doesn't change the fact that God is loving. The Bible testifies to this from beginning to end, perhaps most famously in John 3:16.

But it's not enough to only say, "God is loving." That's an inadequate description of God. Does this surprise you? It shouldn't. After all, humans can be loving too. Yet in our sin, we screw up love all the time. It's embarrassing, really, when you think about it.

As we discuss God's attributes, we need to truly understand who he is and how love relates to God.

What's It Mean?

Just like all of God's other attributes, his love is defined by his holiness. God's love is a holy love. As you might recall, the term holy means "morally pure and blameless," but even more, it also means "set apart." There is nothing in all creation like God's love.

That's why the apostle John uses unique language to describe God's love. In today's verse, rather than saying, "God is loving" (which is true), John writes something much more powerful: "God is *love*" (emphasis added). There's a difference. In other words, John is saying love finds its origin in God. He gives love its definition. Without God, love wouldn't exist.

That sentence bears repeating: without God, love wouldn't exist. It's what John meant a few verses later when he wrote, "We love because he first loved us" (1 John 4:19, ESV). Humanity wouldn't have known how to love at all—whether horizontally (others on earth) or vertically (God in heaven)—if God had not gloriously modeled love for us.

How did he do this? The ways are too numerous to count, but for starters, he created us in his image, and when we sinfully rebelled against him, he provided his Son, Jesus Christ, as a wrath-bearing sacrifice in our place.

That's amazing, holy love.

Now What?

The apostle Paul beautifully expounds upon the eternal effects of God's love for his children in Romans 8:31-39. Check it out!

Did You Know?

This concept was so important to John that he repeated it in the same chapter: "God is love, and all who live in love live in God, and God lives in them" (1 John 4:16).

JANUARY 17

He is the Rock; his deeds are perfect. Everything
he does is just and fair. He is a faithful God who
does no wrong; how just and upright he is!

DEUTERONOMY 32:4

THAT'S NOT FAIR!

Have you ever heard that phrase before? Of course you have. It's the cry that every child has howled at some point in their lives when they sense injustice.

- Someone cut in front of you in line to go to recess? *That's not fair!*
- Billy's LEGO pile looks slightly bigger than yours at playtime? *That's not fair!*
- Betsy's bedtime is thirty minutes later than yours because she's older? *That's not fair!*

Even as we get older, we crave justice. Throughout history, rulers of various kingdoms have been given the laudatory title "The Just" to describe their generally well-received reigns:

- James II "The Just" of Aragon and Sicily (reigned 1285–1327)
- Louis XIII "The Just" of France (reigned 1610–1643)
- Matthias I of Hungary, whose death in 1490 sparked the phrase, "Matthias is dead—justice is lost"

In America, we even name the judges who hold the highest court office in the land "Supreme Court justices." No matter how old we are, the idea of justice—decisions based on fairness, equity, and righteousness—is a big deal to us.

Of course, all human justice fails at some point because of our sin. God's justice, however, does not.

What's It Mean?

God is just. He always does what is right. How does he know what is right? Because his standard of righteousness flows out of his own holy character, which is perfectly pure. As God testifies of himself in Isaiah 45:19, "I the LORD speak the truth; I declare what is right" (ESV).

In this life, you will experience much unfairness and injustice. Chances are, you probably already have. The world can be a cruel place, filled with inequalities. When you do experience injustice, remember those unfortunate situations are always products of sinful humanity's shortcomings.

But take heart! You will never experience injustice from God. He always does what is right in accordance with his righteous character. And if you are his child, that's good news for you!

Now What?

With a trusted adult's permission, do a word search at BibleGateway.com or a similar online search engine with the words *justice* or *righteous* to see how many times Scripture describes God as a just, righteous King.

Did You Know?

Not everyone loves justice. Proverbs 21:15 says, "Justice is a joy to the godly, but it terrifies evildoers."

JANUARY 18

I am the LORD, and I do not change.

MALACHI 3:6

CHANGE IS OFTEN A good thing.

The change in the seasonal cycles from winter, spring, summer, and fall displays the beautiful variety of God's creation. A baby goes through many adorable (and a few not-so-adorable!) changes on his or her way through childhood. All cars need an oil change periodically, or else the engine will break down. What student doesn't long for a change in scenery to get out of classes and start summer break?

And for goodness' sake—please change your underwear every day!

Yes, change is good in so many ways. But the Bible declares that God doesn't change. In fact, God's unchangeable nature—or his immutability—is one of the most important, and beautiful, doctrines of Scripture.

What's It Mean?

Think about it: if God could change, that means he might not have been perfect to begin with—that there could be some room for improvement on his part, some flaw in his character. If this were the case, Christians would be worshiping a God who was only *mostly* good, or *mostly* powerful, or *mostly* wise. That's a frightening thought.

If God could change, another scary possibility would exist: God could change for the worse. He theoretically could choose to do evil at some point. Or he could choose to break some of his promises.

Of course, neither of these options is true. God doesn't change. Scripture consistently affirms this. Everything the Bible declares about him has always been true and always will be true. God has always been holy and will always be holy. All of the Lord's plans will stand firm for eternity (Psalm 33:11).

All these truths should give you great hope. God is the same yesterday, today, and forever. Human nature is fickle, but "the eternal Rock" (Isaiah 26:4) is steadfast. You can trust him because what the Bible has declared about him for thousands of years is still true today.

We serve a God who is wonderfully unchanging in his goodness, wisdom, power, and love!

Now What?

For more verses on God's immutability, read Numbers 23:19; Psalm 102:25-27; and James 1:17.

Did You Know?

Hebrews 13:8 applies the same doctrine of immutability to Jesus when it says, "Jesus Christ is the same yesterday, today, and forever," affirming Jesus' divinity as the eternal Son of God.

JANUARY 19

You are always the same; you will live forever.

PSALM 102:27

GOD DOESN'T CHANGE.

We discussed this topic yesterday, and it's an extremely important part of God's character to understand and believe. But many people don't believe it. In fact, lots of folks—including many who call themselves Christians— have fallen prey to a subtle yet popular lie that claims the God of the Old Testament is different from the God of the New Testament.

"Oh sure, there's only one God," these folks readily admit. But then they go on to say, "Look at the stories in the Bible, and you can clearly see that there are two types of God. First, he's a God of anger and vengeance in the Old Testament, while he's much more loving and compassionate in the New Testament with the arrival of Jesus."

Hogwash! Nothing could be further from the truth.

What's It Mean?

Any attempt to put God in two different categories (Old Testament = God of wrath; New Testament = God of love) is a gross oversimplification, mis-understanding, and discredit to his perfectly unified and wholly consistent character.

It's true that the Old Testament is filled with stories of God's wrath against sin. But it's also filled with countless testimonies of his steadfast love, mercy, and grace. Consider these Old Testament verses:

- The LORD is good. His unfailing love continues forever, and his faithfulness continues to each generation. (Psalm 100:5)
- The LORD is compassionate and merciful, slow to get angry and filled with unfailing love. (Psalm 103:8)
- Do you think that I like to see wicked people die? says the Sovereign LORD. Of course not! I want them to turn from their wicked ways and live. (Ezekiel 18:23)

Likewise, the New Testament is filled with passages of God's coming wrath. A few examples are Romans 1:18–2:11; 1 Thessalonians 1:10; 2 Peter 3:1-12; and much of the book of Revelation. Believe it or not, Jesus taught more about hell than anyone else did in Scripture.

The point is, God doesn't change. God acts in both wrath and love, but he is always perfectly consistent with his holy character. He is always the same!

Now What?

Take some time to scan the book of Psalms (Old Testament) and see how much it mentions God's mercy, compassion, and love.

Did You Know?

God's wrath is his righteous anger toward sin. Unlike human anger, it's always justified and never capricious.

JANUARY 20

Blessed be the God and Father of our Lord Jesus Christ, who has
blessed us in Christ with every spiritual blessing in the heavenly
places, even as he chose us in him before the foundation of the
world, that we should be holy and blameless before him.

EPHESIANS 1:3-4, ESV

STARTING TOMORROW, we will transition from our opening study of
God's character and attributes to an exploration of God's creation of the
universe. But first, we have a big question to tackle: What was God doing
before he created everything?

Have you ever considered this? It's a fascinating question to ponder.
After all, the triune God is eternal, so the Father, Son, and Spirit existed
infinitely before the fixed point in time when they decided to bring the
cosmos into being with powerful words, as described in Genesis 1.

Theologians call the pre-creation period "eternity past." The Bible leaves
much of eternity past an unexplained mystery, yet there are Scripture passages here and there that hint at God's activities.

The brief glimpses we get are amazing.

What's It Mean?

In Jesus' prayer of John 17, he twice refers to the glorious fellowship that the
Father and Son (and by implication, the Spirit) shared in eternity past:

Father, bring me into the glory we shared before the world began. (verse 5)

Then they can see all the glory you gave me because you loved me even
before the world began. (verse 24)

Jesus gives us an incredible peek into his preincarnate relationship with
God the Father and the mutual love and glory they shared before the eternal
Son took on human form to die for our sins. But wait, there's more!

Look at today's verse. Before God laid the foundations of the earth, he
was designing his great plan of salvation for humanity. More specifically,
he "chose" everyone who would be saved by grace through faith in his Son
(Ephesians 2:8-9). In eternity past, God "predestined us for adoption to

himself as sons through Jesus Christ, according to the purpose of his will" (Ephesians 1:5, ESV).

Before he said, "Let there be light," God was sovereignly pouring out love on his children—prior to anyone's birth. Wrap your mind around that!

Now What?

For more of the Son's preincarnate existence with the Father, read John 1:1-3.

Did You Know?

One of God's names that speaks to his eternal nature is the Ancient of Days (Daniel 7:9, ESV).

JANUARY 21

In the beginning God created the heavens and the earth.

GENESIS 1:1

ARE YOU FAMILIAR WITH today's verse? Maybe you've read it before. Maybe you've read it a hundred times.

No matter. Read it again. Its importance cannot be overstated.

These are the words that open Scripture, God's revelation to mankind about himself and his eternal plan to save his people from their sins. When God's Spirit inspired the author of Genesis, likely Moses, to begin this amazing collection of what became sixty-six books spanning at least 1,300 years, God could have told Moses to write anything. So it's instructive that God chose these words, in particular, to begin his great revelation of who he is and what he's done.

In the beginning God created the heavens and the earth.

Do you think God knew what he was doing when he inspired those poignant words?

You'd better believe it.

What's It Mean?

This sentence, in English, is only ten words long. It's so simple and beautiful, yet it's powerful and profound.

These words tell us that God existed "in the beginning"—before anything else. They speak to God's eternal, sovereign, self-existing nature.

They strip away all notions that the universe started through evolution or by random chance.

They repudiate all notions of other gods or belief systems.

In only one sentence—ten words long—Scripture establishes the order of the universe. Genesis 1:1 immediately establishes that there is one God, he has eternally existed, and therefore he has never been created and doesn't answer to anyone or anything else. It tells us that there's an intelligent Creator who intricately designed everything we see.

These truths trickle down to everything else in the Bible—and our lives. If these things weren't true, our existence would look far different.

But they are true! Praise God that before time began, he created all things!

Now What?

As you read Scripture, remember not to read too fast. Even one simple ten-word sentence can have profound spiritual meaning.

Did You Know?

Jesus, the eternal Son of God, was also an active agent in Creation, along with the Father and the Spirit (Colossians 1:16; Hebrews 1:2).

JANUARY 22

In the beginning God created the heavens and the earth.

GENESIS 1:1

PEOPLE ARE INTRIGUED by chance.

Each year, approximately forty million people visit Las Vegas and spend billions on gambling. Yes, you read that correctly—billions of dollars. It's a staggering amount of money for games where randomness rules and most people lose more than they win.

Incredibly, many people credit chance as the "creator" of the universe. Thanks to Charles Darwin's infamous book, *On the Origin of Species*, which espoused the theory of evolution, and other spurious hypotheses such as the "Big Bang Theory," multitudes around the world believe that human life is a product of cosmic randomness. In America, evolution has become so engrained in our culture that public schools teach it as fact rather than theory.

But if we're honest, human experience and observation tell us otherwise. So does Scripture. We look again to the very first verse of the Bible: "In the beginning God created the heavens and the earth."

What's It Mean?

Go outside and look around you. Look at the grass, trees, and sky. Remember the last time you were at the zoo and the incredible array of animals you witnessed. Consider the snow-peaked mountains, vast oceans, lush rain forests, and fiery volcanoes that populate our planet. Contemplate the countless stars that you can see on a cloudless night and the way the planets in our solar system work in perfect orbital harmony together around the sun.

Is this a product of chance and randomness?

Absolutely not.

The world is one of order and design, down to smallest atoms. Romans 1:20 declares, "For ever since the world was created, people have seen the earth and sky. Through everything God made, they can clearly see his invisible qualities—his eternal power and divine nature. So they have no excuse for not knowing God."

In other words, the entire universe speaks—no, screams!—each day of God's existence and his creative handiwork. A loving Creator spoke this world into being in great love and power.

As for the possibility of random Darwinian evolution?

No chance.

Now What?

Read Psalms 8, 19, 104, and 139. They testify to God's creative power in forming various parts of the universe.

Did You Know?

Charles Darwin concocted his theory of evolution after sailing around the world on the HMS *Beagle* from 1831 to 1836. He published *On the Origin of Species* in 1859.

JANUARY 23

The LORD merely spoke, and the heavens were created.
He breathed the word, and all the stars were born.

PSALM 33:6

THIS WORLD IS FULL of creative marvels.

Have you ever looked out from the top of the Empire State Building in New York City or crossed the Golden Gate Bridge in San Francisco? Have you ever visited Nevada's Hoover Dam, which provides electricity to three states thanks to the 90,000 gallons of water that surge through it every second? Have you ever been to an art museum and gazed upon an original Monet, Picasso, Rembrandt, or van Gogh?

Perhaps creativity flows in your veins too. Maybe you can create wonders of art, technology, or engineering for others to enjoy.

But there's a catch. To create anything, humans have to start with something:

- a brush, a can of paint, and a blank canvas
- a stack of lumber, a hammer, and some nails
- a rock and a chisel
- a lump of Play-Doh

To build, to make, to create, we must possess prior materials to work with. But not God.

When God created the universe, he simply spoke!

What's It Mean?

Imagine having the power to bring the entire universe—stars, planets, galaxies, and all forms of life on earth—into existence with mere words. That's how powerful God is. He declared, and it instantly happened. He commanded, and it immediately came to be.

Look at what Genesis 1 says:

- God said, "Let there be light," and there was light. (verse 3)
- God said, "Let there be a space between the waters, to separate the waters of the heavens from the waters of the earth." And that is what happened. (verses 6-7)

And so on. For six days, God used nothing more than his voice—no building materials, no tools, no construction cranes or dump trucks—to intricately craft the cosmos.

That is power beyond human understanding or description! That is the power of the Lord God Almighty!

Now What?

Worship this all-powerful, creative God by meditating on Psalm 33:6-9.

Did You Know?

- Theologians refer to God's work of creation with the Latin term *ex nihilo*, meaning "out of nothing."

JANUARY 24

By faith we understand that the universe was
created by the word of God, so that what is seen
was not made out of things that are visible.

HEBREWS 11:3, ESV

WHERE DID THE UNIVERSE come from? How did life begin? What is the origin of everything?

For the last three days, we have been discussing biblical Creation—how God created the universe by speaking powerful words. It's the doctrine of *ex nihilo*—"out of nothing."

The Bible says that in the beginning, there was only the trinitarian God—Father, Son, and Spirit. Then, God commanded light to appear, and an expanse between the waters and dry land to come forth, then vegetation, planetary bodies, and finally the animal kingdom and humans. The six days of biblical creation is one of the foundations of Christianity.

Does it take faith to believe this? Absolutely. But that's exactly what God's Word calls us to. Just look at today's verse.

What's It Mean?

Simply defined, faith is believing without seeing. No human being was alive at the beginning of the world. Yet Hebrews 11:3 (and the rest of Scripture) calls us to believe that the one true God of the Bible—not a Big Bang, a microscopic organism in a primordial soup, a pantheon of lesser gods, or any other alternate force—began the universe. This is what the Bible testifies to, and so we must believe. You cannot please God without faith (Hebrews 11:6).

Funny as it sounds, the theory of evolution takes great faith too. Think about it: How else is someone to believe that our incredibly beautiful, detailed, and orderly universe began by a fluke of nature and continues to function by sheer evolutionary randomness? And where, by the way, did those first microscopic particles involved in the Big Bang come from? This is a something-from-nothing argument, which has never proven possible in the natural world . . . unless, however, a greater power—or Being—exists who can create something from nothing.

Look around you. Watch a butterfly in fluttery flight or a squirrel hunting for acorns. Consider the clockwork nature and wonderful variety of the meteorological seasons. Or the way the moon's gravitational pull affects ocean tides. Try to find two matching snowflakes or both ends of a rainbow.

Do you see a world thrown together by the impersonal, emotionless evolutionary force of randomness and chance? Or a world of beauty and order, designed by a loving Creator?

By faith, believe that the universe was created by God!

Now What?

Read Revelation 4:11. From its first book to the last, the Bible's consistent witness is of divine creation.

Did You Know?

Genesis 1:14 foreshadowed that humans would use the planets and stars one day to date their calendars.

JANUARY 25

God looked over all he had made, and he saw that it was very good!

GENESIS 1:31

THIS WORLD IS A beautiful place. There are so many parts of creation to marvel at and enjoy.

But sin has also marred God's original design. Read the news on any given day, and you'll quickly see that the paradise of Genesis 1–2 has given way to great pain, suffering, and death because of human rebellion against our Creator.

But it was not so in the very beginning. At Creation, everything was very good. In fact, it was perfect!

After each of the six days of Creation, God declared what he had made "good." Today, we're going to look at that phrase—"And God saw that it was good"—and discuss the meaning behind it.

What's It Mean?

Maybe you've seen rating systems that ask you to rank a product or service on a scale of *excellent, very good, good, fair,* or *poor*. That is *not* what Scripture means here!

When Genesis 1:4 says, "And God saw that the light was good," it's not saying that God could've done one or two levels better with his creation of light. The word good in this verse—and throughout chapter 1 to describe all of God's creative acts—denotes perfection and completeness.

God's original creation reflected his glory. Only God is to be worshiped, but the universe he created dazzled with the radiance of his goodness and attributes. He could've created a bland, boring world of metal and stainless steel. But no! Instead, he designed a world of majestic rolling hills, deep valleys, and waterfalls. He created bumblebees, orangutans, swordfish, and bald eagles. He made stars, comets, and galaxies. His loving, imaginative fingerprints cover the world he created.

God's declaration of creation's goodness was a glorious declaration of the inherent perfection and wholeness of what he made. God is holy and completely separate from any moral impurity. As such, his original creation was wholly good and lacking anything impure. God did not create anything sinful, evil, or deficient in any way. Everything he created was flawless—exactly the way he wanted it to be.

Everything God made was very good indeed!

Now What?

Take some time to prayerfully thank God for all the goodness you enjoy in his creation each day.

Did You Know?

Many biblical scholars agree that the way the Genesis Creation account was written was, in part, to contradict prevailing Near Eastern pagan creation mythology of that era from Mesopotamia, Egypt, and other local cultures.

JANUARY 26

The heavens proclaim the glory of God. The
skies display his craftsmanship.

PSALM 19:1

HAVE YOU EVER TAKEN a walk through a flowery meadow or down an autumn path? Have you ever climbed a mountain and surveyed the seemingly endless landscape before you? Have you ever laid out a blanket on the ground on a cloudless night or gone to a planetarium and stargazed, contemplating the overwhelming size and beauty of our solar system?

The earth is more than our native planet, and the Milky Way galaxy is more than our home solar system. Earth—yes, even the entire universe itself—is a canvas. The Master Artist is God.

What's It Mean?

Have you ever stopped long enough to consider God's breathtaking power and handiwork in creation? That's what today's verse is calling you to do.

There are many other verses like this in Scripture. Here are a few examples:

- The heavens proclaim his righteousness; every nation sees his glory. (Psalm 97:6)
- The earth is the LORD's, and everything in it. The world and all its people belong to him. For he laid the earth's foundation on the seas and built it on the ocean depths. (Psalm 24:1-2)
- Holy, holy, holy is the LORD of Heaven's Armies! The whole earth is filled with his glory! (Isaiah 6:3)

Our universe is full of so many wonders, it's impossible to list them all. From the lowliest worm to the great herds of elephants stampeding across the African plains, from the smallest acorn to the great Himalayas, from the rings of Jupiter to star clusters in distant galaxies that our satellites can't even reach—God has displayed his astounding authority and majesty in his creation in spectacular ways. He did this out of his great love for us so that we might enjoy what he created. He also displayed his awesome glory so that we might worship him.

Sadly, many people throughout the centuries have chosen to worship the created rather than the Creator (Romans 1:25). May it not be so with us. The marvels of his creation should continually draw us closer to him.

The heavens and earth proclaim the glory of God. Let's worship him!

Now What?

Ask your parents or a trusted adult to take you on a day trip somewhere to enjoy the glories of God's creation.

Did You Know?

NASA estimates that there are hundreds of billions of galaxies in the observable universe, perhaps even up to a trillion.

JANUARY 27

*O LORD, you are our Father. We are the clay, and you
are the potter. We all are formed by your hand.*

ISAIAH 64:8

THINK BACK TO WHEN you were a young child.

Did you ever play with Play-Doh? Chances are, you did! Who knew
what fun kids could have with just the right mixture of flour, water, salt,
boric acid, and mineral oil. Ahhh, those were the days—when nothing more
than a young imagination and a carton full of squishy modeling compound
could provide entertainment for hours (or at least twenty minutes).

Now imagine if suddenly that strange-looking Play-Doh humanoid you
had created peeled itself off your kitchen table, stood up, and said, "You
fool! Look what you've done to me! How dare you give me asymmetrical
legs, Picasso eyes, and an arm with a crab claw for a hand! What were you
thinking?"

This, of course, is ridiculous. Created beings would never have the
audacity to question and revolt against their creator, without whom they
wouldn't even exist, right?

Wrong.

What's It Mean?

Sadly, we act like that insolent lump of Play-Doh when we rebel against
God and question his rule in our lives.

As we discuss Creation, it's important to remember one of the chief lessons of Genesis 1: because God is the sovereign Creator and we are the created, we answer to him in everything. We were created in his image. As part
of his creation, we must submit to his authority. He makes the rules and we
obey, not vice versa. To question God would be utterly absurd, like a lumpy,
half-concocted Play-Doh creature going on a power trip.

Thousands of years before Play-Doh was invented, the prophet Isaiah
made several metaphorical references to pottery clay. One of them is today's
verse. Look also at his very blunt message to idolatrous Judah in the eighth

century BC: "How foolish can you be? He is the Potter, and he is certainly greater than you, the clay! Should the created thing say of the one who made it, 'He didn't make me'? Does a jar ever say, 'The potter who made me is stupid'?" (Isaiah 29:16).

The implied answer, of course, is no. We can learn a great deal from this, too. Don't be like a senseless jar or bitter lump of Play-Doh, fighting your Maker. Instead, be moldable clay in the hands of the loving Master Potter.

Now What?
Are you trying to rule areas of your life? Prayerfully submit them to your Creator.

Did You Know?
The putty-like substance that eventually became a wildly popular children's modeling compound known as Play-Doh was first sold as a wallpaper cleaner in the 1930s.

56

JANUARY 28

God created man in his own image, in the image of God
he created him; male and female he created them.

GENESIS 1:27, ESV

WHAT DO YOU SEE when you look in the mirror? Well, if you look in the mirror at 6 a.m., you will probably see droopy eyes, frizzy hair, and creases on your face from your pillowcase.

Attractive!

A mirror, of course, shows an image of yourself. It's a reflection of who you are.

Similarly, humans reflect their Creator. It's not in the way we look. As we've already discussed in the January 4 and 5 devotions, God is spirit (i.e., an immaterial, invisible living being) and we are human (i.e., living beings with physical bodies). Rather, we reflect God in other aspects of how we were made.

As today's verse says, God created us "in his own image." To be created in God's image is a glorious truth that gives every human being great purpose. This leads to several important questions:

- What does it mean to be created in God's image?
- Why did God do that?
- How should this affect the way I live?

We'll tackle the first question today and the other two over the next two days.

What's It Mean?

To be created in God's image means we are uniquely created. The Lord made nothing else in his image—not monkeys, whales, eagles, elephants, daffodils, sycamores, icebergs, planets, or anything else in the universe. Only humans. This is a distinct honor.

To be created in God's image means that we share some of his character-istics but not all of them. Like God, we are moral beings, we can reason and problem-solve, we can communicate in spoken language, we can be creative, and we can experience loving relationships. The greatest relationship we can enjoy is when we become a child of our heavenly Father through faith in his Son, Jesus Christ. Nothing else in creation has this privilege.

While we are not an uncreated eternal spirit like God, the Lord did put an immaterial spirit inside us. Our spirit will exist forever, either with him or apart from him, depending on whether we submit to his rule in our life.

This is by no means an exhaustive list of what it means to be made in God's image. As sinful humans, we neither share all of God's characteristics, nor do we possess any of them perfectly. But what a privilege to share his image at all!

(Even with crazy bed head.)

Now What?

Place a sticky note on your bathroom mirror that says, "Made in God's image."

Did You Know?

When Jesus returns to earth, Christians will bear his glorified image (1 Corinthians 15:49; 1 John 3:2).

JANUARY 29

*God created man in his own image, in the image of God
he created him; male and female he created them.*

GENESIS 1:27, ESV

IN **YESTERDAY'S** DEVOTION, WE discussed mirrors, the wacky bed
head you get at 6 a.m., and what it means to be created in God's image (but
mostly the latter!).

This foundational biblical truth of being created in God's image leads
to two other important questions:

- Why did God create us in his image?
- How should this affect the way we live?

We will consider the first question today and the second in tomorrow's
devotion. When we answer these two questions, many other mysteries about
life and our existence on earth will come into focus.

What's It Mean?

God created us to bring glory to his name. We see that very clearly from
Bible passages such as Isaiah 43:6-7 and 1 Corinthians 10:31.

But all of creation brings God glory. The loftiest angels to the strangest
creatures in the darkest ocean depths all bring praise to God (Psalm 148:2,
7). Look also at Psalm 19:1: "The heavens proclaim the glory of God. The
skies display his craftsmanship."

So if everything in the universe brings God glory, how are we, as
humans, any different? Well, as we learned in yesterday's devotion, only
humans were created in God's image. That's incredibly significant.

God created us in his image to represent him on earth and do the work
he's called us to do—using the various gifts he's given us for his glory. Being
God's image-bearers also means we can experience fellowship with him in a
unique way. We can pray to him, enjoy his Spirit's presence in our life, and
call him our heavenly Father.

Finally, God also created humans in his image to receive glory through his eternal plan of redemption. He knew we would sin and imperfectly represent his image. So he decided to send his perfect Son—not an image of God, but God himself in human form—to pay for our sins.

Are you lying sprawled out on the floor right now? If not, why? Just kidding (sort of). But the point is, when we reflect on these truths, it should send us to our knees, if not literally then figuratively, in worship of our great God!

Now What?
Whatever you do, read tomorrow's devotion to find out how to live as God's image-bearer!

Did You Know?
The New Testament frequently talks about the Kingdom of God. This Kingdom doesn't consist of kangaroos, killer whales, and kittens. It is made up of God's image-bearers who have been redeemed by the blood of Jesus!

JANUARY 30

Whether you eat or drink, or whatever you
do, do it all for the glory of God.

1 CORINTHIANS 10:31

CHIMPANZEES DON'T DO IT.

Neither do cardinals, caribou, cockatoos, catfish, cobras, crocodiles, cheetahs, chickens, chipmunks, or chinchillas.

Massive Jupiter doesn't do it. Neither does Saturn, with its fascinating rings of ice and rock particles, nor the sun, a blazing hot star of immense proportions and power.

Not even the highest, mightiest order of angels can claim this remarkable distinction.

Only humans bear God's image.

Over the last two days, we've learned what that means and why God created us this way. Today, we will explore this question: How should being God's image-bearers affect the way we live?

What's It Mean?

To understand the concept of bearing God's image, we must understand the ancient concept of a viceroy, which was a governor or representative ruling a region on behalf of the overall sovereign of an empire. This is why, as soon as God said, "Let us make man in our image, after our likeness" (Genesis 1:26, ESV), he immediately said that we were to "reign over" the animal kingdom (verse 26) and "fill the earth and govern it" (verse 28).

In ancient times, the king's viceroy often carried a signet ring or another official tool in order to sign documents on the king's behalf. Viceroys were royal emissaries. They literally bore the king's image on that token. Their word was the king's word. If they spoke or acted unfittingly, it reflected poorly on the king, and people could misunderstand who he was and how he ruled.

Do you see the connection? As God's image-bearers, we are given the high calling of representing the eternal King. It's a huge responsibility. But it's one he has well-equipped us to do through the power of his Spirit and his Word.

It wasn't long before sin got in the way of our ambassadorship. The first earthly viceroys—Adam and Eve—fell short of their calling (Genesis 3) and all humans since then have too (Romans 3:23). But the King has mercifully made atonement for our sinful rebellion through the sacrifice of his perfect Son. Through faith in Jesus Christ and obedience to the eternal King, you can fulfill your calling and bring glory to his name as his image bearer until he calls you home!

Now What?
Read 2 Corinthians 5:20 and Ephesians 6:18-20 for references of being an "ambassador" for God.

Did You Know?
• When Joseph rose to power in Egypt in Genesis 41, he became a viceroy under the ruling pharaoh.

JANUARY 31

What are mere mortals that you should think about them,
human beings that you should care for them?

PSALM 8:4

HAVE YOU EVER LAID on your back outside on a clear evening and gazed into the nighttime sky? It is a marvelous thing to behold.

On a cloudless night approximately three thousand years ago, King David did this too. Israel's great shepherd-king didn't have all the high-tech astronomy equipment and scientific knowledge that we now possess. But he knew what his eyes told him, and it was as awesome in 1,000 BC as it is today.

David saw thousands of twinkling stars. He noticed the moon in its glory as it reflected the sun's radiance. Perhaps he even spotted a shooting star or Venus, if the timing was right.

The sight took David's breath away. After soaking it all in, the Bible's greatest songwriter wrote the timeless, inspired words of Psalm 8:3-4: "When I look at the night sky and see the work of your fingers—the moon and the stars you set in place—what are mere mortals that you should think about them, human beings that you should care for them?"

What's It Mean?

Against the backdrop of God's incomprehensible universe, it's easy to feel utterly insignificant and completely irrelevant. And yet we are not.

Although you might feel like a mere blip in the cosmos, God greatly loves you and cares for you, as today's verse says. In fact, Psalm 8:5 goes on to say that God gave us an exalted place in creation as his image-bearers: "Yet you have made him a little lower than the heavenly beings [i.e., angels] and crowned him with glory and honor" (ESV).

In all his majesty and power, God knows you by name. He knows every detail about you, great and small. He has planned out your days. You are loved by him.

Most amazingly, he provided his Son, Jesus Christ, to redeem you from your sins. This Jesus, the eternal second Person of the Trinity, "created the world" and "upholds the universe by the word of his power" (Hebrews 1:2-3, ESV).

Meditate on that blessed gospel truth the next time you stargaze!

Now What?

Read all of Psalm 8 to rejoice in God's majesty and our blessed status as his image-bearers.

Did You Know?

There are about five thousand to ten thousand stars observable to the naked eye from earth (depending on various estimates), but only half of those are visible to us at any given time since the other half is obscured by earth's opposite hemisphere.

FEBRUARY 1

The LORD God formed the man from the dust of the ground.

GENESIS 2:7

DUST.

Like gnats, mosquitoes, and revolving doors, dust is a bothersome fact of life that doesn't seem to serve a purpose. But it's everywhere.

Dust makes us sneeze. We sweep, spray, and vacuum our houses to get rid of it, especially before special guests arrive. During the Great Depression of the 1930s, a severe drought in midwestern America became known as the Dust Bowl.

But let's not be too harsh on poor dust. After all, we originate from it.

In Genesis 2, we get fascinating insight into God's creation of the first humans, learning that God formed Adam "from the dust of the ground" and "breathed the breath of life into the man's nostrils, and the man became a living person" (verse 7). Shortly thereafter, God made Eve, the first woman, from "one of the man's ribs" (verse 21).

Ever since God made Adam and Eve, he has given the gift of human life through procreation. But the first human life came from . . . well, dirt. Kind of sobering, huh?

What's It Mean?

As a human, you are made in God's image, as we've already discussed. This means you are greatly privileged above all else in the universe, even angels. The Lord loves and cherishes you more than anything in creation.

But you are also dust. As part of the curse of sin, God told Adam and Eve that death would be part of human reality, saying, "You were made from dust, and to dust you will return" (Genesis 3:19).

The Bible speaks in other metaphors to remind us of the frailty and brevity of human life. Scripture compares us to "dreams that disappear" (Psalm 90:5), withered "grass" (Isaiah 40:7), and "the morning fog" (James 4:14).

Scripture reminds us of these sad realities to keep us humble and remember our unique place in this world. We are dearly loved by our Creator, but we are also nothing without him—sinners in desperate need of a Savior. We would do well to remember both these truths.

Now What?

Read Psalm 103, which talks about how God "remembers we are only dust" (verse 14) and cares for us in the midst of our weakness.

Did You Know?

Here's glorious news! First Corinthians 15:47-49 compares the imperfect first man (Adam) to the perfect Son of Man (Jesus Christ). Verse 49 says, "Just as we have borne the image of the man of dust, we shall also bear the image of the man of heaven" (ESV). At Jesus' return, every believer's dusty body will be exchanged for eternal resurrection bodies that mirror the Savior's!

FEBRUARY 2

The LORD God planted a garden in Eden in the east,
and there he placed the man he had made.

GENESIS 2:8

WHAT WAS THE GARDEN of Eden like? What was it like to live in
Paradise before the Fall?

The Bible doesn't provide many details about Adam and Eve's daily life
before sin and death entered the world. But it's fascinating to think about
those blissful, early days after Creation.

Here's what we do know from Genesis, chapter 2:

- Eden was a stunning garden filled with "beautiful" trees that
  "produced delicious fruit" (verse 9).
- The garden was well-watered (verse 10).
- The surrounding land was rich in natural resources such as "gold,"
  "aromatic resin," and "onyx stone" (verse 12).
- God gave Adam work to do, but before the Fall, work was a blessing,
  not a curse (verse 15).

If all this sounds like language describing the manicured, royal grounds
of a glorious monarch's kingdom, well, you're exactly right.

What's It Mean?

The Lord is both highly exalted above all his creation, and yet he is also a
wonderfully close and personal God. He lovingly created a world for us to
enjoy his presence. We were not meant to live apart from him but with him.

Before the Fall, the Garden of Eden was literally meant to be heaven
on earth—God's dwelling place with mankind. We see a brief yet beautifully revealing glimpse of this in Genesis 3:8 after Adam and Eve had made
their fateful decision to disobey God: "When the cool evening breezes were
blowing, the man and his wife heard the LORD God walking about in the

garden." Somehow, God made a habit of strolling through the Garden to personally fellowship with Adam and Eve. Amazing!

Sadly, sin has grossly distorted God's earthly dwelling place where he wants to make his presence known. But one day when Jesus returns, the Lord will destroy all evil and restore paradise, which the Bible refers to as "a new heaven and a new earth" (Revelation 21:1). This is God's eternal Kingdom, where all true believers will reign with him forever and enjoy close, personal fellowship with him—without sin and without end.

As Revelation 21:3 says, "I heard a loud shout from the throne, saying, 'Look, God's home is now among his people! He will live with them, and they will be his people. God himself will be with them.'" What a beautiful day that will be!

Now What?

Read Revelation 21:1–22:5 and see how many "paradise restored" references you see relating to Genesis 2.

Did You Know?

Based on Genesis 2, the original Garden of Eden was probably located somewhere in the ancient Fertile Crescent.

FEBRUARY 3

*On the seventh day God had finished his work of
creation, so he rested from all his work.*

GENESIS 2:2

THERE ARE NO HAMMOCKS in heaven. Naptime is not a thing there.
There isn't a need for quiet rooms with a big bed, blackout shades, and a
noisemaker that mimics the sound of a soft, babbling brook.

You probably already knew this, but it's best to make sure. After all,
today's verse says that after the six days of Creation, God "rested from all
his work." The way we think about rest today and God's idea of rest as
expressed in Genesis 2:2 are two completely different concepts.

God wasn't exhausted after creating the universe. He didn't have his
hands on his proverbial hips. He didn't need to wipe his brow, catch his
breath, or use an inhaler.

God is the Ancient of Days. He is the Alpha and Omega, the beginning and the end. He spoke, and solar systems flew into place. He uttered
mere words, and galaxies were born. At his command, the entire earth was
instantly populated with natural wonders that humans have been marveling
at for millennia. No, with this kind of power and authority, God does not
get tired.

Why, then, did God rest?

What's It Mean?

The idea of God resting after his act of Creation signifies a completion of
his work. God wasn't weary! He was simply finished with the grand activity
of creation and exceedingly pleased with the result. As Genesis 1:31 says,
"God looked over all he had made, and he saw that it was very good!"

God's rest on the seventh day also set up the Sabbath cycle—a weekly
holy day when God's people in the Old Testament, the Israelites, would
cease their labors after the pattern of their Creator and worship him
(Exodus 20:8-11).

Think of that: there's a God in heaven who created the entire universe in six days and didn't even break a sweat! Isaiah 40:28 testifies, "The LORD is the everlasting God, the Creator of all the earth. He never grows weak or weary." He made the world as a temple for his glory, and he was glad to share it with his children.

Rest in the greatness, power, and love of this great God!

Now What?

Read Psalm 104, which is a "creation psalm."

Did You Know?

The Jewish Sabbath (day of worship and rest) falls on a Saturday. But starting shortly after Jesus' ascension, Christians have made their weekly worship gathering a Sunday, the first day of the week, to honor the day of Christ's resurrection (Acts 20:7).

FEBRUARY 4

The God of peace will soon crush Satan under your feet.

ROMANS 16:20

IF GENESIS CHAPTERS 1–2 are a sightseeing tour bus that transports us back in time to witness God's beautiful act of Creation, Genesis 3:1 is the ominous sound of screeching brakes. EEERRRRT!!!

Here's what the verse says: "The serpent was the shrewdest of all the wild animals the LORD God had made. One day he asked the woman, 'Did God really say you must not eat the fruit from any of the trees in the garden?'"

This verse is a purposefully stark contrast to the Bible's first two blissful chapters, and it raises plenty of questions:

- Who is this serpent?
- Where did he come from?
- How was he "the shrewdest of all the wild animals" on earth?
- Why was he questioning God?
- And how in the world was he able to talk?!

While the Bible doesn't answer all these questions, Genesis 3:1 introduces us to history's most diabolical character. This is none other than God's cosmic enemy, "the great dragon . . . that ancient serpent, who is called the devil and Satan, the deceiver of the whole world" (Revelation 12:9, ESV).

What's It Mean?

Many people today deny Satan's existence, but the Bible unequivocally affirms his reality. Before we discuss the death and destruction he brought into the world, we need to learn more about who he is.

Satan is a created being and not eternal, although the Bible doesn't explicitly say when God created him or when he and other angels rebelled against God. But God originally made him morally pure, for God cannot create evil.

71

Since his fall, Satan has actively tried to destroy God's plan of salvation on earth "in great anger, knowing that he has little time" (Revelation 12:12). In fact, the name "Satan" means "adversary." He accuses Christians before God night and day—to no avail (Revelation 12:10). He is "a murderer from the beginning" and "the father of lies" (John 8:44).

But Satan has no authority over Christians. Jesus destroyed Satan's power with his victory at the Cross (1 John 3:8), and we can resist the devil through the righteous armor of God (Ephesians 6:10-18). In the end, Jesus will throw Satan into hell forever (Revelation 20:10).

The devil is a defeated foe. Where Adam and Eve failed, you can have victory over the devil's temptations through Christ!

Now What?

When Satan tempts you to sin, answer with Scripture like Jesus did (Matthew 4:1-11).

Did You Know?

Some (but not all) Bible commentators believe Isaiah 14:12-15 and Ezekiel 28:12-19 are prophecies with double meanings—both as warnings against wicked earthly kings in ancient times and as glimpses into the pre-Genesis 3 fall of Satan.

FEBRUARY 5

He is a liar and the father of lies.

JOHN 8:44

THE WORST DAY IN history started with a terrible string of lies.

When Satan, taking the form of a serpent, appeared to Eve in the Garden of Eden, he immediately began whispering fallaciously in her ear about God's character and commands. Earlier, God had given Adam and Eve only one restriction: "You may freely eat the fruit of every tree in the garden—except the tree of the knowledge of good and evil. If you eat its fruit, you are sure to die" (Genesis 2:16-17).

But Satan slithered up to Eve and said, "Did God really say you must not eat the fruit from any of the trees in the garden? . . . You won't die! . . . God knows that your eyes will be opened as soon as you eat it, and you will be like God, knowing both good and evil" (Genesis 3:1, 4-5).

Sadly, Eve succumbed to temptation and ate the fruit. Then Adam did too. They rebelled against God's law, and sin entered the world.

Satan's fatal lies had worked.

What's It Mean?

Satan is a master liar who is constantly trying to destroy God's Kingdom with his deceits. He even lied to Jesus during the wilderness temptations (Matthew 4:1-11) in order to ruin Christ's redemptive mission.

In John 8:44, Jesus said Satan "has always hated the truth, because there is no truth in him. When he lies, it is consistent with his character; for he is a liar and the father of lies." In the Garden of Eden, Satan convinced Adam and Eve to disregard God's authority and doubt his goodness by twisting God's words and uttering bold-faced falsehoods. Adam and Eve's choice to believe Satan's lies instead of obeying God proved disastrous for all of humanity (Romans 5:12).

Satan is still actively opposing God's plan today. He seeks to destroy every person's life—both Christian and non-Christian—with his wicked lies.

But praise God the story doesn't end on such a negative note! God had a plan from the beginning to crush Satan. As 1 John 3:8 says, "The Son of God came to destroy the works of the devil" through his atoning work on the cross for our sins and his powerful resurrection. Through Christ's power, we can "resist the devil, and he will flee" from us (James 4:7).

Thank you, Jesus!

Now What?

Memorize Scripture to combat Satan's lies, just like Jesus did. Here are two great texts to start: Ephesians 6:10-18 and 1 Peter 5:6-11.

Did You Know?

While Satan is a natural liar and brings death, Jesus is "the way, the truth, and the life" (John 14:6).

FEBRUARY 6

*Everyone who sins is breaking God's law, for
all sin is contrary to the law of God.*

1 JOHN 3:4

FALLING IS NEVER a good thing—well, unless you're a skydiver, perhaps.
Then, it's pretty cool. (Just don't forget your parachute.)

But in general, falling hurts. It produces scrapes, bruises, cuts, broken
bones, or worse.

Genesis chapter 3 is often referred to as "The Fall" of mankind. And
boy, did it hurt.

This is when humanity fell from perfect fellowship with God through
Adam and Eve's original sin in the Garden of Eden.

Interestingly, the word sin is not mentioned at all in Genesis 3. But if
you read what the rest of the Bible has to say about sin, it's clear that's what
Adam and Eve did.

This leads us to the question, What is sin? It's a vitally important concept to understand. In fact, it's a matter of life and death.

What's It Mean?

Sin is breaking God's law, as today's verse says. Adam and Eve sinned
because they willfully disobeyed God's command to not eat from the tree of
the knowledge of good and evil.

Every human in history has broken God's law. As Romans 3:23 says,
"All have sinned and fall short of the glory of God" (ESV).

But sin goes much deeper than our actions. Sin is a matter of the heart.
We have also rebelled against God in our attitudes. This is what Jesus was
driving at in passages such as Matthew 5:21-26 and 15:1-20. If we think
hateful thoughts against someone—even if we refrain from speaking or acting maliciously against them—the Bible says we have still broken God's law
to love our neighbor as ourselves.

We are also sinful by nature. Because of Adam's sin, all humans are

75

born inherently guilty before God (Romans 5:12). From birth, we have what's often referred to as indwelling sin. It's in our nature to defy him.

This all sounds pretty bleak, doesn't it? We said earlier that understanding sin was a matter of life and death—because sin brings both physical and spiritual death (Romans 6:23). But there is one who offers hope and eternal life to rebels! As Romans 5:8 says, "God shows his love for us in that while we were still sinners, Christ died for us" (ESV).

Our sin is great, but Jesus is greater!

Now What?
"The law of the Spirit of life has set you free in Christ Jesus from the law of sin and death" (Romans 8:2, ESV). Trust in this Savior!

Did You Know?
Temptation isn't the same as sin. Check out James 1:14-15 and the February 14 devotion for more on this.

76

FEBRUARY 7

Pride goes before destruction, and haughtiness before a fall.

PROVERBS 16:18

HAVE YOU EVER WONDERED what drove Adam and Eve to disobey God in the Garden of Eden? Yes, they were deceived by Satan, but they were not innocently duped. They bore responsibility.

The exchange between Satan and the couple in Genesis 3 is telling. Satan deceitfully told them that by eating the fruit from the tree of the knowledge of good and evil, they would "be like God" (verse 5). Verse 6 says that Eve "wanted the wisdom it would give her. So she took some of the fruit and ate it." Adam did so too.

At the root of original human sin was pride.

What's It Mean?

What is pride? Biblically defined, pride is the desire to please or exalt ourselves rather than God. It's thinking more highly of ourselves than we ought to.

Ultimately, Adam and Eve displayed great arrogance when they ate the forbidden fruit. Not content with their privileged status as God's beloved image-bearers, Adam and Eve proudly desired even more knowledge, power, and prominence in creation.

Pride festers deep within every human being. Whether we're gifted in academics, art, music, sports, or other endeavors, we can all fall prey to thinking too highly of our God-given talents. Worse yet, we all have proudly desired in our hearts to "climb to the highest heavens and be like the Most High" (Isaiah 14:14), wanting to run our lives independent from God.

But as today's verse confirms, pride always precedes disaster. Scripture consistently reserves some of its strongest language to speak against human conceit. In Isaiah 13:11, God says, "I will crush the arrogance of the proud and humble the pride of the mighty." (See also Proverbs 8:13, Isaiah 2:11, and Proverbs 6:16-19.) Sometimes, pride's consequences happen in this life. It's God's way of trying to turn that person toward repentance. But for the person who continues to willfully rebel, eternal consequences await.

The antidote to pride is humility—giving glory to God and considering others better than yourself. "As the Scriptures say, 'God opposes the proud but gives grace to the humble'" (James 4:6).

The best example of humility, of course, was Jesus Christ. The sinless Son of God came to earth in human form to suffer in our place so that we could be redeemed. Pride destroys, but Jesus saves!

Now What?
Learn more about the amazing humility of Christ by reading Philippians 2:3-11.

Did You Know?
If Isaiah 14:12-15 and Ezekiel 28:12-19 truly are descriptions of Satan's original downfall, then Isaiah 14:13-14 and Ezekiel 28:17 show how pride seemed to be the predominant offense.

FEBRUARY 8

The wages of sin is death, but the free gift of God is
eternal life through Christ Jesus our Lord.

ROMANS 6:23

IN MEDIEVAL TIMES, IT became popular for painters to depict Satan as a hideous-looking beast, complete with fangs, horns, claws, fiery eyes, a pointy tail—the whole shebang. That, however, doesn't jive with the biblical record.

Second Corinthians 11:14 says, "Satan disguises himself as an angel of light." This is figurative language, revealing the devil's trickery. He always approaches us deceitfully, under the guise of offering something good, pleasing, or helpful.

His very first temptation in the Garden of Eden is a perfect example. He made the forbidden fruit appear tantalizing to Adam and Eve, even though it brought death. As Genesis 3:6 says, "The woman was convinced. She saw that the tree was beautiful and its fruit looked delicious, and she wanted the wisdom it would give her."

Adam and Eve both fell hard for Satan's wicked lie. But they quickly found out how high the cost of the sin's deceit is.

What's It Mean?

Sin always looks good. That's what Satan wants us to think. But he is "the father of lies" (John 8:44)—history's master con artist.

Sin, like Satan himself, is beguilingly treacherous. It might bring temporary happiness, but it always ends in pain and suffering. It falsely promises great blessings but only delivers terrible curses. It deceptively guarantees satisfaction, but only delivers spiritual death and destruction.

Look at the immediate aftereffects of Adam and Eve's sin in Genesis 3:

- They immediately felt shame and hid from God (verses 7-8).
- They blamed others for their own wrongdoing (verses 12-13).
- Their life experiences became exceedingly harder (verses 16-19).

- Strife entered human relationships (verse 16).
- The ground was cursed (verse 17).
- Physical death became a reality (verse 19).
- They were banished from the Garden and separated from God's presence (verse 23).

So much for Satan's false promises.

Ultimately, sin never satisfies, but there is a Savior who always does! While sin brings death, "the free gift of God is eternal life through Christ Jesus our Lord" (Romans 6:23). Where Adam (as humanity's first representative) failed, Jesus (as humanity's righteous representative) perfectly triumphed over sin's curse. Turn from sin's lies and trust in Christ today!

Now What?
Read Romans 5:12-21 to see how the Bible beautifully contrasts Adam's failure with Jesus' righteousness.

Did You Know?
In another example of figurative language, Revelation 12 calls Satan a "dragon," but its detailed description of the dragon's appearance is meant to be symbolic.

FEBRUARY 9

In the middle of the garden he placed the tree of life
and the tree of the knowledge of good and evil.

GENESIS 2:9

PERHAPS BY NOW—FORTY DEVOTIONS into this book and a couple of chapters into the Bible—you're scratching your head with a puzzled look on your face. Genesis chapters 2–3, in particular, present many extremely difficult questions that have puzzled theologians and sparked debates for centuries. Here are some examples:

- Why did God create Satan if he knew he would eventually rebel, tempt Adam and Eve, and cause such destruction in the world?
- Why did God create the tree of knowledge of good and evil if it eventually became sin's conduit into the world? (See today's verse.)
- Why did God allow evil and death to enter his creation at all?

These theological conundrums keep the most learned biblical scholars awake at night. But none of this, of course, is a puzzle to God. It's perfectly clear to him. And therein lies the heart of the matter. The Lord God Almighty, perfectly holy and righteous, is the grand architect of human history. He knows the answers, even if we don't.

What's It Mean?

When the Bible doesn't provide clear answers to difficult questions, we must be content to acknowledge our human limitations and God's mysterious sovereignty. If you really believe that God is holy and righteous—highly exalted above his creation, morally blameless in all his ways, and just in all his judgments—you can submit to his decisions. But if you question his character or purposes, beware. There's a difference between genuinely wanting to grow in your faith and becoming a skeptic.

The individual who wants to grow seeks to know more about God and worship him. The skeptic begins to accuse God and say, "Why did you do it that way? I would've done things differently. I know better." That's the same prideful response that got Adam and Eve into trouble.

Reading the entire Bible won't answer every single question you have about life. That's okay. You weren't meant to know everything.

But continue to study God's Word and trust in his goodness, sovereignty, and love. And remember: when you're left scratching your head, God still reigns on high—and he loves you very much.

Now What?
Prayerfully ask the Lord to give you a spirit of humility and understanding when considering hard spiritual questions.

Did You Know?
Even the great apostle Paul, who was unsurpassed among the biblical writers at explaining deep spiritual truths, exclaimed, "Oh, how great are God's riches and wisdom and knowledge! How impossible it is for us to understand his decisions and his ways!" (Romans 11:33).

FEBRUARY 10

I will walk among you; I will be your God, and you will be my people.

LEVITICUS 26:12

AS YOU READ THE account of humanity's fall in Genesis 3, has verse 8 ever stuck out to you? Here is what it says:

> When the cool evening breezes were blowing, the man and his wife heard *the LORD God walking about in the garden.* So they hid from the LORD God among the trees. (emphasis added)

When reading Genesis 3, it's natural to get caught up in the negative. It's easy to focus on Satan's temptation, Adam and Eve's disastrous decision to disobey, sin's curses, and all the questions this defining moment produces.

But often lost in these important discussions is another fascinating topic, emphasized in italics above: at the outset of Creation, God himself walked in the Garden of Eden.

Wow!

What's It Mean?

Sin corrupted God's perfect order and separated us from our Creator, but his heart's desire and his original, perfect design was to have close, personal fellowship with his people.

Even after the Fall, God continually sought to dwell with his people and be actively present among them (see today's verse). It's also why he commanded Israel to build a Tabernacle and later a Temple. His glory—a visible manifestation of his holy presence—filled these houses of worship on special occasions.

The greatest example of God's presence with his people is, of course, Jesus Christ. Two thousand years ago, the eternal Son of God left heaven's glory, became human, and walked among us. John 1:14 testifies to this, saying, "The Word became flesh and dwelt among us" (ESV).

One day, Jesus will return to earth in great power and majesty to destroy Satan, death, and all evil. At that time, he will inaugurate his eternal Kingdom, "the new heaven and new earth" of Revelation 21, where God's plan of close, personal fellowship with his image-bearers will never again be broken. "God's home is now among his people! He will live with them, and they will be his people. God himself will be with them" (Revelation 21:3).

Look again at today's verse and compare it to Revelation 21:3. Do you see the connection between what God will say in eternity with what God said in ancient times? His heart has always been to live with his people!

Now What?
For cool stories about how God was actively present among his people, read Exodus 13:17-22; Exodus 40:34-38; and 2 Chronicles 7:1-3, 16.

Did You Know?
Today, God dwells inside every believer through his Holy Spirit (1 Corinthians 3:16; also see the September 9–11 devotions).

FEBRUARY 11

Now he has reconciled you to himself through the
death of Christ in his physical body.

COLOSSIANS 1:22

ONCE ADAM AND EVE sinned, they had to pack their bags . . . or their suitcases . . . or their knapsacks . . . or their fanny packs . . .

Wait, none of these things had been invented yet.

Hmmm.

Well, anyway, they had to leave Eden. Look at Genesis 3:23-24:

The LORD God banished them from the Garden of Eden, and he sent Adam out to cultivate the ground from which he had been made. After sending them out, the LORD God stationed mighty cherubim to the east of the Garden of Eden. And he placed a flaming sword that flashed back and forth to guard the way to the tree of life.

Tragically, Adam and Eve's sin separated them from God.

What's It Mean?

At first glance, this exile from the Garden sounds harsh, doesn't it? But remember: God is holy and righteous in all his ways. He cannot allow una-toned sin in his presence.

Sadly, the unique fellowship Adam and Eve enjoyed with God was broken. Their sin had ended the beautifully unique interactions they experienced with their Creator in Paradise (Genesis 3:8).

But remember this, too: the Fall didn't surprise God. Before time began, he knew all humanity, including you, would rebel against him, and he had a plan to reconcile—or restore broken relationships—with his people through his Son, Jesus Christ.

Look at the magnificent truth found in Colossians 1:19-22:

God in all his fullness was pleased to live in Christ, and through him God reconciled everything to himself. He made peace with everything in heaven and on earth by means of Christ's blood on the cross. This includes you who were once far away from God. You were his enemies, separated from him by your evil thoughts and actions. Yet now he has reconciled you to himself through the death of Christ in his physical body. As a result, he has brought you into his own presence, and you are holy and blameless as you stand before him without a single fault.

Aren't you glad that the story didn't end at Genesis 3? Aren't you glad that God is a loving King who pursues his wayward children? Sin separates us from God, but Jesus beautifully reconciles this broken relationship!

Now What?
To learn more about reconciliation through Christ, read Romans 5:1-11 and 2 Corinthians 5:16-21.

Did You Know?
Before God sent Adam and Eve from the Garden, he killed an animal to make them clothing and cover their nakedness (Genesis 3:21). It was a fore-shadowing of the sacrificial atonement for sins that happened when Jesus died on the cross.

FEBRUARY 12

[God said,] "I will cause hostility between you and the
woman, and between your offspring and her offspring. He
will strike your head, and you will strike his heel."

GENESIS 3:15

ARE YOU SCARED of snakes? Does even the sight of them make your skin crawl—like, well, a serpent slithering through the grass?

If so, it's understandable. Snakes are intriguing and mysterious but also creepy!

Humanity's uneasiness with snakes dates all the way back to the Fall. After the serpent successfully tempted Adam and Eve to sin, God pronounced curses on man, woman, creation, and the serpent. Check out today's verse—part of a larger curse that God decreed on the snake in Genesis 3:14-15:

> Because you have done this, you are cursed more than all animals, domestic and wild. You will crawl on your belly, groveling in the dust as long as you live. And I will cause hostility between you and the woman, and between your offspring and her offspring. He will strike your head, and you will strike his heel.

It's a powerful, harsh curse that still exists today. But amazingly, this terrible curse also contains a wonderful promise. Did you catch it?

What's It Mean?

God's beautiful promise is contained within a conflict. Immediately after the Fall, he foretold "hostility" between Eve's "offspring" and Satan. Who is this offspring? A group of people? Perhaps. Satan certainly has been fighting against humans since Creation.

But these verses speak to a much deeper, more glorious truth. Ultimately, Eve's "offspring" here is an individual—a single man who will battle Satan. The devil will wound this man with a nonfatal blow ("strike his heel"), but this man will deal Satan a death blow ("strike your head").

The mystery man is Jesus! Amazingly, found within the curse of the serpent in Genesis 3:15 is the earliest proclamation of the gospel—the good news of salvation through Christ. The eternal Son of God became Eve's "offspring" through his miraculous incarnation.

Satan struck Jesus' heel, so to speak, thousands of years later by inciting wicked men to crucify him (Luke 22–23), but this was all part of God's sovereign plan to bring lost sinners to salvation. Jesus crushed Satan's head, so to speak, by defeating the power of sin through his death and resurrection (1 Corinthians 15:55-57), and ultimately, he will throw Satan into hell forever one day (Revelation 20:10).

Amid sin's curse and Satan's temporary victory in the Garden, God pronounced final victory through his Son, the coming Savior!

Now What?

Read about Satan's end in Revelation 20.

Did You Know?

There are almost 3,000 snake species in the world, but only about 375 are venomous.

FEBRUARY 13

The King will turn to those on the left and say, "Away with you, you cursed ones, into the eternal fire prepared for the devil and his demons."

MATTHEW 25:41

PARADISE WAS LOST.

Among the many curses that followed Adam and Eve's rebellious choice to eat the forbidden fruit was a new horrible reality: separation from God. Because of their sin, the couple had to leave God's immediate presence in the Garden of Eden. The beautiful fellowship they had once enjoyed with him was fractured.

Because of Adam's disobedience, every person is guilty before God and begins life spiritually "dead because of your disobedience and your many sins" (Ephesians 2:1). Apart from God's saving grace, people are not only separated from God spiritually in this life, but they are also in danger of being cast away into a place of eternal punishment once they die.

The Bible calls this place hell.

What's It Mean?

Why are we talking about hell as we discuss Genesis 3? Because it's extremely important to understand everything the Bible teaches about the effects and outcome of our sin. Left to our wickedness—without divine intervention—each of us would be headed toward an eternity separated from God in hell.

Hell is mysterious and misunderstood, but it's not make-believe. The Bible always refers to it as a real place.

Hell is where God's enemies (anyone who doesn't repent of their sins and trust in Jesus as their Savior) will be punished forever after death. This is the final destination for Satan and his demons too.

The Bible describes hell in the following ways:

- a fiery furnace, where there will be weeping and gnashing of teeth (Matthew 13:42)

- the eternal fire prepared for the devil and his demons (Matthew 25:41)
- gloomy pits of darkness (2 Peter 2:4)
- a place where the smoke of their torment will rise forever and ever, and they will have no relief day or night (Revelation 14:11)
- a lake of fire and the second death (Revelation 20:14)

Hell is a horrific place.

Thankfully, the Lord has mercifully provided a way for us to avoid such a terrible fate. Romans 6:23 says, "For the wages of sin is death, but the free gift of God is eternal life through Christ Jesus our Lord."

God sent his Son to die for our sins so that we wouldn't have to experience eternal separation from him. Through Jesus, we can be forgiven and restored to our Creator's presence forever!

Now What?
Jesus told a parable about heaven and hell. Read it in Luke 16:19-31.

Did You Know?
Jesus mentioned hell more than anyone else did in Scripture.

FEBRUARY 14

*Temptation comes from our own desires, which entice us and
drag us away. These desires give birth to sinful actions. And
when sin is allowed to grow, it gives birth to death.*

JAMES 1:14-15

WHAT WERE YOU AFRAID of most when you were younger? Spiders?
Snakes? Heights? The doctor's office? Being alone?

What about being in a dark room at night?

At some point in our childhood, most, if not all, of us were scared of
what might be lurking in shadowy corners—in the closet, behind a door, or
under the bed.

Of course, bedtime monsters aren't real. However, there is a horrible
monster lurking inside each of us. In fact, the Bible says it is "crouching at
the door, eager to control you" (Genesis 4:7). Do you know what this hideous creature is?

It's our sinful nature. And it manifested itself in a brutal way in Genesis 4.

What's It Mean?

After leaving the Garden of Eden, Adam and Eve had two sons, Cain and
Abel. One day, both of them brought sacrifices to God. Cain (a farmer)
brought some of his crops, while Abel (a shepherd) brought the best portions of his flock's firstborn lambs

The Lord received Abel's gift, but rejected Cain's (although Scripture
doesn't specify why). Cain was furious, and God admonished him: "You will
be accepted if you do what is right. But if you refuse to do what is right,
then watch out! Sin is crouching at the door, eager to control you. But you
must subdue it and be its master" (verse 7).

Shortly afterward, Cain killed Abel in a jealous rage—the first murder,
only two generations into human history. That's how depraved sin is. Cain
completely disregarded God's warning and let the monster of sin consume him.

Sin crouches at the doorstep of every person's heart. But today's verse
masterfully illustrates the progressive nature of sin. Temptation isn't sin.

When you are tempted to disobey, you have a choice. You can give in and let your desires hatch into rebellion against God, or you can choose a righteous, obedient response.

As 1 Corinthians 10:13 says, "He will not allow the temptation to be more than you can stand. When you are tempted, he will show you a way out so that you can endure."

Don't crack open the door for the monster of sin. Slam it shut by God's power!

Now What?

Read the entire account of Cain and Abel in Genesis 4:1-16.

Did You Know?

Psalm 119:11 shows us where to go to shut the door on sin's temptation: "I have hidden your word in my heart, that I might not sin against you."

FEBRUARY 15

The LORD was sorry he had ever made them and
put them on the earth. It broke his heart.

GENESIS 6:6

BY THE TIME OF Noah, at least ten generations since Creation, humanity
had reached its lowest point. People were finding seemingly new ways to
dishonor God every day.

Here's how Genesis 6:5-8 describes it:

> The LORD observed the extent of human wickedness on the earth, and
> he saw that everything they thought or imagined was consistently and
> totally evil. *So the LORD was sorry he had ever made them* and put them
> on the earth. It broke his heart. And the LORD said, "I will wipe this
> human race I have created from the face of the earth. Yes, and I will
> destroy every living thing—all the people, the large animals, the small
> animals that scurry along the ground, and even the birds of the sky. *I*
> *am sorry I ever made them.*" But Noah found favor with the LORD.
> (emphasis added)

Humanity had completely forsaken its Creator and become so wicked that
God actually said he regretted creating them at all. That's quite a statement.

At first glance, though, this seems to pose a theological conundrum: Can
God make a mistake? Can the Lord God Almighty—the omnipotent, omniscient ruler of the universe—actually blunder? Does he need "do-overs" from
time to time, like the rest of us?

Not at all.

What's It Mean?

God is holy. He never makes mistakes. He is perfectly wise and just in all he
does. Every decision he makes comes from his perfectly good, loving character. As we learned in the January 18 and 19 devotions, the clear, consistent
witness of Scripture is that God never changes his mind.

When God said he was sorry for making humanity, he was not apologizing for an error he made. He was expressing divine sorrow over human depravity. God grieved over the sinful choices that people were making. He was cut to the heart over the righteous judgment they would suffer.

Genesis 6:5-8 doesn't present us with a dilemma about God at all. Rather, it powerfully affirms God's hatred of sin and his tender heart for the lost. Remember, as 2 Peter 3:9 says, "He does not want anyone to be destroyed, but wants everyone to repent."

We serve a loving God who grieves over human sin. Praise God for that!

Now What?
Read the entire Noah's ark account in Genesis chapters 6–9.

Did You Know?
A similar example of God's sorrow over human sin is his rejection of King Saul in 1 Samuel 15 (see specifically verses 11 and 35).

FEBRUARY 16

Noah was a righteous man, the only blameless person living on earth at the time, and he walked in close fellowship with God.

GENESIS 6:9

IMAGINE IF THE WORLD was filled with nothing but thousands of dangerous escaped convicts. This was the moral climate of earth in the early days of humanity, as described in Genesis 6:5: "The LORD observed the extent of human wickedness on the earth, and he saw that everything they thought or imagined was consistently and totally evil."

That's a shocking statement.

Verses 11-12 give additional detail: "Now God saw that the earth had become corrupt and was filled with violence. God observed all this corruption in the world, for everyone on earth was corrupt."

Once a beautiful paradise, God's creation sadly had devolved into a realm of brutality and wickedness, thanks to sin. The world was a treacherous place to live. Love and kindness were as rare as an oasis in a vast desert wasteland. Selfishness, pride, and hostility ruled. Violence was the currency of the day (verse 11). It's entirely possible Cain's murderous example was being repeated often. The earth was groaning under the weight of sin.

But one man was different. His name was Noah. As today's verse says, "Noah was a righteous man, the only blameless person living on earth at the time."

What's It Mean?

Noah's decision to follow God in such a hostile environment couldn't have been easy. The entire world was filled with evil and cruelty. He was one man walking one way while the flood of humanity (no pun intended) wickedly raged the opposite way. It would have been much easier to go with the flow. Yet he chose to trust in God, press on, and ultimately, his faith saved him and his family.

Read today's news headlines. Today's world is no different than Noah's. It's a dark, wicked place. Maybe you haven't been confronted yet with tough choices in life. If not, you will eventually. Or maybe you're facing one now. Regardless, when that decision comes, will you go with the flow of godlessness, or like Noah, will you stand against the tide and follow God in obedience and faith?

Now What?

Pray for God to help you stand strong for him, even when it seems the whole world is choosing evil.

Did You Know?

Noah's era was also when God began limiting the extensive age spans of humans. Genesis 6:3 says, "In the future, their normal lifespan will be no more than 120 years."

FEBRUARY 17

It was by faith that Noah built a large boat
to save his family from the flood.

HEBREWS 11:7

HOW MANY TIMES have you read the story of Noah's ark?

Once? Twice? Ten times? Fifty times? Never?

Regardless of your familiarity with this famous story, as a twenty-first-century reader, it's easy to skim it and miss the magnitude of what you're reading.

But look again and marvel at what God told Noah to do:

Build a large boat from cypress wood and waterproof it with tar, inside and out. Then construct decks and stalls throughout its interior. Make the boat 450 feet long, 75 feet wide, and 45 feet high. Leave an 18-inch opening below the roof all the way around the boat. Put the door on the side, and build three decks inside the boat—lower, middle, and upper.

GENESIS 6:14-16

God did not ask Noah to build a schooner, tugboat, pontoon, or a dinghy. The ark was bigger than an NFL-sized football field and roughly four stories tall! Noah couldn't contract the work out to a construction company. He couldn't use a crane, forklift, or even a battery-operated screwdriver to do it himself.

No, he and his three sons found whatever ancient tools were available and painstakingly did the work by hand.

One . . . nail . . . at . . . a . . . time.

What's It Mean?

If Noah's amazing obedience in building something that massive isn't impressive enough, consider his faith. He lived in ancient Mesopotamia, probably a long way from any large bodies of water. What would he do with this gigantic boat after it was built?

That would have been an obvious question for most folks. But God had already told Noah the answer: "Look! I am about to cover the earth with a flood that will destroy every living thing that breathes" (Genesis 6:17).

Thousands of years later, here's how the writer of Hebrews recorded Noah's remarkable response: "It was by faith that Noah built a large boat to save his family from the flood. He obeyed God, who warned him about things that had never happened before" (11:7).

What about you? Ark building might not be in your future, but God does want you to display Noah-like faith. God is far greater than your circumstances. He wants your obedience, even when he asks big things of you. And he will always keep his promises, even if your eyes can't immediately see what he's up to.

Will you trust him?

Now What?
Noah-like faith doesn't happen magically. Pray for God to increase your faith.

Did You Know?
After the Flood, the ark came to rest on "the mountains of Ararat" (Genesis 8:4), which are in modern-day Turkey.

FEBRUARY 18

*I will remember my covenant with you and with all living
creatures. Never again will the floodwaters destroy all life.*

GENESIS 9:15

THE LARGE WOODEN DOOR slowly swung open. Noah peered into the
vast openness before him and squinted. The brightness of the outside world
took some adjusting to.

He stepped foot on Mount Ararat and took a long, deep breath. Can
you imagine how good the fresh oxygen must have felt after more than a
year of being cooped up with smelly animals inside a huge floating zoo?

Once all his family members and the animals had exited the ark,
Noah sacrificed a burnt offering to God for saving them from the great
Flood. Then God made a wonderful promise to Noah—words that no one
on earth had ever heard before. God said, "I am giving you a sign of my
covenant with you and with all living creatures, for all generations to come.
I have placed my rainbow in the clouds. It is the sign of my covenant with
you and with all the earth" (Genesis 9:12-13).

God had made his first covenant.

What's It Mean?

In biblical terms, a covenant is a relationship between two or more parties
that originates with an oath-bound promise. Typically, a covenant in the
Bible looks something like one of these options:

I promise to do such-and-such for you.

If you do this, then I will do this.

There are dozens of references to covenants in the Bible. But whenever
God entered into a covenant with people, he was always the originator.
Sinful humanity never starts a covenant with God. It's always God, in his
sovereign mercy and grace, who initiates a covenant with us.

What's more, God never enters into a covenant promise based on the
inherent goodness of the other party. Look at Noah. Even though Noah was

"a righteous man" (Genesis 6:9), God still said that "the intention of man's heart"—including Noah's—"is evil from his youth" (Genesis 8:21, ESV).

God's rainbow covenant with Noah never to destroy all life again with a flood was a wonderful sign of God's great love. He certainly wasn't obligated to do this.

God is still keeping his rainbow covenant today. He is still pouring out waves of undeserved mercy and grace through Jesus!

Now What?

The next time you see a rainbow in the sky, remember God's covenant of mercy and grace.

Did You Know?

God made some other well-known covenants with Abraham (Genesis 15), David (2 Samuel 7), and with Moses and the Israelites (Exodus 19–24). Check them out!

FEBRUARY 19

*They said, "Come, let's build a great city for ourselves with
a tower that reaches into the sky. This will make us famous
and keep us from being scattered all over the world."*

GENESIS 11:4

NOAH WAS DEAD. THE great Flood was over. The human race was rapidly expanding, thanks to a population explosion growing out of Noah's family.

But there was a problem. In Genesis 9:1, God had commanded Noah's descendants to "fill the earth." But Genesis 11:1-2 says the following: "All the people of the world spoke the same language and used the same words. As the people migrated to the east, they found a plain in the land of Babylonia and settled there."

God hadn't told humanity to settle in one place. He had commanded them to spread out across the earth.

What's It Mean?

In exceedingly great pride, humanity wanted to join together and make a name for themselves by building the tower of Babel (see today's verse). They wanted to celebrate their own strength, skill, creativity, and resourcefulness. Despite the Flood and its warnings, their worship had quickly turned away from their Creator once again.

What was the Lord's response? In both judgment and mercy, he "confused the people with different languages" and "scattered them all over the world" (Genesis 11:9), which meant "they stopped building the city" (verse 8). Mercifully, he didn't destroy them, but he also wouldn't let them continue this outright rebellion together against him.

This same pride of ancient Babylonia inhabits our hearts too. It's quiet and cunning, but it's there. No matter how old you are, where you live, or what you're good at, your inborn human pride calls for you to settle in the Land of Vanity and Self-Sufficiency, apart from God.

In a modern-day twist on today's verse, pride says, Come, let's build a great monument of self-glorification to YOU that reaches into the sky! This will make you famous and will keep you from going unnoticed in the world.

This, of course, is the height of conceit. But we do it subtly, like bragging about our athletic prowess or questioning God's promises.

Watch out for the Babel trap. Avoid constructing towers of self-flattery and praise. God says very clearly in Isaiah 42:8, "I will not give my glory to anyone else." Whatever you build in life, whatever you undertake, do it for God's glory!

Now What?
The next time you hear a different language, remember what happened at the tower of Babel.

Did You Know?
The "tower" that the people in Genesis 11 built was likely a ziggurat, a Mesopotamian pyramid structure of successively smaller levels with a temple shrine on the top.

FEBRUARY 20

I will make you into a great nation.

GENESIS 12:2

LET'S BE HONEST: the first eleven chapters of Genesis, for the most part, are a real downer.

You've got talking serpents, devilish temptations, lies, rebellion, curses, violence, murder, anarchy, and watery worldwide annihilation (save for one family). Oh yeah . . . don't forget a really tall tower of human pride. And we're not even halfway through the first book of the Bible!

Sheesh.

Then, like a sudden breath of fresh air, Genesis 12 arrives, and suddenly, the tone changes.

Amid the chaos of human wickedness in the world, God broke through with a marvelous plan that nobody saw coming. The Lord's sovereign strategy—formed before he created the world—involved a pagan.

Yes, an idol-worshiper.

His name was Abram. Here's what God told him in Genesis 12:1-3:

Leave your native country, your relatives, and your father's family, and go to the land that I will show you. I will make you into a great nation. I will bless you and make you famous, and you will be a blessing to others. I will bless those who bless you and curse those who treat you with contempt. All the families on earth will be blessed through you.

What's It Mean?

We often think of Abram (whose name would soon be changed to Abraham) as one of the great pillars of the faith—and rightfully so. But when the Lord first called him, he was a heathen. Abram grew up in "Ur of the Chaldeans" (Genesis 11:31), an idolatrous Mesopotamian city. Abram's family worshiped false gods (Joshua 24:2).

Did you notice how God initiated the conversation with Abram? Israel's future patriarch wasn't seeking the one true God. There's no evidence that he had even heard of God.

No matter.

God had a plan to change the world. Eventually, he would create a people for his glory and bring his promised Savior through them to bless the whole world. But the story would begin with the call of the people's unsuspecting patriarch, Abram.

God is still doing the same thing today. When it comes to calling us to his plan for salvation, God always initiates the process, not us. That's because we possess no inherent goodness. Colossians 2:13 says, "You were dead because of your sins and because your sinful nature was not yet cut away. Then God made you alive with Christ, for he forgave all our sins."

Praise God that he's still calling people today, just like he called Abram thousands of years ago!

Now What?

For similar references to Colossians 2:13, read Ephesians 2:1-9 and Titus 3:4-7.

Did You Know?

The ancient city of Ur would've been located in modern-day Iraq.

FEBRUARY 21

Abram departed as the LORD had instructed.

GENESIS 12:4

AS WE DISCUSSED **YESTERDAY,** the story of Abram's call is a wonderful example of God's gracious initiative in saving lost sinners and bringing them into his eternal purposes.

But have you ever considered Abram's perspective? When God commanded him, "Leave your native country, your relatives, and your father's family, and go to the land that I will show you" (Genesis 12:1), Abram's head must have been spinning! Perhaps some of the following thoughts and questions ran through his mind:

- Who in the world is speaking to me? (Remember, Abram came from a family who worshiped many gods and idols.)
- This is clearly a powerful God since none of the other gods my family has worshiped ever spoke to me. Does this mean all the others are fake?
- What kind of land is God sending me to? It's an awfully long journey. Is it a dangerous place? What if I don't like it there?
- How can God make me into a great nation (Genesis 12:2) when my wife and I are both old and we don't have children?

Abram had a lot of reasons to say no to God's calling. But thankfully, he said yes. And the world has never been the same.

What's It Mean?

If you are God's child through faith in his Son, Jesus Christ, he will call you to display great faith in him, as he did with Abram. Sometimes, he will pull you out of your comfort zone for your own good. He's probably not going to tell you to hop on a camel and trek hundreds of miles to a foreign country to start a new nation. But whether now or later, God will reveal his plan for various parts of your life, and he will call you to follow his guiding hand.

When he does, his timing and purpose probably won't align with your plan. That's okay—he's God and you're not! Don't question him; just obey. Follow Abram's faith-filled example and "depart as the Lord instructs" (paraphrase of today's verse). When the Lord calls, say yes!

You won't know what the outcome will be. But the Lord does. And you can trust that the almighty, omniscient God has your best interest in mind, and that he will equip you for the journey and will carry you through until the end.

God is calling. Are you ready to answer?

Now What?

Pray for a heart that will say yes to God's call.

Did You Know?

Abram was no spring chicken when he started the journey from Haran to Canaan. He was seventy-five!

FEBRUARY 22

Abram believed the LORD, and the LORD counted
him as righteous because of his faith.

GENESIS 15:6

ONE NIGHT, ABRAM WAS sitting in his tent with the troubles of life and the uncertainty of his future weighing heavily on him.

He had obeyed God's command to go from Haran to Canaan, but he was still childless. By now, Abram was probably in his eighties, and his wife Sarai was in her seventies. How, Abram wondered, would God fulfill his great promise to make me into a great nation?

So on a beautiful, cloudless evening, God powerfully came to Abram in a vision.

"Look up into the sky and count the stars if you can," God said. "That's how many descendants you will have!" (Genesis 15:5).

God's promise was bold . . . incredible . . . and seemingly impossible—impossible, that is, for man. But certainly not for God.

As Abram digested this seemingly audacious covenant, something amazing happened. He didn't waffle between belief and doubt. He didn't ask God for a list of previous miracles or references. As today's verse says, "Abram believed the LORD, and the LORD counted him as righteous."

What's It Mean?

Abram did not just show blind faith that night outside his tent. He showed remarkable, saving faith. Today's verse, Genesis 15:6, is an essential verse in biblical soteriology (the doctrine of salvation), showing how God requires faith for someone to be justified (or considered righteous) before him.

This verse points to a beautiful work of grace in Abram's heart. Abram hadn't done anything noteworthy to merit God's favor. He simply trusted in the Lord's promise of future blessings, and through this faith, God credited righteousness to his account.

God's promise sounded impossible. But in a wonderful display of faith, Abram believed that God could do the impossible, and God counted him as righteous for it. He later blessed Abram with a son, Isaac, through whom the nation of Israel would come.

God wants the same faith from you today. In fact, the Bible says righteousness without faith is not possible (Hebrews 11:6). You can't earn God's favor through works. You just need to believe in what he's already accomplished for you (forgiveness of sins through Christ) and the promise of future blessings (most gloriously, eternal life with him).

Will you believe?

Now What?

The apostle Paul beautifully links Abram's experience four thousand years ago to our lives today in Romans 4:23-25. Check it out!

Did You Know?

New Testament writers quoted today's important verse four times—in Romans 4:3; Romans 4:22; Galatians 3:6; and James 2:23.

FEBRUARY 23

Do what is good and run from evil so that you may live!

AMOS 5:14

Um, excuse me, Mr. Zookeeper, would you please open the lion's cage so I can get a closer look at this ferocious beast?

Uh, pardon me, Mr. NASCAR official, would you mind if I rode my bike on the track during the Daytona 500? I promise to wear my helmet.

Hi, Mr. NASA official. May I please stand near the launch pad as you blast a rocket into outer space so I can roast some marshmallows in the overwhelming inferno of the liftoff?

Would you ever ask any of these questions? No, of course not! Putting yourself in such close proximity to any of these things would put you in grave danger.

Spiritually speaking, though, this is exactly what Abram's nephew, Lot, did as he and Abram settled into their new homes in Canaan. As Genesis 13:12-13 says, "Lot moved his tents to a place near Sodom and settled among the cities of the plain. But the people of this area were extremely wicked and constantly sinned against the LORD."

Maybe Lot didn't know about Sodom's wickedness when he first moved there. But one chapter later, in Genesis 14:12, Lot had moved inside the city gates of Sodom. By Genesis 19:1, "Lot was sitting in the gate of Sodom" (ESV), a place reserved for business and judicial matters in ancient times. He apparently had become a prominent citizen.

Lot was playing with fire—literally. God was about to judge Sodom with "fire and burning sulfur from the sky" (Genesis 19:24). Mercifully, God sent two angels to rescue him and his family.

What's It Mean?

Like Lot, sometimes we put ourselves in harm's way by not taking sin seriously. We try to dip our toes into sin's treacherous waters without fully

109

taking the plunge. Or we hang out with bad influences thinking it won't rub off on us. But sin doesn't work like that. Sin is a slippery slope. In the end, we usually end up way too deep, needing a spiritual life preserver.

Scripture calls us to "run from evil" (today's verse) that we might live. We are not to encamp near sin. Rather, we must turn 180 degrees and sprint the other way.

Don't loiter around sin. Run toward godliness!

Now What?

Sometimes we are blinded to our proximity to sin. Ask a trusted friend or adult to reveal any instances of this to you and pray for the Lord's help to change.

Did You Know?

Despite Lot's terrible decision to live in Sodom, 2 Peter 2:8 interestingly calls him "a righteous man who was tormented in his soul by the wickedness he saw."

FEBRUARY 24

Be still in the presence of the LORD,
and wait patiently for him to act.

PSALM 37:7

THE CALENDAR PAGES SEEMED to flip interminably slowly . . .
Wait—paper calendars hadn't been invented yet.

The hour and minute hands seemed like they were barely moving . . .
Hold on—wall clocks and wristwatches didn't exist yet either.

We'd mention sand slipping slowly through the hourglass . . . But, well,
you know the drill by now—hourglasses were a couple thousand years from
development too.

The point is, from the moment God initially promised to "make
[Abraham] into a great nation" (Genesis 12:2) until the fulfillment of the
promise, Abraham had to wait twenty-five years!

That's a looooong time.

Finally, when Abraham was one hundred years old, his wife, Sarah
(who was ninety), gave birth to Isaac, the child of the promise. Here's how
Genesis 21:1-2 records it:

> The LORD kept his word and did for Sarah exactly what he had
> promised. She became pregnant, and she gave birth to a son for
> Abraham in his old age. This happened at just the time God had
> said it would.

What's It Mean?

Can you imagine waiting twenty-five years for someone to keep their promise to you? That's about one-third of a modern life span. Even for Abraham,
who lived 175 years, that was a long wait.

But God's timing is flawless. He is never slow or forgetful in keeping his
promises. The plans he makes for our lives are perfectly ordered.

God's timing is not like ours. He sees all eternity at once (2 Peter 3:8).
We can't see past the present. He is holy, infinite, and omniscient. We are

sinful, finite, and typically very narrow-minded. He often asks us to wait for things longer than we'd like to.

Ultimately, this is a good thing. As we wait on God's timing, he teaches us patience, perseverance, and trust. Remember, Abraham's faith in God's promise was "counted . . . to him as righteousness" (Genesis 15:6, ESV).

Is God calling you to wait on him right now? Have you been praying for a long time with no discernable answer yet? Be encouraged from the story of Isaac's birth. You might not know the timing or the answer, but God will answer in his own perfect timing. Trust in him. Make today's verse your prayer. He will always do what's best for you.

Now What?
Keep a prayer journal so you can track when and how God answers prayer and faithfully fulfills his promises.

Did You Know?
When Abram was ninety-nine, God changed his name to Abraham, which means "father of a multitude," to reaffirm the covenant God had made with him.

FEBRUARY 25

Now I know that you truly fear God.

GENESIS 22:12

ONE DAY, WHEN ISAAC was a young boy, God gave Abraham a shocking command: "Take your son, your only son—yes, Isaac, whom you love so much—and go to the land of Moriah. Go and sacrifice him as a burnt offering on one of the mountains, which I will show you" (Genesis 22:2).

God's words were chilling and dreadful. Even today, although we know the end of the story, the words are disturbing to read. Imagine how Abraham must have felt, not knowing the outcome.

A million questions must have raced through his mind, not the least of which was how God would keep his promise to make Abraham into a great nation if Isaac died. Yet Abraham faithfully followed God's command.

Abraham climbed the mountain, tied Isaac to an altar he constructed, and raised a sharp dagger. Suddenly, an angel called out to him: "Do not hurt him in any way, for now I know that you truly fear God. You have not withheld from me even your son, your only son" (Genesis 22:12).

What's It Mean?

What are we to make of this fascinating story? First, it's important to remember that God *never* tempts us to sin (James 1:13), but he does test our faith (Genesis 22:1). God is not cruel or sadistic. His plan for Abraham never involved sacrificing his son.

Isaac was the child of God's promise, through whom he would bring forth the nation of Israel and bless the world (Genesis 12:2-3). God was testing Abraham's devotion, and Abraham—in an astounding display of faith and commitment—proved he would sacrifice everything, even what he loved most, to God.

In your life, God will never tempt you to sin, but he might test your faith. He wants to reveal where your heart's allegiance truly lies and show the depth of your commitment to him.

Is there anything you're withholding from him right now? Is there any area of your life that you're telling God, "You can have all of me except that—that part is mine"?

Don't withhold any part of your life from God. Freely give your whole life to him in faith and worship. As today's verse says, this is what it means to "truly fear God."

Now What?
Read Genesis 22 and Hebrews 11:17-19 for the full picture of today's story.

Did You Know?
Somehow, Abraham believed that both he *and* Isaac would return to his servants who traveled to the mountain with them, possibly an allusion to Abraham's belief in God's ability to raise someone from the dead (Genesis 22:5 and Hebrews 11:19).

FEBRUARY 26

*Since he did not spare even his own Son but gave him
up for us all, won't he also give us everything else?*

ROMANS 8:32

WHAT DO YOU HOLD most dear in life?

Sports? Popularity? Academics? Work? Chocolate chip cookie dough ice
cream? (If your answer is the last option, please share!)

As we discussed yesterday, God tested Abraham in Genesis 22 to see
what Abraham held most dearly—his son, Isaac, and God's great promise, or God himself. Isaac, as you recall, was a very special child—the son
through whom God's great promise to Abraham (Genesis 12:2-3) would be
fulfilled. Yet after Isaac was finally born, God shocked Abraham by telling
him to take a three-day journey and sacrifice Isaac on a mountain. God was
testing Abraham to see where Abraham's true allegiance lied.

God had no intention of letting Isaac die, but he wanted to see the full
measure of Abraham's devotion to him. This is reflected in what the angel
said as Abraham raised the dagger: "Do not hurt [Isaac] in any way, for now
I know that you truly fear God. You have not withheld from me even your
son, your only son" (Genesis 22:12).

What's It Mean?

Does that verse sound familiar to you? It should. The Bible is full of historical parallelisms—events that God ordained to occur in Old Testament times
to reflect the gospel—the greater message of salvation through his Son, Jesus
Christ.

Look at today's verse. Do you see the similarities? Just like Abraham
was willing to give up his own son, God took the far greater step and actually sacrificed his own Son on the cross and raised him back to life so that
we could be saved from our sins. God's love for you is unparalleled. There's
nothing more that he could have given up for you than his own Son, who
had committed no wrong (2 Corinthians 5:21) and did nothing deserving
death. What amazing love the Father and Son have for us!

At the beginning of today's devotion, we asked the question, What do you hold most dear in life? Hopefully, the answer is a relationship with God through our Lord and Savior, Jesus Christ.

Now let's flip that question around: What does God hold most dear in life? The answer is you, if you are his child through faith!

Now What?

As you read the Old Testament in your personal quiet times, keep your eyes peeled for gospel-centric parallelisms like this one. They're all over!

Did You Know?

Another parallelism with gospel overtones is found in Genesis 22:8. Can you see the connection?

FEBRUARY 27

On the mountain of the LORD it will be provided.

GENESIS 22:14

WHEN ABRAHAM SADDLED his donkey and set out for Mount Moriah to sacrifice Isaac, the great patriarch had no idea what the outcome of his journey would be. And little did he realize how modern-day Christians would still be reading about his amazing devotion to the Lord and being strengthened in their own faith.

Yet this story also raises a fascinating question: If God is omniscient, why did he test Abraham's faith at all? Didn't he already know the level of Abraham's commitment toward him and how Abraham would respond?

Hmmm . . .

What's It Mean?

Before we answer this question, we need to reiterate a crucial point that the Bible makes clear: God *never* tempts us to sin (James 1:13). Unlike the false gods that many ancient pagan cultures used to worship, God is not cruel, sadistic, or capricious. He doesn't toy with human beings, as if we are merely pawns on a cosmic chess table. He is holy—perfectly good, loving, and just in all his ways.

But God does test our faith. Does he do this to learn something he didn't already know about our love, trust, or commitment toward him?

No.

God knows all things (1 John 3:20), including our hearts and minds. He fully knew Abraham's devotion to him. Ultimately, the test of Isaac's sacrifice wasn't for God's benefit, but for Abraham's—to strengthen his faith and show him that God would provide for all his needs.

Look what happened next:

Abraham looked up and saw a ram caught by its horns in a thicket. So he took the ram and sacrificed it as a burnt offering in place of his son. Abraham named the place *Yahweh-Yireh* (which means "the LORD will provide"). To this day, people still use that name as a proverb: "On the mountain of the LORD it will be provided."

GENESIS 22:13-14

When God tests your faith, remember: God isn't trying to learn something about you he doesn't already know. And don't resist the test. It's for your spiritual good (James 1:2-4). Instead, look for the ways God is meeting your needs, just like he did for Abraham.

Remember, God's name is Yahweh-Yireh. The Lord will provide!

Now What?

When you're being tested in life, keep a journal of how God provides for you so you can remember his faithfulness and praise him later on.

Did You Know?

- We also need to acknowledge the presence of divine mystery here. God sometimes tests our faith despite knowing the outcome of that testing beforehand. If this remains hard for us to understand, that's okay because it's perfectly understood by God.

FEBRUARY 28

God showed his great love for us by sending Christ
to die for us while we were still sinners.

ROMANS 5:8

ANY PREGNANT WOMAN CAN tell you the joys—and discomforts—
of a baby moving inside the womb. It's one of the wonders of the prenatal
period.

But what Rebekah, the wife of Abraham's son, Isaac, felt inside her
was like two mixed martial artists grappling in a steel cage. Rebekah was
carrying twins! Their names were Jacob (younger) and Esau (older). The
boys weren't going to grow up to be best buddies. They even fought in
utero! (See Genesis 25:22.) When they were born, little bro came out grasp-
ing Esau's foot, so he was named Jacob, which means "one who grabs the
heel." Not a compliment!

This strife continued through the family lineage. Jacob became a master
deceiver, while Esau, a "godless" man (Hebrews 12:16), wanted to kill Jacob
for a time. Jacob's twelve sons became the twelve tribes of Israel. But early
on, these men were bloodthirsty scoundrels who sold their brother, Joseph,
into slavery. As you trace ancient Israel's history, it's one moral failure after
another.

Why, then, did God specifically choose Abraham's family to initiate his
plan of salvation? Down the line, this family was filled with thieves, liars, hypocrites, adulterers, murderers, and idolaters. Why didn't he pick a better family?

What's It Mean?

Indeed, Abraham's family was filled with all sorts of rebels, miscreants, and
reprobates. But so is everyone's. "All have sinned and fall short of the glory
of God" (Romans 3:23, ESV).

Thankfully, God not only saves sinners, but also uses them in his
eternal plan of redemption. In fact, he receives more glory because he
accomplishes his eternal purposes while using those whose hearts were once
hardened against him! (See today's verse.)

God didn't choose Abraham's family to change the world because of any inherent righteousness in them. He graciously worked through both their obedience and rebellion to accomplish his sovereign plan of salvation.

God is still saving sinners and using them today. Does he have to? No. But he chooses to! He carries out his redemptive plan not because of us, but rather in spite of our sin. Then he invites us into his plan by grace and helps us become part of it. Praise the Lord!

Now What?
Read the stories of Jacob and Esau in Genesis 25–35.

Did You Know?
In Romans 9:10-13, the apostle Paul uses Jacob and Esau to illustrate the doctrine of election—God's sovereign plan for salvation. For more on election, check out this key passage of Scripture, as well as the October 17–22 devotions.

MARCH 1

I will not leave you until I have finished giving
you everything I have promised you.

GENESIS 28:15

JACOB WAS IN QUITE a predicament. The deceitful "heel-grabber" was on a 550-mile journey from his family's home in Beersheba to Haran, fleeing from Esau, who wanted to kill him after Jacob connivingly stole his older brother's valuable birthright and blessing. Apparently, in his haste, Jacob forgot to pack a pillow and had to fluff a rock before lying down to sleep.

Oops.

While Jacob slept, God came to him in a marvelous dream. In it, a stairway stretched from heaven to earth, with angels ascending and descending and God standing at the top. Then God reaffirmed the covenant he had made with Jacob's forefathers:

> I am the LORD, the God of your grandfather Abraham, and the God
> of your father, Isaac. The ground you are lying on belongs to you. I
> am giving it to you and your descendants. Your descendants will be as
> numerous as the dust of the earth! They will spread out in all directions—
> to the west and the east, to the north and the south. And all the families
> of the earth will be blessed through you and your descendants. What's
> more, I am with you, and I will protect you wherever you go. One day I
> will bring you back to this land. I will not leave you until I have finished
> giving you everything I have promised you.
> GENESIS 28:13-15

What extraordinary promises! Shaken and amazed, Jacob woke up, constructed a memorial pillar, and worshiped God.

What's It Mean?

Jacob had been running from his vengeful brother. But really, he had been fleeing from his calling as God's chosen instrument to bless the nations.

Like his rocky pillow, Jacob's heart had been hard toward God. But through one dream, the Lord unforgettably softened his heart like a down pillow.

God wasn't about to let hard-hearted Jacob go. He is a God who compassionately pursues stubborn heel-grabbers like Jacob . . . and like us.

Are you running from God? Is there a specific area of your life that you're not submitting to him? Or perhaps you are in complete rebellion against him right now. Surrender to him through repentance and faith as Jacob ultimately did. If you do, he will be with you and will protect you wherever you go.

Now What?
Read the entire account of this story in Genesis 28:10-22.

Did You Know?
Jacob and Esau eventually reconciled. You can read about it in Genesis 33.

MARCH 2

You will all see heaven open and the angels of God
going up and down on the Son of Man, the one who
is the stairway between heaven and earth.

JOHN 1:51

JACOB—THE HEEL-GRABBING, rock-headed patriarch—was changed forever when God confronted him with a spectacular dream as he slept on a stone. As God softened his heart, he began to see himself for who he was in God's redemptive plan.

But there's a deeper meaning to this story. It has to do with the stairway that Jacob saw in his dream. Here's what Jacob saw: "As he slept, he dreamed of a stairway that reached from the earth up to heaven. And he saw the angels of God going up and down the stairway" (Genesis 28:12).

To unlock the greater significance of this stairway, we must fast-forward nearly two thousand years from Jacob's era to the time when Jesus walked the earth.

What's It Mean?

Jesus often told parables to his disciples and then explained their meaning. Sometimes, he even reminded them of Old Testament stories and interpreted them in light of his coming. This is what he did one day when he first called Nathanael to be one of his disciples.

Nathanael was a skeptic. He initially didn't believe that the Messiah could come from lowly Nazareth, Jesus' hometown. But when Jesus proved his divinity by displaying supernatural knowledge about Nathanael that only God could know (John 1:47-48), Nathanael humbly exclaimed, "Rabbi, you are the Son of God—the King of Israel!" (verse 49).

Jesus' response was fascinating: "You will see greater things than this. . . . I tell you the truth, you will all see heaven open and the angels of God going up and down on the Son of Man, the one who is the stairway between heaven and earth" (John 1:50-51).

In essence, Jesus was telling Nathanael, "Do you remember the story of Jacob and his dream about the stairway between heaven and earth? Well, I'm the stairway."

Jesus is the only way we can access a holy God in heaven. Only through God's Son can we—as sinful humans on earth—have our sins forgiven.

Jesus descended the staircase, so to speak, to make us right with God through his sacrificial death and resurrection. Through faith in his finished work on the cross, we can ascend to the Father in eternity. Thank you, Jesus!

Now What?
Read John 1:43-51 to learn more about Jesus' conversation with Nathanael.

Did You Know?
By calling himself "the Son of Man" in John 1:51, Jesus linked himself to the mysterious figure referred to in Daniel 7:13-14 and also affirmed his deity and eternal nature as the second Person of the Trinity.

MARCH 3

When he became a man, he even fought with God.

HOSEA 12:3

UNFORTUNATELY FOR JACOB, the ancient Greek Olympics didn't start until long after his death. Otherwise, he might have medaled in running and wrestling.

As a young man, Jacob deceived Esau and fled for his life to his uncle Laban. Then he wore out his welcome with Laban and ran away from him, too.

In Genesis 32, on the night before Jacob was to be reunited with Esau, a mysterious man attacked him. The two wrestled throughout the night. Jacob was no match for his adversary, but he refused to give up, even after the man dislocated his hip socket just by touching it.

At sunrise, Jacob realized his foe was supernatural. He was fighting God himself in human form—a *theophany*. So he pleaded for a blessing.

God said, "Your name will no longer be Jacob. . . . From now on you will be called Israel, because you have fought with God and with men and have won" (Genesis 32:28).

What's It Mean?

Approximately 1,200 years later, the prophet Hosea used Jacob's example to rebuke his generation's stubbornness toward God:

> The LORD is bringing charges against Judah. He is about to punish Jacob for all his deceitful ways, and pay him back for all he has done. Even in the womb, Jacob struggled with his brother; when he became a man, he even fought with God. Yes, he wrestled with the angel and won. He wept and pleaded for a blessing from him. There at Bethel he met God face to face, and God spoke to him— the LORD God of Heaven's Armies, the LORD is his name! So now, come back to your God. Act with love and justice, and always depend on him.
>
> HOSEA 12:2-6

This is a good word for us, too. Are you wrestling against God right now? Is your heart resisting fully submitting to his lordship in your life? If so, you are fighting a losing battle.

Don't think you can win a confrontation with the Lord God Almighty, the Maker of heaven and earth. It's impossible! His power is limitless. Yet he always acts out of holy love, wanting lost sinners to repent and his children to follow him. He changed Jacob's heart, and he can change yours.

If you're struggling with the Lord, listen to the words of Hosea: "Come back to your God . . . and always depend on him."

Now What?
Meditate on James 4:6-10. It's a great passage on submitting to God's rule in your life.

Did You Know?
- Jacob's name change marks the first time "Israel" is used in the Bible. In Hebrew, it means "He strives with God," or "God strives."

MARCH 4

You intended to harm me, but God intended it for good to
accomplish what is now being done, the saving of many lives.

GENESIS 50:20, NIV

YOU'VE HEARD THE STORY of Joseph and his coat of many colors,
right? Jacob dearly loved his son Joseph and gave him an ornate robe.
Perhaps that doesn't sound like a great present to us in the twenty-first century. But for a nomadic, tent-dwelling shepherd in ancient times, this was
quite a gift!

Joseph's coat was all the rage . . . literally! Jacob's favoritism of Joseph
sent his older brothers into a fury. "When his brothers saw that their father
loved him more than any of them, they hated him and could not speak a
kind word to him" (Genesis 37:4, NIV).

Joseph (perhaps a little boastfully) then shared a few dreams he had
about his brothers bowing down to him, and it only increased their anger.
So one day, they tore off his robe, threw him in a pit, and sold him into
slavery to merchants heading to Egypt.

Joseph quickly rose to prominence in his new master's household, but
he was unjustly thrown into prison, where he languished for two years.
Things certainly looked bleak. He must have questioned God's purposes.
But Joseph was about to learn an amazing truth about God.

What's It Mean?

By God's grace, Joseph was released from prison after God allowed him to
accurately interpret Pharaoh's dreams about a coming famine. He became
Pharaoh's second-in-command and saved Egypt from the ravaging food
crisis he had foretold—one that even reached Canaan and threatened to
destroy Jacob's family.

When his brothers arrived in Egypt looking for food, God's divine plan
became clear to Joseph. God had turned their wickedness into good by
sending Joseph ahead of them into Egypt so he could save them years later
and keep God's covenant to Abraham intact. Only the Lord God Almighty

could do such a thing! Joseph exclaimed to his brothers in today's verse, "You intended to harm me, but God intended it for good to accomplish what is now being done, the saving of many lives."

Perhaps you are going through something difficult or downright evil. Take heart! The God who helped Joseph is still active today. He is still turning evil to good in his divine sovereignty and love. As Romans 8:28 says, "We know that God causes everything to work together for the good of those who love God and are called according to his purpose for them." He will do this for you if you trust in him!

Now What?

Read the story of Joseph's life in Genesis 37 and 39–50.

Did You Know?

Joseph's dreams about his brothers bowing down to him came true (Genesis 42:6).

MARCH 5

Love your enemies! Do good to those who hate you. Bless
those who curse you. Pray for those who hurt you.

LUKE 6:27-28

JACOB'S SONS THOUGHT THEY were dead meat.

The man standing before them—the second-most powerful man in Egypt, one of the world's greatest nations at the time—looked so different from the long-lost brother they remembered. Could this really be Joseph, the one they had thrown into a pit and sold into slavery—all because of hatred and petty jealousy—more than twenty years earlier?

Yes, it was.

But they weren't sure at first. The decades in Egypt had changed his appearance. Besides, when they had first arrived seeking food in the midst of a widespread famine, he had concealed his identity, wanting to test their commitment to each other and see if their hearts had changed.

Finally, Joseph's emotions overwhelmed him. "I am Joseph, your brother!" he exclaimed.

His brothers were shocked and dismayed. Joseph was in a position of great power and authority. Revenge would have been so easy. Surely Joseph would pay them back for their heartless cruelty years ago—wouldn't he?

Nope.

Joseph wept with joy, warmly embraced each of his brothers, invited his entire family to Egypt, and explained how God worked through the brothers' wicked deeds to save Jacob's household.

What's It Mean?

Revenge comes so naturally to us, doesn't it? The idea of "paying back" someone who has hurt us is hardwired into our sinful hearts. But retaliation doesn't please God. He calls his children to treat others differently, even when they mistreat us.

Jesus taught us not only to love others, but to love our enemies (today's verse). It's not always easy, but it's always possible by God's power as we pray for him to change our hearts. God wants us to repay evil with good, just like Joseph did.

The greatest example of this is what God did for us through his Son. Because of our sinful nature, we have rebelled against God since birth. But rather than automatically repay our evil with the judgment we deserve, God gave us the good gift of eternal life through Jesus Christ, if we repent and believe.

Now that is loving your enemies!

Now What?
Put the Romans 12:19-20 principle into effect and show kindness to someone who has mistreated you.

Did You Know?
Colossians 1:21 says we were God's "enemies, separated from him by your evil thoughts and actions," before Jesus reconciled us to God.

MARCH 6

*He thought it was better to suffer for the sake of Christ than to own
the treasures of Egypt, for he was looking ahead to his great reward.*

HEBREWS 11:26

MOSES HAD IT ALL.

The wealth of ancient Egypt was there for the taking. As a young
Egyptian prince, money, power, and worldly delights were all his. All he had
to do was reach out and grab them.

Moses was Jewish, but Pharaoh's daughter had taken custody of him
when he was a baby (Exodus 2:1-10) and raised him in Egypt's palace. All
the power, glory, and treasures that the ancient Egyptian empire could offer
were at his fingertips.

Yet Moses grew restless. While he enjoyed a cushy royal life, his fellow Jews endured backbreaking labor under the harsh treatment of their
Egyptian overlords. One day, Moses went out to the fields where he got
a shocking firsthand look at the "brutal slave drivers" (Exodus 1:11) who
"worked the people of Israel without mercy" (verse 13) and "made their lives
bitter" (verse 14).

That day, he made a life-changing choice. He decided to turn his back
on the world's temporal gratifications in favor of following God's calling—
being counted among a nation of poor, helpless slaves.

Why on earth would he do that?

What's It Mean?

The answer to that question is found in Hebrews 11:24-26:

> It was by faith that Moses, when he grew up, refused to be called
> the son of Pharaoh's daughter. He chose to share the oppression of
> God's people instead of enjoying the fleeting pleasures of sin. He
> thought it was better to suffer for the sake of Christ than to own the
> treasures of Egypt, for he was looking ahead to his great reward.

Moses had no idea what God had in store for him when he first left Egypt. But he knew that all the empire's vast riches wouldn't bring him lasting joy. He knew a far greater reward awaited him—an everlasting prize that is beyond worth.

Earthly riches never satisfy, and they always end in this life. But treasuring God brings great spiritual blessings both in this life and the one to come. The joy, contentment, and eternal peace with God that we have through Christ is worth more than anything the world can offer us. Treasure that above all else!

Now What?

Read Matthew 6:19-21 and 1 Timothy 6:9-10 to see what Scripture says about earthly treasures.

Did You Know?

- Moses was forty years old when he left Egypt and its riches (Acts 7:23).

MARCH 7

Remember, dear brothers and sisters, that few of you were wise in the world's eyes or powerful or wealthy when God called you.

1 CORINTHIANS 1:26

WHEN YOU PICTURE MOSES in your mind, what do you see? A bold speaker confronting Pharaoh, one of the most powerful men in the ancient world? A formidable leader guiding more than a million Hebrew slaves out of Egypt? A zealously righteous man hurling the Ten Commandments down Mount Sinai at the sight of Israel's idolatry?

These are often how artists portray Moses. And yes, he certainly was all these things.

But not at the beginning.

The first biblical glimpses we get of Moses are not very flattering. Before he did anything remarkable for God, Moses murdered an Egyptian labor foreman, hid the body, and fled to Midian (Exodus 2:11-15). Years later, when God called him from the burning bush to lead Israel out of Egypt, Moses made lots of excuses not to go (Exodus 3:1–4:17). Even after he became the leader of Israel's Exodus, he still struggled with anger and pride, to the point of rebelling against God in the wilderness and being banished from entering the Promised Land (Numbers 20:2-13; Deuteronomy 34).

What's It Mean?

This isn't "National Pick On Moses Day." Moses was a godly man. In fact, Deuteronomy 34:10 says, "The Lord knew [him] face to face." But he had a lot of faults, just like we do. Here's the point: if God can use a guy like Moses, think of how God can use you!

Too often, we err by thinking that God only uses "super-Christians"— people who somehow were already spiritually mature when God called them. Nothing could be further from the truth.

Look at today's verse. God loves calling weak, ordinary people (like us) to join his mission and accomplish extraordinary things for his Kingdom by his power. That way, we grow in his grace, and God gets all the glory.

God is calling you now—perhaps in a few ways, but at the very least, through this book! You might not be wise, powerful, or wealthy in the world's eyes. That doesn't matter to God. Moses wasn't either, and look how the Lord used him. A true servant of God humbly admits he or she is nothing without God but everything with him.

Follow God's calling and watch his power work in your life!

Now What?

Read 1 Corinthians 1:18-31 to see how God loves using the weak to accomplish mighty things.

Did You Know?

Moses is mentioned by name in nearly half of the Bible's sixty-six books.

MARCH 8

God replied to Moses, "I AM WHO I AM. Say this to
the people of Israel: I AM has sent me to you."

EXODUS 3:14

ONE DAY, MOSES was tending sheep in Midian. His former life as an
Egyptian prince was a distant memory, but he certainly must have thought
of the enslaved Jews, his ethnic people, quite often.

Suddenly, God spoke to Moses from a burning bush that miraculously
wasn't consumed by the fire. Moses reacted like all of us would have: he
recoiled and hid his face, "afraid to look at God" in his overwhelming holiness (Exodus 3:6).

The Lord told Moses that he knew of the terrible oppression that his
people, the Israelites, were suffering in Egypt and was calling Moses to be
his agent of deliverance. The Israelites had lived in a pagan, polytheistic society for four hundred years, so Moses asked a valid question: "If I go to the
people of Israel and tell them, 'The God of your ancestors has sent me to
you,' they will ask me, 'What is his name?' Then what should I tell them?"
(Exodus 3:13).

God's answer, in Exodus 3:14-15, was marvelous, mysterious, and
majestic:

> I AM WHO I AM. Say this to the people of Israel: I AM has sent
> me to you. . . . Yahweh, the God of your ancestors—the God of
> Abraham, the God of Isaac, and the God of Jacob—has sent me
> to you. This is my eternal name, my name to remember for all
> generations.

What's It Mean?

I AM.

For thousands of years, Bible scholars have been studying this fascinating name. It's a deep well full of beautiful truths about God. When God

spoke this name, he was trying to teach Moses, Israel—and us!—some incredible, eternal realities about himself.

For the next two days, we are going to meditate on God's special name of Yahweh, with tomorrow's devotion exclusively dedicated to what I Am and Yahweh mean. But today, rejoice that there is a God in heaven who graciously reveals himself to us. He is not a God who is aloof or far off. He is holy and highly exalted above us, but he is our heavenly Father, and he wants his children to know who he is and how to worship him. Take comfort in this glorious truth!

Now What?

Ask your parents the meaning of your name and the story behind why they gave it to you.

Did You Know?

- Orthodox Jews have long considered the names God, Lord, and Yahweh too sacred to be spoken or written in full, in fear of breaking the third commandment (Exodus 20:7).

MARCH 9

I AM WHO I AM.

EXODUS 3:14

THE BURNING BUSH EPISODE was a turning point in Moses' life and an early milestone in Israel's history as God's chosen nation. The Lord was calling Moses to be his instrument of redemption as he prepared to do mighty, saving wonders for his people.

But that moment in Midian also marked an extraordinary day for all of humanity because of God's gracious decision to reveal important attributes about himself. When Moses asked God whom he should say sent him, here was God's response:

> I AM WHO I AM. Say this to the people of Israel: I AM has sent
> me to you. . . . Yahweh, the God of your ancestors—the God of
> Abraham, the God of Isaac, and the God of Jacob—has sent me
> to you. This is my eternal name, my name to remember for all
> generations.
>
> EXODUS 3:14-15

What's It Mean?

In ancient cultures, a person's name often provided essential information about that individual. In this response, God was giving his name and communicating important truths about himself.

When God called himself "I AM," he was referring to his divine name, "YHWH," which is transliterated from the original ancient Hebrew text into Yahweh or sometimes rendered LORD in small capital letters. The original Hebrew words God used to describe himself in Exodus 3:14-15 that our English Bibles translate into "I AM" and Yahweh were verbs that originally meant "to be." In other words, as God prepared to save Israel from Egypt, he wanted the people to know these truths:

- **God is self-existent.** No one created him, and he doesn't rely on anyone else for his being.
- **God is eternal.** He has no beginning or end.
- **God is the Creator and Sustainer** of the entire universe.
- **God is the perfect standard of truth and goodness** that everything else in the cosmos is judged by.
- **God doesn't change.**

Did you catch that last part? Yahweh doesn't change. He is still the same loving God today that he was more than three thousand years ago when he spoke to Moses. He is still speaking, calling people to follow him, and saving lives today. Will you answer?

Now What?
Read Exodus 3–4 to get the full story and hear what God reveals about himself.

Did You Know?
In some Bible translations, the word Yahweh is translated as LORD in small capital letters. This comes from the ancient Greek word *kyrios* ("Lord"), which was used in place of Yahweh in the Septuagint, the first Greek translation of the Old Testament in the third century BC. The translators used Lord to link Jesus with God the Father. (See John 8, specifically verse 58.)

MARCH 10

*He has paid a full ransom for his people. He
has guaranteed his covenant with them forever.
What a holy, awe-inspiring name he has!*

PSALM 111:9

MOSES WAS FEELING ANGRY, confused, and helpless. This whole "save
Israel from Egypt" thing hadn't started out so well.

When Moses first confronted Pharaoh, he told him everything God
had commanded him to say. But Pharaoh just shrugged and said, "Who
is the LORD? Why should I listen to him and let Israel go? I don't know
the LORD, and I will not let Israel go" (Exodus 5:2).

Moses probably felt like a flustered quarterback. The odds were stacked
against him, and none of his play calls were working. So he glanced at his
coach on the sideline as if to say, "What now?"

Look at God's powerful, reassuring answer in Exodus 6:6-8:

Say to the people of Israel: "I am the LORD. I will free you from
your oppression and will rescue you from your slavery in Egypt. I
will redeem you with a powerful arm and great acts of judgment.
I will claim you as my own people, and I will be your God. Then
you will know that I am the LORD your God who has freed you
from your oppression in Egypt. I will bring you into the land I
swore to give to Abraham, Isaac, and Jacob. I will give it to you as
your very own possession. I am the LORD!"

What's It Mean?

Did you notice how God's response was almost entirely void of specific Xs
and Os? God didn't describe a detailed game plan. He simply reminded
Moses of who *he* was and what *he* had promised to do. He was calling
Moses to trust him.

In his response, God mentioned his name, Yahweh, three times. In
addition to the other things we've said about this special name, it was God's

unique covenantal identity with Israel—a reminder that he is a promise-keeping God.

Look again at all of God's "I" statements in Exodus 6:6-8:

- I will free you.
- I will redeem you.
- I will claim you.
- I will be your God.
- I will bring you into the land.
- I will give it to you as your very own possession.

These are covenantal promises. Israel hadn't earned these blessings by its own righteousness. God was graciously choosing to redeem these people for his glory and their good.

Yahweh, the covenant-keeping God, is still doing this today!

Now What?

The next time you make (or break) a promise, remember the God who always keeps his!

Did You Know?

The English word Yahweh corresponds to the four original Hebrew consonants *YHWH*.

MARCH 11

Let them all praise the name of the LORD. For his name is
very great; his glory towers over the earth and heaven!

PSALM 148:13

ENOCH, WHAT WERE YOU thinking?

Yes, yes—we know you were a godly man who, incredibly, never experienced physical death (Genesis 5:24). But did you have to name your firstborn son Methuselah? The name doesn't really roll off the tongue, you know. What's worse, Methuselah means "to bring death."

Imagine poor Methuselah's response as a teenager: Wow, thanks a million, Dad. Now I'm really gonna be popular with all the other antediluvian kids at school.

Were you trying to be ironic, Enoch? Because your son's biggest claim to fame, of course, is that he lived 969 years, longer than anyone else in history. So perhaps his name should mean "to bring death . . . after nine centuries."

Anyway, Methuselah is just one of many fascinating names in the Bible. Names were a big deal in ancient times. They not only identified you, but they also described what you were like as a person.

For the last three days, we've been learning about God's special name in Scripture, Yahweh. But the Bible uses many other beautiful names to describe God. Today, we will briefly look at some of these.

What's It Mean?

Here are seven more names that reveal God's awesome, holy character:

1. **Elohim.** The standard word for "God" in the Old Testament. Elohim is used more than two thousand times, including in Genesis 1:1.
2. **Adonai.** A reverential title meaning "Lord" or "Master," found more than four hundred times in the Old Testament.
3. **El Elyon.** This name means "The Most High God," found often in Genesis and the Psalms. It speaks of God's sovereignty over his creation.

4. **El Shaddai.** This means "God Almighty," speaking to his power to do everything he wants to accomplish in his perfect will.

5. **El Olam.** This means "The Everlasting God," alluding to his infinite nature. Daniel 7 describes him similarly as "the Ancient of Days" (ESV).

6. **Yahweh-Yireh.** This name, meaning "The LORD Will Provide," is used only once in Scripture—Genesis 22:14—when God provided Abraham a sacrificial ram in Isaac's place on Mount Moriah.

7. **Yahweh-Sabaoth.** This name means "The Lord of Hosts." God sovereignly rules over all spiritual and earthly forces. He controls the fate of all battles.

As today's verse says, the name of the Lord is very great indeed. Praise the name of the Lord!

Now What?

Look up the following verses to learn more names of the Lord: Judges 6:24; Psalm 23:1; and Jeremiah 23:6.

Did You Know?

Other than Enoch, the Bible records only one other human whom God brought straight to heaven without dying: Elijah (2 Kings 2:11).

MARCH 12

*Has any other god dared to take a nation for himself
out of another nation by means of trials, miraculous
signs, wonders, war, a strong hand, a powerful arm,
and terrifying acts? Yet that is what the LORD your
God did for you in Egypt, right before your eyes.*

DEUTERONOMY 4:34

BLOODY RIVERS! RELENTLESS FROGS! Incessant insects! Oozing
infections! Meteorological mania! Oppressive darkness! Catastrophic death!
Is this the latest horror movie out of Hollywood?

Nope.

It's just the book of Exodus, chapters 7–12—the account of the ten
plagues that God inflicted upon Egypt to free Israel. When God sent Moses
and Aaron before Pharaoh, they proclaimed a consistent message from the
Lord: "Let my people go." But Pharaoh's heart was hardened toward God, so
the Lord brought ten destructive judgments on Egypt:

1. water turned to blood
2. frogs
3. gnats
4. flies
5. a deadly plague on Egyptian livestock
6. painful boils
7. a ravaging hailstorm
8. locusts
9. darkness
10. death to all of Egypt's firstborn males

At first glance, the ten plagues seem a bit arbitrary. Why did God bring
these specific plagues on Egypt?

What's It Mean?

The Egyptians were a polytheistic nation, believing in many false gods. In their mythology, the deities they had concocted controlled every aspect of life. Their daily religious practices focused on winning the favor of these supernatural creatures.

The ten plagues were not only God's judgment on Egypt for enslaving his people but also a mighty demonstration of legitimacy: Who was real—the one God of Israel or the many gods of Egypt? The Lord answered unequivocally. When God turned the Nile to blood, he showed Hapi and Isis, the god and goddess of the river, to be false. When God sent devastating hail on the land, he showed Nut (the sky goddess), Osiris (the god of crops and fertility), and Set (the god of storms) to be fakes. When God threw the land into darkness, he showed Ra, the sun god, to be a fabrication. And so on.

Today, you probably don't struggle with worshiping a pantheon of false gods. But know this: the God who did amazing wonders to free his people in Egypt thousands of years ago is the same God working mightily in human hearts to save people today! By his awesome deeds, it's clear that he is Yahweh, the only true God who is worthy of all our praise. There is none like him!

Now What?

Read Exodus chapters 7–12 and be amazed at God's mighty saving works!

Did You Know?

The plagues were also to be a constant reminder to Israel of Yahweh's commitment to them (today's verse).

MARCH 13

The LORD hardened Pharaoh's heart,
and just as the LORD had predicted to
Moses, Pharaoh refused to listen.

EXODUS 9:12

WE LIKE IT when life is easy. But there are some hard things that are good too:

- Hard hats are critical for construction workers.
- Hard candy is always delicious to suck on.
- Hard concrete is always better to walk on than soft, wet concrete.

But a hardened heart? Well, that's another matter entirely.

When Moses and Aaron were preparing to confront Pharaoh, God told Moses,

I will harden Pharaoh's heart, and though I multiply my signs
and wonders in the land of Egypt, Pharaoh will not listen to you.
Then I will lay my hand on Egypt and bring my hosts, my people
the children of Israel, out of the land of Egypt by great acts of
judgment. The Egyptians shall know that I am the LORD, when I
stretch out my hand against Egypt and bring out the people of Israel
from among them.

EXODUS 7:3-5, ESV

Genesis features multiple references about Pharaoh hardening his heart
against God and refusing to let Israel go. But there are other references,
including today's verse and the passage above, that specifically say God hardened Pharaoh's heart.

So which was it? And if God hardened Pharaoh's heart, was Pharaoh responsible for his actions? After all, if God initiated this, how could Pharaoh
resist God's will?

What's It Mean?

These are deep theological questions—deep enough for the apostle Paul to use Pharaoh to illustrate the age-old "God's sovereignty vs. man's free will" debate in Romans 9. (See the October 17–20 devotions on God's election.)

First, we must agree with Scripture that God is always just in his judgments (Deuteronomy 32:4). Next, we need to understand that humans (including Pharaoh) are always accountable for their sinful nature, rebellious deeds, and hardened hearts against God.

Before encountering Yahweh, Pharaoh wasn't an upstanding moral citizen. He was a pagan emperor who had little regard for human life (Exodus 5), constantly broke his word, and "refused to listen" (today's verse). Pharaoh's guilt was justified.

Yes, Pharaoh hardened his heart toward God. But God also hardened Pharaoh's heart to accomplish his sovereign purposes with Israel (Exodus 9:16; Romans 9:17).

How can the two coexist? Ultimately, the Bible doesn't fully explain, but rather it calls us to trust in God. Are you willing to submit your curiosity, questions, and limited understanding of the deep riddles of life to the Lord's sovereignty, goodness, and love?

Now What?

Read Romans 9 to gain a greater understanding and reverence for God's awesome sovereignty.

Did You Know?

God used wicked Pharaoh to accomplish his plan to create a nation through which the Savior of the world would come!

MARCH 14

On that night I will pass through the land of Egypt and strike down every firstborn son and firstborn male animal in the land of Egypt. I will execute judgment against all the gods of Egypt, for I am the LORD!

EXODUS 12:12

PHARAOH WAS UNYIELDING. LIKE the Great Pyramids or the Great Sphinx of Giza, his heart was an unmovable rock fixed in the Egyptian desert. Despite the constant warnings of Moses and Aaron and nine previous plagues that ravaged his nation, he refused to let Israel go. So God was going to send a tenth plague—the final and most terrible judgment—on Egypt.

Every firstborn male of all Egyptian families, even animals, was going to die. But God would spare the entire Israelite nation if each family sacrificed a spotless one-year-old male lamb or goat and sprinkled its blood on the doorframe of their home.

The Israelites obeyed God, and he "passed over" his people, inaugurating the first annual Passover festival that Jews still celebrate today. However, it was a catastrophic night for the Egyptians. "Loud wailing was heard throughout the land of Egypt. There was not a single house where someone had not died" (Exodus 12:30). So Pharaoh drove Israel out.

What's It Mean?

After 430 years of slavery, Israel was free at last! The story of the ten plagues started with Pharaoh's extreme pride, as he defiantly asked Moses, "Who is the LORD? Why should I listen to him and let Israel go?" (Exodus 5:2). But it ends with Pharaoh begging Moses, "Get out! . . . Leave my people . . . but bless me as you leave" (Exodus 12:31-32). In fact, as the Israelites departed, the Egyptians even gave them gifts of clothing and precious jewelry!

Pharaoh changed his mind one more time, pursued Israel, and experienced complete humiliation at the Red Sea (Exodus 14:1–15:21). The mightiest ruler on earth at the time exalted himself against God, but the Lord greatly humbled him. With the establishment of the Passover, God wanted his people to always remember his powerful, saving deliverance for their good and the glory of his name (Exodus 12:25-27).

God still wants his people today to remember how he works on their behalf. How has he worked mightily in your life? Humbly praise him for the great things he has done for you!

Now What?

Record in a journal the mighty ways that God has worked to save and help you.

Did You Know?

The Israelites eventually used their plunder of Egyptian treasures for the worship of the golden calf (bad!) and the building of the Tabernacle (good!).

MARCH 15

When I see the blood, I will pass over you.

EXODUS 12:13

IMAGINE BEING AN ISRAELITE on that first Passover night more than three thousand years ago. You probably would have felt a mixture of excitement, reverence, and fear.

For 430 years, the Jews—the children of God's promise through Abraham—had been cruelly enslaved in Egypt. Now, the night of their salvation was at hand. God was about to send a final plague that would shatter Pharaoh's arrogance and humble an entire nation by striking down all firstborn males in every family. To avoid this terrible judgment, the Israelites had to follow God's specific command (outlined in Exodus 12):

1. Kill a one-year-old male lamb (or goat) without defect.
2. Sprinkle its blood on the sides and top of the doorframe of their house.
3. Roast and eat the edible parts with unleavened bread and bitter herbs.
4. Eat it while dressed in travel clothes and prepared to leave quickly.
5. Remain until morning and then leave Egypt.

While Egypt suffered judgment, all Israel obeyed and God "passed over" them. Why did the Lord use such a unique method to save his people?

What's It Mean?

Through Passover, God wanted to teach Israel (and us!) a vital lesson: the blood of the sacrificial lamb will save you.

Because of our sin, we all deserve God's wrath, just like the ancient Egyptians. God saved Israel by accepting the sacrifice of a spotless lamb—represented by the blood over each Israelite house. To be saved, they had to be "under the blood."

Afterward, God instructed his people to celebrate Passover annually and set up an elaborate system of animal sacrifices—because sin requires blood payment. To save a life from sin, a life must be taken (Hebrews 9:22).

But before you construct an altar in your backyard, remember 1 Corinthians 5:7: "Christ, our Passover Lamb, has been sacrificed for us"!

We don't need to observe Passover or sacrifice spotless lambs today because Jesus died and rose again to take away our sins once and for all. The Old Testament Passover and sacrifices were ultimately pointing forward to God's Son, the perfect Lamb, whose sacrifice was sufficient to wash away our sins.

All Christians who have put their faith in God's Savior are "under the blood" of Christ. The sacrifice of Jesus, the true Passover Lamb, will save you!

Now What?
Read Exodus 12; Isaiah 53:7; John 1:29-36; and 1 Peter 1:19 to make a cool connection between Passover and Jesus.

Did You Know?
Passover was so significant for the Jews that God told them to start their ancient calendar in the month it happened (Exodus 12:2).

MARCH 16

With your unfailing love you lead the people you have redeemed.
In your might, you guide them to your sacred home.

EXODUS 15:13

ISRAEL WAS FINALLY FREE.

After 430 years of Jewish captivity, God had powerfully redeemed his people from Egyptian bondage. For comparison's sake, imagine if Americans had been enslaved by a foreign nation from the 1590s to today.

Wow! That's a long time to be in captivity.

But after the Jews left, Pharaoh stubbornly decided to pursue Israel with his army, including six hundred of his finest chariots. With their backs to the Red Sea and a large Egyptian army moving aggressively toward them in the distance, the Israelites quickly lost faith and began complaining.

"Why did you bring us out here to die in the wilderness?" they bickered to Moses (Exodus 14:11).

Israel had left Egypt with 600,000 men (Exodus 12:37), but these recently freed captives were no match for an expert fighting force with superior training, mobility, and weaponry. By human standards, it wasn't a fair fight at all.

But who said anything about human standards? Yahweh was about to fight for his people! As God told Moses in Exodus 14:18, "When my glory is displayed through them, all Egypt will see my glory and know that I am the LORD!"

All that night, God's presence—represented by a pillar of cloud—separated the Egyptians from the Israelites while he parted the Red Sea into two huge walls of water for his people to walk through in the morning. Israel passed safely through, but when Pharaoh's army pursued, God brought the water crashing back down, drowning all the Egyptians.

What's It Mean?

As Moses and the Israelites marveled at God's salvation, they began singing—the first song recorded in Scripture. They praised the Lord for many things, including his "unfailing love," his redemption, and guiding his people "to your sacred home" (today's verse).

In the immediate context, the "sacred home" meant the Promised Land of Canaan that God had pledged to Abraham hundreds of years earlier. But this verse—and all of Exodus 15—still bears great truth for modern-day believers. The God who redeemed captive Israel still redeems those who are held captive to sin today. The God who parted the Red Sea still works miraculously in human hearts today. The God who guided his people into the Promised Land will one day guide all of his redeemed into the "sacred home" of eternity in his presence.

Praise the Lord!

Now What?

Read the account of the crossing of the Red Sea and Israel's song of praise in Exodus 14:1–15:21.

Did You Know?

Psalm 77:16-20 adds that rain, lightning, and thunder were part of God's miraculous display during the parting of the Red Sea.

MARCH 17

Do everything without complaining and arguing.

PHILIPPIANS 2:14

GRIPE, GRIPE, GRIPE.

Whine, whine, whine.

Grumble, grumble, grumble.

Not long after the Israelites had experienced a lifetime's worth of unforgettable miracles—first the ten plagues, then the parting of the Red Sea—they started bellyaching about, well, their aching bellies.

"If only the LORD had killed us back in Egypt," they moaned. "There we sat around pots filled with meat and ate all the bread we wanted. But now you have brought us into this wilderness to starve us all to death" (Exodus 16:3).

Wait a minute. Did they forget their previous slavery? Surely, they were exaggerating about the amount of food they enjoyed in Egypt. Enslaved people never eat like kings!

While in captivity, they were in "misery" (Exodus 4:31) and they "continued to groan under their burden of slavery" (Exodus 2:23). Their wistful memories of Egypt were nothing more than sinful, ungrateful revisionist history.

God had every right to destroy this wicked, boorish people or leave them to fend for themselves in the desert. Instead, he lovingly and miraculously provided daily manna and quail for forty years until he brought them into the Promised Land.

What's It Mean?

Israel's complaining, thankless attitude was a major problem throughout its wilderness wanderings. For four decades, they groused about being hungry, being thirsty, the food God provided, their perceived inability to conquer Canaan, Moses' leadership, and anything else they could think of! They consistently lacked faith in God and his provision for them.

Sure, they had witnessed God's extraordinary miracles to liberate them from Egyptian bondage, but when it came to the minutiae of daily life—food, drink, money, clothing, etc.—they struggled to trust that Yahweh was going to meet all of their needs.

What about you? When adversity strikes or life's frustrations mount, how do you react? Do you complain like the ancient Israelites did? Do you throw yourself a world-class pity party? Or do you wait patiently on the Lord?

When life gets hard, don't complain against God. He loves you beyond words. Rather, expectantly wait for him to act on your behalf as you rest in his perfect character and promises. He will meet all of your needs!

Now What?

The manna God provided to Israel "tasted like honey wafers" (Exodus 16:31). The next time you eat graham crackers, remember God's provision to Israel . . . and you!

Did You Know?

In John 6:35, Jesus called himself "the bread of life" who provides eternal life, showing that he is far greater than the manna of Israel's exodus generation.

MARCH 18

*Obey the commands of the LORD your God by
walking in his ways and fearing him.*

DEUTERONOMY 8:6

TWO MONTHS HAD PASSED since the Israelites left Egypt amid the wails of firstborn sons dying. Now, they were encamped at Mount Sinai.

Suddenly, the sky darkened. Thunder roared, and lightning flashed above. An earthquake shook the ground violently. The whole mountain appeared as if it was engulfed in flames and smoke. The Israelites were terrified.

The Lord God Almighty had descended from heaven to make an everlasting covenant with his people. Then he called Moses up the mountain where he gave him the Ten Commandments, the most famous rules in history. Here they are from Exodus 20:3-17:

1. You must not have any other god but me.
2. You must not make for yourself an idol of any kind or an image of anything in the heavens or on the earth or in the sea.
3. You must not misuse the name of the LORD your God.
4. Remember to observe the Sabbath day by keeping it holy.
5. Honor your father and mother.
6. You must not murder.
7. You must not commit adultery.
8. You must not steal.
9. You must not testify falsely against your neighbor.
10. You must not covet.

What's It Mean?

So what are twenty-first-century Christians supposed to do with these ancient rules? Follow them!

All of the Ten Commandments apply to believers today. (See the March 20 devotion for specific details on the fourth commandment.) The first four commandments discuss people's relationship with God. The last six discuss people's relationships with each other.

God never meant for the Ten Commandments to be an exhaustive list of rules. They are representative of overall attitudes and actions he expects from his people. For example, "You must not murder" doesn't only mean don't kill someone in anger (thus merely fulfilling the letter of the law), but also avoid harboring bitterness in your heart toward others (thus fulfilling the spirit of the law; Matthew 5:21-26).

God also never meant for salvation to come through rules. The Ten Commandments—and the overall Mosaic law—were to govern Israel's worship and community life. Salvation comes through faith in God's promised Messiah, Jesus Christ, who perfectly fulfilled the law for our sake (Matthew 5:17) so that we could become "the righteousness of God" (2 Corinthians 5:21, ESV).

Now What?
Say a prayer of thanks for Jesus, the perfect Law Keeper!

Did You Know?
God meant for his laws to be spiritually nourishing, not overbearing. As Psalm 119:47 says, "How I delight in your commands! How I love them!"

MARCH 19

You shall not take the name of the LORD your God in vain.

EXODUS 20:7, ESV

WHAT'S IN A NAME? When it comes to the Lord God Almighty, plenty!

When God gave Israel the Ten Commandments, he instructed Israel to worship him alone and never to create idols—whether in an attempt to worship him or another false god. It's easy to see why those two commandments top the list.

Then comes commandment number three: "You shall not take the name of the LORD your God in vain" (Exodus 20:7, ESV). Does its priority on the list of Ten Commandments surprise you? Why did God place it there, and what does it mean to take God's name "in vain"?

What's It Mean?

To take the Lord's name "in vain" means to treat it disrespectfully, use it for a worthless purpose, or empty it of its true significance. Psalm 139:20 puts it bluntly: it is God's "enemies" who "blaspheme" him and "misuse [his] name."

When people say, "Oh, my God!" or "Jesus Christ!" as an expression of surprise, delight, or disgust, etc., this is an unfortunate example of taking it in vain. This brings to mind Leviticus 19:12: "Do not bring shame on the name of your God by using it to swear falsely. I am the LORD."

But the third commandment goes deeper than offhand human expressions. God is holy—completely separate from sin and highly exalted above all creation—and his name is worthy to be praised. He graciously revealed his precious name of "Yahweh, I AM," to ancient Israel—"This is my eternal name, my name to remember for all generations" (Exodus 3:15)—so that all might personally know him. Even today, "Everyone who calls on the name of the LORD will be saved" (Romans 10:13).

We are to glorify his name since it represents his nature and character. Recall that Jesus taught us to pray, "Our Father in heaven, *hallowed* be your name" (Matthew 6:9, ESV, emphasis added).

To take the Lord's name in vain means to make it futile or worthless—the exact opposite of God. Luke 6:45 says, "What you say flows from what is in your heart." If you misuse God's name, it reveals a heart that thinks low, insulting thoughts of God. This is what the third commandment is driving at.

May this not be said of us! Instead, may we give his holy name the honor and adoration it deserves.

Now What?

Memorize Psalm 103:1: "Let all that I am praise the LORD; with my whole heart, I will praise his holy name."

Did You Know?

In ancient Near Eastern cultures, a person's name represented who a person was, including the person's characteristics, accomplishments, etc. To dishonor someone's name was to dishonor the person.

MARCH 20

Remember to observe the Sabbath day by keeping it holy.

EXODUS 20:8

TODAY, WE'RE GOING to look at the fourth of the Ten Commandments, which is all about honoring the Sabbath.

"On that day," the commandment says, "no one in your household may do any work" (Exodus 20:10). (FYI: This was not to accommodate all-day NFL watch parties.)

From ancient times until now, the Jewish Sabbath starts at sundown Friday and lasts until sundown Saturday. The commandment finds its roots in God's creative order. Exodus 20:11 declares, "In six days the LORD made the heavens, the earth, the sea, and everything in them; but on the seventh day he rested. That is why the LORD blessed the Sabbath day and set it apart as holy."

Some of the Ten Commandments are repeated in the New Testament. But the fourth commandment is not. So the question lingers: now that believers live under the "new covenant" thanks to Jesus' death and resurrection (Hebrews 8), do we still have to observe the Sabbath today?

What's It Mean?

While the New Testament doesn't explicitly command us to "keep the Sabbath," it makes it clear that gathering regularly (i.e., weekly) with other believers is an important part of the Christian life. Hebrews 10:25 says, "Let us not neglect our meeting together, as some people do, but encourage one another, especially now that the day of his return is drawing near."

Acts 2:42-47; 4:31; 5:12; 20:7; and 1 Corinthians 16:1-2 all allude to the frequent fellowship of believers, which was to be done around the teaching of God's Word. And in Revelation 1:10, the apostle John said he was "worshiping in the Spirit" on "the Lord's Day" (i.e., Sunday). Clearly, the biblical pattern is for God's people to set aside a day each week to gather together to worship him.

Gathering together weekly with other believers isn't a social club. God's people meet together to grow spiritually as they worship the Lord, hear the teaching of Scripture, partake of the Lord's Supper, serve one another, and seek to fulfill the great commission.

Most of all, God wants our hearts. More than perfect church attendance, the Lord wants people who worship him "in spirit and in truth" (John 4:24) every day of the week.

Now What?

Read Jesus' interaction with the Pharisees on Sabbath law in Mark 2:23-28, especially noting the last two verses.

Did You Know?

In the Old Testament, breaking the Sabbath, if premeditated, was punishable by death (Exodus 31:14; Numbers 15:32-36). This was because observing the Sabbath was one way that Israel was separated from the pagan nations as holy to God.

MARCH 21

Honor your father and mother.

EXODUS 20:12

ONCE UPON A TIME, way back in the 1950s through 1970s, television networks produced a lot of popular sitcoms featuring stories about the idealized American family.

Shows such as *Father Knows Best, Leave It to Beaver, The Adventures of Ozzie and Harriet,* and *The Brady Bunch* showcased traditional family values with a dad, mom, and several children (including at least one rambunctious boy to drive the narrative). Every series followed a formulaic story arc each week: the family would encounter a problem that ultimately would be solved by the episode's end, all within thirty minutes—commercial breaks and corny laugh tracks included.

Real life rarely works out so tidily, but one of the hallmarks of those old shows is the children's respect for their parents, which is often lacking in today's society.

Honoring your parents isn't just a nice idea or a quaint, outdated notion from a bygone era. It's the fifth of the Ten Commandments—one of the most important commands of Scripture.

What's It Mean?

"Honor your father and mother" is the preeminent of the latter six commandments—those that the Lord issued to govern life in Israel's covenant community. God knew that obeying one's parents is foundational to obeying God himself. In other words, how can you obey God, whom you cannot see, if you don't first learn to obey your parents, whom you *can* see? You can't. You must learn to do the latter before doing the former.

God graciously gave you parents to raise you, protect you, teach you about life, and ultimately, train you in godliness (Deuteronomy 6:6-7). Your parents aren't perfect, but they are a God-given gift and an authority in your life you must submit to in reverence to God (Romans 13:1-2).

By honoring and obeying your parents, you learn to put away your selfish and prideful tendencies. You learn that your way isn't always best. You learn to submit to a higher authority.

"Honor your father and mother" is so important, in fact, that the apostle Paul emphasized it several times in the New Testament. He cited the fifth commandment in Ephesians 6:1-3, and in Colossians 3:20 he wrote, "Children, always obey your parents, *for this pleases the Lord*" (emphasis added).

You don't need to be a squeaky-clean 1950s TV sitcom kid. But you do need to honor your parents in everything!

Now What?

Do something unexpectedly kind for your parents to express your love for them.

Did You Know?

- Not every family looks like the picture-perfect, black-and-white TV household. If your family isn't picture perfect, you'll be especially interested in tomorrow's devotion.

MARCH 22

Honor your father and mother.

EXODUS 20:12

YESTERDAY, WE DISCUSSED the importance of obeying the fifth commandment to "honor your father and mother." Your sinful nature is never going to make this perfectly easy. But it'd be a lot simpler if every parent were like a 1950s TV sitcom dad or mom, with impeccable manners, sage advice at every turn, and nary a hair out of place!

Of course, that's not real life. Parents are sinners, too. They need God's grace, just like you. But many of them are fulfilling their God-given role: training their children to walk with the Lord.

Sadly, though, some aren't. Maybe you don't enjoy that picture-perfect TV family. Maybe you come from a broken home, where genuine expressions of love are virtually nonexistent. Maybe you've experienced the nightmare of abuse.

If any of this is your reality, "honor your father and mother" probably isn't a simple command for you. It might spur a million thoughts, causing you to wonder, How in the world do I do that?

And that's okay. Let's talk about it.

What's It Mean?

We live in a fallen world. Sin has affected every inch of the human experience, including many parent-child relationships. If this brokenness has extended to your family, and a parent's words or actions have made it difficult to honor them, remember the following truths from Scripture:

- Broken families weren't God's original design. That's Satan's handiwork. (He fights against everything found in the godly family model of Ephesians 5:22–6:4.)
- God loves the parent(s) you're struggling with. He sent his only Son, Jesus Christ, to die for your sins—and theirs (John 3:16-17).
- God is your perfect, loving heavenly Father. You can "give all your worries and cares to God, for he cares about you" (1 Peter 5:7).

- In his divine providence, God sometimes allows us to go through great trials that seem unbearable at the time but will ultimately strengthen our faith in him (James 1:2-4).
- Amazingly, God works all things in his children's lives for ultimate good, even trials (Romans 8:28).
- If Scripture calls us to love our enemies and "pray for those who persecute you" (Matthew 5:44), pray for the parent(s) you are struggling with.
- God wants love and forgiveness, not bitterness, to reign in your heart toward those who have wronged you (Ephesians 4:31-32).

There are so many complex family situations out there that one devotion can't adequately address them all. But God knows your situation completely. Cry out to him. He always takes care of his children.

Now What?
Meditate on Psalm 147:3 and Isaiah 42:3.

Did You Know?
If you're suffering abuse, that is not God's design for your life, and you don't have to navigate this alone. Seek help from a trusted adult.

MARCH 23

The LORD has made known his salvation; he has revealed
his righteousness in the sight of the nations.

PSALM 98:2, ESV

BEFORE MOSES CLIMBED up Mount Sinai for an extended stay, the
Israelites got a dazzling display of God's awesome power.

Lightning flashed, thunder roared, and a thick cloud descended upon
the mountain. The sky filled with black smoke, and the mountain trembled
violently, causing the people to shake with fear. The Lord had manifested
his presence.

But of all the remarkable events that transpired over the next forty days
on Mount Sinai, that shocking display might have been the least amazing
thing that happened. When God gave Moses the Mosaic law, it signaled to
Israel that he is a God of self-revelation.

Today, God has revealed himself to us sufficiently in his Word, the
sixty-six books of the Bible. For the next five days, we're going to discuss the
blessing that God has given to us in Scripture.

What's It Mean?

God has revealed himself in many different ways throughout history:

- through his creation
- through mighty signs and wonders
- directly to individuals in the Bible through a divine visit, vision, or
  audible interaction
- to a person or people group through a prophet or other mediator in
  Scripture
- through holy men who wrote down his words under the Holy Spirit's
  guidance

The last point, in particular, was how the Bible was written. As 2
Peter 1:20-21 says, "No prophecy of Scripture comes from someone's own

interpretation. For no prophecy was ever produced by the will of man, but men spoke from God as they were carried along by the Holy Spirit" (ESV).

The Bible doesn't tell us everything about God—not even the universe can contain his greatness, let alone one book—but it does sufficiently reveal everything we need to know about him for life, truth, and salvation.

Praise the Lord that he's a God of revelation! He certainly didn't owe this to rebels like us. Without God's initiative, we'd be hopelessly lost in sin. But God mercifully revealed his nature, laws, and salvation to us. He loves us dearly and wants us to know him, love him, and worship him forever.

Now What?

Whenever you read any of the following phrases in the Bible . . .

The word of the Lord came to . . .
Then the Lord told . . .
Thus says the Lord . . .
Tell my people Israel . . .

. . . remember that God was graciously revealing himself to people!

Did You Know?

Most incredibly, God has revealed himself to us by *becoming one of us*. See the March 26 and December 14–17 devotions for more details!

MARCH 24

*All Scripture is breathed out by God and profitable for teaching,
for reproof, for correction, and for training in righteousness.*

2 TIMOTHY 3:16, ESV

ALTHOUGH HE DIED IN 1616, William Shakespeare is still widely regarded as the greatest playwright and poet who ever lived. His plays, poems, and sonnets have had an enormous influence on language, literature, and the creative arts in the western hemisphere. In fact, "The Bard" is even credited with introducing as many as 1,700 words and phrases to the English language.

While it's unclear whether Shakespeare coined them all, he often receives the credit since his published works are the first examples of the terms being used. Below are five examples:

- Swagger (Henry V)
- Good riddance (The Merchant of Venice)
- Vanish into thin air (Othello)
- Lonely (Coriolanus)
- For goodness' sake (Henry VIII)

Fifteen hundred years before Shakespeare, the apostle Paul might have enjoyed a little term-coining fun, too. The original Greek text of today's verse features a word that, to date, has not been found in any other ancient Greek text (biblical or secular) before Paul wrote the letter of 2 Timothy (c. AD 64–67).

The word is *theopneustos*. It literally means "God-breathed," and it goes a long way in helping us understand critical truths about the Bible.

What's It Mean?

For all Scripture to be "breathed out by God" means God inspired it through the direction of his Spirit. Remember the powerful words of 2 Peter 1:21: "No prophecy was ever produced by the will of man, but men spoke from God as they were carried along by the Holy Spirit" (ESV). In other words, the

Holy Spirit guided all forty (or so) biblical authors as they wrote Scripture's sixty-six books over an approximately 1,300- to 1,500-year period.

Because God inspired them, here's what's true of every word of Scripture:

- They have divine authority over us. (Luke 11:28; James 1:25)
- They are inerrant. (Psalm 119:160; Proverbs 30:5)
- They are infallible (i.e., incapable of containing error) because God is their source. (Titus 1:2; Hebrews 6:18)
- They are pure. (Psalm 12:6)
- They are eternal. (1 Peter 1:24-25)
- They are sufficient for our life, salvation, and obedience to God. (2 Timothy 3:15)
- They provide us great spiritual wisdom. (Psalm 19:7)
- They work powerfully in us to produce spiritual fruit. (Isaiah 55:11; Hebrews 4:12)

Amazing!

So props to Shakespeare for Macbeth, King Lear, and the rest. But that's all much ado about nothing (heh, heh) when compared to God's inspired Word!

Now What?
Memorize 2 Timothy 3:16 and look up the biblical references listed above.

Did You Know?
Shakespeare, along with other shareholders, commissioned the Globe Theatre in London to perform in.

MARCH 25

You have been acquainted with the sacred writings, which are able to make you wise for salvation through faith in Christ Jesus.

2 TIMOTHY 3:15, ESV

AS HE SAT IN a dark, lonely, Roman dungeon near the end of his life, the apostle Paul wrote to his dear friend, Timothy. Paul likely met Timothy some twenty years earlier on his first missionary journey as he passed through the Galatian city of Lystra.

Timothy had a strong heritage in the faith. His Jewish grandmother and mother were Christians who had taught him the Old Testament. Timothy had either come to know Christ at a young age through their witness or later through Paul's ministry (2 Timothy 1:2, 5). Paul took Timothy on his second missionary journey (Acts 16:1) and tasked him with strengthening various churches throughout the Roman Empire.

But now, as Paul faced imminent execution (c. AD 64–67), his mind turned to encouraging his protégé to remain strong in the faith by remaining faithful to Scripture. Here's what he wrote in 2 Timothy 3:14-15:

As for you, continue in what you have learned and have firmly believed, knowing from whom you learned it and how from childhood you have been acquainted with the sacred writings, *which are able to make you wise for salvation through faith in Christ Jesus* (ESV, emphasis added).

Those words ring as true today as they did in the first century AD!

What's It Mean?

There are lots of books that will make you smart. Dictionaries and thesauruses will help increase your vocabulary. School textbooks will increase your learning in specific subject matters. Encyclopedias will expand your general knowledge in a variety of topics. And cookbooks will help you learn, uh, how to cook.

But there's only one book in the whole world that is "able to make you wise for salvation through faith in Christ Jesus." That's God's Word—the Bible.

No other religious book can do this—not the Koran, Book of Mormon, or any other supposedly sacred text. Why? Because no other book is "breathed out by God" (2 Timothy 3:16, ESV). As such, only the Bible is inerrant, infallible, and eternal—revealing God's full plan of redemption for sinners through his Son, Jesus Christ.

Take a cue from Paul. "Continue in what you have learned" and soak up the life-giving words of Scripture, "which are able to make you wise for salvation through faith in Christ Jesus"!

Now What?
Check out James 1:21, which is similar to today's verse.

Did You Know?
Paul wrote the entire letter of 1 Timothy to equip Timothy to lead the church in Ephesus (1 Timothy 1:3).

MARCH 26

I have revealed you to them, and I will continue to do so.

JOHN 17:26

THOUSANDS OF PEOPLE from all walks of life saw Jesus during his earthly ministry. But very few fully understood his true nature or one of the main reasons for his mission while he was on earth.

Even his own disciples struggled to understand this. During the Last Supper, Jesus told Thomas, "I am the way, the truth, and the life. No one can come to the Father except through me. If you had really known me, you would know who my Father is. From now on, you do know him and have seen him" (John 14:6-7).

His disciple Philip said, "Lord, show us the Father, and we will be satisfied."

Jesus replied, "Have I been with you all this time, Philip, and yet you still don't know who I am? Anyone who has seen me has seen the Father!" (verses 8-9).

This, dear reader, is an amazing truth! For the last three days, we've been discussing how God has revealed himself to us through his holy Word, the Bible. But he also revealed himself to us through the incarnate Word—his Son.

What's It Mean?

When Jesus descended to earth to be born in Bethlehem's manger, the Second Person of the Trinity—God himself—incarnated into humanity. That's the message the apostle John beautifully conveys in John 1:14: "The Word became human and made his home among us."

Jesus did this, of course, to fulfill the Father's eternal plan of redemption for lost sinners like us. But he also came to reveal the Father to us in ways that weren't possible otherwise. As Jesus prayed in his High Priestly Prayer, "I have revealed you to them, and I will continue to do so" (today's verse).

While he walked this earth, Jesus gave us a living, breathing example of what the Father is like. Colossians 1:15 says, "Christ is the visible image of the invisible God." In Jesus' incarnation, we see God's unfathomably deep love for us in ways that wouldn't have been feasible from a distance. In the Cross, we see God's overwhelming mercy, grace, and forgiveness toward us. In the empty tomb, we see God's breathless power over sin, death, and the cosmic forces of evil for our sake.

Praise God for revealing himself to us through his Son!

Now What?
Read the following Bible passages to see how the Father reveals himself through the Son: John 1:18; Philippians 2:6; Colossians 1:19-20; and Hebrews 1:3.

Did You Know?
Jesus said the only people who truly know the Father are "those to whom the Son chooses to reveal him" (Matthew 11:27).

MARCH 27

I will bless those who have humble and contrite
hearts, who tremble at my word.

ISAIAH 66:2

THE AVERAGE HUMAN CAN read 200–300 words a minute. Yet there are self-proclaimed speed-readers in the world who claim to be able to read 25,000 words a minute.

That's a lot of Dostoyevsky in sixty seconds. Hey, that's a lot of Dr. Seuss in sixty seconds!

Regardless of the reading proficiency of these supposed speed-readers, this is not the way to read the Bible! When it comes to God's Word, the point is not to skim large amounts of information quickly just to say you did it. The point is to prayerfully meditate, learn, and grow.

As we have been discussing the last four days, God is a God of self-revelation. Most beautifully, he has revealed himself in Scripture. This leads to the natural question: How should we respond to his Word?

As today's verse says, we should "tremble."

What's It Mean?

The Bible is a beautiful gift that we should continually explore and treasure. No other book in the world is like it. As God's inspired, inerrant Word, it offers eternal life. It holds spiritual truth for today and promises for the future.

If you read Scripture and it doesn't move you, the problem is not Scripture. You might need to take a long, hard look at your heart.

We all have hard days and stretches where the Bible's words feel like dry pages in a textbook. We're human, after all. But if you suffer through an abnormally long period where the truth of Scripture doesn't amaze, encourage, and exhort you—causing you to worship the Lord—you need to prayerfully examine yourself.

That's because Scripture is a divine tool designed for heart penetration. As Hebrews 4:12 says, "The word of God is alive and powerful. It is sharper than the sharpest two-edged sword, cutting between soul and spirit, between joint and marrow. It exposes our innermost thoughts and desires."

God's Word shows who we really are (helpless sinners apart from sovereign grace) and who God really is (the Savior of the lost). It proclaims how much God loves us and what Christ did on our behalf. It reveals how we need to grow spiritually in loving obedience to our heavenly King. Therefore, we tremble—not in fear, but in awe and worship.

Is this how you approach God's Word?

Now What?

If you don't already, pray before reading Scripture to focus your mind and prepare your heart for what God wants to teach you during time in his Word.

Did You Know?

Jeremiah 23:29 features a fascinating description of Scripture.

MARCH 28

*Don't you realize that your body is the temple of the Holy
Spirit, who lives in you and was given to you by God?*

1 CORINTHIANS 6:19

TODAY, WE'RE TALKING about tents.

No, this isn't a discussion about camping. We're talking about the Old
Testament Tabernacle.

As God was giving Israel the Old Testament law, he told Moses, "Have
the people of Israel build me a holy sanctuary so I can live among them"
(Exodus 25:8). This "holy sanctuary" was called the Tabernacle, which
means "tent," or "dwelling." The Creator of heaven and earth wanted a special place to manifest his presence among his chosen people despite their
sin. Incredible!

Because God is holy and to be revered, he gave the Israelites exact speci-
fications regarding the Tabernacle (and later, the Temple) construction and
worship practices. Today, the Tabernacle no longer exists. The Israelites used
it for hundreds of years until King Solomon replaced it with the more permanent Temple around 960 BC. But Solomon's Temple and its replacement
were ultimately both destroyed.

God, however, never meant for the Tabernacle and Temple to last forever. He wanted to dwell with his people in something far better than physical buildings.

What's It Mean?

God's plan has always been to live among his people. First, he walked with
Adam and Eve in the Garden of Eden (Genesis 3:8). Then, he made his
presence known in Israel through the Tabernacle and Temple. Most beautifully, the Lord literally became flesh and walked among us when Jesus came
to earth as *Immanuel*, which means "God is with us" (Matthew 1:23)!

When Jesus died on the cross, the Temple curtain—signifying separation between a holy God and sinful man—was supernaturally torn in two
(Matthew 27:51).

Jesus' death removed that barrier because he is the perfect sacrifice, fully sufficient to forgive our sins. Tabernacles and temples are no longer needed. Thanks to Jesus, God now indwells his people through his Spirit, as today's verse says.

The Spirit's indwelling allows us to freely worship the Lord at all times. He convicts us of sin and makes us more like Jesus day by day (sanctification). These are just a few of the many benefits of being God's flesh-and-blood temple!

That's sure better than worshiping in a tent, wouldn't you say?

Now What?

Read Exodus 25–30 to see the care and detail God wanted the Israelites to take in worshiping him at the Tabernacle.

Did You Know?

- The Babylonians destroyed Solomon's Temple in 586 BC. The Romans destroyed the rebuilt Temple in AD 70.

MARCH 29

How quickly they have turned away from the way I commanded
them to live! They have melted down gold and made a
calf, and they have bowed down and sacrificed to it.

EXODUS 32:8

HOLY COW!

The Israelites had a big problem: they, uh, thought a cow was holy.

Moses had been on Mount Sinai for many days with God, receiving the law. But the Israelites grew impatient. They wanted to worship a god they could see, so they told Aaron, Moses' brother, to "make us some gods who can lead us" (Exodus 32:1). Sadly, Aaron complied and built the infamous golden calf idol. This was a direct violation of the first two commandments.

The Israelites had experienced an incredible amount of God's love and power since leaving Egypt:

- He delivered them from slavery with ten plagues and the parting of the Red Sea.
- He led them through the desert with a pillar of cloud and fire.
- He provided water from a rock to drink and manna and quail to eat.
- He descended in smoke, fire, and thunder on Mount Sinai.
- He expressed a desire to live among them through the Tabernacle.

Why would they reject God and do something so foolish?

What's It Mean?

Most likely, the Israelites were mimicking what they saw in Egypt. The Egyptians worshiped many deities, including two called Hathor and Apis that were represented with a cow's and bull's head, respectively. The Israelites seemed to be mixing pagan worship with the worship of the Lord, perhaps even making the golden calf to represent God (Exodus 32:4-5).

This was both wicked and ridiculous. Remember, God had destroyed many of Egypt's cows with a plague on livestock and then further wiped them out with a plague of hail. If God was a mighty cow or bull, why would he kill his own kind with plagues? And for that matter, why would he later command Israel to sacrifice bulls to him?

Do you see how deceptive sin is? It deludes us into believing bold-faced lies about God and causes us to behave irrationally, far outside the boundaries of our calling as God's image-bearers.

Today, your biggest struggle likely isn't worshiping a golden calf. However, we all struggle with idols of the heart—things we desire instead of God. Guard your heart against sin's deceitfulness and the idols that can creep in and take the place of rightful worship of our Creator!

Now What?
Pray and meditate on Psalm 51:10: "Create in me a clean heart, O God. Renew a loyal spirit within me."

Did You Know?
Centuries later, Israel was still struggling with golden calf worship. Check out 1 Kings 12:28.

MARCH 30

All honor and glory to God forever and ever! He is the eternal
King, the unseen one who never dies; he alone is God.

1 TIMOTHY 1:17

FOR AN OLD GUY, Moses could still bring the noise when needed!

When the Israelites worshiped the golden calf, God was prepared to destroy his rebellious and idolatrous people. But Moses interceded for them, and the Lord mercifully relented from his righteous anger.

But when Moses personally witnessed the people's wickedness, he smashed the Ten Commandments in a rage, burned the golden calf, ground it into powder, and forced the people to drink it. Then he instructed the Levites to kill everyone who remained stubbornly unrepentant toward the Lord—about three thousand people.

Wow! Pretty fiery for an eighty-year-old!

But Moses had every right to be angry. The Israelites had been exceedingly wicked and unfaithful toward God. They had broken both the first and second of the Ten Commandments (Exodus 20:3-4):

1. You must not have any other god but me.
2. You must not make for yourself an idol of any kind or an image of anything in the heavens or on the earth or in the sea.

What's It Mean?

God is different, far greater, and far more glorious than anything else in his creation. Nothing in the universe can come close to adequately representing God, so in the second commandment, he forbids us to even try.

Idolatry was a constant snare to the ancient Israelites. God is "the eternal King, the unseen one" (today's verse), but they wanted a god they could see and touch. It's partially why they built the golden calf and struggled with idolatry throughout much of their pre-exile history.

Don't think you're above this. You might not be tempted to worship false gods of metal, wood, or stone, but every human heart is prone to be deceived and lose faith when our eyes don't see empirical evidence of the supernatural.

You've certainly heard the popular phrase, "I'll believe it when I see it." But God calls us to adopt a different mentality. We are to believe even when we don't "see it." In other words, we are to have faith in God even though we don't see him.

God is alive today! He is ruling the universe and ruling in human hearts. Even though you can't see him, will you allow him to rule in your heart?

Now What?

Read the account of the golden calf in Exodus 32.

Did You Know?

More than one billion people in the world today still worship man-made idols. Pray for their salvation.

MARCH 31

Christ has already accomplished the purpose for which the law was given. As a result, all who believe in him are made right with God.

ROMANS 10:4

NO MATTER WHO YOU are, you must follow lots of rules in life. There are rules at home, at school, at work, on the road, on planes, in the library, in stores—everywhere!

But check out these unique rules:

- All small animals that scurry along the ground are detestable, and you must never eat them.
- Do not wear clothing woven from two different kinds of thread.
- Do not trim off the hair on your temples or trim your beards.

These rules all come from Leviticus. Let's be honest: Leviticus is one of the toughest books in the Bible to read. Sometimes, it can sound antiquated, obscure, and overbearing.

But Leviticus—which is part of the Pentateuch, the first five books of the Bible (or the Torah, as Jews call it)—is also inspired Scripture, just like the rest of God's Word. So how are we supposed to understand this difficult book today, with all of its ancient rules and regulations?

What's It Mean?
In essence, Leviticus, like the rest of the Mosaic law (including parts of Exodus, Numbers, and Deuteronomy), is a holiness code, teaching sinful Israel how to properly worship and honor a holy God as his covenant community.

But there was a three-letter problem: sin. Our sinful nature took advantage of the law, and everything the law forbade (e.g., covetousness, Exodus 20:17) sin gladly produced in our corrupt hearts (Romans 7:7-12). Subsequently, Israel could never follow Leviticus—let alone the entire Mosaic law—perfectly. "It is clear that no one can be made right with God by trying to keep the law" (Galatians 3:11).

Ultimately, the law revealed that we are all miserable rule-breakers. As funny as it sounds, this was a wonderful aspect of the law, for it showed we are helpless, but not hopeless. It pointed ahead to a perfect Rule-Keeper who would fully accomplish the law's purpose for us, as today's verse says.

God's Son, Jesus Christ, perfectly kept the law. As such, he was able to represent us before the Father as both our High Priest and our sacrificial Lamb. Thank you, Jesus!

Now What?

Today, Christians don't need to follow the sacrificial system or many other ritualistic purity laws in Leviticus since we are under the new covenant of grace. But we do need to grow in sanctification, becoming more like Christ. As God says in Leviticus 11:45, "Be holy because I am holy."

Did You Know?

- Leviticus is a Latin word meaning "things concerning Levites."

APRIL 1

Our High Priest offered himself to God as a single sacrifice for sins, good for all time.

HEBREWS 10:12

THE DAY STARTED EARLY with a meticulous bath. Next came a meticulous outfit. Everything had to be just so.

Then several choice animals had to be chosen from the herds: a bull, a ram, and two goats. Finally, the high priest would solemnly make his way to the Tabernacle.

The Day of Atonement was at hand.

God called his people to regularly offer sacrifices through the priests for the forgiveness of their sins. But the Day of Atonement was different. Besides the weekly Sabbath and annual Passover festival, the annual Day of Atonement (as described in Leviticus 16) was one of the most sacred observances on the ancient Jewish calendar. It was the day the high priest would atone for the nation's sins and for the Tabernacle itself (verse 16), making it possible for a holy God to remain present among sinful people.

This was the only day all year when the high priest could pass beyond the veil into the Most Holy Place of the Tabernacle (and later, the Temple). There, God would appear to him uniquely in a cloud above the Ark of the Covenant's "mercy seat" (verse 2, ESV).

The Day of Atonement also featured the "scapegoat" ceremony. The high priest would slaughter one goat as a sacrifice and keep the other alive, laying his hands on its head and releasing it into the wilderness, outside Israel's camp. This symbolized the transfer and removal of sins from God's people to a substitute.

What's It Mean?

Human sin requires atonement, a term that means payment for an offense. In biblical terms, it's when God's righteous wrath toward sin is appeased by offering a blood sacrifice.

All of the Day of Atonement's rituals symbolized a far greater atonement that was coming. As Hebrews 10:4 says, "It is not possible for the blood of bulls and goats to take away sins."

That's why Jesus came into the world. He is our great High Priest. He perfectly represented his people before the Father.

Jesus also became our scapegoat. The Father laid all our sins on his Son, and Jesus died outside the camp, so to speak—beyond the walls of Jerusalem on a hill called Golgotha.

The Day of Atonement is no longer needed. God's Son atoned for our sins in every way through his sinless life, death, and resurrection!

Now What?

Read Hebrews 8–10 to learn more about Jesus' high priestly work.

Did You Know?

Today, Jews observe the Day of Atonement annually as Yom Kippur.

APRIL 2

The LORD is with us!
Don't be afraid of them!

NUMBERS 14:9

GIANT WARRIORS!

Giant fortresses!

Giant fruit and other agricultural produce!

The Land of Canaan Welcomes You!

Okay, maybe that's not the greatest Board of Tourism campaign. But that's how Israel initially viewed their future home.

After spending almost a year at Mount Sinai, the Israelites finally arrived at the southern tip of Canaan. They were so close to entering the Promised Land—the land that God had promised to give to Abraham's descendants.

God told Moses to send twelve spies to scout Canaan before the entire nation entered. Forty days later, they returned, and ten of them gave a frightful report: "The people living there are powerful, and their towns are large and fortified. . . . The land we traveled through and explored will devour anyone who goes to live there. All the people we saw were huge. We even saw giants there!" (Numbers 13:28, 32-33).

Two of the spies, Caleb and Joshua, remained faithful to God, imploring the people to trust in him. "They have no protection," they said, "but the LORD is with us! Don't be afraid of them!" (14:9).

In the end, the people listened to the ten faithless spies and rebelled against God. They even considered stoning Caleb and Joshua and returning to Egypt. How quickly they forgot all the mighty works God had performed for them in Egypt, at the Red Sea, and on the way to Canaan!

As a result, God sentenced Israel to wander in the wilderness for forty years before entering Canaan until the faithless generation perished. He also sent a deadly plague on the ten cowardly spies.

What's It Mean?

This is a somber story, to say the least! But there's much we can learn both from Israel's faithless response to the spies' report and Caleb and Joshua's praiseworthy reaction.

In the face of overwhelming pressure to go with the crowd, Caleb and Joshua remained faithful to the Lord. They stood their ground even when threatened with death. They looked beyond what their eyes told them and remembered God's promises, which always come true.

What about you? Are you in a situation where people are testing your faith or trying to drag you into unbelief? Are you tempted to believe that the challenges facing you are greater than God's limitless power?

Remember the Lord's promises! He is faithful, and he will be with you.

Now What?

Prayerfully meditate on five biblical promises of God, thanking him for his faithfulness. One to start with is Psalm 103:8.

Did You Know?

Caleb's nephew, Othniel, became Israel's first judge during that period (Judges 1:13 and 3:7-11).

APRIL 3

He does not punish us for all our sins; he does not
deal harshly with us, as we deserve.

PSALM 103:10

FORTY YEARS HAD PASSED.

The wicked generation that believed the ten spies' cowardly report of Canaan had died. Now, the Israelites were back at Kadesh, a normally well-watered oasis south of the Promised Land, where their wilderness wanderings had started.

But there was a problem: the oasis was bone dry. How do you think Israel reacted?

(Drumroll, please.) That's right, they complained and lost faith . . . again! (See Numbers 20:3-5.)

God showed mercy to Israel, commanding Moses to speak to a nearby rock to miraculously bring a water flow. Moses, however, was seething with anger at the people's constant complaining.

"Listen, you rebels!" he shouted. "Must we bring you water from this rock?" (verse 10). Then he struck the rock twice with his staff.

Amazingly, water still flowed from the rock. But Moses and Aaron (who was with him at the time) had brazenly defied God's command in sight of the people, so God had to discipline them: "Because you did not trust me enough to demonstrate my holiness to the people of Israel, you will not lead them into the land I am giving them!" (verse 12).

What's It Mean?

After leading Israel for forty years, Moses and Aaron died outside the Promised Land for their prideful rebellion at Kadesh ("Must *we* bring you water from this rock?"). Was this an unfair, harsh punishment? No. Because God is holy, any disobedience toward him is sinful insurrection, worthy of death (Romans 6:23).

Where Moses and his stubborn people deserved wrath, God showed great love and mercy. They complained and their leader raged, yet the water still flowed from the rock.

Lest we judge the obstinate Israelites too harshly, we must admit we bear a lot of similarities:

- Israel sinned and complained countless times. So do we.
- Israel frequently forgot God's prior displays of love and power. So do we.
- Israel often lacked faith. So do we.

Our sin is great, but God's mercy is greater. As today's verse says, he does not treat us as our sins deserve.

God showed abundant mercy to Israel, and he does with us, too. When Moses struck the rock, despite his disobedience, God provided life-giving water to nourish his people. Many years later, despite our sin, God sent his own Son to the Cross to provide life-giving salvation to anyone who believes. Thank the Lord for that!

Now What?

Read Psalm 103 for a great reminder of his steadfast love toward those who don't deserve it.

Did You Know?

Aaron died on Mount Hor, south of Canaan (Numbers 20:22-29). God allowed Moses to overlook Canaan on a mountain in Moab before he died (Deuteronomy 34).

APRIL 4

As Moses lifted up the bronze snake on a pole in the
wilderness, so the Son of Man must be lifted up, so that
everyone who believes in him will have eternal life.

JOHN 3:14-15

MIRIAM WAS DEAD. Aaron was dead. The forty years of wilderness wandering for believing the ten spies' bad report about Canaan was at an end. The Israelites were so close to the Promised Land.

And then they started grumbling . . . again.

"'Why have you brought us out of Egypt to die here in the wilderness?' they complained. 'There is nothing to eat here and nothing to drink. And we hate this horrible manna!'" (Numbers 21:5).

If the Ancient Moaning and Groaning Olympics existed, the Israelites would have won a gold medal!

This time, God judged his people by sending venomous snakes into their camp, and many died from the bites. When the people cried out for help, God did something interesting: instead of removing the snakes, he told Moses to make a bronze snake on a pole so everyone bitten could be healed simply by looking at it.

The Israelites needed to understand that their sin brought terrible consequences, but that faith in God's plan of salvation would save them.

What's It Mean?

Do you know we've all been bitten by a poisonous snake? "The ancient serpent called the devil, or Satan, the one deceiving the whole world" (Revelation 12:9) has been at work since the Garden of Eden. Because of the Fall, the venom of sin has utterly corrupted each of us since birth (Psalm 51:5; Romans 3:9-18, 23). That's why Jesus said, "You must be born again" in John 3:7—a spiritual rebirth.

In fact, when Jesus was explaining this process, he used Old Testament Israel's experience with the bronze snake to illustrate his point (see today's verse). The story of the bronze snake isn't just a story about judgment and death. It's about God showing his people how they must be saved—and pointing ahead to the greater Savior.

Just like the Old Testament Jews had to look to God's appointed way of deliverance (a bronze snake, lifted up) to be saved from their rebellion, we must look in faith to Jesus, who was lifted up on the cross, to be saved from our sins.

The poison of sin runs deep, but by looking to Jesus, we can receive the antidote of God's love, mercy, and grace!

Now What?
Read Numbers 21:4-9 (the account of the bronze snake) and John 3:1-21 (the account of Jesus and Nicodemus).

Did You Know?
By King Hezekiah's reign (at least six centuries later), the bronze serpent had become an idolatrous object of worship in Judah (2 Kings 18:4).

APRIL 5

Look, I have come to block your way because
you are stubbornly resisting me.

NUMBERS 22:32

THE BIBLE IS a profound book. It's God's marvelous revelation of his eternal plan of redemption for mankind.

Sometimes, though, certain Bible stories are just downright funny! Take, for instance, the story of Balaam and his talking donkey. Now, before you start connecting this with the movie Shrek, an explanation is needed.

In Numbers 22, Israel had just entered Moab after two significant military victories. Terrified, the Moabite king, Balak, tried to hire Balaam, a well-known soothsayer, to curse Israel. But God intervened and commanded Balaam to bless Israel.

Balaam feigned obedience, but his heart was filled with idolatry and wickedness. So as Balaam traveled with Balak's messengers, God sent a mighty angel to block his way. The angel was invisible to Balaam but, remarkably, not to his donkey! Three times the donkey changed course to avoid the heavenly warrior, and three times Balaam beat the animal.

Then, God miraculously opened the donkey's mouth!

"What have I done to you that deserves your beating me three times?" [the donkey] asked Balaam.

"You have made me look like a fool!" Balaam shouted. "If I had a sword with me, I would kill you!"

"But I am the same donkey you have ridden all your life," the donkey answered. "Have I ever done anything like this before?"

"No," Balaam admitted.

NUMBERS 22:28-30

Then God opened Balaam's eyes to see the angel blocking his path. The angel rebuked Balaam, telling him that if the donkey hadn't stopped, the angel would have killed Balaam for "stubbornly resisting" God (verse 32).

What's It Mean?

As humorous as this story is, there's a serious message, too. While Balaam obeyed God and pronounced three blessings on Israel (much to Balak's chagrin), his heart wasn't fully devoted to the Lord. In Numbers 31, we learn that because of Balaam, Israel committed terrible idolatry, which led to Balaam's ultimate demise.

What about your heart? Like Balaam, do you only pay lip service to God? Do you say the right things in the right situations to look godly while your heart runs after other things? Or are you fully devoted to the Lord?

God wants people who love him wholeheartedly (Deuteronomy 6:5). Don't be like Balaam, who was more mulish toward God than a donkey! Humble yourself before the Lord, and he will lift you up.

Now What?

Read about Balaam in Numbers 22–24, his treachery against Israel in chapter 25, and his death in 31:8.

Did You Know?

"The angel of the LORD" (Numbers 22:22) who confronted Balaam and his donkey might have been a "theophany"—a physical manifestation of God himself.

APRIL 6

Teach us to number our days that we may get a heart of wisdom.

PSALM 90:12, ESV

MOSES WAS MANY THINGS.

He was a godly leader, a powerful prophet, a wise judge, and a Spirit-inspired biblical author. He was also a tablet expert: thousands of years before electronic tablets with Internet capability, he was receiving new Ten Commandment tablets after angrily throwing the first set down a mountain!

But did you know he was also a poet? It's true! While King David wrote at least half of the book of Psalms, Moses wrote one—Psalm 90, making it the oldest of the 150 psalms.

Moses likely penned Psalm 90 during Israel's wilderness wanderings. It's a beautiful song that juxtaposes the brevity of human life against God's awe-inspiring eternality and sovereign purposes.

Moses experienced many highs and lows in life. He had much wisdom to dispense. Mostly, he wanted the readers of Psalm 90 to understand how awesome God is and how—as mere mortals but also privileged image-bearers of the King—they fit into the grand scope of this big, fallen world.

"Teach us," he wrote in today's verse, "to number our days that we may get a heart of wisdom."

What's It Mean?

God is eternal—without beginning or end. But human life is short—about seventy years or so, maybe eighty if we're really blessed (verse 10). Much of it, though, is filled with "pain and trouble" (verse 10). As such, Moses says, we would be wise to "number our days."

Was Moses the world's biggest pessimist? Was he taking a morbid, fatalistic view of life, like counting down the days until you die?

No. When Moses says, "Teach us to number our days that we may get a heart of wisdom," he is asking God to help us make the most of the beautiful, albeit relatively brief, gift of human life on earth. How do we get a heart of wisdom? That begins with fearing the Lord (Proverbs 9:10; see the April 22 devotion), seeking him through his Word, and walking in his ways.

Life is hard. Time zips by relentlessly. Are you numbering your days for the Lord? Are you seeking a heart of wisdom? Are you pursuing God wholeheartedly?

You should—because his love for you is never-ending. As Moses sang in verse 14, "Satisfy us each morning with your unfailing love, so we may sing for joy to the end of our lives."

Now What?
Read Psalm 90.

Did You Know?
Moses lived to be 120 years old (Deuteronomy 34:7), beating the average life span he wrote about in his own psalm! (But hey, who's counting?)

APRIL 7

You shall teach them diligently to your children, and shall
talk of them when you sit in your house, and when you walk
by the way, and when you lie down, and when you rise.

DEUTERONOMY 6:7, ESV

ISRAEL HAD DEFEATED KING Sihon of Heshbon and King Og of
Bashan, two powerful Amorite rulers. Now, God's people were encamped
just east of the Promised Land. Moses addressed them as they prepared to
enter their long-awaited home. Battles followed by a sermon? Now there's a
long-lost concept in warfare!

Moses' lengthy discourse fills nearly the entire book of Deuteronomy.
But chapter 6 features some of his most important words:

Hear, O Israel: The LORD our God, the LORD is one. You shall love
the LORD your God with all your heart and with all your soul and
with all your might. And these words that I command you today shall
be on your heart. You shall teach them diligently to your children, and
shall talk of them when you sit in your house, and when you walk by
the way, and when you lie down, and when you rise.

VERSES 4-7, ESV

What's It Mean?

This is a critical Old Testament passage—one that most ancient Jewish children would know by heart. Every Israelite was to be wholeheartedly devoted
only to God, and parents were to take daily opportunities to teach their
children to love and obey him.

Similarly, Psalm 78:4 says, "We will not hide these truths from our children; we will tell the next generation about the glorious deeds of the LORD,
about his power and his mighty wonders." God's most glorious deed, of
course, is providing his Son, Jesus Christ, as an atoning sacrifice for our sins.
Verses 5-6 describe a process where multiple generations would hear about
God's powerful works of salvation.

The point is clear: God wants the good news of salvation to be passed down primarily through families. Pastors, evangelists, Christian schoolteachers, and Christian organizations are all important to spread the gospel. But for children, God wants the gospel message to start with parents, in the home.

Are your parents faithfully teaching you Scripture? If so, praise God! If not, you can commit to starting that generational trend with your children one day—and thank the Lord that he graciously enlightened you with the truth of the gospel in a different way!

Now What?

Start serving in your church's children's ministry or elsewhere to make a gospel impact on the next generation.

Did You Know?

Both the Old and New Testaments attest to God's heart for strong families rooted in his Word.

APRIL 8

Study this Book of Instruction continually. Meditate on it day
and night so you will be sure to obey everything written in it.
Only then will you prosper and succeed in all you do.

JOSHUA 1:8

IMAGINE, FOR A MOMENT, this scenario: you are the newly appointed leader of a young nation. The previous leader—your mentor, a beloved and incomparable prophet whom God knew face-to-face—is dead. Now, all of the responsibility to lead approximately two million grumbling rebels falls on your shoulders. In addition, you are about to guide them into a land filled with fierce pagan people groups, who dwell in well-fortified cities and are superior to you in warfare. Plus, you will face giants!

This was the overwhelming challenge that Joshua faced after Moses died. You can imagine his potential trepidation as he prepared to lead Israel into the Promised Land.

How, then, would Joshua and Israel succeed in driving out the Canaanites and fulfilling God's promise to Abraham, Isaac, and Jacob? God did not tell Joshua to hold an emergency boot camp, or quickly form military alliances with neighboring nations, or deploy his tanks, fighter planes, and nuclear submarines.

God told him to study Scripture.

What's It Mean?

Here's what God specifically told Joshua:

> Be strong and very courageous. Be careful to obey all the instructions Moses gave you. Do not deviate from them, turning either to the right or to the left. Then you will be successful in everything you do. Study this Book of Instruction continually. Meditate on it day and night so you will be sure to obey everything written in it. Only then will you prosper and succeed in all you do. This is my command—be strong

and courageous! Do not be afraid or discouraged. For the LORD your God is with you wherever you go.

JOSHUA 1:7-9

Are you surprised at God's answer? You shouldn't be!

Rather than relying on military might or human power, God wanted Joshua to rely on him. Drawing strength from God can only come from knowing and obeying Scripture.

This is a powerful reminder for us today, too. We cannot succeed spiritually in life without planting God's Word into our hearts. Unlike Joshua, we have the benefit of God's full revealed canon of Scripture—all sixty-six books of the Bible.

Read the Bible daily. Study it. Memorize it. Love it. Obey it. Treasure it. "Only then will you prosper and succeed in all you do."

Now What?

Memorize today's verse!

Did You Know?

Meditating on Scripture has nothing to do with meditation linked to Eastern transcendentalism. It simply means to prayerfully think through what you read.

APRIL 9

The LORD is for me.

PSALM 118:6

GOD HAD MIRACULOUSLY BROUGHT Israel across the Jordan River. Spies had been sent to scout out Jericho. The conquest of Canaan was about to begin.

But on the eve of battle, a fascinating encounter between Joshua and a mysterious stranger occurred. Joshua 5:13-15 records it:

> When Joshua was near the town of Jericho, he looked up and saw a man standing in front of him with sword in hand. Joshua went up to him and demanded, "Are you friend or foe?"
>
> "Neither one," he replied. "I am the commander of the LORD's army."
>
> At this, Joshua fell with his face to the ground in reverence. "I am at your command," Joshua said. "What do you want your servant to do?"
>
> The commander of the LORD's army replied, "Take off your sandals, for the place where you are standing is holy." And Joshua did as he was told.

Joshua likely remembered this brief meeting the rest of his life. We can learn a great deal from it too.

What's It Mean?

Confronted by a startling warrior, Joshua wanted to know, "Whose side are you on?" It seemed to be a legitimate question. However, based on the warrior's response, the better question for Joshua (and us) is this: Are *you* on the Lord's side? In other words, do you have the Lord's plans in mind?

Too often, we want God on our side in selfish ways. We want him to approve all the goals and plans we've already mapped out for our lives. This often shows up in the way we pray.

But God doesn't work like that. He is the eternal, sovereign Ruler of the universe. He is not obligated to follow our plans, but we are obligated to follow his. He calls us to humble ourselves in repentance and faith and join his purposes, which are always for his glory and our good.

Is the Lord "for" his people? Yes! Scripture clearly teaches this. (Psalm 118:6 and Romans 8:31-39.) But he always does this within the framework of his greater purposes.

If God is committed to his people out of his abundant love and grace, how much more should we be committed to him out of worshipful obedience? So follow the example of Joshua, who wisely humbled himself before God in Joshua 5:14 and asked, "What do you want your servant to do?" May we do the same!

Now What?

When you pray, seek the Lord's will to be done in your life (Matthew 6:10), not your own.

Did You Know?

Many theologians believe that "the commander of the LORD's army" in Joshua 5:13-15 was actually a preincarnate appearance of Christ.

APRIL 10

The seventh time around, as the priests sounded the long
blast on their horns, Joshua commanded the people,
"Shout! For the LORD has given you the town!"

JOSHUA 6:16

THE PEOPLE OF JERICHO were shaking in their tunics and sandals!

Word had spread quickly throughout Canaan about Joshua and Israel. Jericho's residents knew all about God's miraculous acts and powerful victories as he led his chosen people from Egypt to Canaan's doorstep.

Now, Israel had its sights set on Jericho. So the city was sealed up airtight. Nobody in. Nobody out.

Then the Lord told his people to do something strange:

I have given you Jericho, its king, and all its strong warriors. You
and your fighting men should march around the town once a day
for six days. Seven priests will walk ahead of the Ark, each carrying
a ram's horn. On the seventh day you are to march around the town
seven times, with the priests blowing the horns. When you hear the
priests give one long blast on the rams' horns, have all the people
shout as loud as they can. Then the walls of the town will collapse,
and the people can charge straight into the town.

JOSHUA 6:2-5

Has there ever been such an unusual command given in the history of warfare?

What's It Mean?

As the story of Jericho in Joshua 6 unfolds, God's intentions become very clear: he wanted to test Israel's faith and show his people that their victory was completely by his power ("*I* have given you Jericho," Joshua 6:2, emphasis added), not their military strength.

There must have been times during that weeklong march where Israel's soldiers felt pretty ridiculous. After all, who defeats a well-fortified city by quietly circling it, then shouting? Nobody does—except God. On the seventh day, Israel achieved a remarkable victory through faith and obedience.

How big is your faith in God? Do you believe he can do the impossible? Do you believe he created the universe, flooded the earth, and plagued one nation to begin another? Do you believe he can part the seas, thunder from on high, and topple city walls?

Yes, the Lord God Almighty can do all these things—and much more. Let any disbelief crumble away like Jericho's walls and trust in him!

Now What?
Read the story of Jericho in Joshua 6.

Did You Know?
• Archaeologists have discovered that ancient biblical Jericho was surrounded by two walls, and that the inner wall was 4 meters (13 feet) thick at certain points.

APRIL 11

*Jericho and everything in it must be completely
destroyed as an offering to the LORD.*

JOSHUA 6:17

THE TOWERING WALLS OF Jericho were ready to fall. Israel's first conquest in the land of Canaan was at hand.

"Shout!" Joshua told his troops. "For the LORD has given you the town!" Joshua continued: "Jericho and everything in it must be completely destroyed as an offering to the Lord" (Joshua 6:16-17).

This directive was in obedience to God's earlier command through Moses in Deuteronomy 7:2: "When the LORD your God hands these nations over to you and you conquer them, you must completely destroy them." In other words, Israel was to kill every man, woman, and child—not just in Jericho, but everywhere in Canaan.

Some people read this and question God's goodness. They ask, "How can a loving God give such an order?" But when we truly understand God's character, we see how this command is perfectly consistent with his holiness, justice, and overall plan of salvation.

What's It Mean?

It's critical that we think correctly about God, and this is a subject we can easily misinterpret. So we need to remember a few key truths in light of today's verse:

- When God renders judgment, it is always perfectly just.
- As Creator, God rules over the entire earth and can allot land to whomever he chooses, whenever he desires.
- As sinful creatures, all humans—including the ancient Canaanites—are subject to God's judgment. We owe God everything, but he owes us nothing. Any good he gives us above the outpouring of his justly deserved wrath is beautiful mercy and grace.

The Canaanites were a notoriously wicked, idolatrous people that God had patiently given many centuries to repent, but they didn't. So in his sovereign plan, he used Israel to execute judgment—not because Israel was more righteous than the Canaanites, but because he had chosen to use Israel for his sovereign purposes (Deuteronomy 7; 9:1-6).

God also knew that if the Canaanites lingered in the land, they would drag Israel into their godless practices (Deuteronomy 7:4).

Additionally, God chose Israel to be a holy people set apart to the Lord (Deuteronomy 7:6) and the nation through which the Messiah would come—the Savior for both Jews and Gentiles.

Sin is egregious before a holy God. Were it not for God's mercy and grace, our fate would be like the Canaanites'. Praise the Lord for Jesus, who bore God's righteous wrath toward sin on our behalf!

Now What?

To better understand this difficult subject, read Deuteronomy 7–12.

Did You Know?

Israel never fully eradicated the Canaanites from the Promised Land.

APRIL 12

*As for me and my family,
we will serve the LORD.*

JOSHUA 24:15

LET'S BRIEFLY REVIEW some important choices you might have to
make in life:

- Getting a closer look at a lion pride by approaching it in a gazelle
  costume OR staying in the enclosed safari SUV.
- Going spelunking in an active volcano OR choosing a normal cave
  without 1,600-degree lava.
- Riding your rusty dirty bike from 1996 OR accepting a free, cherry-
  red Lamborghini from your insanely rich uncle.

These are all "no-brainer" choices. In Joshua 24:14-15, Israel's aging
leader gave the people a similar choice in his final address:

Fear the LORD and serve him wholeheartedly. Put away forever
the idols your ancestors worshiped when they lived beyond the
Euphrates River and in Egypt. Serve the LORD alone. But if
you refuse to serve the LORD, then choose today whom you will
serve. Would you prefer the gods your ancestors served beyond
the Euphrates? Or will it be the gods of the Amorites in whose
land you now live? But as for me and my family, we will serve
the LORD.

Joshua's no-brainer was for the Israelites to fully commit to God, who
had miraculously worked on their behalf as his chosen people. But if they
decided to reject him, Joshua basically said, "Don't waste my time or God's:
choose now which false, worthless gods to worship—the ones the Lord
exposed as frauds in Egypt or in Canaan."

What's It Mean?

As today's verse says, Joshua made his choice clear: he and his family committed their lives to the Lord.

What about you? Your biggest dilemma probably isn't whether to serve false gods or the one true God of the Bible. Idolatry for twenty-first century Americans is an entirely different problem than it was for ancient Israel. Our hearts are prone to worship the "gods" of personal comfort, money, fame, selfish ambition, and worldly pleasures, to name a few. These idols might not be made of wood or stone, but they are just as worthless and spiritually enslaving as lifeless statues. May your mantra instead echo Joshua's: "As for me and my family, we will serve the LORD."

There's a God in heaven who created you and lovingly sacrificed his own Son to atone for your sins. Serving this God leads to eternal life. All other false gods lead to spiritual death.

Your choice should be clear. In fact, you could say it's a no-brainer.

Now What?

Prayerfully examine your heart for any "gods" you are worshiping, and confess them to the Lord.

Did You Know?

Joshua lived to be 110—almost as old as Moses!

APRIL 13

In those days Israel had no king; all the people did
whatever seemed right in their own eyes.

JUDGES 21:25

CYCLES CAN BE GOOD in life.

Bicycles are great for fun, exercise, and competition. A washing and drying cycle helps us clean our clothing. Then there are various cycles that are vital to life on earth, such as the water cycle, where water evaporates from the earth, condenses in the atmosphere, and falls to the earth as precipitation over and over.

These are all good cycles. But the book of Judges describes a terrible cycle.

Once Joshua died, a new generation of Israelites who didn't follow the Lord grew up. Because they failed to drive out all the idolatrous Canaanites, God's earlier warnings came true: "They abandoned the LORD, the God of their ancestors, who had brought them out of Egypt. They went after other gods, worshiping the gods of the people around them. And they angered the LORD" (Judges 2:12).

And so began Israel's maddening cycle of rebellion, judgment, and forgiveness. God punished Israel's wickedness by allowing enemies to oppress them. When the people cried out in despair, God mercifully raised up judges to save them. But then they quickly fell away from the Lord, beginning the maddening cycle again. This period spanned approximately four hundred years.

Perhaps the most accurate, chilling summary of this regrettable period in Israel's history comes from today's verse: "All the people did whatever seemed right in their own eyes."

What's It Mean?

Doing what is right in your own eyes means you are giving in to pride. It means you are acting like you are the final arbiter between good and evil. It means you are trying to arrogantly rule your own life, as if you don't have to answer to a higher authority.

Ultimately, it means you are buying into Satan's original lies in the Garden of Eden:

"Did God really say . . ."
"You won't die."
"You will be like God!"

Left to ourselves, we are poor judges of right and wrong. Jeremiah 17:9 says, "The human heart is the most deceitful of all things, and desperately wicked." We need God's wisdom to rightly discern what is pleasing to the Lord.

Praise God that he willingly gives us his wisdom in abundance! Call on the Lord to help you do what is right.

Now What?

Want to see constant examples of God's steadfast love, patience, and mercy with a stubborn people? Read the entire book of Judges!

Did You Know?

The book of Judges mentions twelve judges, and eleven were male. The wisest seemed to be Deborah, the lone female (Judges 4–5).

APRIL 14

*Not to us, O LORD, not to us, but to your name goes all
the glory for your unfailing love and faithfulness.*

PSALM 115:1

WHEN YOU THINK of the greatest military leaders of all time, who comes
to mind?

Alexander the Great?
Hannibal?
Julius Caesar?
Genghis Khan?
Napoleon Bonaparte?
George Washington?
Mickey Mouse? *(Just wanted to see if you were paying attention!)*

You probably don't immediately think of Gideon, do you? Gideon was
a judge whom God called to save his people from Midianite oppression.
When the angel of the Lord first called Gideon, he was threshing wheat in a
winepress to hide from Israel's overpowering enemies (Judges 6:11).

"Mighty hero!" the angel said. "The LORD is with you!" The scene was
dripping with humorous irony.

Gideon's task was daunting. Midian's army was 135,000 strong with
countless camels. Gideon had 32,000 foot soldiers. He was already facing
more than 4-to-1 odds.

Then God did something shocking. Through a series of dismissals,
God had Gideon whittle his army down to 300 soldiers. The odds were
now utterly ridiculous: 450-to-1. Every Israelite had to kill more than
450 Midianites to win the battle! What's more, God told them to attack
Midian's camp with strange weapons—empty jars, torches, and trumpets.

Why on earth did God do all this? Was he trying to get Israel killed?
No! Actually, it was the exact opposite.

What's It Mean?

God was going to save Israel. But he was going to do it with a heavenly display of power they would never forget.

"If I let all of you fight the Midianites, the Israelites will boast to me that they saved themselves by their own strength," God told Gideon (Judges 7:2).

God could see inside his people's hearts. He knew how quickly they would take credit for a victory they didn't earn and glory that wasn't theirs.

We are no different. Too often, we sinfully want the glory for ourselves even though all our gifts and abilities and everything we accomplish are only by God's grace and power.

Prayerfully search your heart. Are there areas in your life where you need to actively give God the glory? Maybe it's sports, academics, work, music, or something else. Whatever it is, offer praise and honor where it's due—to your Creator. He alone is worthy of it!

Now What?

Read about the miraculous way God gave victory to Gideon and his three hundred men in Judges 7.

Did You Know?

Gideon was also called Jerub-baal, meaning "Let Baal defend himself," because he had broken down Baal's altar earlier in life (Judges 6:28-32).

APRIL 15

Let the Holy Spirit guide your lives. Then you won't
be doing what your sinful nature craves.

GALATIANS 5:16

CAN YOU IMAGINE what a job interview with Samson, the famous
Israelite judge, might have sounded like?

> **Hiring manager:** So Mr. Samson, what do you currently do for a living?
> **Samson:** I harass and destroy my archenemies, the Philistines, at every
> opportunity.
> **Hiring manager:** I see. Hmmm. Well, what are your most impressive
> accomplishments?
> **Samson:** I don't want to brag, but I have quite a few. I've destroyed
> a lion with my bare hands, killed one thousand Philistines with a
> donkey's jawbone, uprooted massive city gates and carried them
> dozens of miles to escape my enemies, and flexed my biceps to snap
> virtually anything people try to bind me with.
> **Hiring manager:** So you're probably not cut out for a desk job. . . . Is
> there anything else you'd like to share about yourself?
> **Samson:** Yes, actually. I was dedicated to the Lord by a Nazirite vow since
> birth for a special purpose. But I've broken the vow many times.
> **Hiring manager:** Well, uh, thanks for coming in today. Don't call us.
> We'll call you!

Samson certainly led a fascinating life. For twenty years, he fought
against the Philistines on Israel's behalf, performing extraordinary deeds by
God's empowering Spirit.

But too often, Samson followed his own sinful passions and worldly
pleasures. He got involved with ungodly Philistine women. He impulsively
tried to seek vengeance on his enemies. And he often forsook his vows and
forgot God's calling on his life.

At the end, he was a blinded, shackled Philistine captive. His final prayer was, "Let me die with the Philistines" (Judges 16:30). Then he brought an entire temple down on thousands of people, including himself.

What's It Mean?

Samson's life reads like an epic Greek tragedy. The Lord gave Samson a unique gift, but he continually squandered his opportunity through bad choices. Perhaps Samson's biggest downfall was his penchant for following his sinful desires.

This is a powerful warning for us. Left to our own flesh, we will continually make bad choices, too. Only when we allow God's mighty, life-changing Spirit to lead us can we make godly choices that are pleasing to the Lord. Galatians 5:16-26 talks about this vital difference.

Samson performed some remarkable deeds. But more than anything his life serves as a tragic warning for those who choose sinful passions over the Spirit's power. The choice is clear!

Now What?

Read about Samson's life in Judges 13–16. Then read Galatians 5:16-26.

Did You Know?

Samson's unique Nazirite vow included never drinking alcohol, eating anything ceremonially unclean, or shaving his head.

APRIL 16

He has delivered us from the domain of darkness and
transferred us to the kingdom of his beloved Son, in
whom we have redemption, the forgiveness of sins.

COLOSSIANS 1:13-14, ESV

SOME COUPLES MEET for the first time at their workplace. Others meet
at parties or are set up on a blind date by a mutual friend. Some start out as
high school sweethearts.

In the book of Ruth (which took place during the time of Israel's
judges), we read that one of history's most poignant love stories began
in a hot, sweaty grainfield. You're probably not going to see that on the
Hallmark Channel.

Ruth was a woman from Moab (a pagan nation often hostile toward
Israel) who put her faith in the one true God of Israel. Her mother-in-law,
Naomi (a Jew), had a husband and two sons. When all three men died
within a ten-year span, Ruth selflessly vowed to stay by Naomi's side (Ruth
1:16-17). But how would Ruth take care of herself and Naomi? Her husband was dead, and she had no job prospects.

Enter a man named Boaz.

What's It Mean?

Boaz was Naomi's relative. In the Old Testament, whenever a woman's husband died childless (as Ruth's had), the deceased husband's brother or other
kin was responsible to marry the widow, provide for her, and try to have a
son to keep the family name alive. This was a beautiful act of redemption,
which is why Boaz is called a "kinsman-redeemer."

Boaz met Ruth as she was working in his fields. He eventually married
her, and they had a son named Obed, who was the grandfather of King
David, Israel's greatest king. This was the earthly ancestral line of Jesus. Do
you see God's sovereign hand at work here?

The book of Ruth is a wonderful story about the concept of redemption. The word *redeem* can mean the following:

- to buy back or repurchase
- to free from captivity by payment of a ransom
- to release from blame or debt
- to repair or restore

These are all things God has graciously and powerfully done for us. Through the practice of the kinsman-redeemer, God was preparing his people for a much greater Redeemer, the coming Messiah.

Jesus purchased our spiritual freedom with his blood, as today's verse says. He freed us from the captivity of sin and death by paying a terrible ransom: his own life. Through his sacrifice, he fulfilled the debt we couldn't pay and restored our damaged relationship with the Father.

God's Son is our great Redeemer!

Now What?
Read the book of Ruth to learn about the kinsman-redeemer principle— and a great love story!

Did You Know?
Ruth 1:16-17 is a passage many married couples etch into each other's wedding rings.

APRIL 17

No one is holy like the LORD! There is no one
besides you; there is no Rock like our God.

1 SAMUEL 2:2

TODAY'S DEVOTION BEGINS with a man named Elkanah who had two wives. (Bad move, brother!)

Elkanah's favorite wife, Hannah, couldn't have children. Elkanah's other wife, Peninnah, who had given Elkanah many children, often mocked Hannah for her barrenness. First Samuel 1:5 says God had purposefully closed Hannah's womb.

Hannah could have responded many different ways. She could've said any of the following prayers:

"Dear Lord, please give me as many children as Peninnah so we can play them in basketball and crush them by fifty points."

"Dear Lord, lots of people look down on me for not having children. Please inflict them with rare, itchy skin diseases."

"Dear Lord, I'm tired of washing the dishes, taking out the trash, and doing the laundry every day. Please give me kids so I can make them do it."

"Dear Lord, why won't you let me have children? Don't you care? Don't you love me?"

This, of course, is not how Hannah prayed. Instead, she made a beautiful vow to God in 1 Samuel 1:11: "O LORD of Heaven's Armies, if you will look upon my sorrow and answer my prayer and give me a son, then I will give him back to you. He will be yours for his entire lifetime."

Instead of reacting angrily to Peninnah or even to God, Hannah humbly petitioned the Lord for a son—not for her own benefit, but for his glory. And the Lord answered her prayer! Eventually, Hannah gave birth to Samuel, who became one of Israel's greatest prophets.

What's It Mean?

Hannah's wonderful prayer of praise in 1 Samuel 2:1-10 can teach us a few things about prayer. Her prayer was

- all about God, not Hannah;
- a prayer of praise and thanksgiving; and
- focused on who God is and the wonderful things he has done.

In other words, Hannah's prayer was God-centric. Our prayers should glorify the Lord and make much of him. If you look at the greatest prayers in Scripture, they recall God's faithfulness, extol his name, and look forward to his continued salvation.

Whatever we're facing in life, we can bring it to the Lord. Our prayers, meanwhile, should never be haughty or self-serving but worshipful of the God who hears our petitions and answers them according to his perfect will.

Now What?

Read Hannah's prayer in 1 Samuel 2:1-10. Using it as your model, start praying more God-centrically every day.

Did You Know?

Hannah's prayer closely resembles Mary's Magnificat in Luke 1:46-56.

APRIL 18

The LORD doesn't see things the way you see them. People judge by outward appearance, but the LORD looks at the heart.

1 SAMUEL 16:7

SAUL WAS NOT FIT to rule over God's people. Time and time again, Israel's first king had violated God's commands. He made unlawful sacrifices (1 Samuel 13:8-14) and rash vows (14:24), flagrantly disregarded God's military orders (chapter 15), consulted a medium (chapter 28), and even threw a spear at his own son, Jonathan (20:33)!

First Samuel 16:1-13 tells the story of God choosing a new king through the prophet, Samuel. "Go to Bethlehem," God told Samuel. "Find a man named Jesse who lives there, for I have selected one of his sons to be my king."

One by one, Jesse paraded his sons before the prophet. Samuel was impressed with Eliab, the oldest. To Samuel, Eliab looked like great king material! But God quickly interjected: "Don't judge by his appearance or height, for I have rejected him. The LORD doesn't see things the way you see them. People judge by outward appearance, but the LORD looks at the heart" (today's verse).

Under God's guidance, Samuel passed over Jesse's seven oldest children before anointing his young shepherd-boy son. David—"a man after [God's] own heart" (1 Samuel 13:14)—would be Israel's next king.

What's It Mean?

In 1893, Dr. Daniel Hale Williams performed the world's first recorded successful open-heart surgery in Chicago. These days, open-heart surgeries are commonplace. This, however, is as close as we will get to looking inside the human heart.

Modern-day doctors might be able to physically peer into someone's heart to repair bodily maladies. But only God can truly examine someone's spiritual status.

Outward appearances are extremely important to us. We judge

others—and ourselves—by them all the time. (Why do you think the fashion and cosmetic industries are multibillion-dollar global enterprises?)

Thankfully, God doesn't judge us by standards of height, weight, skin color, hair length, muscle tone, or anything else so superficial. (He made us in his image, so we are all beautiful to him, no matter what we look like.) God cares about things of eternal significance: Are we seeking him and his will through Christ? Are we loving? Do we sacrifice our needs for the good of others? Do we walk in humility? These are the things that God values.

We would be wise to prioritize what God does—both in ourselves and in those whom we associate with.

Now What?
When you choose friends, look below the surface for godly characteristics such as love, kindness, patience, humility, etc.

Did You Know?
Superficial human judgment is nothing new. Look up the ancient Greek myth of Narcissus!

APRIL 19

Everyone assembled here will know that the LORD
rescues his people, but not with sword and spear.

1 SAMUEL 17:47

TODAY'S DEVOTION INVOLVES a scared army, a shepherd boy, a slingshot, and a very surly giant. This story, found in 1 Samuel 17, is one of the
most famous narratives in the Bible.

If you guessed "David versus Goliath," you're correct!

Israel and its chief enemy at the time, Philistia, had drawn up battle
lines in the valley of Elah. Day after day, a Philistine giant named Goliath
brazenly marched out and dared Israel to send someone to fight him.
Goliath stood about nine feet, nine inches tall, and with all his armor and
weaponry, he was like a human tank!

No one from Israel—not even King Saul—was brave enough to take
Goliath's challenge. But when David arrived from tending his father's sheep,
he courageously took the challenge.

The heart of the story is found in 1 Samuel 17:45-47, when David laid
out the true odds for the menacing giant: "You come to me with sword,
spear, and javelin, but I come to you in the name of the LORD of Heaven's
Armies—the God of the armies of Israel, whom you have defied" (verse 45).
In other words, Goliath had no chance.

Enraged, Goliath rushed to meet David, who swung his slingshot
and—bull's-eye!—sunk a stone right between Goliath's eyes.

Battle over. No more giant.

What's It Mean?

David versus Goliath is an incredible story. But too often, we focus solely on
David. We marvel at his remarkable faith—and rightfully so. We would do
well to display that level of faith in difficult times.

But don't walk away from this story simply being wowed by a man or
asking yourself, "What are the giants in my life that I need to slay?" That

completely misses the point. This story isn't in the Bible to glorify David. It's there to glorify the God who saved him!

When David faced one of the biggest challenges of his life, he turned to the God of the universe who gave him a mighty victory. God is greater than all our enemies, trials, fears, and doubts. He can deliver us from all trouble through faith.

The focus of this story is not on mortal man, but on the immortal God who is powerful to save. May that be your focus, as well!

Now What?
When you are faced with a big problem, read Proverbs 3:5-6 and trust in the Lord of Heaven's Armies.

Did You Know?
After defeating Goliath, David cut off his head and took it to Jerusalem to display as a victor's trophy (1 Samuel 17:54). Creepy!

APRIL 20

*Worship the LORD in all his holy splendor. Let
all the earth tremble before him.*

PSALM 96:9

KING DAVID'S EARLY REIGN was rolling.

He had united Israel's tribes, captured the strategic city of Jerusalem for his new capital, and defeated the Philistines in a miraculous victory. Now, he desired to bring the Ark of the Covenant from Kiriath-jearim to Jerusalem.

David summoned every Israelite to make it a celebratory parade (1 Chronicles 13:8).

Then things went wrong—very wrong.

They placed the Ark on a cart behind a pair of oxen. Because of his holiness, God specifically commanded Levites to carry the Ark using poles that would slide through rings on the Ark's sides (Exodus 25:14-15; Deuteronomy 10:8). Touching the Ark was expressly forbidden (Numbers 4:15).

At one point in the journey, the oxen stumbled, and the cart tipped. A man named Uzzah instinctively reached out to keep the Ark from falling. Instantly, "the LORD's anger was aroused against Uzzah, and he struck him dead because he had laid his hand on the Ark" (1 Chronicles 13:10).

Instant party deflater.

David immediately stopped the procession. He was frightened, angry, and confused. "How can I ever bring the Ark of God back into my care?" he asked (1 Chronicles 13:12).

What's It Mean?

Perhaps, like David, you're thinking, *Wasn't instant death for Uzzah a little harsh? After all, wasn't he trying to help by keeping the Ark from hitting the ground?*

Here we must understand God's holiness and our sin. The Ark wasn't just a special religious object. In his lovingkindness, God used it to manifest

221

his presence among his people, physically appearing in a cloud of glory above the mercy seat (i.e., the lid) between two golden cherubim. He told Moses in Exodus 25:22, "I will meet with you there and . . . give you my commands for the people of Israel."

But God is holy, and we are pervasively sinful. We must approach him according to his terms (through atonement), not ours. This was Uzzah's mistake and David's confusion.

David had no right to be angry at God. But in some respects, David had a right to be frightened. God is perfectly loving, but his holiness is an awesome, fearsome thing (see today's verse). It should not be taken lightly.

If you are God's child, you don't need to dread him, but you do need to take his commands seriously and give him the proper worship he deserves.

Now What?
Read the account of Uzzah in 1 Chronicles 13 and 2 Samuel 6:1-11. Also review the January 10 and 11 devotions on God's holiness.

Did You Know?
David finally moved the Ark to Jerusalem three months after Uzzah's death.

APRIL 21

Create in me a clean heart, O God. Renew a loyal spirit within me.

PSALM 51:10

DAVID WAS THE GREATEST king in Israel's long, tumultuous history—"a man after [God's] own heart" (1 Samuel 13:14).

But David was certainly not perfect. When he failed, he failed spectacularly. Take for instance the infamous story of David and Bathsheba in 2 Samuel 11–12.

One day, as David was gazing down from his palace terrace into the city, he noticed a beautiful woman—Bathsheba—bathing. She was the wife of Uriah, one of David's most trusted soldiers. No matter. In a moment of wickedness, David brought Bathsheba into his palace, where she became pregnant with his child. Later, in a heinous attempt to cover his sin, he callously ordered Uriah to the front lines of battle, where he died. David then married Bathsheba.

David couldn't hide his sin from God. Through the prophet Nathan, the Lord condemned David's immoral actions. David was cut to the heart and repented. "I have sinned against the LORD," he said (2 Samuel 12:13).

God disciplined David by allowing his child to die. Later, much of David's family and reign was marked by violence and rebellion. It was an unfortunate conclusion for an otherwise great king.

What's It Mean?

David's terrible sins brought tragic consequences that had a domino effect on future generations. But his repentance was real. After the gravity of his transgressions had sunk in, David penned Psalm 51, one of the most beautiful psalms in Scripture.

The psalm is a humble cry for God's mercy, appealing to his "unfailing love" and "great compassion" to "blot out the stain of my sins" and "wash me clean from my guilt" (verses 1-2). David consistently acknowledged his own depravity and God's righteousness. But he didn't wallow in his sad state. Rather, he exulted in the hope of forgiveness available to him through the "God who saves" (verse 14) and expectantly asked for a renewed heart and a loyal spirit to better obey the Lord (today's verse).

David's heart of contrition in Psalm 51 is a great model for all of us. Whenever you sin, you can rest assured that you have a heavenly Father who is ready to forgive if you humbly repent and confess your sins. God doesn't want to banish you from his presence (verse 11); rather, he wants to "restore . . . the joy of your salvation" (verse 12).

Praise God!

Now What?
Read 2 Samuel 11–12 and Psalm 51 to see David's path from terrible sin to humble confession and repentance.

Did You Know?
Long before Paul developed the doctrine of inherited sin more extensively in the New Testament (e.g., Romans 5–7), David mentioned it in Psalm 51:5.

APRIL 22

Fear of the LORD is the foundation of wisdom. Knowledge
of the Holy One results in good judgment.

PROVERBS 9:10

AFTER KING DAVID DIED, his son Solomon ascended to Israel's throne.

Solomon quickly ordered the deaths of a handful of men who had acted
treacherously against his father. He also banished a disloyal priest and married the daughter of Egypt's Pharaoh for a strategic political alliance.

Phew! Being an ancient king was a dangerous, complicated business!

But even as he consolidated his power, Solomon loved the Lord and
wanted to follow him. One night, God appeared to him in a dream.

"What do you want?" God said. "Ask, and I will give it to you!" (1
Kings 3:5).

Wow! What an opportunity! Heaven's treasures were at Solomon's dis-
posal. What would you have asked for in his place? Riches? Fame? A huge
mansion? Never-ending detention for all school bullies? A lifetime's supply
of fudge brownies? The options were endless.

Here's how Solomon responded: "Give me an understanding heart so
that I can govern your people well and know the difference between right
and wrong. For who by himself is able to govern this great people of yours?"
(1 Kings 3:9).

God was so pleased with Solomon's humble response that he granted
his request—and much more. Solomon became the richest, wisest, most
famous king in antiquity. (You can read the whole story in 1 Kings 3:1-15;
see also 4:20-34.)

What's It Mean?

Solomon knew leading Israel would be a huge job—one he couldn't possibly do by himself. That's why he sought divine wisdom. God granted his
request in spades.

Everyone needs wisdom. But few people know where to find it.
True spiritual wisdom doesn't come from libraries, school textbooks,

the entertainment industry, or an old sage sitting cross-legged on a mountaintop.

As today's verse says, true wisdom starts with the "fear of the LORD." This has nothing to do with fright or terror. This refers to a reverential awe of God and worshipful devotion to him. Seeking God is like laying a "foundation of wisdom" in life. As we grow in our faith and pursue God, he will build a sturdy structure of spiritual knowledge on that rock-solid base. All other pursuits of spiritual wisdom are in vain.

God has done unimaginable things to show you his love and save you through his Son. Fear him. Worship him. Adore him. Love him. Follow him.

This is the foundation—the starting point—of true wisdom in life.

Now What?
Read Solomon's thoughts about godly wisdom in Proverbs 1–4.

Did You Know?
Israel's kingdom was the largest and wealthiest under Solomon's reign (c. 970–930 BC). He also replaced the Tabernacle with God's magnificent Temple in Jerusalem.

APRIL 23

If you think you are standing strong, be careful not to fall.

1 CORINTHIANS 10:12

KING SOLOMON had seven hundred wives. Wrap your mind around that!

That's a lot of birthdays and anniversaries to celebrate. That's a reality TV show just screaming to be made!

Solomon's spousal surplus is a ready-made punch line, but the wealthy king's spiritual state was no laughing matter. After 1 Kings 3–10 outlines Solomon's great successes, chapter 11 feels like a bit of a shock.

In it, we read how Solomon's many wives led to his rampant idolatry later in life. These Canaanite women "turned his heart to worship other gods instead of being completely faithful to the LORD his God" (verse 4). Solomon built altars to pagan deities that represented child sacrifice and other abominable practices.

Wow! Was this really the same king who humbly asked God for wisdom, built God's Temple, prayed a beautiful prayer (1 Kings 8), and wrote inspired Scripture?

How did Solomon fall so far?

What's It Mean?

Sadly, the king once renowned for godly wisdom turned into a wicked fool. The fall of Solomon feels abrupt. But there were early warning signs.

He accumulated many horses (1 Kings 4:26), directly violating Deuteronomy 17:16. He spent nearly twice as long building his own palace as God's Temple (1 Kings 6:38 and 7:1). And of course, his rebellious decision to intermarry with pagan nations (Deuteronomy 7:3) must have been going on for years.

That's how sin works. It's devious and subtle. It tricks us into believing everything is okay. Sin never says, "Jump off a cliff to your doom." Instead, it asks us to slowly rappel into a treacherous ravine of ruin—just a few feet at a time. But it never looks that bad as we're going down.

No one will ever know.

If it feels good, it can't be that bad.

God is too restrictive anyway. You're free to enjoy this.

It's a web of deceit spun by Satan himself.

Look at today's verse. Solomon, the great king, surrounded by riches and fame, thought he was standing strong. But he scorned God's Word, and by the end of his life, he was ruined.

Don't be like Solomon! Put on your spiritual armor (Ephesians 6:10-18) so that you can resist Satan, his subtle lies, and the strong pull of sin.

And for goodness' sake, don't have hundreds of spouses. Sheesh!

Now What?

Reread the February 8 devotion on sin's terrible deception. Also check out James 1:12-15 and 1 Corinthians 10:12-13.

Did You Know?

- After Solomon died, Israel split into two kingdoms as part of God's judgment on Solomon's idolatry (1 Kings 11:11-13).

APRIL 24

After the fire there was the sound of a gentle whisper.

1 KINGS 19:12

ELIJAH WAS ONE of Israel's greatest prophets.

For many years, he courageously proclaimed God's truth to Israel in the midst of King Ahab and Queen Jezebel's wicked idolatry. God did some astounding miracles through him, too, including a successfully predicted drought (1 Kings 17:1), raising a boy from the dead (17:17-24), and the remarkable fire-from-heaven showdown with 450 prophets of Baal on Mount Carmel (18:17-40).

But now Elijah was on the run.

Jezebel had threatened his life, and rather than trust God, Elijah bolted—hundreds of miles, in fact—to Mount Sinai.

"What are you doing here, Elijah?" God asked him.

"The people of Israel have broken their covenant with you, torn down your altars, and killed every one of your prophets. I am the only one left, and now they are trying to kill me, too," he said, in a bit of a pity party (1 Kings 19:10).

Suddenly, one by one, a supernatural windstorm, earthquake, and fire appeared before Elijah—each awesome in power. But God wasn't in any of them. Then everything grew eerily quiet. And in the stillness, the stubborn, bewildered prophet heard a small, hushed voice.

"What are you doing here, Elijah?"

The Lord God Almighty was speaking to him in a whisper.

What's It Mean?

Elijah had witnessed God's power in incredible ways. But when his faith was at an all-time low—he even wanted to die (1 Kings 19:4)—God didn't wow him with miracles. He whispered in his ear.

"Elijah, stop feeling sorry for yourself. I'm not always going to get your attention through great wonders. Sometimes, you're going to have to listen

229

for my quiet voice. Trust in me. I am always with you. Now I have more for you to do. Are you ready to listen and obey?"

This story has much to teach us today. God is still fully capable of grabbing our attention with fire from heaven. But mostly, he speaks to us through his Word and the gentle inner "whisper" of his Holy Spirit. We need to stop running and listen to his voice.

Maybe, like Elijah, you are feeling alone, abandoned, and hopeless. But remember, God is always with you (Deuteronomy 31:6). He might not reveal himself visibly. But if you are his child, his Spirit lives inside you.

Listen for his voice. Heed his beautiful, gentle whisper. You are never alone.

Now What?
Feeling alone like Elijah? Pray! God promises you will find him when you "look for me wholeheartedly" in prayer (Jeremiah 29:13).

Did You Know?
Elijah (and Moses) briefly returned from the dead during Jesus' Transfiguration (Matthew 17:1-13). Whoa!

APRIL 25

The word of God is alive and powerful. It is sharper
than the sharpest two-edged sword, cutting between
soul and spirit, between joint and marrow. It
exposes our innermost thoughts and desires.

HEBREWS 4:12

DOES BEING A POWERFUL king and ruling over an entire nation sound exciting to you—or intimidating? What about being made a king while you're still losing your baby teeth?

Welcome to Josiah's world.

Josiah ascended to Judah's throne at age eight when his father, Amon, was assassinated just two years into his evil reign. On top of that, Josiah's grandfather, Manasseh, was the worst king in Judah's long history. His rampant idolatry provoked God's future judgment on Judah.

Poor Josiah. While other kids his age were learning how to read, write, and properly milk a goat, his skinny shoulders carried large burdens.

In the eighteenth year of Josiah's reign, his officials found the Book of the Law (2 Kings 22:8) in the Temple—likely a dusty, long-overlooked scroll of Deuteronomy—and read it to the king. Josiah "tore his clothes in despair" (2 Kings 22:11). He knew Judah's sins were exceedingly great.

So he swiftly enacted reforms:

- He read God's law to the people and called for their obedience (23:1-4).
- He cleansed the land of idolatrous worship objects (23:4-19).
- He executed pagan priests (23:20).
- He restored the annual Passover (23:21-23).
- He banished psychics, mediums, and household gods throughout the land (23:24).

God was pleased with Josiah's humble, obedient response. "You will not see the disaster I am going to bring on this city," God said (2 Kings 22:20).

231

What's It Mean?

When Josiah heard God's Word, he was cut to the heart. He immediately repented, asked for God's forgiveness on behalf of himself and the nation, and sought to faithfully obey.

As today's verse says, Scripture "is alive and powerful." That's because it contains the words of the living God, graciously given to us to help us know him and live righteously.

Reading Scripture is a beautiful thing. But it's not always pleasant. "It exposes our innermost thoughts and desires," and they aren't always godly. We must be willing to change based on the conviction God brings, just like Josiah.

When we read the Bible, it has an amazing way of piercing our hearts with conviction and bringing change—as long as we remain humble before the Lord. Is this what happens when you read God's Word? Hopefully so! Let his Spirit speak, convict, and guide you.

Now What?

Do you often approach Bible reading only out of habit or duty? Ask God to replace that attitude with love and desire for his Word.

Did You Know?

Pharaoh Neco killed Josiah in battle at Megiddo in 609 BC.

APRIL 26

They scoffed at the prophets until the LORD's anger could
no longer be restrained and nothing could be done.

2 CHRONICLES 36:16

JERUSALEM'S WALLS WERE a charred heap of rubble. God's great
Temple was a burning pile of ruins. Dead bodies were everywhere. Most of
those who had escaped the sword were forced into exile.

The year was 586 BC, and the vicious Babylonian army of King
Nebuchadnezzar had accomplished its mission. The kingdom of Judah was
conquered.

More than a century earlier, the mighty Assyrians had destroyed the
northern kingdom of Israel. Judah had survived the ominous threat, thanks
to God's grace and a few righteous kings. Overall, though, Judah didn't
learn from the mistakes of idolatrous Israel. For centuries, Judah rebelled
against God, following the detestable practices of the pagan nations around
them, despite God's continual, compassionate attempts to turn his people's
hearts back through his prophets.

But as today's Scripture passage says, "The people mocked these messengers of God and despised their words. They scoffed at the prophets until
the LORD's anger could no longer be restrained and nothing could be done."

Yet all was not lost. Because of God, there was still hope!

What's It Mean?

God didn't completely abandon his people. They had done absolutely
nothing—*zero, zilch, nada*—to deserve his mercy and grace. Yet they would
still be part of his cosmic plan to offer salvation to the nations through
Christ.

Before long, God would turn the heart of Persia's King Cyrus toward
them, allowing them to return to the Promised Land and rebuild the
Temple. Eventually, God would send his Son into the world through a
young Jewish girl named Mary. Then, after Jesus' ascension, God would
start his worldwide church through Christ's apostles (all Jews) and give us

the New Testament almost exclusively through Jewish authors. No, God was definitely not through with Israel yet!

God is "slow to anger and abounding in steadfast love" (Psalm 86:15, ESV). But we must never presume upon his mercy, grace, and forgiveness. A day is coming when God will judge everyone once and for all—no retries, second chances, or do-overs.

God's true children—those who trust in Jesus for salvation—don't have to fear this judgment. They are secure in Christ. But those who still mock, despise, and scoff at his message have everything to fear.

Have you received God's message of salvation in faith?

Now What?
Read the accounts of Judah's fall in 2 Kings 25; 2 Chronicles 36; and Jeremiah 39.

Did You Know?
The only known Gentile New Testament author was Luke, who wrote the Gospel of Luke and Acts. (The author of Hebrews is unknown.)

APRIL 27

Blessed be the LORD, the God of our fathers, who put
such a thing as this into the heart of the king, to beautify
the house of the LORD that is in Jerusalem.

EZRA 7:27, ESV

TAKE A MOMENT TO look at a globe or a map of the world. Notice how there are hundreds of countries, but no empires?

Today's world is vastly different from what the Old Testament Jews experienced. The ancient world was one of competing empires. Democracy? Hah! Most kingdoms were ruled by emperors who wielded enormous power and were often worshiped as demigods. Everyone had to live by their rules . . . or else.

That's why what we read in Ezra and Nehemiah is so remarkable. Despite being under no compulsion to show kindness to conquered peoples, mighty Persian rulers allowed the exiled Jews to begin worshiping God again in Jerusalem. Look at the following examples:

- In 538 BC, King Cyrus decreed that the Jews could return to Jerusalem and rebuild the Temple (Ezra 1:1-4).
- After the Temple's construction was halted for about twenty years, King Darius reaffirmed Cyrus's earlier edict, allowing the Temple to be finished in 516 BC (Ezra 6:1-22).
- In 458 BC, King Artaxerxes allowed Ezra to teach the Mosaic law in Judea (Ezra 7:1-28).
- In 445 BC, Artaxerxes allowed Nehemiah to begin rebuilding Jerusalem's walls (Nehemiah 2:1-8).

What prompted these powerful, pagan potentates to care about a helpless, scattered people like the Jews?

Today's verse provides a big hint.

What's It Mean?

As we discussed in yesterday's devotion, Israel and Judah's terrible rebellion against God led to divine judgment. Yet God still had great plans for his people. Amazingly, this plan involved the unexpected benevolence of secular kings.

The Cyruses, Dariuses, and Artaxerxeses of the world never would have thought to promote God's plans if it weren't for—well, God himself! No king is too powerful to supersede God's designs. He orchestrates all things on earth according to his sovereign purposes. As Proverbs 21:1 says, "The king's heart is like a stream of water directed by the LORD; he guides it wherever he pleases."

This gives us great comfort today. No matter who is in charge—from the small-town mayor, to the president of the United States, throughout every nation on earth—God's plans will prevail. "The earth is the LORD's, and everything in it. The world and all its people belong to him" (Psalm 24:1).

Now What?

- Read the book of Ezra to see how God both intimately cares for his people and sovereignly rules over the nations.

Did You Know?

Old Testament books are not all ordered chronologically. Ezra and Nehemiah are the fifteenth and sixteenth books in the Bible, yet they detail events that happen last in the Old Testament timeline.

APRIL 28

O Lord, please hear my prayer! Listen to the prayers
of those of us who delight in honoring you.

NEHEMIAH 1:11

THROUGHOUT HISTORY, there have been many things once considered impossible—or not previously conceived—that humans have accomplished. Here's a list of a few:

- sailing around the globe
- human flight
- automobile transportation for the general public
- television
- personal computer ownership for most American households
- the Internet
- short lines at Disney World in July

Well, at least we got the first six out of seven.

But you get the point. God has given us the ability to achieve many things that were once considered impossible.

When Nehemiah surveyed the charred ruins of once-mighty Jerusalem in 445 BC, he faced what must have felt like insurmountable odds. Yet in a mere fifty-two days, he rebuilt an entire city wall despite significant challenges and constant opposition.

How did he do it? Here's one way to categorize his divinely blessed success, as he records firsthand in the fascinating book of Nehemiah:

1. He humbly submitted his plans to the Lord.
2. He bathed his endeavor in prayer.
3. He acknowledged God's blessings.
4. He met opposition with godly courage and wisdom.

What's It Mean?

Do you want to accomplish great, even seemingly impossible things for God? Then follow Nehemiah's blueprint for success!

1. **Humbly submit your plans to the Lord.** Is your idea from God (Nehemiah 2:12), or something you've fabricated for personal gain? To determine which, pray and seek godly counsel about it.
2. **Bathe your endeavor in prayer.** Nehemiah was constantly in prayer throughout his wall-building enterprise for all kinds of requests (1:4-11; 2:4; 4:9; 6:9; 13:14, 22, 29, 31). We would do well to follow his example.
3. **Acknowledge God's blessings.** Pride goes before a fall (Proverbs 16:18). We can never accomplish anything apart from God's empowering grace. Nehemiah knew this (Nehemiah 2:8), and we need to also.
4. **Meet opposition with godly courage and wisdom.** Nehemiah had to fight hostility throughout his campaign. You should expect spiritual resistance too (Ephesians 6:16). Fight it with "the sword of the Spirit, which is the word of God" (Ephesians 6:17) and prayer.

There is a great deal involved in accomplishing great things for God. But following Nehemiah's model is a great place to start!

Now What?

Dream big and pray big about how God wants to use you in his Kingdom—all for his glory—and see where he leads you.

Did You Know?

The area of Jerusalem that Nehemiah walled in 445 BC—while still impressive—was much smaller than the city that Babylon destroyed in 586.

APRIL 29

*Who knows if perhaps you were made
queen for just such a time as this?*

ESTHER 4:14

DID YOU KNOW THERE'S a book in the Bible that never mentions God at all?

It's true!

It's the book of Esther, a beautiful work of Old Testament prose. Even though Esther never mentions God explicitly, his presence and sovereignty are felt throughout the book.

The story begins in the Persian capital of Susa, during the third year (483 BC) of King Ahasuerus's reign. When Queen Vashti disobeyed Ahasuerus's orders, he divorced her and eventually replaced her with a young exiled Jewish girl named Esther after a yearlong search.

Through her cousin, Mordecai, Esther learned of a plot by the wicked Haman, one of Ahasuerus's powerful officials, to destroy all the Jews in the empire. Fueled largely by his hateful jealousy of Mordecai, Haman had tricked Ahasuerus into ordering the ethnic cleansing.

Esther was deeply troubled, but she was in a tricky position. Ahasuerus didn't know she was Jewish, and to reveal her heritage or displease the king could prove fatal. But to remain quiet and betray her own people was unthinkable.

So Esther cleverly invited the king and Haman to a great feast. There, she risked her life by revealing her ethnicity and Haman's plot. Ahasuerus was enraged and—in an ironic twist of justice—ordered Haman to be hanged on the gallows that Haman had built for Mordecai.

The Jews were saved, and Esther and Mordecai became national heroes!

What's It Mean?

Although God is never mentioned explicitly in Esther, his fingerprints are obvious throughout her story and the Jews' deliverance. If Haman had succeeded in wiping out the Jews, God's eternal plan of salvation would have failed. Of course, God wasn't going to let that happen. But he used the courageous efforts of Esther and Mordecai to further his plans.

Maybe, like Esther's story, God is working quietly in your life, almost to the point where you're questioning his presence. Make no mistake—he is always there!

God is completely sovereign over both the affairs of nations and individual lives. But we have a responsibility to stand up for righteousness and God's truth, too, just like Esther did.

As God directs your life, where can you courageously take a stand for righteousness? How can you accomplish his purposes? Is there a situation in your life where God is calling you to stand for just such a time as this?

Now What?

Read the book of Esther for a wonderful example of how to take a stand for righteousness amid difficult circumstances.

Did You Know?

Jews still observe the annual festival of Purim to celebrate their deliverance from Haman's plot (Esther 9:20-32).

APRIL 30

"Should we accept only good things from the hand of God and never anything bad?" So in all this, Job said nothing wrong.

JOB 2:10

WHAT WOULD YOU DO if you had everything this life has to offer, then suddenly all of it—even your health—was inexplicably stripped away and your only "comfort" (if you can call it that) was some misguided friends who were heavy on advice and light on compassion? Sounds like a pretty rotten deal, huh?

Welcome to Job's world.

Job was both exceedingly wealthy and "a man of complete integrity" (Job 1:1). But in a short period of time, he lost all ten of his children, his riches, and his house. Then he contracted "terrible boils from head to foot" (2:7).

Most of the book of Job details Job's spiritual struggle to understand his plight as several companions poorly attempt to comfort their suffering friend. This book is a treasure trove of insight for us as we navigate the trials in our lives.

What's It Mean?

There's no way to sugarcoat it: trials can be incredibly difficult and painful—physically, emotionally, and spiritually.

Like Job, you might experience friends who question your faith or offer unhelpful advice. Be patient with them.

Sometimes, like Job's ordeal, trials seem interminable, pointless, and intolerable. You might wonder where God is in the midst of your hardship. You might cry out for days, months, or even years for relief.

But God is always there. As Philippians 4:5 says, "The Lord is at hand" (ESV). That truth then makes the following verse possible: "Don't worry about anything." If we fully believe in God's love, goodness, and sovereignty, trials don't have to produce worry.

Remember, God allows difficulties in your life for a purpose—to

241

build your faith. (See today's verse, James 1:2-4, and the November 20–27 devotions.)

God may never reveal why you're experiencing a trial. The book of Job devotes thirty-seven chapters to Job's laments and debates with his friends over the purposes of his sufferings. Then, for four chapters, God addresses Job "from the whirlwind" (Job 38:1), but he never offers any reasons for Job's suffering.

Instead, God challenges Job to remember his place and trust in God's holiness, power, and sovereignty. "Where were you when I laid the foundations of the earth?" God says in Job 38:4. "Tell me, if you know so much."

The message is clear: God is God. Job was not—and neither are we. It's a hard truth, but a crucial one to accept during trials.

Now What?

Read God's response to Job in chapters 38–41. It's awesome!

Did You Know?

God eventually healed Job and blessed him even more abundantly (Job 42:10-17).

MAY 1

My family is gone, and my close friends have forgotten me.

JOB 19:14

ALL TEN OF HIS children were dead. His house was in ruins, and bandits had stolen his possessions. Festering boils blanketed his body.

Job was in utter misery.

Sitting among the ashes of his former life, he picked up a piece of broken pottery. He knew it would provide only temporary relief. But his skin was crawling with irritation.

Scraaaaape. Scraaaaape. Scraaaaape.

"Curse God and die," his wife implored.

Even Job's wife provided no solace—nor did any other friends or family members. Look how he described his plight in Job 19:14-19:

My family is gone, and my close friends have forgotten me. My servants and maids consider me a stranger. I am like a foreigner to them. When I call my servant, he doesn't come; I have to plead with him! My breath is repulsive to my wife. I am rejected by my own family. Even young children despise me. When I stand to speak, they turn their backs on me. My close friends detest me. Those I loved have turned against me.

Of all of Job's woes, the betrayal from loved ones was one of the worst.

What's It Mean?

Have you ever been hurt by a close friend or family member? Wounds from loved ones are always more painful because there's more invested in those relationships—more trust that's broken.

As King David mourned in Psalm 55:12-13, "It is not an enemy who taunts me—I could bear that. It is not my foes who so arrogantly insult me—I could have hidden from them. Instead, it is you—my equal, my companion and close friend."

Here's a harsh truth: your loved ones will probably fail you in life. And you will fail those you love. That's life in a fallen world.

But God will never fail you. Because of his holiness, he is faithful and perfect (Deuteronomy 32:4). You can always count on his unchanging character, promises, and steadfast love.

As Job lamented the unfaithfulness of those closest to him, look at what brought him hope: "As for me, I know that my Redeemer lives, and he will stand upon the earth at last" (Job 19:25). What glorious truth!

Now What?

Be quick to ask forgiveness when you fail someone else, and don't hold a grudge when someone else fails you (Colossians 3:13).

Did You Know?

Job's experience was not unique in Scripture. Samson (Judges 16), David (2 Samuel 15–18), and Paul (2 Timothy 4:10) all experienced painful betrayals. Then, of course, there was Judas Iscariot, who betrayed Jesus for thirty measly pieces of silver.

MAY 2

May all who are godly rejoice in the LORD and praise his holy name!

PSALM 97:12

WHERE CAN YOU GO to find joy, sadness, anger, fear, disgust, and a range of other emotions all in one place—well, other than the movie *Inside Out* or morning drop-off time at your local preschool?

The book of Psalms!

The psalms are 150 songs and poems, written by seven identified authors over at least eight hundred years, from the time of Moses to the Jews' post-exilic period in Babylon. The book of Psalms is like a hymnbook for God's people to sing about his character and his mighty acts throughout history.

As a whole, the book of Psalms is beloved because of the beauty, breadth, and "realness" of its contents. For every psalm that urges the reader to exalt God for his majesty, there's a surprisingly candid psalm that explores suffering.

Are you bursting with joy and thankfulness toward the Lord for his blessings? Do you feel downtrodden by life? Are God-haters criticizing you? Do you need God's rescuing hand? Are you astounded at the overwhelming beauty and majesty of God's creation?

Then there are psalms for you! The book of Psalms truly has something for everyone. For ten days, we're going to worship God by reflecting on a handful of beautiful psalms.

What's It Mean?

The very fact that the book of Psalms is in the Bible should greatly encourage you. It means that Christianity is not a pie-in-the-sky religion—and God is not an unrealistic, aloof deity who expects his followers to be robotic slaves. No! The psalms prove exactly the opposite.

Here are a few of the beautiful spiritual realities that the psalms gloriously magnify:

- God is holy, majestic, and worthy of all of our praise (today's verse).
- God deeply loves his creation and has revealed himself to us (Psalm 19:1-6).
- He is a God who we can turn to in all circumstances—in success and failure, fear and happiness, in joy and despair. (See Psalm 69 for an example of faith amid suffering and Psalm 100 as an example of thanksgiving.)

All of these truths cause us to joyfully join David in declaring, "O LORD, our Lord, your majestic name fills the earth!" (Psalm 8:1).

Turn to the psalms often to worship God, marvel at him, and draw near to him. They will bless you spiritually from the inside out!

Now What?
Memorize Psalm 8, a short, beautiful psalm that magnifies God's glory.

Did You Know?
King David wrote almost half of the psalms. Asaph, Moses, Solomon, Heman, Ethan, and the sons of Korah wrote some too. Many psalms are anonymously written.

MAY 3

Some trust in chariots and some in horses, but we
trust in the name of the LORD our God.

PSALM 20:7, ESV

TODAY, WARFARE FEATURES IMPRESSIVE, yet frightening, state-of-the-art technology. Nations can rain explosives from the skies, fire missiles from miles away to pinpoint locations, and wipe out entire cities with the push of a button.

King David never would've dreamed of this weaponry. Back in the tenth century BC, horses and chariots ruled the day.

Since the Israelites entered Canaan, they have always been surrounded by hostile neighbors. In David's era, those enemies were Syria (north); Ammon, Moab, and Edom across the Jordan River (east); Amalek and Egypt (south); and of course, Philistia, Israel's age-old nemesis, along the Mediterranean coastline (west). Danger lurked at every side. National defense was a top priority.

Yet look at what God told Israel in Deuteronomy 17:16: "The king must not build up a large stable of horses for himself."

Wait. Hold on a minute. What was Israel supposed to do to defend itself?

Of course Israel could have an army. But ultimately, God wanted the people to trust him rather than military might.

David took this to heart. We see this in Psalm 20, specifically today's verse—a beautiful exclamation of dependence on God.

What's It Mean?

Obviously, fighting with horses and chariots is antiquated. No modern-day nation will win any wars like that! But the principle of today's verse is timeless.

So the question is, where are you placing your trust?

Many people trust in money. They stockpile wealth as an insurance policy against the future (Luke 12:16-21).

Others hope that the next presidential candidate, self-help guru, or religious leader can solve their problems. (Let us know how that works out!)

Others put their trust in good deeds, education, hard work, or their faith in humanity. Many people, often unwittingly, don't really trust in anything. They just coast through life like a boat set adrift.

The problem is, none of these things will save you from your greatest enemies—sin and Satan. But God can! He sent his only Son to crush your foes by his redemptive work on the cross and offer you salvation through faith.

Don't trust in worldly things for salvation. They will ultimately fail you. Trust in the name of the Lord our God. He will never let you down!

Now What?
Today, spend time in prayer asking God to reveal if your heart is trusting in things other than him.

Did You Know?
Chariots were used in warfare as early as 1800 BC, perhaps even earlier.

MAY 4

The LORD is my shepherd; I shall not want.

PSALM 23:1, ESV

AMONG ALL THE PSALMS, Psalm 23 is one of the greats. It is a superlative biblical poem written by David, Israel's famous shepherd-turned-king, about the ultimate Shepherd-King of the universe, the Lord God Almighty.

Let's briefly stroll through "green pastures" and "beside still waters" with David as he helps us rejoice in God's loving care and protection.

What's It Mean?

"The Lord is my shepherd; I shall not want" (verse 1, ESV). Unlike aloof false deities of other religions, God is an attentive, loving shepherd who cares for all of our needs (Matthew 6:25-34).

"He makes me lie down in green pastures. He leads me beside still waters. He restores my soul" (verses 2-3, ESV). As a shepherd leads sheep to lush meadows and babbling brooks for nourishment, God gives us spiritual rest and refreshment through his Word and his Spirit.

"He leads me in paths of righteousness for his name's sake" (verse 3, ESV). God graciously guides us toward obedience—again, through his Word and Spirit—as he sanctifies us for our good and his glory (1 Thessalonians 5:23).

"Even though I walk through the valley of the shadow of death, I will fear no evil, for you are with me; your rod and your staff, they comfort me" (verse 4, ESV). Even in our deepest, darkest hours, God is always with us, giving us hope and allowing us to avoid fear. The rod and staff— a shepherd's instruments of protection—provide a further metaphor of God's comforting watchfulness over us.

"You prepare a table before me in the presence of my enemies; you anoint my head with oil; my cup overflows" (verse 5, ESV). Here, the psalm transitions from picturing God as the Chief Shepherd to the gracious Host of a great feast (Revelation 19:6-10). Our enemies (e.g., sin,

Satan, the world) will try to assail us, but the Lord will provide for and richly bless his children.

"Surely goodness and mercy shall follow me all the days of my life, and I shall dwell in the house of the Lord forever" (verse 6, ESV). In ancient Israel, "the house of the Lord" meant the Tabernacle/Temple. For modern believers, we can look forward to enjoying God's "goodness and mercy" in this life as we anticipate eternally dwelling with him in heaven (Revelation 21:3). Praise God!

Now What?

Memorize Psalm 23. It's good to have this in your heart!

Did You Know?

God as shepherd is a common biblical motif. Other examples include Genesis 48:15; Psalm 80:1; and Psalm 100:3. Jesus called himself the "Good Shepherd" (John 10:11) and is presented as a shepherd in places such as Matthew 26:31; Hebrews 13:20; 1 Peter 5:4; and Revelation 7:17.

MAY 5

Be still, and know that I am God!

PSALM 46:10

WHATEVER YOU DO, DON'T LISTEN TO THE NEWS TODAY!
DON'T TURN ON THE TV!
DON'T SCROLL THROUGH SOCIAL MEDIA!
DON'T PICK UP A NEWSPAPER!

At least, don't do any of those things if you want to avoid negative headlines and discouraging stories.

This world is a crazy, messed-up place. Ever since sin entered the picture, the human experience has been filled with sadness, suffering, and death.

Sometimes, it can feel like life is coming apart, at least if you read the national and international headlines. All over the world, people are treating each other savagely. We shouldn't be surprised at this. It's the effects of the Fall.

Psalm 46 describes this through several powerful metaphors: trembling earthquakes, crumbling mountains, roaring oceans! "The nations are in chaos, and their kingdoms crumble" (verse 6).

It's easy to be shaken at the world's volatility. But the Creator of heaven and earth calls us to respond in faith.

"Be still, and know that I am God! I will be honored by every nation. I will be honored throughout the world" (verse 10).

What's It Mean?

Stillness.

It's not something we're accustomed to anymore in this fast-paced age. But when chaos reigns around us, there's nothing better to do than quiet our lives, humble our hearts, and listen to God.

Psalm 46, especially God's personal command above, is a beautiful reminder of his sovereign rule over all creation. Sin might be wreaking havoc in the world, but there is complete peace in heaven. The Lord "is our refuge and strength, always ready to help in times of trouble" (verse 1).

You can be still in God. You can trust his goodness, be assured of his power, and rest in his love. He has things completely in control.

How? you ask. It sure doesn't look like it from down here.

That's because we only see the here and now. Our knowledge is finite, our sight is myopic, and our strength is limited. God is transcendent. He sees eternity all at once (see the January 13 devotion). The universe is spread out before him like a map. He will accomplish all of his purposes for the glory of his name and the good of his chosen people.

Be still and know that he is God!

Now What?

Get into the habit of pausing to pray whenever breaking news causes you concern.

Did You Know?

- In the midst of sin's disorder, God calls Christians to be peacemakers (Matthew 5:9).

MAY 6

May they be like snails that dissolve into slime.

PSALM 58:8

IMAGINE SINGING THIS at your next worship service at church:

Break off their fangs, O God!
 Smash the jaws of these lions, O LORD!
May they disappear like water into thirsty ground.
 Make their weapons useless in their hands.
May they be like snails that dissolve into slime,
 Like a stillborn child who will never see the sun.
God will sweep them away, both young and old,
 Faster than a pot heats over burning thorns.
The godly will rejoice when they see injustice avenged.
 They will wash their feet in the blood of the wicked.

Ooooohhh-kay, then.

Believe it or not, this is a section of Psalm 58, written by King David. Like most psalms, this was a song meant to be sung by Israelites gathered to worship.

Hmmm. These days, that'd be tough to insert between "Amazing Grace" and "What a Friend We Have in Jesus" while ushers pass the offering plates.

Psalm 58 is just one of many so-called imprecatory psalms—psalms that call down curses upon the wicked. They include harsh language that, at first glance, seems inconsistent with the Bible's message to "love your neighbor as yourself" (Mark 12:31).

So what are we to make of these unique contributions to the biblical canon?

What's It Mean?

There are several important factors to remember when reading the "imprecatory psalms":

- Above all else, the psalmists were passionate for God's glory and his Kingdom.
- The psalmists' adversaries were always terribly immoral enemies of God who were trying to subvert his ways and destroy his people.
- Even in their anger and passion, the psalmists never endorsed personal vendettas against the wicked. Rather, they asked *God* to uphold justice, save the righteous, and defend his holy name.

What does this mean for us today?

We must be careful with our prayers, attitudes, and actions. While it's right to abhor evil (Romans 12:9; the September 28 devotion), seek justice, and want righteousness to prevail, we must never adopt a hateful attitude toward the lost.

Remember, judgment and vengeance belong to God (Deuteronomy 32:35; Romans 12:19). Your job is to proclaim God's truth in love while praying for his Spirit to bring repentance to unbelievers' hearts (2 Timothy 2:24-26).

Now What?

Don't pray, "Dear Lord, please turn the people I don't like into snails that dissolve into slime."

Do pray, "Dear Lord, please give me the grace to show your love to those who fight against you and show unkindness to me."

Did You Know?

Other examples of psalms featuring curses include Psalm 5; 10; 34; 59; 69; 94; 109; and 137.

MAY 7

O God, you are my God; I earnestly search for you. My soul thirsts for you; my whole body longs for you in this parched and weary land where there is no water.

PSALM 63:1

DAVID WAS ON THE RUN.

His enemies were hotly pursuing him, so he ventured into an arid wilderness to lose them. In Psalm 63, David describes his plight. He was far away from the luxuries of palace life. Water was scarce. The delectable foods of the royal banquet table were a distant memory. Nights were filled with fitful sleep.

Most of all, though, David longed to set foot again in God's sanctuary (verse 2)—the Tabernacle, where God's presence resided most powerfully over the Ark of the Covenant's mercy seat. David had "gazed upon [God's] power and glory" (verse 2) before, and now he longed to do so again.

In today's verse, he expressed his deep spiritual desire to leave the wilderness and worship God among the faithful congregation.

"I lie awake thinking of you, meditating on you through the night. Because you are my helper, I sing for joy in the shadow of your wings. I cling to you; your strong right hand holds me securely" (verses 6-8).

What's It Mean?

To David, true, unencumbered worship of God was like water to a desert wanderer.

Satisfying.

Refreshing.

Rejuvenating.

Energizing.

Life-giving.

What is your individual worship of God like? Does your soul thirst for God? Do you earnestly search for him? Do you long for him like a desert wanderer seeking an oasis in a parched and weary land, finding rest for your soul through prayer, Scripture reading, and meditation on his Word? Or are your devotional times hum-drum affairs that you fit in whenever it's convenient?

What is your corporate worship of God like? Do you gather with other believers regularly out of a deep-seated hunger to praise the Lord, grow in your faith, and encourage the body of Christ? Or do you go out of a perceived obligation?

Remember, hunger and thirst come from need. God doesn't "need" our worship, but he desires it. However, we desperately need him. We need him for salvation through Christ, and we need him for our daily spiritual growth.

The more you understand your need for God, the more you will hunger and thirst for worship.

Now What?

Get in the habit of daily devotions, not for habit's sake but for honoring the Lord with your time and maturing spiritually.

Did You Know?

David was likely either fleeing Saul or his own son, Absalom, when he wrote Psalm 63.

MAY 8

*Whom have I in heaven but you? I desire you
more than anything on earth.*

PSALM 73:25

DO YOU KNOW ASAPH'S story?

Asaph lived during King David's reign. As a Levite, he had the privilege of caring for God's Tabernacle. He was also one of David's chief musicians (1 Chronicles 16:5).

Asaph's entire life was devoted to worshiping God—a noble purpose. But his calling was a strict, often solitary one—and it certainly didn't pay well!

As he looked around him, he saw wicked people prospering, and it troubled him greatly. He grew embittered, and his faith was severely shaken. Why, he wondered, did he pour so much time and energy into faithfully serving the Lord—only to suffer many hardships—while godless people seemed to enjoy a wealthy and carefree life?

In Psalm 73, Asaph laid bare his soul. Here's a portion of his refreshingly raw honesty:

> As for me, I almost lost my footing. My feet were slipping, and I was almost gone. For I envied the proud when I saw them prosper despite their wickedness. They seem to live such painless lives; their bodies are so healthy and strong. They don't have troubles like other people; they're not plagued with problems like everyone else.
> VERSES 2-5

Envy of worldly success was tearing Asaph apart.

What's It Mean?

Today is no different from Asaph's era. Everywhere you look, people with no regard for God are becoming wealthier. It's easy to longingly look at their luxurious lifestyles and wistfully echo Asaph's doubts: "Did I keep my heart pure for nothing? Did I keep myself innocent for no reason?" (verse 13).

But when Asaph sought the Lord, his heart turned and he "finally understood the destiny of the wicked" (verse 17). Ultimately, they will be destroyed (verses 18-19). God will give all evildoers what their actions deserve—certainly in the life to come, if not before.

Are you asking similar questions to Asaph's? Do you find yourself envying the wicked's success and pining for worldly pleasures? Have you been tempted to wonder whether living righteously matters at all? Take a cue from Asaph: when he remembered the eternal destiny of evildoers, he realized that his fleshly desires for temporary pleasures were "foolish and ignorant" (verse 22). This knowledge led him to a beautiful new refrain in today's verse: "Whom have I in heaven but you? I desire you more than anything on earth."

May this be your refrain, as well.

Now What?

Do you know someone who has no regard for God? Pray for opportunities to share his love with them.

Did You Know?

Levites like Asaph had to enforce the death penalty on unauthorized individuals who entered God's Tabernacle (Numbers 3:10).

258

MAY 9

I honor and love your commands. I meditate on your decrees.

PSALM 119:48

WHAT EXCITES YOU MOST in life?

Hold on. Don't blurt it out. Is it one of the following?

- laws
- commandments
- regulations
- instructions
- decrees

What's that? You say those things don't excite you? This is shocking news! After all, don't you love being told what to do?

(Deafening silence.)

Hopefully, you get the joke here. Most people don't do cartwheels and sing for joy over following rules. But the writer of Psalm 119 did. Look at today's verse. The psalmist was head-over-heels excited about God's "commands" and "decrees." He had fully embraced the beauty and blessing of God's laws.

This is such a foreign concept to many of us that it's worth exploring in more detail.

What's It Mean?

Psalm 119—the longest chapter in the Bible and longer than many *books* of Scripture—is a celebration of the Torah, the first five books of the Bible, specifically the law-giving sections in Exodus, Leviticus, Numbers, and Deuteronomy. Due to our sinful nature, we inherently want to throw off laws and regulations.

So why did the writer of Psalm 119 exult in God's commandments? Because as a Spirit-led believer, he joyfully acknowledged that the Old Testament moral code was a gracious gift, not a burden, from God to guide his covenant community.

With unabashed enthusiasm, the psalmist says God's laws help keep us from sin (verse 11), reveal "wonderful truths" (verse 18), give "wise advice" (verse 24), "expand [our] understanding" (verse 32), give life (verse 37), comfort us in our troubles (verse 50), bestow more value than all the world's riches (verse 72), and provide spiritual "light" (verse 130).

Yet we face a tension. Although good, God's laws can't save. Ultimately, they reveal God's righteous standard, our sinful inadequacy, and our great need for a Savior.

That's where Jesus comes in! Since Psalm 119 was written, Christ fulfilled his redemptive mission and the full canon of Scripture was completed. Now, as twenty-first-century Christians, we can read this psalm with even greater significance, understanding that God's "laws," "commandments," and "decrees," etc., include the whole counsel of Scripture—Old and New Testaments.

Jesus has perfectly satisfied every word of God's law (Matthew 5:17) so that we might have a perfect High Priest and Savior.

Yes, God's "regulations are good" (Psalm 119:39). But Jesus is greater!

Now What?

Read Psalm 119 and thank God not only for his Word, the Bible, but the *living* Word—Jesus Christ!

Did You Know?

In the original Hebrew, Psalm 119 is an acrostic featuring the twenty-two letters of the Hebrew alphabet.

MAY 10

O LORD, you have examined my heart and know everything about me.

PSALM 139:1

THESE DAYS, WE GO to great lengths for virtual privacy—and rightfully so. Identity theft is a big deal.

The world is teeming with scoundrels who would love to know your personal information for nefarious purposes. So we password-protect everything. We carefully monitor our financial accounts, social security numbers, and other sensitive personal information. We put our credit cards in safety sleeves to guard against "electronic pickpocketing."

But what if there was someone who knew everything about you—your name, what you look like, your address, family life, favorite dessert, biggest pet peeve, worst fear . . . EVERYTHING. If that person was a stranger, that would be creepy.

But what if that someone was perfectly good and used that knowledge to consistently bless you—both now and for all eternity? Imagine that!

Well, that's exactly what Psalm 139 is all about.

What's It Mean?

In other psalms, David marvels at God's creation, his majesty, and his faithfulness to Israel, to name just a few topics. In Psalm 139, he expresses awe at how the Lord of heaven and earth knows every detail about him.

God is holy and highly exalted. His greatness is beyond human description. Yet he is also a God who is intimately involved with his children, even before they were born. As David proclaims in verse 13, "You made all the delicate, inner parts of my body and knit me together in my mother's womb." God even knows all our thoughts (verse 2) and each word we speak before we say it (verse 4).

The Lord's sovereign, loving care lasts throughout our lifetime. "Every day of my life was recorded in your book. Every moment was laid out before a single day had passed" (verse 16).

In verse 7, David confesses, "I can never escape from your Spirit! I can never get away from your presence!" To the wicked, this might seem scary or oppressive. To the righteous, this is wonderfully reassuring.

God's loving knowledge of you is profound. It should overwhelm you—in a good way! Like David, you should walk away from Psalm 139 utterly dumbstruck by God's steadfast commitment to you. It should cause you to echo David's words in verse 6: "Such knowledge is too wonderful for me, too great for me to understand!"

Now What?
Read through Psalm 139—slowly and prayerfully—thanking God for his intimate knowledge of you.

Did You Know?
Like Psalm 139:13-16, Job 10:8-12 speaks of God's intimate design of each human being before they are born.

MAY 11

The LORD is merciful and compassionate, slow to
get angry and filled with unfailing love.

PSALM 145:8

DO YOU KNOW ANYONE who is short-tempered? Is there someone in
your life who, like a stick of dynamite with a short fuse, blows up quickly
and without much warning? They're probably not much fun to be around.

Many people think God is short-tempered, ready to strike us down
at the smallest offense. They might base this on Old Testament stories
that show his wrath toward sin. But this reveals a terribly mistaken understanding of God's character.

We need to fill our minds with true thoughts of God. Psalm 145 is a
great place to go!

Look particularly at today's verse. This is a common refrain throughout
the Old Testament—the very place where "angry God" theorists go to find
their faulty arguments. (How ironic!)

God originally spoke these words about himself to Moses on Mount
Sinai (Exodus 34:6). David repeats them several times elsewhere in
the Psalms (86:15; 103:8). Joel (2:13), Jonah (4:2), Nahum (1:3), and
Nehemiah (9:17) all reiterated these glorious attributes of God, as well.

What's It Mean?

God is "slow to get angry," but that doesn't mean he *never* gets angry. Here's
where we must proceed carefully and biblically.

God doesn't have a "temper." You won't find that word associated with
him anywhere in Scripture. Yes, his anger burns hotly toward sin. But this
is a holy wrath—fully justified toward our wicked rebellion, but never
fickle.

What's more, in God's holiness, his wrath is balanced perfectly by his
other characteristics such as justice, love, and mercy. Any claim otherwise is,
at best, misguided theology, and at worst, a lie from hell.

Psalm 145 reveals what God is really like:

- He "is good to everyone" and "showers compassion on all his creation" (verse 9).
- He "always keeps his promises" (verse 13).
- He "helps the fallen and lifts those bent beneath their loads" (verse 14).
- He "satisf[ies] the hunger and thirst of every living thing" (verse 16).
- He "is filled with kindness" (verse 17).
- He "is close to all who call on him" (verse 18).
- "He grants the desires of those who fear him" (verse 19).

Is this an angry, short-tempered God? Or an amazing God who "is merciful and compassionate, slow to get angry and filled with unfailing love"?

The answer is as clear as the Scripture before you!

Now What?

Read Psalm 145 to gain a better understanding of God and his goodness toward us.

Did You Know?

James 1:19 calls Christians to imitate God's character when it says, "You must all be . . . slow to get angry."

MAY 12

Our God is in the heavens, and he does as he wishes.

PSALM 115:3

TIME FOR A BRAINTEASER! Try to reconcile these two biblical truths:

- In Exodus 23:7, God commanded, "Never sentence an innocent or blameless person to death."
- Yet in Isaiah 53:10, we read, "It was the LORD's good plan to crush" Jesus on the cross. Furthermore, Acts 4:27-28 says that everything Herod, Pilate, the Roman soldiers, and the wicked Jewish leaders did against Jesus during his crucifixion "was determined beforehand according to [God's] will."

How can God's will—the sacrificial death of his blameless Son on the cross—also be something he outlawed? It's a fascinating question—one that might appear to present a spiritual conundrum. But a closer look at Scripture reveals no contradiction. That's because "the will of God" is a far broader subject than it initially appears. The Bible seems to indicate three different aspects to what is generally referred to as "God's will"—his decretive will, his preceptive will, and his will of disposition.

Today's psalm, which alludes to the Lord's decretive will (more on that in a moment), kicks off a four-day study of this important topic. Time to put on your swimsuit, because we're diving into the deep end of the theological pool!

What's It Mean?

God's decretive will is sometimes called his sovereign will, or his will of decree. These are the things God sovereignly commands that cannot be thwarted or altered. For instance, when God commanded, "Let there be light" (Genesis 1:3), light instantly appeared. Nothing could hinder that decree. (Today's verse speaks to this.)

There is also God's preceptive will. This refers to God's moral laws in Scripture (i.e., his precepts) that he commands us to obey. Sadly, both Christians and non-Christians disobey God's preceptive will.

Finally, there is God's will of disposition, which is perhaps the trickiest to understand. This describes what God may allow to transpire, although not sanction. This is where Jesus' crucifixion comes into play. God's sovereign will (thankfully for us!) was for Jesus to die for our sins. Yet God condemned the wicked actions of those who humanly instigated Jesus' crucifixion. Scripturally speaking, all this can coexist without contradiction in the Lord's inscrutable sovereignty.

We could say much more about God's will, but today's pool time is over. Bring your swimsuit tomorrow for another deep-dive into this gloriously rich topic!

Now What?

Exploring the beautifully mysterious nature of God's will should drive us to worship the one who transcends our understanding. Praise him!

Did You Know?

When it comes to God's will of disposition, just because he allows things to happen that he doesn't approve of doesn't mean he is powerless to stop them.

266

MAY 13

The secret things belong to the LORD our God, but the
things that are revealed belong to us and to our children
forever, that we may do all the words of this law.

DEUTERONOMY 29:29, ESV

DO YOU STILL HAVE your swimsuit from yesterday? Hope so!

Today is a beautiful day for another plunge into the subject of God's
will. It's a vast theological pool that's as infinitely wide as it is deep. We
could swim the length of it or dive the depth of it and never come close to
reaching its limits. God is that far beyond our finite comprehension.

Yet he has graciously revealed much of himself to us through Holy
Scripture, and for this, we should be eternally grateful. He certainly didn't
owe it to us.

In yesterday's devotion, we discussed the three different aspects of God's
will—his decretive will, his preceptive will, and his will of disposition. As
we study God's will, there's another facet we need to understand: God's
"revealed will" and "hidden will."

Wow! you might be thinking. How many wills does God have?

Valid question. But remember: we are mere mortals trying to grasp his
infinite greatness and describe it in human terms. So grab a life jacket, inner
tube, buoy, water noodle—or whatever you need to stay afloat—and let's
keep swimming out into the wonderful waters of God's will!

What's It Mean?

When theologians talk about God's "revealed will," they are usually referring to his preceptive will—the moral precepts and commands that God
has revealed to us in Scripture so we may always obey them (today's verse).

However, as today's verse also shows, there are "secret things" that
God chooses not to reveal to us—his "hidden," or secret, will. This is
important to understand because it involves things in life that require
great faith:

- life circumstances that don't make sense to us
- trials we endure that seem illogical or unending
- specific details about the future, such as Jesus' second coming, what heaven will be like, etc., that Scripture remains mostly vague—or silent—on

Sometimes, we find out God's hidden will in retrospect, after something happens. Other times, we never learn it. Either way, we must bow before God's sovereignty, humbly accept that there are many things in life that God decrees which we may never know about, and worship him.

Now What?
We are treading in deep theological waters here! Pray for spiritual understanding.

Did You Know?
There is nothing in God's hidden will we have to fear because God is holy (Revelation 4:8) and he always deals righteously with his creation (Psalm 89:14).

MAY 14

Do not be conformed to this world, but be transformed by the renewal of your mind, that by testing you may discern what is the will of God, what is good and acceptable and perfect.

ROMANS 12:2, ESV

HAVE YOU EVER WANTED to know your future? Of course! We all have. Humans have long desired to look past the mysterious veil that separates the present from the future and find the answer to questions like these:

- What will tomorrow look like?
- What does the distant future hold?
- What should I do with this particular decision?

In the ancient world, pagans would go to extreme measures to answer these questions, even examining the entrails (liver, intestines, lungs) of sacrificed animals in search of omens about the future—a practice known as *extispicy*. Ewwww!

Christians aren't immune to this desire to know the future. From a biblical perspective, all believers should want to know God's will for their lives. But as we discussed in yesterday's devotion, not all of it has been revealed to us. In our desire to know God's will, we must seek wisely and reverently.

Now we turn to the burning question every Christian wants to know: How can I know God's will for my life?

What's It Mean?

Knowing God's will is not like baking brownies: *Follow these ten easy steps, and* voilà*! Done in thirty minutes!*

God's will doesn't work like that.

Knowing God's will is a spiritual process that involves obedience to his Word, prayer, and patient faith. The first step is a spiritual renewal of your mind (today's verse). Without God's justifying and sanctifying work in your life, you can't know his will.

Sometimes God makes his will immediately clear to his children in specific situations. But if you're waiting for him to appear to you in a burning bush, you're probably going to be disappointed. God certainly can (and still does) speak in miraculous ways, but nowadays, he primarily communicates through his inspired Word. (This, by the way, is far better than one-time visions—see 1 Peter 1:10-12.)

Above all, God's will for you is to bring glory to his name with the spiritual gifts that he has given you (1 Corinthians 10:31). He desires that you become more like his Son (Romans 8:29) and make disciples of others (Matthew 28:19-20).

He will reveal other parts of his will to you as you faithfully walk in his ways, read his Word, seek him in prayer, and seek the counsel of godly believers in your life.

Now What?
Read 1 John 2:17 to learn more about God's will.

Did You Know?
God repeatedly condemned extispicy, often called divination, in the Old Testament.

MAY 15

*If you need wisdom, ask our generous God, and he will
give it to you. He will not rebuke you for asking.*

JAMES 1:5

AT THE START OF today's devotion, just so we're all on the same page,
does everyone agree that cutting open sheep and examining their livers for
mystical signs about the future is

- pretty creepy,
- really kooky and completely useless, and
- a pagan practice that's abominable to the Lord?

(Just nod your head yes.)

Good. Glad we're all in agreement on that.

We joke about this ancient practice of extispicy—or divination, as the
Bible calls it—but it shows the lengths people went to throughout history to
discover the will of the gods.

For the last three days, we've been discussing God's will in broad terms.
Now, it's time to get more detailed. After all, everyone has wondered how to
apply God's will to specific questions, such as, "Should I date this person?"
or "What career path should I take?" or "Is it morally okay for me to watch
this movie?"

Let's discuss!

What's It Mean?

When you wonder what God's will is for you in a specific situation, your
first step should always be to pray. Seek God's wisdom prayerfully in faith,
and he will answer (James 1:5-8).

Next, apply biblical wisdom. Even when God's Word doesn't specifically
address a particular situation, you can always trust the general principles
found within Scripture to keep you in God's will. For instance, movies obviously didn't exist when Scripture was being written, but if you're wondering

if you should watch a film filled with inappropriate sexual content and vulgar language, God's Word has plenty to say about setting your mind on righteousness, not worldliness (e.g., Psalm 101:3; Colossians 3:2; Ephesians 5:3-14). Biblical discernment often leads to the discovery of God's will in specific situations.

Also, it's vital to keep in mind the truth of Romans 12:2 (yesterday's verse of the day). To truly know God's will, we must allow him to transform our minds from craving earthly passions to desiring heavenly things. It will become easier for you to discern his will in specific situations as you develop the "mind of Christ" (1 Corinthians 2:16).

Lastly, God's Spirit will guide you into his will, if you walk humbly before him. This is part of the sanctification process—being made more like Jesus.

Now What?
Matthew 6:10 reveals what your attitude should be in prayer and life regarding God's will. Read it!

Did You Know?
Even when "we don't know what God wants us to pray for," God's Spirit intercedes for believers "in harmony with God's own will" (Romans 8:26-27). Incredible!

MAY 16

Trust in the LORD with all your heart, and do not lean on
your own understanding. In all your ways acknowledge
him, and he will make straight your paths.

PROVERBS 3:5-6, ESV

TAKE A LOOK AT today's Scripture passage. Do you know who wrote it?

King Solomon, Scripture's Mr. Wasted Potential.

Solomon had it all, but he fell so far. His father was Israel's beloved King David, the courageous shepherd boy who slayed a giant, ascended to the throne, and unified a nation. God made an everlasting covenant that David's "kingdom [would] continue before me for all time" (2 Samuel 7:16)—ultimately an incredible Messianic promise that Christ would come through David's lineage (Matthew 1:1-17). Talk about being set up for success!

Before he died, David solemnly charged Solomon to honor the Lord. For a time, it seemed like Solomon got the message. Early on, his wisdom and riches were unmatched in the ancient world.

Yet as we discussed in the April 23 devotion, marrying hundreds of idol-worshiping wives and making other bad choices turned his heart from the Lord. Solomon wrote today's verses, but sadly, he ultimately didn't practice what he preached, and it led to his downfall.

What's It Mean?

Leaning on human understanding has caused much strife in the course of history. Human understanding has produced all the false religions, as sinners have vainly tried to claw their way to heaven apart from the one true God's perfect rescue plan. It has caused neglect, abuse, oppression, vice, greed, violence, homicide, genocide, and worldwide war.

Go all the way back to the Garden of Eden in Genesis 3. Our original forebears, Adam and Eve, leaned on their human understanding, and it caused the Fall itself.

Trusting in ourselves has only brought us pain and misery. God made

273

us to trust in him for everything—from our routine needs (Matthew 6:25-34) to help in our greatest trials (Psalm 69).

When your decision-making acknowledges God—his authority, wisdom, and love—your life will change. You'll still have to make tough decisions. You'll still encounter trials. But God will make straight paths for you—ones that bring you to his appointed will for your life.

But you must trust him with all your heart.

Now What?

Check out these additional passages of Scripture that exhort believers to trust in the Lord: Psalm 20:7; 37:5; 71:5; 84:12; 91:2; and Isaiah 12:2; 26:4.

Did You Know?

Solomon "composed some 3,000 proverbs and wrote 1,005 songs" (1 Kings 4:32).

MAY 17

Walk with the wise and become wise; associate
with fools and get in trouble.

PROVERBS 13:20

KING REHOBOAM FACED A momentous decision. The fate of the kingdom rested in his hands.

After his father, Solomon, died, Rehoboam went to Shechem to be
crowned king. But Jeroboam, who had fled from Solomon, returned, and
with a delegation from the northern tribes of Israel, he told Rehoboam,
"Lighten the harsh labor demands and heavy taxes that your father imposed
on us" (1 Kings 12:4).

Rehoboam told Jeroboam to return in three days for an answer. In the
meantime, he sought wisdom—first from an older group of counselors who
had served under Solomon. They wisely advised him to meet the people's
request.

Then Rehoboam did something foolish: he conferred with some childhood buddies, who told him to threaten the people with even heavier burdens, just to show them who was boss.

You can imagine how well that went over. Jeroboam and ten tribes
rebelled. The nation split into the northern kingdom of Israel and the
southern kingdom of Judah—never to fully recover.

Apparently, Rehoboam did not read his own dad's proverb!

What's It Mean?

Read today's verse again from the book of Proverbs. It sounds so easy—
almost as if it goes without saying. But if it wasn't worth mentioning, God
wouldn't have included it in Scripture.

Clearly, we do need to hear this important message. If we don't take it
to heart, we can quickly fall into Rehoboam's trap. He associated with fools
and got into big trouble, sparking "constant war" between the tribes of Israel
during his lifetime (1 Kings 14:30).

Your choice of friends is one of the most important decisions you'll make in life. Carefully think about the people in your life: Are they spiritually wise or foolish?

True friends don't pressure one another into doing things that are completely against God's laws. Quite the opposite! True friends exhort each other to obey God and grow in their faith. True friends pray with—and for—each other. True friends encourage each other with kind words. True friends put each other first in humility and Christlike love.

Do you have friends like that?

Don't think you're immune to the negative influence of bad friends. No one is! As 1 Corinthians 15:33 says, "Do not be deceived: 'Bad company ruins good morals'" (ESV).

Don't pull a "Rehoboam." Choose your friends wisely!

Now What?

Read Proverbs 17:17 and 18:24.

Did You Know?

David and Jonathan are a great example of a godly, loyal friendship. You can read their story in 1 Samuel 18–20 and 23:15-18.

MAY 18

Let someone else praise you, not your own
mouth—a stranger, not your own lips.

PROVERBS 27:2

HE IS SIMPLY CALLED "The Greatest." And given the chance, he would've happily—and excessively—agreed with that title.

We are speaking, of course, about Muhammad Ali, who is generally considered the greatest heavyweight boxer of all time. Ali finished his remarkable career with a 56–5 record, including thirty-seven knockouts and three world heavyweight championships between 1960 and 1981.

Ali was not only the greatest in the ring; he was also the greatest at declaring himself to be "The Greatest." Among his nicknames was "The Louisville Lip," acquired for his constant, colorful bragging.

Here are some of his most memorable boasts:

"Float like a butterfly, sting like a bee; his hands can't hit what his eyes can't see."
"If you even dream of beating me, you'd better wake up and apologize."
"I've wrestled with alligators. I've tussled with a whale. I done handcuffed lightning. And throw thunder in jail."
"I am the astronaut of boxing. Joe Louis and Dempsey were just jet pilots. I'm in a world of my own."
"It's hard to be humble when you're as great as I am."

When it came to self-praise, Ali was a champ indeed!

What's It Mean?

Today's proverb is straightforward: any praise we receive should come from others, not our own lips. This isn't easy! Our human desire is to draw attention to our talents. Human praise feels good, and we often seek it by talking about ourselves.

But this goes against God's will for us, and it has dire consequences since it exposes sinful pride in our hearts. Proverbs 16:18 tells us, "Pride goes before destruction, and haughtiness before a fall."

As for all the great things you've done, remember this: everything you have and do is a gift from God (1 Corinthians 4:7). Also recall Jesus' words in Matthew 23:12: "Those who exalt themselves will be humbled, and those who humble themselves will be exalted."

But if you must brag about something, you have an outlet! Jeremiah 9:24 says, "Those who wish to boast should boast in this alone: that they truly know me and understand that I am the LORD who demonstrates unfailing love and who brings justice and righteousness to the earth, and that I delight in these things."

So go ahead and boast away! But always boast about God and what he has done for you.

Now What?

List ten things God has done for you recently and prayerfully boast in them, thanking him.

Did You Know?

Muhammad Ali was exiled from boxing during his prime (1967–70) for refusing to serve in the Vietnam War.

MAY 19

Fear God and obey his commands, for this is everyone's duty.

ECCLESIASTES 12:13

WHAT WOULD YOU DO if someone told you the following?

- I observed everything going on under the sun, and really, it is all meaningless—like chasing the wind.
- In this life, good people are often treated as though they were wicked, and wicked people are often treated as though they were good. This is so meaningless!
- The dead are better off than the living. But most fortunate of all are those who are not yet born. For they have not seen all the evil that is done under the sun.

Would you consider that person a wise counselor? Would you ask them to colead a Bible study with you? Would you want them as your pastor? Hmmm . . .

Believe it or not, those quotes are all inspired Scripture, pulled directly from Ecclesiastes. This remarkable, often-confusing book of the Bible features some difficult, timeless topics:

- the search for meaning and purpose in life
- how sin affects the daily human experience
- grappling with injustice—real or perceived
- trying to understand how some of life's greatest gifts are ultimately short-lived

A cursory reading of Ecclesiastes could lead to cynicism, questioning God's sovereignty, wondering why the book is included in the Bible—or all of the above. Clearly, that's not what God intended. We must read and interpret Ecclesiastes carefully, with a biblically informed mindset.

What's It Mean?

Ecclesiastes was an attempt to make sense of life and its perplexing inconsistencies. We often experience joy and despair in the same day. Evil people thrive while righteous people suffer. This is all part of living in a world stained by sin.

How do we make sense of it all? At the end of his pondering, Ecclesiastes' ancient author concluded, "Fear God and obey his commands, for this is everyone's duty. God will judge us for everything we do, including every secret thing, whether good or bad" (Ecclesiastes 12:13-14).

But if you are a Christian, you can go a step further than the author! You live on the other side of the Cross. You know that Christ's great work of redemption is completely finished, and as such, life has great meaning for every believer. You know that when the Savior returns, he'll destroy the sin that makes our daily experiences so vexing.

Thanks to Jesus, one day everything meaningless will become beautifully meaningful!

Now What?

Are you struggling with things in life that you think are meaningless? Offer them in prayer to God.

Did You Know?

Ecclesiastes' anonymous author (possibly Solomon) self-identifies as "the Preacher, the son of David, king in Jerusalem" (Ecclesiastes 1:1, ESV).

MAY 20

My beloved is mine, and I am his.

SONG OF SOLOMON 2:16, ESV

SPOILER ALERT: THIS IS the part of the devotional where it gets a little lovey-dovey.

Yep, today we're discussing the Song of Solomon, one of the most unique books of the Bible. For starters, this book features some great one-liners that any guy or girl can use when trying to impress a member of the opposite gender. A few examples are listed below.

Phrases for girls:

- **To the gentleman who *doesn't* smell like a middle school boys' locker room:** "He is like a bouquet of sweet henna blossoms from the vineyards of En-gedi" (1:14).
- **When a guy writes nonrhyming poetry to you:** "Strengthen me with raisin cakes, refresh me with apples, for I am weak with love" (2:5).

Phrases for guys:

- **To a girl with cool hair:** "Your hair is like a flock of goats leaping down the slopes of Gilead" (4:1, ESV).
- **To a girl who prioritizes dental hygiene:** "Your teeth are like a flock of shorn ewes that have come up from the washing, all of which bear twins, and not one among them has lost its young" (4:2, ESV).
- **To a young lady whose nose stuns you . . . in a good way:** "Your nose is like a tower of Lebanon, which looks toward Damascus" (7:4, ESV).

Yes, Song of Solomon is matchmaking gold.

What's It Mean?

What's shared above, of course, is all tongue-in-cheek. Song of Solomon is actually a magnificent love poem about a young man and woman expressing romantic feelings for one another as they prepare for marriage.

There is great beauty in the affection a husband and wife can share in the God-ordained covenant of marriage. But these strong romantic feelings should only be acted upon in marriage, as is modeled in Song of Solomon. This is God's perfect design, going all the way back to Creation in Genesis 1.

The Bible clearly teaches that sex outside marriage is sin (see the "Did You Know?" section). Even the young woman in Song of Solomon, stirred with passion for her beloved, counsels her friends "not to awaken love until the time is right" (2:7).

Follow God's good plan for your life. Wait to show that physical affection until marriage. You won't regret it!

Now What?

Commit to sexual purity and pray for your future spouse.

Did You Know?

God's design for sex within marriage was first outlined in Genesis 2:18-25 and 4:1-2; codified into law in Exodus 20:14 and Deuteronomy 22:13-30; and expounded on in the New Testament in places such as Galatians 5:19-21; Colossians 3:5; 1 Corinthians 6:9-10, 18-20; 1 Thessalonians 4:3-4, 7; and Hebrews 13:4.

MAY 21

They were calling out to each other, "Holy, holy, holy is the LORD of
Heaven's Armies! The whole earth is filled with his glory!"

ISAIAH 6:3

I . . . am . . . doomed.

Isaiah, the Old Testament prophet, did not like his chances for survival.
In fact, he didn't think he'd be alive the next day.

Was he caught in a burning building with no escape? Lost at sea surrounded by a circle of shark fins? Falling from the sky with no parachute
(because, well, they hadn't been invented yet)?

No, Isaiah had seen a glimpse of God's holiness.

In 740 BC, with the wicked northern kingdom of Israel heading toward
its fall to Assyria and the southern kingdom of Judah dangerously following
the same path of idolatry, God commissioned Isaiah to preach the truth to his
wayward people through an astounding vision. Isaiah was allowed to peer into
God's throne room, where powerful seraphim, a special class of six-winged
angels, constantly hovered nearby, calling out in worship, "Holy, holy, holy is
the LORD of Heaven's Armies! The whole earth is filled with his glory!"

Sounds amazing to behold, right? But when Isaiah saw the Lord, he
feared for his life.

What's It Mean?

Isaiah's once-in-a-lifetime privilege to stand in God's presence was a terrifying
experience. It was like standing in front of the most revealing mirror in the
universe, seeing himself truthfully, instead of who he'd *like* to think he was.

Compared to God's overwhelming holiness, Isaiah was rightfully
undone. He saw his own sinfulness and knew he had transgressed God's
laws countless times.

"I am doomed," he exclaimed, "for I am a sinful man! I have filthy
lips, and I live among a people with filthy lips. Yet I have seen the King,
the LORD of Heaven's Armies" (verse 5).

Have you had an Isaiah 6 moment? Have you considered your sins in light of God's holiness? Far too often, we live our lives with a much higher opinion of ourselves than Scripture allows. But if we are completely honest, we are wretched sinners who are doomed apart from God's saving grace. Praise the Lord for that very grace he gives us in his Son, Jesus Christ!

Now What?

Read Isaiah 6 to learn more about Isaiah's life-changing vision of God. Also read Ephesians 2:8-9.

Did You Know?

Isaiah survived his heavenly revelation! God mercifully forgave his sins by sending one of the seraphim to touch his lips with a burning coal from the altar—representing the Old Testament sacrifices required for atonement and, ultimately, a foreshadowing of Jesus' atoning work on the cross for us.

MAY 22

I dwell in the high and holy place, and also with
him who is of a contrite and lowly spirit.

ISAIAH 57:15, ESV

ON NOVEMBER 13, 1861, M. R. Watkinson, a Pennsylvania minister, wrote a letter to Salmon P. Chase, the US Department of the Treasury secretary. Watkinson knew Chase was about to submit an annual financial report to Congress. So he asked for "the recognition of the Almighty God in some form on our coins," specifically requesting the engraving of the words "GOD, LIBERTY, LAW."

Chase agreed. By 1864, "IN GOD WE TRUST" first appeared on the two-cent coin, and the phrase has been printed on various forms of US currency ever since.

But what kind of God do we trust in? It's often said that the United States was founded on Judeo-Christian ethics and that our Founding Fathers were Bible-believing Christians. Certainly some might have been. But a number of the founders seem to have been deists.

Deism claims that a supreme being (i.e., God) initially created the universe but has had little interaction with it since. This philosophical system was especially popular during the Enlightenment era of the seventeenth and eighteenth centuries in Europe (and later, America), when various advancements and discoveries led people to value human reason and intellect above spiritual matters.

To deists, the idea of a loving, caring God is utterly irrational. God—to the deist—is nothing more than a distant, cosmic Clockmaker who wound up the universe like a timepiece, then stepped back to let it run on its own.

This, of course, is ludicrous, contradicting the entire testimony of Scripture.

What's It Mean?

Look at today's verse from Isaiah again. One of the most beautiful realities about God is that he is both indescribably majestic and amazingly relational. These are not paradoxical statements. They are *both* true!

285

God is so holy and exalted; he cannot be contained by the vast universe he created. As Psalm 113:4 says, "For the LORD is high above the nations; his glory is higher than the heavens."

Yet he is a heavenly Father, showing great love to his children through Christ, and his Spirit dwells in the hearts of those who call on his name. He is near, always accessible through prayer, and he loves showering us with spiritual blessings. What glorious truths!

This is the God in whom we trust.

Now What?

Deism prizes human reason. Scripture calls us to desire godly wisdom. With that in mind, read 1 Corinthians 1:18–2:16.

Did You Know?

Benjamin Franklin confessed to being "a thorough Deist" in his *Autobiography*, but interestingly, he proposed that he and his fellow delegates open the 1787 Constitutional Convention in prayer.

MAY 23

The LORD replied, "Don't say, 'I'm too young,' for you must go wherever I send you and say whatever I tell you."

JEREMIAH 1:7

BEFORE JEREMIAH WAS a great prophet, he was a normal youth with parents, chores, dreams, and questions about the future. One day, the Lord rocked the daily monotony from his life.

"Before you were born," God said, "I set you apart and appointed you as my prophet to the nations" (Jeremiah 1:5).

Wow! Talk about a wake-up call! How would you react if God told you this? Would you jump up and down for joy? Faint in shock? Fall down in worship?

Jeremiah hesitated.

"O Sovereign LORD," he replied, "I can't speak for you! I'm too young!" (verse 6).

If you're familiar with biblical callings, that type of response really doesn't fly with God.

"Don't say, 'I'm too young,'" God said, "for you must go wherever I send you and say whatever I tell you. And don't be afraid of the people, for I will be with you and will protect you. I, the LORD, have spoken!" (verses 7-8).

Jeremiah, of course, became one of history's greatest prophets—and one of the most persecuted saints in the Bible. As he ministered to a rebellious, idolatrous people, he was beaten, put in stocks, imprisoned, thrown into a muddy cistern, and eventually exiled to Egypt.

Yet he remained faithful to the calling of his youth.

What's It Mean?

The book of Jeremiah's fifty-two chapters are power-packed with truth. God's revelation of his future new covenant in Jeremiah 31:31-34—fulfilled through Christ's work on the cross—is particularly powerful.

Yet like Moses, Gideon, and others before him, Jeremiah tried avoiding God's initial calling. He tried using his age and inexperience as an excuse.

Not good enough! As Paul told young Timothy centuries later, "Let no one despise you for your youth, but set the believers an example in speech, in conduct, in love, in faith, in purity" (1 Timothy 4:12, ESV).

What about you? Are you trying to use your age as an excuse to God? In his eyes, that's no reason to be spiritually unfruitful. God used youth to slay giants (1 Samuel 17), rule nations (2 Chronicles 34:1-2), and miraculously heal military generals (2 Kings 5). His power and plans aren't limited by something as insignificant as human age.

God wants to do great things through you, too. Humble yourself before him. Be open to his calling and see where he takes you—all for his glory!

Now What?

When God calls, answer willingly!

Did You Know?

- Jeremiah's prophetic ministry—concurrent with the Babylonian Empire's conquest of Judah—spanned forty-plus years and a half-dozen kings.

MAY 24

The faithful love of the LORD never ends! His mercies never cease.

LAMENTATIONS 3:22

WHAT KIND OF MUSIC do you like? Songs that are tearjerkers, requiems, and funeral marches?

No, probably not.

Most of us enjoy upbeat music that isn't about disheartening topics. Perhaps that's why Lamentations is often an overlooked book of the Bible. This is unfortunate because it's a fascinating, spiritually rich collection of poetic dirges about the plight of Jerusalem and the Jews after the Babylonians destroyed the city in 586 BC. It's filled with wonderful theology, real-life anguish, and heartfelt cries to God.

In many ways, the horrors of ancient siege warfare are incomprehensible to us. Deprivation, starvation, and panic were everywhere. Shockingly, some mothers even resorted to cannibalizing their children (Lamentations 2:20; 4:10).

Once the Babylonians broke through the city walls, the destruction was overwhelming. They reduced the city to rubble and littered Jerusalem's streets with dead bodies (2:21). Survivors were either exiled or left to somehow cobble together a new life among the ruins. They would never be the same.

And yet one survivor—the author of Lamentations—found hope:

The thought of my suffering and homelessness is bitter beyond words. I will never forget this awful time, as I grieve over my loss. Yet I still dare to hope when I remember this: The faithful love of the LORD never ends! His mercies never cease. Great is his faithfulness; his mercies begin afresh each morning. I say to myself, "The LORD is my inheritance; therefore, I will hope in him!"

LAMENTATIONS 3:19-24

What beautiful words!

What's It Mean?

Those words were written to Jews of the sixth century BC who had suffered catastrophic loss. But God's Word is just as relevant today, even though time and circumstances change. In fact, take a few moments now to reread that passage of Scripture as if *you* had written it.

Do you see how powerful and pertinent Lamentations 3:19-24 is today?

Are you currently suffering through an awful time or a trial that feels bitter beyond words? Always remember that "the faithful love of the LORD never ends"!

Maybe, like Israel, the challenges you're facing are self-inflicted because of sinful choices you've made. Or perhaps your hardship is simply the perplexing result of living in a fallen world.

Whatever the case, remember this: what was true for ancient Israel is true for you: reasons to lament may come, but we can dare to hope in the God whose "mercies never cease"!

Now What?

It's okay to lament to God (Lamentations 2:19; 3:55). Cry out to him for help.

Did You Know?

Lamentations was anonymously authored, probably sometime in the sixth century BC.

MAY 25

I will give you a new heart, and I will put a new spirit in you.
I will take out your stony, stubborn heart and give you a tender,
responsive heart. And I will put my Spirit in you so that you
will follow my decrees and be careful to obey my regulations.

EZEKIEL 36:26-27

IF YOU'RE LOOKING TO turn a portion of the Bible into a thriller movie, try Ezekiel 37. It's hair-raisingly cool!

Ezekiel was a Jewish prophet-priest who was exiled by Babylonian King Nebuchadnezzar in 597 BC (2 Kings 24:10-17; Ezekiel 1:1-3). Years later, God gave Ezekiel a startling vision of a valley littered with human bones, recounting a great battlefield of dead soldiers, now reduced to skeletal remains (Ezekiel 37:1-2).

Then God said, "Dry bones, listen to the word of the LORD! . . . Look! I am going to put breath into you and make you live again! I will put flesh and muscles on you and cover you with skin. I will put breath into you, and you will come to life. Then you will know that I am the LORD" (37:4-6).

Suddenly, Ezekiel heard a great rattling noise as the bones supernaturally reformed into human bodies before muscles, tendons, and flesh covered them. Then he spoke a prophetic word, and God's "breath" resurrected the corpses.

What a creepy but cool visual! The dead had returned to life.

What's It Mean?

The valley of dry bones was a shockingly vivid metaphor depicting Israel in Ezekiel's day. Like a wasteland of skeletons, God's people were spiritually dead, rotting away under God's judgment for their sins. But thanks to his incredible love and mercy, God would soon breathe new life into them—making them a new people and returning them to the Promised Land.

How did he accomplish this marvelous feat? The answer is found in Ezekiel 37:5-6 and in today's Scripture passage. He removed their stubborn, stony hearts, replaced them with hearts of obedience, and breathed his Holy Spirit into their lives.

That is what he has done for you, too, if you are a follower of Christ! Part of our salvation process is God awakening our spiritually dead hearts—like scattered dry bones coming to life—to receive the gospel through repentance and faith (Ephesians 2:1-10; Colossians 2:13).

The initiative is gloriously all God's, and we get the benefit!

Now What?

Praise the God who graciously turns dry bones and dead hearts into his spiritually alive children!

Did You Know?

Why did God restore rebellious Israel? Ultimately for the sake of his holy name (Ezekiel 36:21-23) and so that others may know that he is the Lord (verses 36, 38).

MAY 26

Beloved, I urge you as sojourners and exiles
to abstain from the passions of the flesh,
which wage war against your soul.

1 PETER 2:11, ESV

IF THE FOLLOWING DINNER options were placed before you, which
would you choose?

A. a mouthwatering six-course meal filled with cheese and crackers, an
   appetizer, fresh fruit, a Caesar salad, a chicken or steak entree made
   to order, and your favorite ice cream
B. steamed spinach and water

It's a no-brainer, right? Option A! Who would ever choose option B?
Well, Daniel and his three friends did.

Daniel and his friends—Hananiah, Mishael, and Azariah—were Jewish
prisoners exiled to Babylon when King Nebuchadnezzar invaded Judah
in 605 BC. The Babylonians tried to strip the conquered people of their
national and spiritual identities and assimilate them into Babylonian culture. So upon their arrival, Daniel and his friends were forced to change
their names, diets, language—everything.

But "Daniel was determined not to defile himself by eating the food
and wine given to them by the king" (Daniel 1:8)—possibly because the
king's food was at odds with Old Testament food regulations (Leviticus 11)
and also perhaps to retain their identity as God's people.

Daniel and his friends boldly asked to eat only veggies and water for
ten days while their peers ate from Nebuchadnezzar's menu. "At the end
of the ten days, Daniel and his three friends looked healthier and better
nourished than the young men who had been eating the food assigned by
the king" (Daniel 1:15). So they were allowed to continue eating veggies
and water.

What's It Mean?

While exiles, Daniel and his friends remained committed to their identity as God's people, despite incredible pressure to conform—and God blessed them for it.

If you are a Christian, you are an exile, too. This doesn't mean you're a deported individual from a conquered nation. It's referring to your identity in Christ and your eternal destiny.

This world is only our temporary home. As today's verse says, we are "sojourners and exiles" here, momentarily passing through as we await our forever heavenly dwelling. As such, don't let the world's sinful enticements and "the passions of the flesh, which wage war against your soul" allure you.

Like Daniel and his friends, remain committed to your identity as a child of God, despite the intense pressure around you to conform to the world's standards.

Now What?

Are you conforming to the world's standards? Prayerfully read through Romans 12:1-2 and ask God to help you remain faithful to your true identity in him.

Did You Know?

Daniel and his friends' new names—Belteshazzar, Shadrach, Meshach, and Abednego—were in honor of various Babylonian deities.

MAY 27

The Most High rules over the kingdoms of the world. He gives them to anyone he chooses—even to the lowliest of people.

DANIEL 4:17

PROVERBS 16:18 SAYS, "Pride goes before destruction, and haughtiness before a fall." In King Nebuchadnezzar's case, pride went before grass-grazing and a complete disregard for personal grooming habits.

Perhaps an explanation is needed.

Nebuchadnezzar was one of the ancient world's greatest emperors. During his reign (605–562 BC), he brought the Babylonian Empire to its greatest height, conquering other nations and building the city of Babylon into a world-class metropolis.

But Nebuchadnezzar grew quite conceited over his accomplishments. One day, God cautioned Nebuchadnezzar to repent of his great pride through a unique dream—which Daniel interpreted for him—or else he would be driven insane. But Nebuchadnezzar ignored the divine warning.

One year later, as he was strolling on his palace rooftop, he boasted, "Look at this great city of Babylon! By my own mighty power, I have built this beautiful city as my royal residence to display my majestic splendor" (Daniel 4:30).

Instantly, God's judgment fell on him. For a long time, "he ate grass like a cow, and he was drenched with the dew of heaven. He lived this way until his hair was as long as eagles' feathers and his nails were like birds' claws" (verse 33).

The great king—deprived of all sanity—had been completely humbled.

What's It Mean?

Nebuchadnezzar was an incredibly powerful ruler. God even used him as an instrument of punishment against his own people, the Jews, for their idolatrous rebellion. But like any other mighty king—righteous or pagan—Nebuchadnezzar was completely under God's control (Proverbs 21:1). When he didn't give glory to God, he learned the truth of today's verse in an unforgettable way: "The Most High rules over the kingdoms of the world."

Today's world is a much different place. But God still reigns supreme. This should provide great peace and hope as you hear about troubling national and world events.

As Daniel testified earlier in his book, God "controls the course of world events; he removes kings and sets up other kings" (2:21). The world might seem out of control, but God is working all things according to his sovereign purpose.

Don't hold your breath waiting for wicked world leaders to go insane and start eating grass, though! Rather, trust in the almighty God who rules over all the affairs of mankind.

Now What?

Each day, pray for the light of the gospel to shine on a different country.

Did You Know?

Nebuchadnezzar's sanity was eventually restored. He returned to the throne, praising God (Daniel 4:34-37).

MAY 28

Daniel . . . still prays to his God three times a day.

DANIEL 6:13

LIONS, AND PERSIANS, and edicts . . . oh my!

Well, it doesn't exactly have quite the same ring to it as the famous phrase uttered by Dorothy in *The Wizard of Oz*. Then again, these were the things threatening Daniel's life—not tigers and bears.

The story in question, of course, is Daniel and the lions' den. After the Persian Empire conquered the Babylonians, Daniel continued serving the new royal court.

But when his fellow government officials grew jealous of his success, they tricked King Darius into enacting a terrible law: every person who prayed to anyone except Darius would be thrown to hungry lions. What a gruesome way to die! They did this, of course, with Daniel in mind, knowing that he faithfully prayed to God in his room three times every day.

Despite the intense pressure to conform, Daniel continued to pray to God. The wicked Persian officials tattled on him, and Darius reluctantly gave the order: Daniel would become lion food!

Early the next morning, Darius rushed to the pit and called out, "Daniel, servant of the living God! Was your God, whom you serve so faithfully, able to rescue you from the lions?"

Daniel answered, "My God sent his angel to shut the lions' mouths so that they would not hurt me, for I have been found innocent in his sight" (Daniel 6:20-22).

What a miracle!

What's It Mean?

This story is a powerful example of following the Lord faithfully in a very secular setting, no matter what the cost. Daniel knew that worshiping anyone else but God was out of the question, even if it endangered his life.

God never said following him would always be easy. But he still calls us to faithfully love and obey him. He has promised that he will always be with us (Deuteronomy 31:6) and he will strengthen us in our times of need (Isaiah 41:10).

All around you, the crowd might be going one way. But stand strong like Daniel and follow God, no matter what the cost!

Now What?

Along with Daniel 6, also read chapter 3—the similar story of Shadrach, Meshach, and Abednego miraculously surviving the fiery furnace after refusing to bow down to King Nebuchadnezzar's golden image. Then think about how God specifically wants you to follow him, no matter what the cost.

Did You Know?

If Daniel was a teenager when he was exiled to Babylon in 605 BC (Daniel 1:1-6), he would've been at least in his eighties when he was thrown into the lions' den.

MAY 29

We are not fighting against flesh-and-blood enemies,
but against evil rulers and authorities of the unseen
world, against mighty powers in this dark world,
and against evil spirits in the heavenly places.

EPHESIANS 6:12

AS HUMANS, WE ARE often bound by our five senses—sight, smell, hearing, taste, and touch. But God calls us to live by faith and believe in things that our senses can't detect. Occasionally, he'll give us a glimpse into that realm. Case in point: Daniel 7–12.

These chapters in the book of Daniel describe a series of remarkable visions that foretold the future rise and fall of various empires in striking detail. Amid these prophetic revelations, God unveiled to Daniel the constant—yet unseen—supernatural activity that accompanied these seismic world events. In Daniel 10:12-14, for instance, a magnificent angel visits Daniel with a stunning message:

> I have come in answer to your prayer. But for twenty-one days
> the spirit prince of the kingdom of Persia blocked my way. Then
> Michael, one of the archangels, came to help me, and I left him
> there with the spirit prince of the kingdom of Persia. Now I am here
> to explain what will happen to your people in the future, for this
> vision concerns a time yet to come.

Talk about a backstage pass to the spirit realm!

What's It Mean?

The instability of the world around him was greatly troubling to Daniel (Daniel 7:28; 8:27; 10:8-9) and his fellow exiles. God gave Daniel his visions to reassure his persecuted people that the Lord was still sovereignly in control.

He also wanted Daniel—and us—to know that there's far more to life than meets the eye. In addition to the physical element of life that we experience every day, there is an unseen spiritual dimension too.

Read today's verse again. Spiritual warfare is real. It was raging in Daniel's day, and it's still happening today. Our true enemy—the devil and his spiritual forces of evil—consistently wage war against God's saints.

But Satan is a defeated enemy. God—described as the "Ancient of Days" in Daniel 7:9 (ESV)—is enthroned in heaven, already triumphant. One day, Jesus, the "son of man" (Daniel 7:13), will return to earth to claim this victory and inaugurate his eternal Kingdom (Daniel 7:14). Until then, we fight our enemy with "the sword of the Spirit, which is the word of God" (Ephesians 6:17) and "pray in the Spirit at all times and on every occasion" (Ephesians 6:18).

This is how we win at spiritual warfare!

Now What?

Read Daniel 7–12 to see how God remarkably predicted world events in Daniel's day before fulfilling them in the centuries to come.

Did You Know?

Both angels specifically named in the Bible—Gabriel and Michael—are mentioned in Daniel.

MAY 30

*I desire steadfast love and not sacrifice, the knowledge
of God rather than burnt offerings.*

HOSEA 6:6, ESV

IN THE LATE EIGHTH century BC, Israel was in total chaos.

Within about thirty years, six kings ruled the northern kingdom as failed international treaties, court intrigue, and assassinations threw the nation into utter disarray. One king (Zechariah) was assassinated only six months after assuming the throne in 753 BC. His killer, Shallum, was murdered a month later. On and on it went.

Spiritually speaking, things were no better. God's people had completely abandoned the Lord. They had assimilated into the pagan Canaanite culture around them, worshiping false gods and practicing all sorts of wickedness. Yet they still tried to appease God through ceremonial adherence to the Mosaic law and animal sacrifice. It was shallow, heartless religion.

Finally, in 722 BC, the dreaded Assyrian Empire overwhelmed Israel, captured the capital city of Samaria, and deported most of the nation's inhabitants.

Sadly, the people of Judah were also heading down the same path of immorality. The southern kingdom would be overthrown by the Babylonians by 586 BC.

Into the midst of this political and spiritual anarchy, God graciously sent the prophet Hosea to speak his words to his rebellious people. One of the powerful messages he gave was the words of today's verse.

What's It Mean?

You might be thinking to yourself, *Wait, didn't God give Israel the Mosaic law, which included the sacrificial system?* Yes, he did! But the Old Testament covenant was always meant to point to something far greater.

The old covenant ultimately points to God's holiness, humanity's sin, and our need for a Savior. That Savior, of course, is Jesus Christ, who most gloriously reveals the steadfast love of God that today's verse mentions.

Through faith in Christ—not animal sacrifice—our sins are forever atoned for. Jesus called this the new covenant in his blood (Luke 22:20).

Even in the Old Testament, God never wanted the end result to simply be thousands of slaughtered sacrificial bulls and goats. That's shallow, heartless religion. He wanted his people to look forward to the redemption that the sacrifices pointed toward.

God wants our hearts, not religious conformity. He wants us to truly know him and seek him, not just mindlessly follow a bunch of liturgical rules and regulations. He wants us to experience his steadfast love through the incredible, redemptive work of Christ!

Now What?

Prayerfully assess your daily spiritual practices to make sure they are being done out of love for God, not ritual.

Did You Know?

Jesus quoted today's verse on several occasions to condemn the hypocritical religious leaders of his day (Matthew 9:13; 12:7; Mark 12:33).

MAY 31

The day of the LORD is great and very awesome; who can endure it?

JOEL 2:11, ESV

CATACLYSMIC PESTILENCES DON'T only happen in biblical times!

In 1874, the skies grew dark over various parts of America's Great Plains, as trillions of locusts descended from the north. The swarm—which covered an estimated area 1,800 miles long and 110 miles wide—devastated crops and forced many wishful homesteaders to return east.

Of course, the Bible contains its fair share of stories about catastrophic events—the most famous of which were the ten plagues of Egypt in Exodus chapters 7–12. But did you know that the Old Testament book of Joel focuses on a destructive locust invasion too? This fascinating minor prophetic book—only three chapters long—describes this unique natural phenomenon as a way to warn God's people, Israel, about the coming "day of the LORD" (see today's verse).

Was the locust invasion that Joel referred to in chapter 1 an actual historical event or a metaphorical device the prophet was using to illustrate coming destruction if his readers didn't repent? Biblical scholars have been debating that for centuries.

What's clear is the message he wanted to convey.

What's It Mean?

Depending on the context, Joel's—and the rest of Scripture's—references to "the day of the LORD" can mean a coming day of judgment for God's wicked enemies, a time of divine blessing, or future salvation for God's redeemed people.

God's message through Joel was an exhortation to his wayward people. "Turn to me now, while there is time. Give me your hearts," he told them (Joel 2:12). Later, God promised one day to "pour out [his] Spirit upon all people" (Joel 2:28). God's heart is clearly to bless, love, and forgive. "He is eager to relent and not punish" (Joel 2:13).

Israel had turned away from the Lord. If they didn't repent, judgment would overwhelm them like a swarm of devouring locusts. But God's forgiveness was available.

That message is true for us today, too. The day of the Lord is coming. For those who reject Christ, that day will be one of terrible judgment. For the righteous, it will begin a time of eternal blessings in God's presence.

Turn to the Lord while there is still time!

Now What?
Look up the other references to the "day of the Lord" outside Joel: Isaiah 13:6, 9; Jeremiah 46:10; Ezekiel 13:5 and 30:3; Amos 5:18-20; Obadiah 15; Zephaniah 1:7, 14; and Malachi 4:5.

Did You Know?
Laura Ingalls Wilder, author of the famous Little House on the Prairie series, describes the 1870s Rocky Mountain locust invasion in her book, *On the Banks of Plum Creek.*

JUNE 1

I will bring my exiled people of Israel back from distant lands, and they will rebuild their ruined cities and live in them again.

AMOS 9:14

IMAGINE THIS: ONE DAY you're overseeing livestock and tending sycamore-fig trees in a small, hillside town. The days are peaceful and quiet—well, as quiet as possible with the bleating of all those sheep—and your life keeps rolling along as usual.

Suddenly, God calls you to boldly proclaim a shocking message of future judgment to your countrymen who have rebelled against the Lord. Just like that, you have officially become a prophet of God.

Welcome to Amos's world!

Amos lived in the eighth century BC, during a brief period of prosperity for Israel and Judah. Israel viewed its wealth and blessings as a sign of divine favor. But this wasn't the case.

Israel's surface-level religion and adherence to Temple worship ceremonies (Amos 4:4-5) betrayed a moral corruption nationwide within the people's hearts. Israel had ignored the prophets (2:12), mistreated the poor (2:6-7), flaunted injustice (5:10-12), committed sexual immorality (2:7), and practiced forms of syncretism (combining different religions) and outright idolatry (8:14).

"Hate evil and love what is good; turn your courts into true halls of justice. Perhaps even yet the LORD God of Heaven's Armies will have mercy on the remnant of his people," Amos told the people (5:15). With many other words, he implored them to turn back to God.

But Israel paid no attention. Within a few decades, the Assyrian Empire destroyed Samaria, Israel's capital city, and conquered the northern kingdom (in 722 BC).

What's It Mean?

The book of Amos is a sad reminder of the effects of sin. Willful rebellion against God brings judgment.

But even so, the book ends on a note of glorious hope. In the last five verses, Amos describes God's beautiful promise to "restore the fallen house of David" (9:11) and "firmly plant them there in their own land. They will never again be uprooted from the land I have given them" (9:15). (Also see today's verse.) There are unspoken hints here of the Messiah, Jesus Christ. All people, including Israel, must trust in him to receive God's salvation.

Now think about your life. Are you prospering? Don't be lulled to sleep by worldly blessings. They are not automatic signs of spiritual favor with the Lord. God requires repentance and faith in his Son, the perfect Sin-Bearer.

Eschew superficial religion. And above all, follow the Messiah!

Now What?

Read the book of Amos. It's an often-forgotten treasure!

Did You Know?

- Amos was a contemporary of prophets such as Jonah and Hosea, and quite possibly Isaiah and Micah also.

306

JUNE 2

The day of the LORD is near upon all the nations. As you have done,
it shall be done to you; your deeds shall return on your own head.

OBADIAH 1:15, ESV

THINK ABOUT YOUR COUSINS. What are they like? You probably have
some really cool cousins that you enjoy hanging out with and some really
wacky ones that make family gatherings, uh, awkward.

As a nation, ancient Judah had cousins, too. One of them was Edom.
The Edomites were descendants of Jacob's brother, Esau (Genesis 36).

Historically, there was constant strife between the Jews and Edomites.
The worst offense came in 586 BC, when Edom showed no pity toward
Judah during the Babylonian's destruction of Jerusalem and deportation of
its citizens. The short book of Obadiah, in fact, is devoted to a prophecy of
judgment against Edom for these atrocities.

According to Obadiah, the Edomites "rejoiced when the people of
Judah suffered such misfortune" (verse 12) and "plundered the land of
Israel" (verse 13). They even killed some refugees who were trying to escape
and possibly sold others into the slave trade (verse 14; Amos 1:6, 9).

As a result, God judged the Edomites. In 553 BC, the Babylonians
marched against them, fulfilling Obadiah 7: "All your allies . . . will help to
chase you from your land."

What's It Mean?

In Judah's greatest hour of need, Edom had a chance to extend a compassionate hand. Instead, it resorted to vindictiveness based on centuries of
conflict, hatred, and rivalry.

Today's verse was spoken as a warning to Edom to stop persecuting
Judah. But the message still rings true today.

God is just in all his judgments. He never punishes where there is no
sin. Nor does he reward where there is no righteousness.

A day is coming when God will judge the wicked and the righteous for
their deeds (Ecclesiastes 3:17; Matthew 16:27; 2 Corinthians 5:10; Romans

2:6-11). Ultimately, a Christian's righteousness doesn't come from works, but from the atoning work of Jesus Christ on our behalf. Through repentance and faith in him, we can be saved. But good works matter, in the sense of showing that a believer's faith is living and active and that our love for God is real (James 2:14-26).

Remember, God will judge everyone according to what they've done. Those who have been covered in Christ's righteousness have no reason to worry. Those who live godlessly like the Edomites, treating others with contempt, have much to fear.

Now What?
Look up Deuteronomy 23:7 to see how God wanted Israel to treat Edom.

Did You Know?
Ancient Edom is now part of present-day Jordan.

JUNE 3

I knew that you are a merciful and compassionate God, slow to get angry and filled with unfailing love. You are eager to turn back from destroying people.

JONAH 4:2

TODAY'S DEVOTION IS ABOUT big fish and repenting.

No, this isn't to correct you for that time you hooked a big one at the lake during catch-and-release season and stealthily kept it for dinner. That's for you and the local Fish and Wildlife Department to work out.

We're talking about the book of Jonah!

Jonah was a prophet in Israel during the eighth century BC, when Assyria was the world's dominant superpower. So Jonah must have been shocked when God told him to go northeast to Nineveh, one of Assyria's chief cities, and announce God's judgment against its wicked people (Jonah 1:2).

Instead, Jonah disobeyed God and boarded a ship headed west toward Tarshish. But God sent a huge storm, and only when the sailors threw Jonah overboard did the squall subside. Then God miraculously sent a "great fish" (1:17) that swallowed Jonah and spit him on land three days later.

When Jonah arrived at Nineveh, he preached a powerful message of repentance to the people. Then he waited outside the city—almost giddily—for God's fiery judgment to descend from heaven.

But it never came. The Ninevites repented, and God showed compassion on them.

Jonah was incensed. "Didn't I say before I left home that you would do this, LORD?" he complained. "That is why I ran away to Tarshish! I knew that you are a merciful and compassionate God, slow to get angry and filled with unfailing love. You are eager to turn back from destroying people. Just kill me now, LORD! I'd rather be dead than alive if what I predicted will not happen" (4:2-3).

What's It Mean?

Jonah should have been thrilled with God's mercy on 120,000 people (4:11). Instead, he cruelly wanted to watch them burn. God chastised him for this sinful, callous attitude (4:4, 9-11).

Our posture toward others should mirror God's compassionate heart. There is no one "bad enough" to be outside the bounds of his love if they turn to Christ. We should actively seek the salvation of the lost because God "does not want anyone to be destroyed, but wants everyone to repent" (2 Peter 3:9; 1 Timothy 2:4). Colossians 3:12 instructs us to "put on . . . compassionate hearts" (ESV).

Don't be like Jonah! Seek ways to show God's compassion to others around you, especially unbelievers.

Now What?
Read the book of Jonah for a vivid look at God's mercy and compassion.

Did You Know?
Approximately thirty to sixty years after Jonah's visit to Nineveh, Assyria conquered Israel (722 BC).

JUNE 4

I am the LORD, the God of all the peoples of the world. Is anything too hard for me?

JEREMIAH 32:27

"NOW THE LORD HAD ARRANGED FOR a great fish to swallow Jonah. And Jonah was inside the fish for three days and three nights."

These are the well-known words of Jonah 1:17. Many people, though, refuse to take these words literally.

"How," they ask, "can a man live inside the belly of a great fish for three days? It's not humanly possible."

Because of the incredible nature of the story, they dismiss it as a fable. They use it as Exhibit A in a larger argument for why the Bible can't be trusted and Christianity is a bunch of hooey. Others tiptoe around the issue by saying, "Well, Jonah is simply an allegorical tale. He didn't literally get swallowed by a great fish."

But really, the debate is much bigger than one Old Testament story. Because once you start questioning validity or literalness of Jonah, you have to question other miracles, too. You quickly get a patchwork Bible devoid of power, fashioned by man's fallen imagination rather than God's holy inspiration (2 Timothy 3:16; 2 Peter 1:20-21).

So did Jonah exist? Did he really get swallowed by a great fish and live to prophesy in Nineveh?

Today's verse is a great place to find the answer.

What's It Mean?

Nothing is too hard for God. He is the Creator of the universe, including men like Jonah and big fish. If that's the case, why can't he also miraculously keep a man alive inside a fish for three days?

Why can't he flood the earth?

Why can't he part the sea?

Why can't he stop the sun?

Why can't he raise the dead?

He can do all these things and so much more. He can also awaken spiritually dead hearts and justify sinners like us through faith in his Son, Jesus Christ.

Attacks against biblical miracles like the one in Jonah are attacks against God. These kind of criticisms put more stock in human reasoning than in faith. But God clearly calls us to live by faith (Habakkuk 2:4; Romans 1:17; 2 Corinthians 5:7; Galatians 3:11; Hebrews 10:38 and 11:6).

So we come back to the argument: How can a man live inside the belly of a great fish for three days? It's not humanly possible.

No, it's not. But as Jesus said in Luke 18:27, "What is impossible for people is possible with God."

Do you believe?

Now What?
Pray for God's help whenever your faith wavers (Mark 9:24).

Did You Know?
Jesus (Matthew 12:41) and 2 Kings 14:23-25 treat Jonah as a real historical figure.

JUNE 5

Where is another God like you, who pardons the guilt of the
remnant, overlooking the sins of his special people?

MICAH 7:18

OLD TESTAMENT PROPHETS OFTEN acted like prosecuting attorneys.
Their job was to present God's case of divine justice against the accused—a
person, group, or nation who broke his holy laws. Such was the case with
Micah, a prophet to Israel and Judah in the eighth century BC.

Look at the legal language found in Micah 6:2:

Now, O mountains, listen to the LORD's complaint! He has a case
against his people. He will bring charges against Israel.

Israel and Judah's list of offenses was long and serious. Here is a sampling:

- idolatry (Micah 1:7; 5:13-14)
- greedy seizure of property (2:2)
- injustice and violence from rulers (3:1-3, 9-11)
- prevalence of false prophets (3:5-7)
- witchcraft and fortune-telling (5:12)
- dishonest gain (6:11)
- lies and deceit (6:12)

The people had broken their covenant relationship with God. They
were guilty as charged. Tragically, because of Israel and Judah's unrepen-
tance, divine judgment would soon overwhelm them in the forms of the
invading Assyrian and Babylonian armies.

What's It Mean?

Thankfully, the book of Micah—and the story of God's chosen people—
doesn't end with judgment. God doesn't work like that. Micah ends on a
beautiful note of hope:

Where is another God like you, who pardons the guilt of the remnant, overlooking the sins of his special people? You will not stay angry with your people forever, because you delight in showing unfailing love. Once again you will have compassion on us. You will trample our sins under your feet and throw them into the depths of the ocean! You will show us your faithfulness and unfailing love as you promised to our ancestors Abraham and Jacob long ago.

MICAH 7:18-20

The Jews experienced God's amazing love and compassion when he restored the exiles to Judea and fulfilled the prophecy of Micah 5:2 many years later.

Today, God's character remains the same. He still pardons guilt and overlooks the sins of his people. He still shows great compassion. He still tramples our sins and shows faithfulness and unfailing love.

How does the great Judge do this for guilty sinners? Through heaven's Mediator—"our Lord Jesus Christ, through whom we have now received reconciliation" (Romans 5:11, ESV).

Thanks to his Son, God rules in our favor when we trust in Christ. Case closed!

Now What?

Check out Micah 5:2—one of the Bible's most famous messianic prophecies.

Did You Know?

Micah was a contemporary of Isaiah's, and their respective "mountain of the Lord" oracles in Micah 4:1-5 and Isaiah 2:1-5 are nearly identical.

JUNE 6

The LORD is avenging and wrathful.

NAHUM 1:2, ESV

THE ASSYRIAN ARMY was once the most feared fighting force in the world. Better than any empire beforehand, Assyria perfected the art of ancient warfare—such as mass-producing iron weaponry, employing siege engines, and using archers and slingshot-carrying infantry as specialists—to crush its enemies.

Once a city's walls were breached, the Assyrians displayed their now-notorious cruelty. They often slaughtered all the inhabitants—men, women, and children—and impaled the civic leaders on stakes. Survivors were commonly deported elsewhere in the kingdom.

When Jonah preached a message of repentance to Nineveh, one of Assyria's chief cities, in the mid-eighth century BC, the people repented—for a time. But roughly a century later, the scene was quite different in Nineveh. The city was violent, idolatrous, and thoroughly evil. So God called another prophet, Nahum, to speak out against Nineveh. In fact, the entire book of Nahum is an oracle of God's looming judgment against the infamous Assyrian city.

"What sorrow awaits Nineveh, the city of murder and lies!" Nahum proclaimed (3:1).

What's It Mean?

Nahum isn't a pick-me-up book. There's no happy ending. But the prophet's most shocking words aren't those directed toward a godless city. They are about God himself.

Look at how Nahum 1 (ESV) describes God:

- The LORD is avenging and wrathful. (today's verse)
- The LORD will by no means clear the guilty. (verse 3)
- Who can stand before his indignation? Who can endure the heat of his anger? His wrath is poured out like fire, and the rocks are broken into pieces by him. (verse 6)

- With an overflowing flood he will make a complete end of the adversaries, and will pursue his enemies into darkness. (verse 8)

As fearsome as Assyria's warriors were during a siege, Nahum presents the Lord as infinitely more terrifying.

So which is he? Is he a God of love, mercy, and grace? Or a God of fiery anger, vengeance, and wrath?

Actually, he's both.

God will endlessly bless those who become his children through faith in Christ, but those who reject him will suffer his frightful, righteous wrath. In love, he has given us Scripture as a warning to turn from our sin before it's too late. All will be held accountable.

Don't reject God like Nineveh did and suffer his righteous wrath. Choose his love, mercy, and grace through Jesus!

Now What?

Read Romans 8:1 and remember this: true Christians never have to fear God's wrath.

Did You Know?

In 612 BC, Nahum's prophecy was fulfilled when Nineveh fell to a Babylonian-led alliance, spelling the end of the once-mighty Assyrian Empire.

JUNE 7

*Even though the flocks die in the fields, and the cattle
barns are empty, yet I will rejoice in the LORD!*

HABAKKUK 3:17-18

AMONG ALL THE OLD Testament prophets, poor Habakkuk often gets
overlooked. But cheer up, buddy! We're going to give you "The Prophet
with the Coolest Name" award. You deserve it.

Habakkuk, who probably lived during the mid-seventh century BC,
started his book crying out to God about the pervasive violence and injustice within Judah (Habakkuk 1:2-4). But when God responded that he
would use the Babylonians—"a cruel and violent people" (1:6)—to discipline Judah, Habakkuk was stunned. He couldn't fathom how a holy God
could use—at least in his mind—a more wicked empire to punish a less
wicked nation.

"You are pure and cannot stand the sight of evil," Habakkuk said. "Will
you wink at their treachery? Should you be silent while the wicked swallow
up people more righteous than they?" (1:13).

In other words, Habakkuk was wondering, *God, where is your justice?*

What's It Mean?

Look around you. Read the headlines. Injustice is everywhere. Maybe you
are personally experiencing it right now. It can be easy to ask questions
similar to Habakkuk's: *God, you are holy and good. How can you allow this to
happen?*

But within that question is an admittance of God's transcendence and
majesty. If he is holy (which he is), then he is fully qualified to sovereignly
rule his universe on a large scale (nations) and a small scale (individual lives)
in ways we might not always fully comprehend. That's okay. Our job is to
trust him.

Eventually, Habakkuk realized that. He started his book questioning
God's justice. He ended it praising God in the midst of uncertainty. Look at
his ending prayer:

Even though the fig trees have no blossoms, and there are no grapes on the vines; even though the olive crop fails, and the fields lie empty and barren; even though the flocks die in the fields, and the cattle barns are empty, yet I will rejoice in the LORD! I will be joyful in the God of my salvation!

HABAKKUK 3:17-18

What about you? Are there areas in your life where you question God's plan or his justice? Trust him even when you don't understand. Submit to him even when you can't comprehend. God will always do what is best for his children!

Now What?
If you are enduring hardship and uncertainty, pray through Habakkuk 3:17-18 and apply it to your situation.

Did You Know?
New Testament writers quoted Habakkuk 2:4—"the righteous shall live by his faith" (ESV)—three times (Romans 1:17; Galatians 3:11; and Hebrews 10:38) in various contexts. Check them out!

JUNE 8

*I will search with lanterns in Jerusalem's darkest corners to
punish those who sit complacent in their sins. They think
the LORD will do nothing to them, either good or bad.*

ZEPHANIAH 1:12

HAVE YOU EVER HAD a drink of something—fruit juice, hot chocolate,
eggnog, etc.—that tastes great ninety-five percent of the way, but the last
five percent is pretty gross because all the sediment settled to the bottom
and made it sludgy and distasteful?

Sadly, this is the picture that the prophet Zephaniah painted of the
rebellious nation of Judah shortly before God judged it through Babylon. As
a book, Zephaniah describes a nation that, overall, believed in God but had
become like the syrupy sludge at the bottom of a drink.

Look again at today's verse. The Hebrew term for our English word
complacent tells us much about Judah's spiritual state in Zephaniah's day. It
literally means "thickening on the dregs." This is a reference to the wine that
was commonly enjoyed during meals in ancient Israel.

What's It Mean?

Like old wine sitting undisturbed and fermenting at the bottom of a stone
jar, the Judeans had grown spiritually complacent. Their sin had led them
into a warped theology that God doesn't care one way or another about how
people act.

It seems the people were also resting on a false sense of security due to
their privileged Jewish ethnicity as descendants of Abraham—God's chosen
nation.

They had become spiritually motionless, like liquid dregs. They couldn't
fathom that God would judge them through pagan Babylon (Habakkuk
1:12-13).

Today, it's just as easy to fall into the trap of spiritual complacency.
Some people don't perceive God actively working in their lives, so they

319

wrongly assume he is aloof. They feel safe and secure in his love because of the spiritual heritage of their ancestors:

My parents are Christians.
I come from a good, religious family.
I was raised in church.

Does this describe your mentality? If so, beware! You are becoming complacent in fake religiosity, just like the ancient Judeans. You are placing your eternal hope in things that cannot save you. You are thickening on the dregs.

Second-generation Christians don't exist. God requires you to repent and believe in the name of his Son for salvation (Mark 1:15).

God is not distant. "The eyes of the LORD search the whole earth in order to strengthen those whose hearts are fully committed to him" (2 Chronicles 16:9). Don't drink the dregs of spiritual complacency. Enjoy the Lord in all his goodness!

Now What?

Zephaniah doesn't get enough love today. Read it!

Did You Know?

Zephaniah was a contemporary of fellow prophets Habakkuk, Nahum, and Jeremiah.

JUNE 9

Why are you living in luxurious houses while my house lies in ruins?

HAGGAI 1:4

PRIORITIES.

They are so important in life, but so often neglected. The Old Testament book of Haggai is about proper spiritual priorities.

In 538 BC, after overthrowing the Babylonian Empire a year earlier, Persian King Cyrus issued a remarkable decree that any Jew wishing to return to Jerusalem to rebuild God's Temple could do so.

Under Zerubbabel, a civic leader, and Joshua, the high priest, the initial returnees started rebuilding their lives, their homes, and God's Temple amid the rubble left behind by Babylon's former conquest. But intense persecution from local adversaries halted Temple reconstruction for sixteen years (Ezra 4). While the Temple languished in ruins, the people constructed nice houses to live in, replanted farms, and built vineyards.

They didn't have their priorities in order.

Through the prophet Haggai, God called the people to reprioritize their lives around him, not their personal desires of comfort and wealth. In 520 BC, God confronted Zerubbabel, Joshua, and the returned exiles with a piercing question: "Why are you living in luxurious houses while my house lies in ruins?" (today's verse).

"Now go up into the hills, bring down timber, and rebuild my house. Then I will take pleasure in it and be honored," God said (Haggai 1:8).

What's It Mean?

Prioritizing God and worshiping him were vital to Israel's well-being. The same is true for us today.

All Christians would agree that putting God first in our lives is crucial. But it's easier said than done. Sadly, we often allow selfishness, sinful desires, and life's busyness to crowd God out of the picture.

So how do we prioritize God? Here are some questions to consider:

- Are you spending daily time in prayer and God's Word?
- Do you faithfully worship at a gospel-centered church?
- Are you currently being discipled and/or discipling others?
- Do you actively use your spiritual gifts to serve others and build the church?
- Are you actively looking for ways to share your faith and fulfill the great commission?

This is not a complete list by any means. But it's a good start. Don't shelter yourself in a luxurious home of self-centeredness and allow God to remain homeless (so to speak) in your life. Give him the glory and honor—and priority—he deserves!

Now What?

Schedule your daily devotions at the beginning of each day. It's a great way to say, *God, before anything else distracts me, you come first.*

Did You Know?

The Jews completed the Temple construction in 516 BC. Herod the Great significantly expanded it and the surrounding complex starting about 20 BC.

JUNE 10

The LORD will go out to fight against those
nations, as he has fought in times past.

ZECHARIAH 14:3

WHERE CAN YOU GO in the Bible to find eight remarkable visions involving angelic horsemen, flying scrolls, and filthy priests; Messianic predictions; heavenly courtroom exchanges between God and Satan; apocalyptic prophecy; and the following verse that sounds as if it comes straight out of a zombie movie?

> The LORD will send a plague on all the nations that fought against Jerusalem. Their people will become like walking corpses, their flesh rotting away. Their eyes will rot in their sockets, and their tongues will rot in their mouths.

The book of Zechariah, of course!

(By the way, that incredibly creepy verse above is Zechariah 14:12!)

Zechariah was a prophet and priest who (alongside Haggai) ministered to the Jewish exiles that had returned to Jerusalem after Persian King Cyrus's favorable decree in 538 BC. Zechariah's book is one of the most unique works in Scripture, combining angelically assisted visions and prophetic oracles of judgment and salvation into one massive tour de force. It doesn't really have a unified theme, but rather bounces between important topics such as the returned exiles' need to remain faithful to God, the Lord's plan to bless Jerusalem in the future, the long-awaited coming of the Messiah, God's judgment against Israel's enemies, and his future reign over all nations.

So how could we summarize this wonderfully fascinating, diverse, and sometimes difficult book? Perhaps this way: the sovereign God of the universe loves and fights for his people.

What's It Mean?

In chapter 3, Zechariah sees a vision of Satan accusing Joshua, the high priest at that time, because of Joshua's "filthy clothes" (verse 4), a priestly disqualification. But God intervened, rebuking Satan and exchanging Joshua's soiled garments for "fine new clothes" (verse 4), signifying the imputation of God's righteousness.

God also decreed judgment on the nations that destroyed Judah (1:18-21), the religious "shepherds" who harassed his people (11:4-17), and any future nations who arose against Jerusalem (chapter 14). These are just a few of the examples Zechariah provides of God personally advocating for his chosen people.

Today, God still fights for his people. Romans 8:31 says, "If God is for us, who can ever be against us?" Talk about a beautiful rhetorical question!

If you are a believer, aren't you glad the Lord God Almighty goes to battle for you? His Son is your Advocate (1 John 2:1). The Divine Warrior is on your side!

Now What?

Read Romans 8:31-39 to glory in one of Scripture's great passages on the God who loves and fights for his people.

Did You Know?

The New Testament authors heavily quoted Zechariah, referencing many of its Messianic prophecies, such as Zechariah 9:9 (Matthew 21:15 and John 12:15), Zechariah 12:10 (John 19:37), and Zechariah 13:7 (Matthew 26:31 and Mark 14:27).

JUNE 11

You have wearied him by asking, "Where is the God of justice?"

MALACHI 2:17

WHEN WAS THE LAST time you were in a really long line? Perhaps it was during holiday shopping at the mall or waiting for an amusement park ride.

Inevitably, when forced to wait, some people start to complain. Kids start to get fidgety. Babies begin to cry. It's basically the end of the world.

As humans, we hate waiting. We want to get to our destination. Not in five minutes. Not in thirty seconds. NOW.

The book of Malachi—the Old Testament's final book—is about waiting. Malachi was a prophet who probably lived in the mid-fifth century BC. At that time, the Jews had been back in Palestine for nearly a century after their Babylonian exile.

In the post-exilic era, God had promised to restore Jerusalem and the Temple to great glory (Haggai 2:9; Zechariah 8:1-23), punish his people's tormentors (Zechariah 9), and send the Messiah (Zechariah 9:9-10). But none of that had transpired by Malachi's lifetime. The Temple was a shell of its former self, and so was Jerusalem. The people were Persian subjects—a conquered nation, without a Davidic king on the throne—and morale was low.

This affected many people's spiritual lives. Their love of God had grown cold. Their present reality was hindering their faith, and their struggles had warped their theology.

"Where," they asked, "is the God of justice?" (today's verse).

Malachi called them to repent and trust in God as they waited for his promises to be fulfilled.

What's It Mean?

The Jews from Malachi's day until Christ's birth approximately four hundred years later had to live by faith, not by sight. For those who considered only what their eyes could see, it's no wonder they easily became discouraged and spiritually derailed.

Today is no different. We live in troubling times, just like the ancient Jews of Malachi's era. We will face many hardships. We must rely on more than what we see and physically experience in this difficult life. We must live by faith as we wait for Jesus' return.

Many fell away in Malachi's day. But the waiting wasn't for naught. It was all part of God's sovereign plan to introduce his Son, the Redeemer, at the perfect time (Galatians 4:4-5).

One day, Jesus will return again once and for all, as God has promised. Don't lose faith! Don't fall away! The wait can be challenging. But live by faith, even when it's hard not to live by sight.

The God of justice will be faithful to his promises.

Now What?

Read the book of Malachi for a fascinating look at God's last prophetic word in Old Testament times until the coming of Christ.

Did You Know?

In Hebrew, Malachi means "my messenger."

JUNE 12

*When the fullness of time had come, God sent forth his
Son, born of woman, born under the law, to redeem those who
were under the law, so that we might receive adoption as sons.*

GALATIANS 4:4-5, ESV

SILENCE.

Years and years of deafening silence.

The Jews already had been waiting a long time for God's promised
Messiah. Then the last of the great Old Testament prophecies had ceased
and the final Old Testament authors had laid down their ink-stained quills.
Now, it appeared, the seemingly endless wait would continue without the
benefit of hearing God's voice.

Today, we call this silent era the "intertestamental period"—a roughly
four-hundred-year span between the Old and New Testaments. God had
promised a great Deliverer as far back as the Garden of Eden (Genesis
3:15). Moses predicted that God would "raise up for you a prophet like
me" (Deuteronomy 18:15). Old Testament saints such as David, Isaiah,
Jeremiah, and many others proclaimed the same message: one day, God
would send his Anointed One to save his people.

But when? Ever since the Assyrians and Babylonians had conquered
the northern and southern kingdoms of Israel and Judah, respectively, in
722 and 586 BC, the Jews had been languishing under the rule of foreign
empires—the Persians, Greeks, Syrians, and finally the Romans. If ever a
people needed hope, it was the Jews.

So God's people waited . . . and waited . . . and waited. They had to
be wondering, Will God ever fulfill his promise? Will the Messiah ever
come?

What's It Mean?

Oh yes, the Savior was coming. The Lord God Almighty always keeps his
promises. But he does not keep time like we do. He sees eternity all at once.
"A day is like a thousand years to the Lord, and a thousand years is like

a day. The Lord isn't really being slow about his promise, as some people think" (2 Peter 3:8-9).

At just the right time, when the human stage was perfectly set according to God's sovereign plan, the Messiah would come. He would be like nothing anyone expected and more than anyone could have hoped for. He would be God made flesh. And the silence of centuries would be shattered by the chorus of heavenly hosts.

Now What?

Find a study Bible with notes on the intertestamental period, and read more about this fascinating era of history that led up to Christ's birth.

Did You Know?

Malachi is the last book of the Old Testament. But chronologically speaking, some biblical scholars believe that Nehemiah was the last Old Testament book written (no earlier than 423 BC.).

JUNE 13

*Repent of your sins and turn to God, for
the Kingdom of Heaven is near.*

MATTHEW 3:2

PEOPLE FLOCKED INTO THE wilderness in droves.

By the dozens, hundreds, perhaps even the thousands, they left their homes all over the Judean countryside and even Jerusalem to see him—the extraordinary man in the scratchy camel-hair outfit.

"Let's go! He's preaching and baptizing at the Jordan River again! Rumor has it he even eats locusts dipped in honey!"

His name was John, son of Zechariah, the priest. John proclaimed God's message fearlessly, like no one they had ever heard before. God hadn't spoken through a prophet since the days of Malachi, more than four hundred years earlier. Clearly God was speaking through John. But something else was on people's minds: Could this be the long-awaited *Mashiach*—God's promised Messiah from the Davidic kingly line?

No. John admitted as much. But he was the forerunner to the Messiah, announcing his arrival (Matthew 3:3; Isaiah 40:3).

"Repent of your sins and turn to God," John declared, "for the Kingdom of Heaven is near" (today's verse).

What's It Mean?

John the Baptist's words sparked much anticipation and confusion among his original audience. At that time, the Jews had been living under foreign rule for more than six hundred years. They were certainly ready for the Kingdom of Heaven to break through in the form of a political/military messiah who would crush their Roman overlords and restore the nation of Israel.

But the Kingdom of Heaven has nothing to do with politics, armies, or earthly matters at all. That's why John said, "Repent of your sins and turn to God"—and not "Take up your swords and spears"—"for the Kingdom of Heaven is near."

The Kingdom of Heaven is not a physical kingdom, but a spiritual one. The Kingdom of Heaven—far greater than any earthly domain—is a matter of the Holy Spirit's work as he regenerates sinful human hearts to saving faith. To be part of the Kingdom of Heaven, you must repent of your sins and turn to God by trusting in the Savior he provided—his Son, Jesus Christ.

As John was ministering in the wilderness one day, he saw Jesus coming toward him. "Look!" he said. "The Lamb of God who takes away the sin of the world!" (John 1:29). God's Son, the true Messiah, gives us access to the Kingdom of Heaven!

Now What?

Jesus referenced the "Kingdom of Heaven" many times in many different contexts. Read through the Gospel of Matthew to find them!

Did You Know?

- John the Baptist was eventually arrested and beheaded by King Herod (Matthew 14:1-12; Mark 6:14-29).

JUNE 14

Have you forgotten that when we were joined with Christ
Jesus in baptism, we joined him in his death?

ROMANS 6:3

JOHN THE BAPTIST COULDN'T believe his ears.

He had been baptizing many people at the Jordan River to prepare their hearts for God's long-awaited Messiah. Now, Jesus was standing before him, and much to John's surprise, the Savior was asking to be baptized.

"I am the one who needs to be baptized by you," John said, "so why are you coming to me?"

"It should be done," Jesus replied, "for we must carry out all that God requires."

As Jesus came out of the water, God's Spirit descended on him "like a dove" and God spoke: "This is my dearly loved Son, who brings me great joy" (Matthew 3:13-17).

What's It Mean?

Jesus' baptism inaugurated his earthly ministry; authenticated his eternal, triune relationship with the Father and Spirit; and identified him (though he was holy) with sinners he came to save. It also gave all future Christians a pattern to follow. In the great commission before his ascension, Jesus commanded baptism for all believers: "Go and make disciples of all the nations, baptizing them in the name of the Father and the Son and the Holy Spirit" (Matthew 28:19).

Baptism is one of two sacraments for Christians today. (The other is the Lord's Supper, which we'll cover in the August 6 devotion.) A sacrament is a religious ritual that symbolizes a spiritual truth. Neither baptism nor the Lord's Supper is necessary for salvation, but both are important parts of every Christian's life. Baptism is a one-time event that should be done as a public profession of faith after you have trusted in Christ. (See the "Did You Know?" section below.)

As Romans 6:3-4 says, baptism is a visual representation of Jesus' death and resurrection on our behalf. Just as Jesus went down into the tomb and was raised up three days later, a person being baptized goes down into the water and is raised up out of it to show their union with him. Baptism also symbolizes the new creation we are in Christ, as he forgives our sins and spiritually cleanses us before God (1 Peter 3:21).

Baptism is a beautiful representation of the gospel. All believers should be baptized in obedience to God's Son!

Now What?

If you are a follower of Jesus and haven't been baptized, ask your parents about doing so.

Did You Know?

The New Testament apostles always connected baptism with faith and repentance, which is only possible for those who truly understand the gospel (Acts 2:37-38; 8:12; 10:46-48; 18:8; and 22:16).

JUNE 15

*Because one person disobeyed God, many became sinners. But because
one other person obeyed God, many will be made righteous.*

ROMANS 5:19

THE SUN BLAZED OVERHEAD. The wilderness was barren of food and
human interaction. For forty days, Jesus was alone in the desert. Only God's
Spirit and prayer sustained him.

Then he heard a voice. It offered a sinister suggestion, almost as if a
snake had slowly slithered up and started whispering in his ear. "If you are
the Son of God, tell these stones to become loaves of bread" (Matthew 4:3).

The voice was Satan's. He was no longer in serpentine form, as he had
been in the Garden of Eden. But make no mistake: his purposes were just
as diabolical. As he tempted Jesus three times, the devil hoped to swiftly
destroy God's plan of salvation for mankind.

Jesus—fully God and fully man—was hungry and physically weak. But
he knew his purpose, and he wasn't about to let Satan ruin what the Son,
the Father, and the Spirit had planned together in eternity past to save us.

"Get out of here, Satan!" Jesus commanded. "For the Scriptures say,
'You must worship the LORD your God and serve only him'" (Matthew
4:10).

Then Satan fled. Jesus had won.

What's It Mean?

When you read about Jesus' temptations, do you see any parallels to
Satan's temptations of Adam and Eve in the Garden of Eden? You should!
The Gospel writers wanted you to notice some similarities—and a major
difference.

Where Adam failed, Jesus prevailed! The apostle Paul talks about this
in Romans 5 (see today's verse). God provided his Son to be "the better
Adam"—to fulfill God's law where Adam fell short. Because Jesus is a High
Priest "who in every respect has been tempted as we are, yet without sin"
(Hebrews 4:15, ESV), he was able to perfectly represent us as our sin-sacrifice.

Also, by enduring various temptations like we do—but remaining holy—Jesus "understands our weaknesses" (Hebrews 4:15). We have a sympathetic Savior who can relate to the difficulties of the human experience.

Satan's sneaky attempts to ensnare Jesus failed. Our Savior triumphed. Nothing can stop God's saving plan for us in Christ!

Now What?

If you read about Christ's temptations, you'll notice how he always answered Satan by quoting Scripture. Make Bible memorization a regular part of your life. Psalm 119:11 says, "I have hidden your word in my heart, that I might not sin against you."

Did You Know?

Matthew 4:2 said Jesus "fasted" before his temptations. Biblical fasting is always for the purpose of prayerfully seeking God's will. Jesus likely was preparing himself spiritually for the extreme hardships of his redemptive ministry.

JUNE 16

I tell you the truth, unless you are born again,
you cannot see the Kingdom of God.

JOHN 3:3

QUIZ TIME!

In John 3:1-2, we read the following:

There was a man named Nicodemus, a Jewish religious leader who was a Pharisee. After dark one evening, he came to speak with Jesus.

So here's the quiz: Why does Scripture make a point of telling us that Nicodemus came to Jesus "after dark"? Was it because Nicodemus

A. had worked a long day at the Pharisee legalism factory?
B. wanted to catch a 9 p.m. movie with Jesus at the Galilean Multiplex?
C. wanted to play oil lamp tag—the ancient precursor to flashlight tag?

Correct answer: None of the above!

Nicodemus was a member of the Sanhedrin, the seventy-one-member religious ruling body of the Jews. Most of the Sanhedrin vehemently opposed Jesus. But not Nicodemus. Jesus' powerful teaching and miracles had stirred his soul. So he sought an audience with Jesus—but privately, so none of his peers would know.

"Rabbi," Nicodemus said, "we all know that God has sent you to teach us. Your miraculous signs are evidence that God is with you."

Jesus cut through the polite chitchat. "I tell you the truth," he said, "unless you are born again, you cannot see the Kingdom of God."

"What do you mean?" Nicodemus replied, stunned. "How can an old man go back into his mother's womb and be born again?" (See the full story in John 3:1-21.)

What's It Mean?

Being "born again" has nothing to do with physical birth. To enter heaven ("the Kingdom of God"), we need a spiritual rebirth. The Bible also refers to being "born again" as "regeneration" (Titus 3:5, ESV). It's a miraculous heart transformation every human desperately needs.

But we have a problem. Because of our inherited guilt from Adam and indwelling sin, Ephesians 2 says we were born spiritually "dead" (verse 1) and "subject to God's anger" (verse 3). Dead people can't resuscitate their own lifeless hearts. Only one person can help people in such spiritual destitution: God himself!

In his great love and mercy, God sends his Spirit to radically transform dead, sinful hearts, awakening in his chosen people a recognition of sin, a desire to repent, and a heart to believe in Christ for salvation.

Just like human birth, spiritual rebirth is a gift from God!

Now What?

The apostle John, who wrote today's verse, had much to say about being born again. Read 1 John 2:29; 3:9; 4:7; 5:1; and 5:18.

Did You Know?

Scripture alludes to spiritual regeneration in the days of the Old Testament prophet Ezekiel, roughly six hundred years before Jesus' earthly ministry. Check out Ezekiel 11:19-20 and 36:25-27.

JUNE 17

He saved us, not because of works done by us in righteousness, but according to his own mercy, by the washing of regeneration and renewal of the Holy Spirit.

TITUS 3:5, ESV

WIND.

It's one of the most wonderful, mysterious forces in God's creation. We can't actually see wind; we can only see or feel its effects. It is without shape, size, or color.

But wind makes its presence known in obvious ways when we look outside: tree limbs swaying to and fro, litter swirling down the street, a balding man's toupee threatening to fly away, etc. Wind delights us as we watch kites soar, and it wreaks destruction through hurricanes and tornadoes.

When Nicodemus, the Pharisee, visited Jesus at night, the Savior used wind to describe the mystery of regeneration. Here's what he said in John 3:5-8:

I assure you, no one can enter the Kingdom of God without being born of water and the Spirit. Humans can reproduce only human life, but the Holy Spirit gives birth to spiritual life. So don't be surprised when I say, "You must be born again." The wind blows wherever it wants. Just as you can hear the wind but can't tell where it comes from or where it is going, so you can't explain how people are born of the Spirit.

Because it's so important, we're spending a second day on the subject of regeneration, or being spiritually "born again."

What's It Mean?

Like wind, spiritual regeneration is an invisible, hard-to-describe occurrence. God beautifully works in human hearts in inexplicable, miraculous ways that are not fully comprehensible to us. But regeneration is real, and Scripture speaks of it often.

Regeneration is a one-time, life-changing event, initiated by God, to bring a spiritually dead person to life through Christ. God's sovereign initiative here is crucial to understand. Human faith is necessary for salvation (Hebrews 11:6), but we can't manufacture faith on our own because of our sinful nature. It is God who awakens our spiritually dead hearts to see our great need for a Savior, repent, and receive the good news of Jesus. This is what it means to be "born again." At that point, we respond in faith and repentance toward Christ.

The wind of God's gracious regeneration is blowing. Have you answered?

Now What?

Prayerfully meditate on the following verses on regeneration: Ezekiel 36:26-27; John 1:12-13; Colossians 2:13; James 1:18; and 1 Peter 1:3.

Did You Know?

Carefully read Ephesians 2:8-9. God's "gift" is not only the grace and salvation he offers, but the *faith* he produces in you—through spiritual regeneration—to *receive* the gift!

JUNE 18

God so loved the world, that he gave his only Son, that whoever believes in him should not perish but have eternal life.

JOHN 3:16, ESV

YOU SEE IT ON T-shirts, coffee mugs, and wall art. You see it on bumper stickers, billboards, and handheld signs at major sporting events.

It's probably the most well-known verse in Scripture, and certainly one of the best summaries of the gospel: John 3:16.

This verse has become so ubiquitous that we sometimes forget the context. Jesus spoke the words of John 3:16 as he was teaching Nicodemus, the Pharisee, what it truly means to be "born again" and enter God's Kingdom. But this beautiful verse was only part of Jesus' overall message about important themes of darkness, light, judgment, and salvation in John 3:16-21.

Let's take a closer look at this important passage.

What's It Mean?

All Christians love John 3:16. We love it because it focuses on God's gracious initiative, the provision of Jesus, and eternal life. We should always rejoice in these wonderful biblical truths.

But there is also an ominous undertone to John 3:16. Did you notice it? It's in the word "perish." The Father gave up his Son to save us from a terrible fate: the eternal destruction of our souls in hell. This is the just punishment for anyone who doesn't repent and believe in Christ, God's provided sacrifice for sins.

Look at Jesus' words in John 3:17-19:

God sent his Son into the world not to judge the world, but to save the world through him. There is no judgment against anyone who believes in him. But anyone who does not believe in him has already been judged for not believing in God's one and only Son. And the judgment is based on this fact: God's light came into the world, but people loved the darkness more than the light, for their actions were evil.

339

Jesus' first coming was to bring salvation through his atoning work on the cross and resurrection. But as he alludes to here, his future second coming will be for judgment.

We dare not spurn God's loving invitation to salvation. Judgment is coming. Those who have trusted in Christ have no reason to fear. Their eternal reward is beautifully secure! But those who "[do] not believe in him" and have "loved the darkness more than the light" will be condemned.

Now What?
Among Scripture's many references to future judgment, check out the following: Matthew 25:31-46; 1 Corinthians 4:5; and Revelation 20:11-15.

Did You Know?
The original New Testament Greek word for *perish* is *apollymi*, which means "to be destroyed."

JUNE 19

They left their nets at once and followed him.

MATTHEW 4:20

YOU'VE LIKELY HEARD the stories of Jesus calling some of his first disciples.

Peter, Andrew, James, and John were all fishermen who worked in the Sea of Galilee. Yet when Jesus uttered his famous words, "Follow me, and I will make you fishers of men" (Matthew 4:19, ESV), the two sets of brothers instantly dropped everything and followed the Messiah. Likewise, Matthew the tax collector (Matthew 9:9-13) and Philip (John 1:43-45) followed Jesus right away.

The immediacy of these responses is striking. However, there was one man who hesitated when Jesus called.

Philip was so excited about his encounter with Jesus, he went to tell his friend, Nathanael. "We have found the very person Moses and the prophets wrote about!" Philip said. "His name is Jesus, the son of Joseph from Nazareth."

"Nazareth!" Nathanael exclaimed. "Can anything good come from Nazareth?" (John 1:45-46).

Skepticism and sarcasm were dripping from Nathanael's words. Yet Philip persisted, and when Nathanael finally met Jesus, the Savior told Nathanael things that only the omniscient Son of God could know. Nathanael quickly realized he had been sinfully presumptuous.

"Rabbi," he confessed, "you are the Son of God—the King of Israel!" (verse 49).

What's It Mean?

When called, many of Jesus' twelve disciples followed him immediately. Nathanael, however, was slower to follow. Fortunately, though, faith overcame doubt.

What about you? When God calls you for his purposes, what's your response? Do you waver in skepticism and unbelief, or are you willing to drop everything and follow him in complete submission?

Perhaps God is calling you right now—through this book and elsewhere in your life. Are you a follower of Jesus? If not, the first step of answering God's call, like Nathanael, is confessing belief about who his Son really is (Romans 10:9-10).

If you have trusted in Jesus for the forgiveness of your sins, how is God calling you to actively obey him now? What is he calling you to do?

Jesus won't call you face-to-face like he did with the original twelve disciples. Instead, God now calls us through his Spirit working in our hearts. When God calls, don't waver or doubt—leave your nets at once, so to speak, and follow him!

Now What?

Read about Jesus' calling of the disciples in Matthew 4:18-22 and 9:9-13; Luke 5:1-11; and John 1:35-51.

Did You Know?

Many biblical scholars believe Nathanael was also called Bartholomew in the synoptic gospels' list of disciples (Matthew 10:2-4; Mark 3:16-18; and Luke 6:13-16).

JUNE 20

God blesses those whose hearts are pure, for they will see God.

MATTHEW 5:8

THOUSANDS OF YEARS BEFORE the television, Internet, social media, and everything else that drives news and popularity, Jesus was A BIG DEAL. Huge crowds followed him as he traveled throughout Galilee proclaiming the gospel and healing people.

Seeing the multitudes, he climbed a mountainside and taught the people in what we call "The Sermon on the Mount" (Matthew 5–7). Jesus began with a series of blessings we refer to as "The Beatitudes" (from the Latin word *beatus*, meaning "blessed" or "happy"), featuring nine types of people whom God blesses. Today's verse—"God blesses those whose hearts are pure"—is one example.

The Beatitudes, like the rest of the Sermon on the Mount, were unlike anything the crowds had ever heard.

What's It Mean?

Just like John the Baptist before him, Jesus came declaring, "Repent of your sins and turn to God, for the Kingdom of Heaven is near" (Matthew 4:17). But quite frankly, his original audience didn't know how to do that—or that they even *needed* to. The hard-hearted, hypocritical Pharisees and religious leaders of first-century Palestine had taught the people for centuries that God's blessings were for (1) Abraham's descendants and (2) scrupulous adherents to the Old Testament law and traditions of the Jewish elders.

However, a right relationship with God is not a matter of religious observances, but a matter of the heart. So Jesus taught the people what true "blessedness" really looks like.

He taught them that God blesses those whose hearts are pure (today's verse). He told them God blesses those who "mourn" over their sin (Matthew 5:4), show humility before God (verse 5), "hunger and thirst for justice" (verse 6), are "merciful" (verse 7), and so on.

Of course, no one can earn salvation—or a "blessed" relationship with

God—through these actions and traits. Rather, these things are indicative of people whose hearts have already been changed by God's Spirit and are now part of his Kingdom—enjoying and seeking his blessings.

What is your relationship with God like? Are you seeking his blessings through external performance? If so, you'll be nothing more than a hypocritical Pharisee. But if you trust in Christ for your righteousness and seek to honor God with a "Beatitude heart," you will be blessed!

Now What?

Read through the Beatitudes in Matthew 5:1-12 and pray about the areas you need to grow in.

Did You Know?

Luke 6:17-49 bears many similarities to the Sermon on the Mount. Biblical scholars, who sometimes refer to this as the Sermon on the Plain, are divided regarding whether it describes the same event featured in Matthew 5–7.

JUNE 21

*Let your good deeds shine out for all to see, so that
everyone will praise your heavenly Father.*

MATTHEW 5:16

SALT AND LIGHT.

We take them for granted every day. Whenever we need more salt or light,
we can simply purchase extra quantities at our local stores or flip a switch.

This wasn't the case in ancient times. Back then, salt and light were
precious commodities. Salt was used to preserve food. It was so valuable, in
fact, it was sometimes used as currency.

Likewise, light was extremely valuable and harder to come by. Without
electricity, people relied on oil lamps, torches, and lanterns to illuminate
their lives and chase away the darkness once the sun went down.

In the Sermon on the Mount, Jesus famously used the metaphors of salt
and light to teach an important lesson:

> You are the salt of the earth. But what good is salt if it has lost
> its flavor? Can you make it salty again? It will be thrown out and
> trampled underfoot as worthless. You are the light of the world—
> like a city on a hilltop that cannot be hidden. No one lights a lamp
> and then puts it under a basket. Instead, a lamp is placed on a stand,
> where it gives light to everyone in the house. In the same way, let
> your good deeds shine out for all to see, so that everyone will praise
> your heavenly Father. (Matthew 5:13-16)

What's It Mean?

Jesus' point is clear: just like salt preserves and flavors food, Christians
preserve and flavor a lost, fallen world by their positive, godly influence.
Similarly, Christians shine the gospel's light into a world darkened by sin.

But did you notice how Jesus ends his analogy? When believers are salt
and light, it brings praise to God. The question is how, exactly, do our good
deeds do this?

First and foremost, as his image-bearers, we were created to worship and glorify God. When we live righteously, we fulfill our chief purpose on earth.

Our good works can also help others. This fulfills the second greatest commandment to love our neighbors (Mark 12:31), which also honors God!

Additionally, the Holy Spirit can use our good deeds to stir an unbeliever to saving faith in Jesus. What a joy it would be if, through your faithful obedience to the Lord, a nonbeliever becomes a new creation in Christ!

Be salt and light for the glory of God!

Now What?
To be salt and light, get out and serve others somewhere in your church or community.

Did You Know?
Ancient Roman soldiers sometimes received their wages in salt.

JUNE 22

Never take revenge. Leave that to the righteous anger of God.

ROMANS 12:19

DURING THE SERMON ON the Mount, Jesus told his audience, "You have heard the law that says the punishment must match the injury: 'An eye for an eye, and a tooth for a tooth.' But I say, do not resist an evil person! If someone slaps you on the right cheek, offer the other cheek also" (Matthew 5:38-39).

Many people have misunderstood this topic. When Jesus made the "eye for an eye" reference, he was quoting several Old Testament passages (Exodus 21:24; Leviticus 24:20; and Deuteronomy 19:21). God never intended those laws to allow an Israelite to exact personal revenge. Rather, "eye for an eye" was a standard for Israel's judges to apply in legal proceedings to ensure that the punishment fit the crime.

Jesus was correctly interpreting Old Testament law. Because he knows the human heart is weak and prone to sinful anger and revenge, he was also helping us understand ourselves better!

What's It Mean?

We get offended easily, don't we? Sometimes, we get bent out of shape over the smallest things, such as a funny look or a misinterpreted conversation. Other times, we can be legitimately hurt by incredible cruelty from others. Either way, our sinful hearts often crave revenge.

Scripture, though, calls us to be different. When hurt or angered, our response should be to love and forgive. Vengeance is God's domain, not ours. Why? Because God's vengeance is never vindictive or sinful like ours, but is always righteous and governed by his holy character.

God is both graciously loving and justly wrathful. A day is coming when he will punish the wicked for their evil deeds. But this is not a day to gloat over, because God desires that all unbelievers repent (1 Timothy 2:3-4).

In Romans 12:14-21, the apostle Paul beautifully elaborates on Jesus'

Sermon on the Mount teaching on vengeance and loving your enemies. "Dear friends," he writes, "never take revenge. Leave that to the righteous anger of God" (today's verse).

The "eye for an eye" principle might be good for the courtroom, but not for your life! Rather, follow Paul's advice in Romans 12:18: "Do all that you can to live in peace with everyone."

Now What?

Read Romans 12:14-21 and ask God if there's someone you should forgive.

Did You Know?

When Jesus said "offer the other cheek" in his "eye for an eye" teaching, he was simply using hyperbole to make a point: don't return the insult. He certainly wasn't advocating that people take a beating without defending themselves.

JUNE 23

Love your enemies! Pray for those who persecute you!

MATTHEW 5:44

IMAGINE YOU ARE A JEW living in the first century AD.

From the time of Moses, your people have been taught, through Scripture, to be holy to the one true God by separating yourself from the surrounding nations. But you've also been taught by ungodly religious leaders to look down on anyone who is not a "true Israelite" in ethnicity or piety. As such, you've developed an unhealthy superiority complex.

You've also become angry and bitter. For six-hundred-plus years, your people have endured the harsh rule of foreign empires. You hate your current overlords, the Romans, and you dream about future Jewish independence.

Then a remarkable man named Jesus comes along, attracts huge crowds, and preaches an entirely new message:

> You have heard the law that says, "Love your neighbor" and hate your enemy. But I say, love your enemies! Pray for those who persecute you! In that way, you will be acting as true children of your Father in heaven.
>
> MATTHEW 5:43-45

Whoa! Mind blown!

What's It Mean?

Jesus' teaching was a radical new way of thinking for first-century Jews. The Old Testament never says, "Hate your enemy." But it seems somewhere along the way, the Jewish religious leaders had begun grossly misinterpreting certain passages (perhaps like Psalm 5:4-5) to condone bigotry and condescension in the name of law-keeping.

Jesus refuted this terrible error and presented a simple point: if you only love your friends, that's not particularly admirable. Even the wicked do that.

But if you show love to someone whom you're at odds with, then you've done something worthwhile.

But there's a greater truth here: when you love your enemy, you put the gospel on display. Because that is what God did for you.

You were once dead in your sins and transgressions (Ephesians 2:1). In fact, Romans 5:10 says you were actually God's enemy apart from Christ. That's bad—real bad.

Yet God stretched out hands of reconciliation from heaven. This incredible act of grace came at a great price. Do you see the nail scars in those hands? You were the enemy, but he suffered the cost.

If God did this for you while you were his enemy, how much more will he do for you when you are his child? And if God loved you like this while you were his enemy, how much more should you love and pray for those who mistreat you?

Now What?

Are you at odds with anyone? Pray for reconciliation. Then pursue it humbly.

Did You Know?

"Friendship with the world makes you an enemy of God" (James 4:4).

JUNE 24

Pray then like this: "Our Father in heaven, hallowed be your name."

MATTHEW 6:9, ESV

HAVE YOU TRIED STRIKING up a friendship with someone without ever speaking to them? No, of course not! That friendship would be doomed to failure. Communication is key to a healthy relationship.

It's the same in our relationship with God. Talking with God is called prayer. It isn't hard, yet we often don't do it enough, and sometimes we struggle with what to say.

Jesus knows all this, so he gave his listeners (and us) a prayer model that's known as "The Lord's Prayer":

> Pray then like this: "Our Father in heaven, hallowed be your name. Your kingdom come, your will be done, on earth as it is in heaven. Give us this day our daily bread, and forgive us our debts, as we also have forgiven our debtors. And lead us not into temptation, but deliver us from evil."

MATTHEW 6:9-13, ESV

What's It Mean?

Prayer is vital to the Christian life. For the next eight days, we're going to study prayer, starting with the Lord's Prayer. Let's take a closer look at it, phrase by phrase:

Our Father in heaven. As you pray, remember that you are approaching the Lord of heaven and earth. But rejoice that he is also a God who loves you intimately as your Father.

Hallowed be your name. Our prayers should always include praise and worship for God's "hallowed" (i.e., "holy" or "honored") name.

Your kingdom come, your will be done, on earth as it is in heaven. As God's image-bearers, we are to prayerfully seek how we can use our spiritual gifts to reflect Christ ("the Kingdom of Heaven") to others in this world.

351

Give us this day our daily bread. We should never take for granted God's gracious provision but rather acknowledge our daily dependence on him.

And forgive us our debts, as we also have forgiven our debtors. Confession and repentance are crucial parts of prayer (1 John 1:8-10), as well as asking God to help us love others well.

And lead us not into temptation, but deliver us from evil. Our battle is a spiritual one (Ephesians 6:12), so we should pray to that end!

Now What?

Memorize the Lord's Prayer to help your prayer life!

Did You Know?

The Lord's Prayer is a model and is not meant to be all-inclusive. It's perfectly fine to pray it when needed, but Jesus intended it to be used more as a pattern for prayer, rather than a daily script to be recited.

JUNE 25

When you pray, don't babble on and on as the Gentiles do.
They think their prayers are answered merely by repeating their
words again and again. Don't be like them, for your Father
knows exactly what you need even before you ask him!

MATTHEW 6:7-8

HAVE YOU EVER BEEN around a know-it-all?

This is someone who thinks they know something (or everything!) about everything, and they will be oh so happy to grace you with their astounding treasure trove of wisdom (even if, truthfully, their wisdom is neither astounding nor entirely wise).

There is Someone, though, who truly knows it all. By the capital S in Someone, you've probably guessed that we're talking about God. He possesses all wisdom, but unlike human know-it-alls, God never uses this understanding pridefully. His omniscience is governed by his holiness, meaning he always uses his wisdom justly, benevolently, and for the good of his children.

But as we continue our study of prayer, this presents an interesting question: If God knows everything, then why should you pray? The answer will greatly help inform your prayer life.

What's It Mean?

God is the eternal, omniscient Creator and Ruler of the universe. He has always existed and always will. There is nothing that escapes his knowledge, including the innermost thoughts of human hearts. Before a word is on our lips, he knows what we are going to say (Psalm 139:4 and today's verse).

When you pray, you're not telling him anything he doesn't already know. Your prayers are not "Breaking Headline News!" to him about events in your life or the state of your heart.

In other words, prayer is for our benefit, not God's. This is why we pray.

Prayer is about worship. God gave us prayer to glorify his name (Matthew 6:9) and increase our faith. Prayer humbles us. Prayer drives us to our knees for all of our needs. When we pray, it's an inherent acknowledgment that we are not in control—and that's a very good thing.

Prayer is a beautiful gift from God. It humbles prideful sinners with know-it-all tendencies like us and prompts us to seek the one who truly knows all. God's omniscience shouldn't stop you from praying. In fact, it should increase your faith and wonder as you consider his greatness. Pray for his glory and your good!

Now What?
Commit to beginning your prayers with adoration of God.

Did You Know?
In the first-century AD, both Jews and pagans alike said long-winded prayers, thinking God (or their many false gods) would be more impressed by lengthy orations. But Jesus corrected these erroneous practices during the Sermon on the Mount (Matthew 6:5-8).

JUNE 26

Never stop praying.

1 THESSALONIANS 5:17

PRAYER IS A WONDERFUL gift from God. Prayer is an important spiritual discipline in the Christian life. Prayer is something we should do regularly with joy.

Nobody argues with any of that.

But then we run across today's verse from 1 Thessalonians 5:17—"Never stop praying"—and we have to wonder, What exactly does that mean?

Does "never stop praying" mean you need to cease everything else you're doing, shut yourself in a room, pray for eighteen hours a day, sleep for six (maybe), and ask for meals to be slid through an opening in the door at appropriate intervals?

No, of course not!

Knowing what this brief verse doesn't mean isn't hard. But understanding what it does mean will unlock some beautiful spiritual truths about prayer and help us grow in this important area of our lives.

What's It Mean?

Every follower of Jesus Christ should set aside specific daily time to seek the Lord through prayer, Scripture reading, and meditation on God's Word. But prayer should not be limited to a once-a-day occurrence. We should go through our days in a prayerful mindset, being in continual fellowship with God.

When God blesses you, offer a prayer of thanksgiving on the spot. When you are tempted to sin, ask him to deliver you. When you fall prey to temptation, confess your sin and rejoice in the gospel. When you need direction in life, pray for godly wisdom. When life's trials overwhelm you, cry out to him for help. When you meet someone else who is struggling, ask God how you can shine Christ's light on them.

Life is so much more than the mundane, material things we allow ourselves to get wrapped up in. This constant prayerfulness is part of developing a Christlike mindset in alignment with what the apostle Paul says in Colossians 3:2: "Think about the things of heaven, not the things of earth."

Throughout every day, lift up your heart and mind toward your Redeemer in prayers of worship, thanksgiving, confession, and supplication. He is worthy of it all, and your faith will grow!

Now What?

Look at the broader context of today's verse in 1 Thessalonians 5:16-18: "Always be joyful. Never stop praying. Be thankful in all circumstances, for this is God's will for you who belong to Christ Jesus." It seems as if Paul wanted us—among other things—to never stop joyfully thanking God for all his blessings to us.

Did You Know?

You won't wear out God with your prayers. He is a heavenly Father who delights in hearing from his children (Proverbs 15:8).

JUNE 27

*You did not choose me, but I chose you and appointed you that
you should go and bear fruit and that your fruit should abide, so
that whatever you ask the Father in my name, he may give it to you.*

JOHN 15:16, ESV

DO YOU KNOW THE legend of Aladdin?

Perhaps you're most familiar with the 1992 or 2019 Disney adaptations,
where a Middle Eastern street urchin rises to fame and fortune as he tries
to win the heart of a beautiful princess with the help of a magic genie in a
lamp, who obediently grants his wishes.

Sadly, we often pray like God is our personal genie: God, I want this.
God, I need that. God, please do this.

Likewise, many people have misinterpreted verses like Matthew 21:22,
where Jesus says, "You can pray for anything, and if you have faith, you will
receive it."

Rub a lamp! Make a wish! Have all your dreams come true . . . just like
the legend of Aladdin!

But that's not how prayer works. We need a higher view of God. We
need to accurately interpret Scripture. We need a better understanding of
prayer.

What's It Mean?

God is not a magical genie trapped in a lamp, waiting to do our bidding.
He is the Lord God Almighty, Ruler of heaven and earth, who created a perfect, sovereign plan for the universe in eternity past. He wants to hear from
us, but he is not swayed by our selfish, myopic whims. Rather, he graciously
calls us to be part of *his* infinitely greater Kingdom.

By God's grace, our prayers can play an important role in this. Look
at today's verse. In it, Jesus tells his disciples that he chose them to "bear
fruit" so that they might "abide," or remain spiritually faithful, in him. Then
whatever they asked "in [his] name," they would receive.

In other words, when our heart's desires are aligned with God's and we are praying for his purposes in faith, he will answer our prayers. (This is also what Matthew 21:22, and other related verses, are referring to.)

Our prayers don't manipulate God. When your life is united with his will, you'll enjoy many answers to prayer and much spiritual fruit!

Now What?
Meditate on these prayer verses: Psalm 37:4; John 14:13; John 16:23-24; and 1 John 5:14-15.

Did You Know?
While understanding that God's perfect, sovereign will is preeminent, there's nothing wrong with praying for our needs—Jesus instructed this in the Lord's Prayer (Matthew 6:11)—or even certain desires ("God, please heal my loved one," etc.). See tomorrow's devotion for more!

JUNE 28

Give all your worries and cares to God, for he cares about you.

1 PETER 5:7

AS HE SAT WALLOWING in ashes, scraping his festering sores with pottery shards, Job wrestled with God. When Hannah suffered through a long bout of childlessness, she tearfully cried out to God. When Assyrian soldiers were encroaching upon Jerusalem like ants on a sticky summer picnic basket, Hezekiah rushed to the Temple and prayed to God for deliverance.

The book of Psalms is filled with prayers to God for help and deliverance from trials and tribulations. Even the Lord Jesus, as he was experiencing inexplicable grief shortly before his arrest, lifted his voice to the Father in Gethsemane. There are countless other biblical examples of people bringing their troubles and heart's desires to God in prayer.

In yesterday's devotion, we discussed how God is not like a subservient genie in a magic lamp, who exists merely to grant our wishes. Thankfully, there's a vast difference between that and who God really is.

What's It Mean?

God is a caring, sovereign heavenly Father who has showered you with indescribable love. He sacrificed his own Son so you, a lost sinner, could be reconciled to himself and live in his glorious presence for all eternity.

But in this life, you will experience many hardships. God wants you to bring those to him in prayer. As today's verse says, "Give all your worries and cares to God, for he cares about you." Similarly, David writes in Psalm 34:4-5, "I prayed to the LORD, and he answered me. He freed me from all my fears. Those who look to him for help will be radiant with joy; no shadow of shame will darken their faces."

This is amazing! Not only do we have a God who rules the universe, but he also desires to hear about and answer our troubles in prayer. Your Father loves you beyond description. Cry out to him during your times of need. He cares, and he is powerful to save.

Now What?

What are you worried about now? Pause and bring it to God in prayer!

Did You Know?

Praying about your troubles won't make them magically disappear, but prayer builds faith, provides peace, and progresses sanctification (becoming more like Christ).

JUNE 29

Do not be anxious about anything, but in everything by prayer and
supplication with thanksgiving let your requests be made known
to God. And the peace of God, which surpasses all understanding,
will guard your hearts and your minds in Christ Jesus.

PHILIPPIANS 4:6-7, ESV

ANXIETY! STRESS! WORRY! FEAR! Strife! Trouble! Pain! Suffering!

Nobody wants to go through these things, but they are all an unfortunate part of life in a fallen world.

In yesterday's devotion, we discussed how God lovingly desires to hear from his children when we are feeling burdened or enduring trials. Today's Scripture is one of the Bible's great passages in providing a road map to help believers walk through life's challenges.

But questions linger. The passage says, "The peace of God, which surpasses all understanding, will guard your hearts and your minds in Christ Jesus" as we prayerfully offer our anxieties to the Lord. How, though, does this actually work? How does prayer translate into peace?

What's It Mean?

Prayer isn't sorcery. When we pray, our problems don't magically evaporate. Prayer is also not like a retail transaction, where when we pray (payment) we should always expect to receive instantaneous peace (the paid-for item).

No, prayer is a God-given blessing and spiritual discipline of communicating with our heavenly Father. Prayer builds faith because it puts our trust in Someone greater than our problems and something more powerful than our circumstances.

Anxiety comes when we inaccurately view our troubles as existing outside God's concern, power, or control. But when we recall the promises of Scripture, remember God's holy character, and relinquish our anxieties to him "by prayer and supplication with thanksgiving," we begin to tap into heavenly peace.

Prayer brings peace because it

- reminds us how great God is and how dependent upon him we are;
- allows God's Spirit to work in our lives;
- helps us release the tightfisted clench on life's circumstances and give control to our omniscient, omnipotent Creator;
- helps "guard your hearts and your minds in Christ Jesus" when we think big thoughts of God and put our anxieties in their proper context in regard to God's holiness, sovereignty, and love; and
- sanctifies us and makes us more like our Savior.

Are you struggling with anxiety, worries, and trials? God's beautifully indescribable peace is waiting for you. Seek it today through humble prayer!

Now What?
Memorize Philippians 4:6-7. It will be a great help to you in times of trouble.

Did You Know?
Godly peace is not only an abiding, prayerful calmness and trust in the Lord during trials, as we discussed today; peace is also listed as a "fruit of the Spirit" in Galatians 5:22. In other words, it's a godly character trait.

JUNE 30

*I waited patiently for the LORD to help me, and
he turned to me and heard my cry.*

PSALM 40:1

HAVE YOU EVER PRAYED . . . and prayed . . . and prayed for
something—only to feel like your words vanished like the morning mist?

You're not alone. Some of the greatest saints of the Bible prayed for
months, years, or even decades, waiting for God to answer their anguished
pleas. King David, ancient Israel's greatest monarch, was among them. He
experienced many severe trials in life, and in Psalm 22:1-2, he expressed the
heartache of seemingly unanswered prayer:

> My God, my God, why have you abandoned me? Why are you so
> far away when I groan for help? Every day I call to you, my God,
> but you do not answer. Every night I lift my voice, but I find no
> relief.

As we continue our study on prayer, we need to consider a burning
question: What happens when it seems like God isn't answering our prayers?
Or when it feels like he doesn't hear at all?

What's It Mean?

First, it's important to remember that God *always* hears the prayers of
believers. He never ignores his people. As 1 Peter 3:12 says, "The eyes of
the LORD watch over those who do right, and his ears are open to their
prayers."

But some things can hinder our prayers, such as unconfessed sin (Psalm
66:18), lack of faith (James 1:5-7), or improper motives (James 4:3).
However, don't equate unanswered prayer with negligence or indifference on
God's part. And remember, God's timing is not like ours (2 Peter 3:8). He is
eternal and sees all time—past, present, and future—concurrently. To teach
us trust and patience, he often asks us to wait.

Sometimes, God just tells us no. He did this to the apostle Paul (2 Corinthians 12:1-10). And we have to be okay with that—he is God, and we are not!

But what about David in Psalm 22? Did God leave Israel's king hanging without an answer? No. Here's what David said in verse 24: "He has not ignored or belittled the suffering of the needy. He has not turned his back on them, but has listened to their cries for help."

God always answers the prayers of the righteous. His answers might not always be what we want, or according to our timetable, but they are always in alignment with his sovereign will, which is best for us.

Now What?
Read Luke 18:1-8, Jesus' parable about persisting in prayer.

Did You Know?
- Jesus quoted David's cry of anguish in Psalm 22:1 on the cross.

JULY 1

You can ask for anything in my name, and I will do it,
so that the Son can bring glory to the Father. Yes, ask
me for anything in my name, and I will do it!

JOHN 14:13-14

IN THE POPULAR HARRY POTTER book and movie series, Harry and
his wizard friends utter plenty of magical incantations in their battle against
Voldemort and his evil minions. There are spells for opening locks, levitat-
ing, erasing someone's memory, starting fires, paralyzing foes, and many
others.

Then there's "muffliato." This might sound like fixing your car's sput-
tering exhaust system. Alas, it's only meant to afflict someone with a strange
buzzing noise in their ears.

Humans have always been fascinated by the power to speak things into
being through magical words. (See the "Did You Know?" section below.)
That's why we must be careful with a passage like John 14:13-14 (today's
verse), where Jesus says, "Ask me for anything in my name, and I will do it."
Is it really that simple? If we tack on "In Jesus' name, amen" at the end of a
prayer, will we get whatever we ask for?

Not exactly.

What's It Mean?

The Bible never commands us to say, "In Jesus' name, amen" at the end of
our prayers. So why do we do it?

First, when we pray, it's important to remember the only way that sinners can approach a holy God is through Jesus, our "great High Priest"
(Hebrews 4:14) whose atoning sacrifice allows us to "come boldly to the
throne of our gracious God" (Hebrews 4:16). While it's not biblically man-
dated, saying the words "in Jesus' name" at the end of our prayers can help
us remember who makes it possible for us to approach God.

Praying in Jesus' name also means praying for his will to be done. This is
reflected in Jesus saying he will "bring glory to the Father" (John 14:13) when

he answers our prayer. But if you ask "in Jesus' name" for something that won't glorify God, do you think he will honor that prayer? Absolutely not!

To ask for anything in Jesus' name, you must know God's will, and to know God's will, you must know his Word. When your prayers align with God's will as revealed in his Word, you'll see answered prayer!

Now What?

If you say, "In Jesus' name" at the end of your prayers, remember why you do it!

Did You Know?

The first known use of the term *hocus-pocus* dates back to jugglers or magicians in the early to mid-1600s. *Abracadabra*, which dates to at least the second century AD, was once a superstitious charm used in the hopes of dispelling illnesses.

JULY 2

Wherever your treasure is, there the desires of your heart will also be.

MATTHEW 6:21

ON JULY 12, 1987, Valerio Viccei strolled into the Knightsbridge Safe Deposit Centre in London asking to rent a deposit box. Once inside the vault, he and another man brandished guns and stole an estimated $98 million.

For several days, Viccei ran free. Newspapers dubbed it "the crime of the century." Indeed, the heist remains one of the biggest bank robberies in history. But eventually, authorities caught Viccei. In April 2000, on day release from prison, Viccei was killed during a shootout with police.

The allure of earthly treasures can be so tempting. Fame, fortune, big houses, fast cars—it all sounds so glamorous. But spiritually, it leads to a dead end.

During the Sermon on the Mount, Jesus spoke about chasing worldly riches:

> Don't store up treasures here on earth, where moths eat them and rust destroys them, and where thieves break in and steal. Store your treasures in heaven, where moths and rust cannot destroy, and thieves do not break in and steal. Wherever your treasure is, there the desires of your heart will also be.
>
> MATTHEW 6:19-21

You don't have to be a vicious, gun-wielding bank robber to need this biblical truth. We all need to hear it.

What's It Mean?

Every human heart—sinful by nature—desires worldly treasure. That's why Jesus addressed the issue. Deep down, we all want another few zeros at the end of our bank account balances.

But money, mansions, cars, jewelry, and so on are all ephemeral possessions that come and go with the wind. When we die, our money and possessions won't do us any good.

Are these fleeting treasures what your heart truly desires? If so, it says a lot about you. That's because, according to Scripture, the heart is our moral center where a person's emotions, reason, and will reside.

What do you long for most—more stuff on earth, or treasure in heaven? The false idols of worldly wealth or everlasting riches of eternal life with God himself?

You can't have both. As Jesus said in Matthew 6:24, "No one can serve two masters. For you will hate one and love the other; you will be devoted to one and despise the other. You cannot serve God and be enslaved to money."

The choice seems clear. But it's up to you to make it!

Now What?

With a parent's help, give some of your clothing and other possessions to a local shelter or other charitable organization.

Did You Know?

The largest bank robbery in US history was a $30 million heist at the United California Bank in 1972.

JULY 3

Do not be anxious about your life, what you will eat or what
you will drink, nor about your body, what you will put on. Is
not life more than food, and the body more than clothing?

MATTHEW 6:25, ESV

FOR YEARS, ORNITHOLOGISTS—scientists who study birds—believed
that there were approximately nine thousand to ten thousand bird species
worldwide. However, in December 2016, the American Museum of Natural
History in New York City published a study suggesting that there are as
many as eighteen thousand avian species.

Boy, if that's true, things are really going to the birds!

In the Sermon on the Mount, Jesus used our feathered friends to teach
an important lesson on anxiety and trust in God. Jesus' original audience
had plenty of cares. Life was hard. Many people didn't know where the next
day's meals would come from.

Yet Jesus told the crowd, "Do not be anxious about your life, what you
will eat or what you will drink, nor about your body, what you will put on.
. . . Look at the birds of the air: they neither sow nor reap nor gather into
barns, and yet your heavenly Father feeds them. Are you not of more value
than they?" (Matthew 6:25-26, ESV).

He made a similar point about how God beautifully adorns flowers:
"Why worry about your clothing? Look at the lilies of the field and how
they grow. . . . If God cares so wonderfully for wildflowers that are here
today and thrown into the fire tomorrow, he will certainly care for you.
Why do you have so little faith?" (verses 28, 30).

What's It Mean?

Jesus' point is simple: if God invests so much care into the lesser parts of his
creation like birds and flowers, he will certainly provide for the daily needs
of humans, who are his image-bearers (Genesis 1:26-27)—and even more so
for those who are his redeemed children!

So there is no room for worrying on our part. Worrying, in fact, is sin. Worry reveals a lack of trust in God and his goodness.

God is not distant or miserly. Our loving heavenly Father is near, he knows all our needs, and he tenderly cares for his children.

Anxiously chasing after life's basic necessities is a bird-brained idea! Jesus said it's the mark of an unbeliever (Matthew 6:31-32). Instead, "seek the Kingdom of God above all else, and live righteously, and he will give you everything you need" (verse 33).

Now What?
Read Matthew 6:25-34 and give your worries to God.

Did You Know?
The largest bird in the world is the ostrich. The smallest bird is the two-inch-long bee hummingbird.

JULY 4

Do not judge others.

MATTHEW 7:1

ON OCTOBER 5, 1931, at a federal courthouse in Chicago, a trial began for one of the most notorious criminals in American history.

From 1920 to 1931, Al Capone slowly built a powerful, wealthy, and dangerous crime syndicate in the Windy City through bootlegging, extortion, police payoffs, murder, and other offenses. But in the end, he went to jail for—*drum roll, please*—not paying his taxes!

Knowing Capone often resorted to bribery to get favorable results, federal judge James H. Wilkerson cleverly sent the twelve-person jury assigned to Capone's trial into another courtroom and brought that jury into his courtroom. After thirteen days, the jury found Capone guilty of income tax evasion. Judge Wilkerson sentenced him to eleven years in federal prison. Thank goodness for honest judges and the criminal justice system!

But what, then, are we supposed to do with today's verse, where Jesus says, "Do not judge others"? Does this mean that we should abolish our entire justice system, encourage judges to look for other jobs, and let villains run amok?

No, of course not!

What's It Mean?

When Jesus commanded us not to judge others, he was referring to an improper heart attitude toward people. Biblically speaking, to judge someone is to

- hold a grudge,
- pridefully look down on them and/or think you're better than they are,
- make assumptions about their motives or character that may not be true, and
- even go so far as to pronounce God's judgment on them in your heart for something they've said or done in the past.

When you judge another person, you are, in essence, playing judge and jury against them, declaring them guilty before God. That's dangerous territory. As James 4:12 says, "God alone, who gave the law, is the Judge. He alone has the power to save or to destroy. So what right do you have to judge your neighbor?"

Instead of worrying about others, Jesus said, focus on honoring God yourself. That's what Jesus meant with his powerful hyperbole in Matthew 7:3: "And why worry about a speck in your friend's eye when you have a log in your own?"

If God were as quick to judge us as we are to judge others, we would be eternally condemned because of our sins. Thankfully, he is patient and loves to extend mercy and grace to sinners through his Son, Jesus Christ.

Go and do likewise.

Now What?

Read Matthew 7:1-5 and ask God to reveal any glaring "logs" in your eye.

Did You Know?

Al Capone served less than eight years of his prison sentence. He died of cardiac arrest in 1947 at the age of forty-eight.

JULY 5

You can enter God's Kingdom only through the narrow gate.
The highway to hell is broad, and its gate is wide for the many
who choose that way. But the gateway to life is very narrow
and the road is difficult, and only a few ever find it.

MATTHEW 7:13-14

ENGINE PROBLEMS. FLAT TIRES. Potholes. Speed bumps. Speed traps. People who text while driving. People who run red lights. People who cut you off without signaling. Rush-hour traffic. Roadkill.

And that's *before* you leave your neighborhood!

Hazards and annoyances abound when you drive a car. But one of a motorist's worst nightmares is seeing this warning sign: "Road narrows ahead. Expect delays."

Aaaaarrrrgh.

Narrow roads are no fun to navigate. But in today's Scripture passage from the Sermon on the Mount, Jesus told the crowd to seek a different kind of narrow path. Jesus' message goes against societal norms, even much of what is preached in many churches.

Let's take a closer look at the Savior's profound words.

What's It Mean?

In 2017, the Pew Research Center published a report saying that 2.3 billion (31 percent) of the world's 7.3 billion people claimed to be Christian. But does nearly one-third of the earth *really* follow Christ as their Lord and Savior?

Not according to the Bible.

Today's passage—and Scripture's complete testimony—is clear: true Christians will always be a significant minority. Look, too, at Jesus' interchange with someone in Luke 13:23-24: "Someone asked him, 'Lord, will only a few be saved?' He replied, 'Work hard to enter the narrow door to God's Kingdom, for many will try to enter but will fail.'"

Sadly, many people lead a blatantly wicked life, willfully rejecting God.

Many others believe their "religiosity" will get them through heaven's door, so to speak. Thus, the "highway to hell," as Matthew 7:13 says, is wide and well-traveled. The end of that road is horrific: eternal destruction and separation from God.

By comparison, the road into God's Kingdom is narrow and lightly traveled. Why? Because it's "difficult" (verse 14). The Christian life is full of wonderful blessings but also great hardships. It weeds out the pretenders. You can't be a half-hearted follower of Christ (Revelation 3:16). But that road's end is a glorious eternity where weary travelers will rejoice in God's presence forever.

The path is clear: choose the narrow gate and follow Christ as your Lord and Savior!

Now What?
Read Luke 13:22-30 for a similar allegory from Jesus about God's Kingdom.

Did You Know?
Jesus likely used a gate metaphor in Matthew 7:13-14 because city gates were vital parts of daily life in the ancient Greco-Roman world.

JULY 6

Not everyone who calls out to me, "Lord! Lord!"
will enter the Kingdom of Heaven.

MATTHEW 7:21

JESUS WAS NEARLY FINISHED with his Sermon on the Mount. He had
given the people plenty to think about.

As he surveyed the huge crowds on the mountainside, his heart must
have ached with compassion and love—but also a righteous passion for
them to hear hard truth. Many of them had tagged along, hoping to see a
fantastic miracle (Matthew 4:23-25).

Jesus didn't want tagalongs. Nor did he want people to have a false per-
ception of salvation. So he drove home a very important point about true
discipleship:

> Not everyone who calls out to me, "Lord! Lord!" will enter the
> Kingdom of Heaven. Only those who actually do the will of my Father
> in heaven will enter. On judgment day many will say to me, "Lord!
> Lord! We prophesied in your name and cast out demons in your name
> and performed many miracles in your name." But I will reply, "I never
> knew you. Get away from me, you who break God's laws."
> MATTHEW 7:21-23

Let's discuss what the Savior meant by these strong words.

What's It Mean?

Jesus was a master of word economy. In only three verses, he said a great
deal about false assurances of salvation and true discipleship.

Look at the people's response in Jesus' story. What were they basing
their entrance into heaven on? It wasn't Jesus' righteousness. It was their
own warped sense of works-based morality. They gladly pointed out that
they had "prophesied," "cast out demons," and "performed many miracles"
in his name.

Jesus was thoroughly unimpressed. On their own merit, our good deeds "are nothing but filthy rags" (Isaiah 64:6) in God's sight.

To enter heaven, Jesus said, one must "do the will of my Father" (Matthew 7:21). Naturally, then, we ask, *What is that?* Jesus tells us in John 6:40: "It is my Father's will that all who see his Son and believe in him should have eternal life."

Many of the mountainside crowd that day were willing to call Jesus Lord. But they lacked faith in him as their Savior from sins.

What about you? Are you willing to call Jesus Lord *and* follow God's will by believing in him as Savior?

Now What?

Make sure to read tomorrow's devotion, which answers the ensuing question: "So how can I be assured of my salvation?"

Did You Know?

The Bible records many instances of miracles being done outside of true discipleship and faith in Jesus (Exodus 7:11-12, 22; 8:7; Acts 19:13-16; 2 Thessalonians 2:9; Revelation 13:13-14).

JULY 7

Not everyone who calls out to me, "Lord! Lord!"
will enter the Kingdom of Heaven.

MATTHEW 7:21

BIRTH CERTIFICATES, SOCIAL SECURITY cards, graduation diplomas, product warranties . . .

Life is full of tangible documents that validate various aspects of our lives. They confirm our status, inform us of our rights, and so on.

But Christians don't receive a certificate or any other physical evidence when they trust in Jesus. Yes, God's regenerative, justifying work of salvation is genuine and transformative. But it's an unseen act of his Spirit, accomplished miraculously in human hearts.

This returns us to Matthew 7:21. One day, countless people will stand before God's judgment throne thinking they did everything necessary for entrance into heaven, only to be turned away. It's a sobering thought. Naturally, this leads some Christians to wonder, *Will that be me? How can I be assured of my salvation?*

Take heart! God answers this clearly in his Word.

What's It Mean?

First, remember that salvation doesn't depend upon us or our performance. (Thank goodness!) It rests on God's character, his promises, and Christ's finished work of redemption. What God started in eternity past—choosing all believers "to be holy and without fault in his eyes" (Ephesians 1:4)—he will certainly bring to completion for his glory and their good (Romans 8:28-39).

What's more, God has placed his Spirit inside every believer as an authenticating mark. "For his Spirit joins with our spirit to affirm that we are God's children" (Romans 8:16). The Holy Spirit produces spiritual fruit that wouldn't be possible apart from a regenerated heart.

With that in mind, ask yourself if you're growing in these ways:

- in your love of God, devotion to Christ, and obedience to his Word
- in your hatred of sin and worldly temptations
- in the fruits of the Spirit
- in your love of Scripture reading, prayer, regular worship with other believers, etc.

These are some marks of true faith. Does every Christian do these things perfectly all the time? No, of course not! Indwelling sin still remains. But true faith manifests itself in maturing spiritual fruit (James 2:14-26; Galatians 5:22-23).

There are, of course, false assurances of faith. These normally stem from a misunderstanding of salvation and misapplication of Scripture. But when we rightly apply God's Word and rest in his Spirit, true Christians can "confirm your calling and election" (2 Peter 1:10, ESV).

Now What?

For more on God's Spirit as our guaranteed "seal" of an authentic faith (or his "mark," as some versions put it), see 2 Corinthians 1:22; Ephesians 1:13; and Ephesians 4:30.

Did You Know?

Moments of doubt don't disqualify God's children. The more you grow in your understanding of God, Scripture, and the Christian walk, the more your doubts will fade (Mark 9:24).

JULY 8

*Anyone who listens to my teaching and follows it is wise,
like a person who builds a house on solid rock.*

MATTHEW 7:24

HAVE YOU EVER WANTED to live in a window-filled mansion overlooking America's beautiful coastlines?

Well, you may want to reconsider.

In recent years, plenty of scientific studies have been published showing how rising sea levels, increased storm activity, and other factors are causing the nation's shorelines to erode. That's bad news for houses built on seaside bluffs. Sure, you might enjoy gorgeous vistas, but they won't last long if the ground beneath the house is giving way!

This brings to mind Jesus' metaphorical parable about building your house on the proper foundation. Here's what he said:

> Anyone who listens to my teaching and follows it is wise, like a person who builds a house on solid rock. Though the rain comes in torrents and the floodwaters rise and the winds beat against that house, it won't collapse because it is built on bedrock. But anyone who hears my teaching and doesn't obey it is foolish, like a person who builds a house on sand. When the rains and floods come and the winds beat against that house, it will collapse with a mighty crash.
>
> MATTHEW 7:24-27

When Jesus concluded the Sermon on the Mount with these words, he wasn't giving real estate advice. He was showing concern for the eternal state of our souls.

What's It Mean?

What are you basing your life on? This was Jesus' question to his original audience—and to us today.

God has given us the words of *the* Word—his Son, Jesus—to build our lives upon. There is no other true spiritual foundation in life. Pharisaical righteousness—trying to please God through good works—won't get us into heaven. If we build our lives upon fame, fortune, pleasure, or any other worldly pursuits, the "rains and floods" of life (i.e., trials and hardships) will reveal the shakiness of those foundations.

The floodwaters of trouble will come in life. Don't build your hope on the unstable sand of self-righteous pursuits or worldly vanity. Build on Christ! He is the true Foundation, the Rock (1 Corinthians 10:4), and the Cornerstone (Ephesians 2:20) on which our eternal hope stands firm!

Now What?

Next time you're at the beach, take time to read Matthew 7:24-27.

Did You Know?

When Jesus finished his Sermon on the Mount, "the crowds were amazed at his teaching, for he taught with real authority—quite unlike their teachers of religious law" (Matthew 7:28-29). Unlike the religious leaders, who quoted other rabbis when they lectured, Jesus powerfully spoke with his own divine authority as the Son of God.

JULY 9

*My dear brothers and sisters, how can you claim to have faith in our
glorious Lord Jesus Christ if you favor some people over others?*

JAMES 2:1

FIRST-CENTURY PALESTINE WAS A hotbed of frustration and animosity. The Jews hated being ruled and taxed by their cruel Roman overlords. But when they saw their own countrymen collecting taxes on Rome's
behalf—well, that really got them steamed!

In addition to what Rome required, many tax collectors charged the
people an extra percentage to enrich themselves (Luke 3:13; 19:8). The
Romans didn't care, and the oppressed Jewish citizenry were often helpless
to resist. As such, Jewish tax collectors were considered reprehensible traitors
and hopelessly outside of God's grace. They were often used to illustrate the
worst of society (Matthew 5:46; 18:17; and 21:31).

All this made what Jesus did in Matthew 9:9-13 unthinkable to the
Jewish religious leaders. One day, Jesus called Matthew, a Jewish tax collector, to be one of his twelve disciples, and he later went to dine at Matthew's
house with some other tax collectors and social outcasts. Huffing and puff-
ing with self-righteous indignation, the Pharisees asked Jesus' disciples,
"Why does your teacher eat with such scum?" (verse 11).

Jesus' answer was beautiful: "I have come to call not those who think
they are righteous, but those who know they are sinners" (verse 13).

What's It Mean?

Jesus doesn't play favorites, and he doesn't want us to either. As today's verse
and many other Bible passages make clear, God hates preferential treatment.
In fact, Romans 2:11 spells it out clearly: "God does not show favoritism."

That's because he created all people equal, as his image-bearers. We
must never show partiality toward others based on race, gender, popularity,
outward appearance, money, or any other trivial, human means of segrega-
tion (Psalm 82:2; Proverbs 24:23; James 2:1-13; and 1 Timothy 5:21).

When God's Son lived on the earth, he consistently made time for the marginalized, outcasts, and riffraff of society. Jesus showed love to tax collectors, lepers, Samaritans, the demon-possessed, the poor, sick, crippled, and many others whom Israel's religious elite deemed "unworthy."

What about you? Do you consistently drift toward the "in" crowd? Do you show favoritism in your interactions with others based on shallow human factors?

Or do you treat everyone as God's image-bearer and love them equally, reaching out to those who are hurting and rejected? There is no place for showing favoritism as a Christian!

Now What?
Befriend someone outside your normal social circles today.

Did You Know?
According to the ancient historian Philo, some first-century tax collectors would resort to extortion and/or imprisoning a man's family members if he fled without paying his debts.

JULY 10

You search the Scriptures because you think they give
you eternal life. But the Scriptures point to me!

JOHN 5:39

QUIZ TIME!

It's time to put your Old Testament knowledge to the test.

1. What kind of animal did God require for the annual Passover
   sacrifice?
2. What tribe of Israel did David descend from?
3. Which Assyrian king attacked Judah during Hezekiah's reign?
4. How long did it take Nehemiah to rebuild Jerusalem's walls?
5. Where is the prophecy of Jesus' birthplace found?

(Answers are below in the "Did You Know?" section.)

Head knowledge of Scripture is great, and it might win you a trivia contest or make you look pretty clever in front of others. But when it comes to
salvation, Bible facts alone are no more useful than a chariot without wheels.

This brings us to today's Scripture passage. In John 5, Jesus was talking
to some of the Jewish Sanhedrin members who wanted to kill him for healing a man on the Sabbath and claiming deity.

The religious leaders knew what the Old Testament said. They had
studied it their whole lives. But their great error was that they missed its
fundamental meaning. They didn't understand that it all pointed to Jesus as
our only Savior from sins.

What's It Mean?

You can memorize all the books of the Bible. You can rattle off the Ten
Commandments, the ten plagues of Egypt, the twelve tribes of Israel, and
the fruits of the Spirit. You can even recite some famous chapters such as
Psalm 23, Isaiah 53, and Romans 8. But it won't matter if you don't trust in
Jesus as Savior and Lord.

This isn't to minimize Scripture. Hebrews 4:12 says, "The word of God is alive and powerful." It softens hardened hearts to hear the gospel.

But our response to Christ makes all the difference. The ancient Jewish religious leaders got it completely wrong. They were blinded to the truth by pride, self-righteousness, greed, and corruption.

God's Word reveals God's Son. As you study it, be receptive as God's Spirit speaks to your heart. Let Scripture deepen your love and commitment to the Savior who gave his life for yours. Use the Bible to grow in your faith in the God who created you and his Son who died so that you might live.

Knowing Scripture is so important. But Bible knowledge is worthless without personally knowing the one whom Scripture reveals. Without Jesus, knowledge is simply a trivial pursuit.

Now What?

Read John 5 to see Jesus' relationship to God the Father and the Old Testament.

Did You Know?

Here's the answer key to the quiz above:

1. a spotless one-year-old male lamb
2. Judah
3. Sennacherib
4. fifty-two days
5. Micah 5:2

JULY 11

Everyone who acknowledges me publicly here on earth, I will also acknowledge before my Father in heaven. But everyone who denies me here on earth, I will also deny before my Father in heaven.

MATTHEW 10:32-33

THERE HAVE BEEN MANY infamous denials in American history. Perhaps the most notorious is Richard Nixon's televised rebuttal on November 17, 1973.

At the time, Nixon, serving his second term as president of the United States, was under investigation for a huge political scandal. Seventeen months earlier, burglars had broken into the Democratic National Convention headquarters, located in the Watergate Hotel complex in Washington, DC, during the 1972 presidential campaign. The prowlers were caught wiretapping phones and stealing documents.

Within several months, investigators traced the Watergate crimes to Nixon's Republican reelection campaign. While several of his administration officials were eventually convicted on related cover-up charges, Nixon initially denied any involvement. As the scandal intensified, he made this now-infamous statement on TV: "I welcome this kind of examination because people have got to know whether or not their president's a crook. Well, I'm not a crook! I've earned everything I've got."

Ironic words indeed. As the investigation continued, the evidence undoubtedly pointed to Nixon's involvement. Facing impeachment, Nixon resigned in August 1974.

Denying the truth is a bad idea. Yet as today's verse says, it's far worse to deny Christ.

What's It Mean?

What is there to deny? Jesus suffered the horrors of the Cross for our sake. He has done everything for us! It's a privilege to claim allegiance to him.

Yet there are many who are false disciples, only wanting the benefits of Christianity but none of its hardships.

385

Jesus, though, requires our total allegiance. Saying you're a Christian only when it's convenient is an insult to Jesus. No true Christ follower publicly denies their commitment to him. The apostle Peter did this three times one night—and regretted it terribly (Matthew 26:69-75). Peter repented, received forgiveness, and never denied his relationship with Jesus again. But for those who consistently deny Jesus on earth, he will deny them in eternity.

That's the stern warning for choosing wrongly. However, there's a beautiful promise for choosing rightly. If you consistently honor and give witness to Christ, you will stand before heaven's throne one day as the Son proudly acknowledges you before the Father. What a glorious day that will be!

Now What?
Read Mark 8:38; 2 Timothy 2:12; and 1 John 2:23.

Did You Know?
In 2019, Donald Trump became only the third president in US history to be impeached. The others were Andrew Johnson and Bill Clinton. Nixon resigned from office before formal impeachment hearings began in 1974.

JULY 12

My Father has entrusted everything to me. No one truly knows the Son except the Father, and no one truly knows the Father except the Son and those to whom the Son chooses to reveal him.

MATTHEW 11:27

ON A SCALE OF 1 to 100, how well do you know God?

(Hint: Nobody should say 100—or anywhere close. God is far too holy and majestic to be fully known. So don't be too presumptuous!)

But the beautiful thing is, God *can* be known in many ways! However, none of that knowledge of, or relationship with, him that you possess is possible without the redemptive work of his Son, Jesus Christ.

Look at today's verse. Does this sound like a great mystery to you? Let's unpack its truth.

What's It Mean?

God is our Creator. We wouldn't exist without him. But he didn't just create us and leave us, like a clockmaker winding up timepieces and letting them endlessly *ticktock* away with no other interaction. No, he is a loving, personal God of *revelation*. He wants his creation to know him.

If you search the whole Bible, you'll notice that the great saints of Scripture didn't get their start by actively searching for God. As humans, our desire to know God never inherently comes from within our corrupt, sinful nature. Rather, any true believer—in Scripture or in modern times—starts desiring God when *God* takes the initiative. He does this through his Spirit's work in our hearts—calling our hearts to himself. Then God's Spirit graciously regenerates, justifies, and sanctifies us as we grow in our faith.

The linchpin, though, is Jesus. You cannot know the Father unless you truly know the Son through faith and repentance. That's because, as the incarnate second Person of the Trinity, Jesus is God! "For God in all his fullness was pleased to live in Christ" (Colossians 1:19).

Perhaps you're thinking to yourself, *I'm not sure if the Son has ever revealed God the Father to me.* Guess what? He's doing it right now! Through this devotional, you are learning about God's character, his dealings with humanity, truths from his Word, and his great love for you through Christ.

The Son is revealing the Father to you today. Worship him!

Now What?

In today's verse, Jesus said the Father "has entrusted everything to me." Look up Matthew 28:18 to find out what he means by "everything."

Did You Know?

In today's verse, Jesus implies that he "chooses" to reveal the Father to some, but not all. This speaks to God's sovereign election, which we'll discuss more in the October 17–20 devotions.

JULY 13

Still other seeds fell on fertile soil, and they produced a crop that was
thirty, sixty, and even a hundred times as much as had been planted!

MATTHEW 13:8

UNTAMED AMERICA, back in the eighteenth and nineteenth centuries, was a much more agricultural nation than it is today. But over the years, our "amber waves of grain"—as hailed in the opening stanza of the old folk song, "America the Beautiful"—have continued to shrink as the population booms and technology advances.

Back in first-century Palestine, agriculture was the heart and soul of Jewish life. That's why Jesus told the parable of the sower in Matthew 13:1-23.

In this parable, Jesus describes a farmer who sows seed in his field. The seed falls on four different kinds of soil—a footpath, rocky terrain, a thorny patch, and fertile ground.

But Jesus' parable wasn't about the latest ancient crop-raising techniques or which seeds produce the best beans, beets, or broccoli. No, he wanted to teach an important lesson on how our hearts receive God's Word.

What's It Mean?

The farmer in Jesus' parable is God. He graciously sows his Word (the seed) into the hearts (the soil) of people, including you. But different people respond many different ways to God's Word.

Let's look at what happened to the seeds that fell among the different types of soil in Jesus' parable:

- **On the footpath.** These people hear God's Word but don't understand it, and like a bird who notices seeds lying helpless on a path, Satan "snatches away" what they've received (verse 19).
- **On the rocky soil.** These people receive God's Word joyfully at first, but when spiritual persecution or life's hardships come, they fall away "since they don't have deep roots" (verses 20-21).

389

- **Among the thorns.** These people initially express a love for God's Word, but like good plants among briars, they quickly get choked by the worries and enticements of the world, "so no fruit is produced" (verse 22).
- **On fertile soil.** These are people "who truly hear and understand God's word and produce a [spiritual] harvest" far greater than what was planted (verses 8, 23).

Where do you fall on this list? Does your heart joyfully receive God's Word and its calling upon your life? Do you believe all of the Bible's claims about God and his Son, Jesus Christ? Are you allowing God's Word to germinate in your heart while sowing hope in others for a great spiritual harvest?

Just planting some seeds for thought.

Now What?
Read the full parable of the sower in Matthew 13:1-23.

Did You Know?
Katharine Lee Bates, the composer of "America the Beautiful," was inspired to write the song on a trip up Pike's Peak in Colorado in 1893.

JULY 14

*These people honor me with their lips, but their hearts
are far from me. Their worship is a farce.*

MATTHEW 15:8-9

WHAT'S THE ONE INSTRUCTION your parents always gave you (and maybe still do!) before you sat down to eat?

WASH YOUR HANDS!

Every child has probably heard this instruction ad nauseam. But perhaps no one in history has washed their hands more than pious Jews in ancient Palestine.

In Matthew 15, the Pharisees and scribes confronted Jesus because his disciples had disobeyed their "age-old tradition . . . of ceremonial hand washing before they eat" (verse 2).

Jesus had no time for these hypocrites. These were the same religious leaders who tithed the smallest garden herbs yet neglected to show mercy to others (Matthew 23:23), fastidiously scrubbed all their eating utensils to remain outwardly clean yet were inwardly filled with wickedness (Matthew 23:25), and adorned the tombs of famous prophets (Matthew 23:29) yet conspired to kill Christ.

No wonder Jesus condemned their surface-level religion and worthless adherence to manmade traditions by quoting Isaiah 29:13 in today's verse.

What's It Mean?

The Pharisees and scribes thought the more sacred laws they observed, the more righteous they would be before God. Nothing could be further from the truth. Worshiping God isn't a matter of rule-keeping or ceremony. It's a matter of the heart.

This is where Christianity differs from religion. Religion is man's way of trying to please God. But no amount of literal or symbolic handwashing can atone for our sins. Only God's Son can do that. Jesus' finished work on the cross was fully sufficient for propitiation—appeasing God's just wrath toward our sins and turning it to favor.

This is the message of the gospel and true Christianity: Jesus came to accomplish for us what no laws, rules, observances, rituals, ceremonies, liturgies, or any other earthly systems ever could. The Pharisees tried everything they could think of to impress God. But it was all in vain. "Their worship is a farce," Jesus said in today's passage.

What are *you* basing your relationship with God on? Good works? Church attendance? Your parents' faith? Something else?

If it's not solely on Jesus' atoning work, it's all in vain. Avoid pharisaical religion, and trust in Christ today!

Now What?

For more on Jesus' condemnation of the hypocritical scribes and Pharisees, read Matthew 23:1-36.

Did You Know?

In Exodus 30:17-21, God commanded the priests to wash their hands and feet before serving in the Tabernacle/Temple. But by the first century AD, the Pharisees had unnecessarily extended this rule to all Israelites to (in their minds) maintain strict ritual purity.

JULY 15

*If you confess with your mouth that Jesus is Lord and believe
in your heart that God raised him from the dead, you will
be saved. For with the heart one believes and is justified,
and with the mouth one confesses and is saved.*

ROMANS 10:9-10, ESV

GOSSIP! RUMORS! SPECULATION! THEORIES! Hearsay!

As Jesus traveled through Palestine teaching, healing, and performing astounding miracles, huge crowds followed him. Yet people's opinions
greatly differed regarding Jesus' true identity.

So one day, when Jesus and his disciples entered Caesarea Philippi, he
asked them, "Who do people say I am?"

"Well," they replied, "some say John the Baptist, some say Elijah, and
others say Jeremiah or one of the other prophets."

Interesting guesses . . . but all wrong.

Then Jesus got personal with his disciples: "But who do you say I am?"

Peter, never shy about speaking first, boldly answered in one of
Scripture's great confessions: "You are the Messiah, the Son of the living
God" (Matthew 16:13-20).

Peter's confession hit the mark. He acknowledged Jesus was God's Son
(implying Christ's deity) and the Messiah—God's promised Savior for the
sins of the world. Bull's-eye, Peter!

What's It Mean?

In the first century AD, lots of people mistook Jesus' true identity. It's no
different today. Ask ten people on the street who Jesus is, and you might get
ten different answers, including some of the following:

- a good man
- a great prophet
- a martyr
- the leader of a religious movement

Sadly, many people today might not know what to say because they haven't given Jesus any thought at all.

But the topic of Jesus' identity is as relevant today as it was two thousand years ago. So now the Savior's question comes to you: Who do *you* say Jesus is?

As today's passage from Romans 10 implies, it's a question of eternal significance. No sinner is justified (or made right with God) apart from faith in Christ (Romans 5:1; Galatians 2:16). To receive God's forgiveness and experience his salvation, you must believe in Jesus' true identity, trust in his saving power for your life, and be willing to openly declare it.

If you haven't already, confess Jesus as Lord, trust in his saving work on your behalf, and receive his salvation today!

Now What?
Read the full account of Peter's great confession of Christ in Matthew 16:13-20.

Did You Know?
After Peter's confession, Jesus told Peter he was "blessed . . . because my Father in heaven has revealed this to you. You did not learn this from any human being" (Matthew 16:17). Our saving faith doesn't spring from our own sinful hearts; it is a gracious gift from God.

JULY 16

You are seeing things merely from a human point of view, not from God's.

MATTHEW 16:23

AS SOON AS THE APOSTLE PETER had reached a peak of his young faith, he tumbled down quickly.

In yesterday's devotion, we learned about Peter's great confession. Many people had wild ideas about Jesus' true identity. But Peter nailed it: "You are the Messiah, the Son of the living God" (Matthew 16:16).

Shortly after Peter's confession, Jesus began telling his disciples plainly that he would suffer at the hands of the Jewish leaders, die, and then rise again. This sounded like nonsense to Peter. So he scolded Jesus. (Bad mistake!)

"Heaven forbid, Lord," Peter exclaimed. "This will never happen to you!" (Matthew 16:22).

Jesus instantly rebuked Peter, attributing his impulsive friend's words to a much more diabolical source: "Get away from me, Satan! You are a dangerous trap to me. You are seeing things merely from a human point of view, not from God's" (Matthew 16:23).

What's It Mean?

Peter, like most first-century Jews, expected a Messiah who would liberate Israel from Roman tyranny and reestablish them as a sovereign nation. Peter couldn't fathom God's promised Savior suffering the horrible torture, indignity, and divine curse associated with Roman crucifixion (Deuteronomy 21:23 and Galatians 3:13).

Peter, though, had forgotten the Old Testament messianic prophecies—or at least not applied them to Jesus. He was trying to fit God's incredibly comprehensive plan of redemption into his tiny little box of human understanding. (Another mistake!)

We can learn a lot from Peter. If you're not careful, your life experiences (family, friends, church, school, etc.) can easily shape how you view God, the Bible, and your faith overall. But this is backward thinking!

Don't view spiritual matters solely through the tainted lens of your experiences and understanding. Don't try to superimpose your inferior plans or understanding over God's far greater design for your life—and the world. Your assumptions, preconceived notions, and sin will only blind you to God's truth, as it did with Peter. Jesus, then, would offer this reminder: "You are seeing things merely from a human point of view, not from God's" (today's verse).

When you allow Scripture and the Holy Spirit to be your guides, you can build a God-glorifying framework for your life, instead of trying to apply a misinformed framework on Scripture!

Now What?
Read the account of Peter's excited but incorrect answer in Matthew 16:21-23.

Did You Know?
Psalm 22; Isaiah 53; Zechariah 12:10; and Zechariah 13:7 all predicted that God's Savior would be a suffering Messiah.

JULY 17

This is my dearly loved Son, who brings me great joy. Listen to him.

MATTHEW 17:5

HAVE YOU EVER HEARD someone mention having "a mountaintop experience"? Usually that's figurative language for enjoying a great moment in life.

Well, Peter, James, and John had a literal mountaintop experience with Jesus. We call it "The Transfiguration," and no one today has ever seen or felt anything comparable.

Here's how Matthew 17:2-8 describes what happened once they reached the summit:

> As the men watched, Jesus' appearance was transformed so that his face shone like the sun, and his clothes became as white as light. Suddenly, Moses and Elijah appeared and began talking with Jesus.
>
> Peter exclaimed, "Lord, it's wonderful for us to be here! If you want, I'll make three shelters as memorials—one for you, one for Moses, and one for Elijah."
>
> But even as he spoke, a bright cloud overshadowed them, and a voice from the cloud said, "This is my dearly loved Son, who brings me great joy. Listen to him." The disciples were terrified and fell face down on the ground.
>
> Then Jesus came over and touched them. "Get up," he said. "Don't be afraid." And when they looked up, Moses and Elijah were gone, and they saw only Jesus.

Bet you've never seen that on your latest climbing expedition!

What's It Mean?

There's so much to learn from the Transfiguration as Jesus revealed a glimpse of his true glory. But don't miss what God the Father (the voice from the cloud) said about his Son.

Jesus brings God great joy. (God was reiterating what he had said at

Jesus' baptism in Matthew 3:17.) Jesus perfectly accomplished everything that the triune God had planned, before creating the world, for the salvation of his chosen people (Ephesians 1:3-14). This filled the Father with "great joy," and he instructed Jesus' three disciples, "Listen to him."

Today, through his Spirit and Scripture, God is still telling us, "Listen to my Son." Drink in the Savior's words like a desert wanderer who finds an oasis. Hide Jesus' words in your heart. Feed them to your soul. Christ himself said, "The very words I have spoken to you are spirit and life" (John 6:63).

Then one day, you will join Peter, James, John, and all the other believers in witnessing and exulting in the Savior's indescribable glory—not just during a brief mountaintop experience, but for all eternity!

Now What?

Read the other Transfiguration accounts in Mark 9:2-13 and Luke 9:28-36.

Did You Know?

The Transfiguration also teaches us about Jesus' preincarnate/current glory (Matthew 17:2), and it affirms his fulfillment of the Old Testament and life after death, as evidenced by Moses and Elijah's appearance.

JULY 18

Anyone who becomes as humble as this little child
is the greatest in the Kingdom of Heaven.

MATTHEW 18:4

KIDS HAVE IT MADE TODAY!

Think of all the amenities children have specifically geared toward them: video games, sports leagues, museums, playgrounds, trampoline centers, theme parks, toy stores, restaurant menus . . .

That wasn't the case for boys and girls in ancient times. They were generally afterthoughts until they grew old enough to become "productive members of society."

With that in mind, what Jesus said in Matthew 18:1-4 must have been shocking to his original audience. Look at the passage:

> About that time the disciples came to Jesus and asked, "Who is greatest in the Kingdom of Heaven?" Jesus called a little child to him and put the child among them. Then he said, "I tell you the truth, unless you turn from your sins and become like little children, you will never get into the Kingdom of Heaven. So anyone who becomes as humble as this little child is the greatest in the Kingdom of Heaven."

No one in that society considered childlike humility a prerequisite for greatness in God's Kingdom. But Jesus did.

What's It Mean?

Both then and now, the world says greatness is achieved through fame, fortune, pleasure, power, and self-promotion. *Make a name for yourself! Look out for number one! Climb the social ladder!*

But God's Kingdom is not like man's. When Jesus presented a little child as the template for true spiritual greatness, he flipped humanity's script. Little children aren't perfect (ask any parent!), but generally speaking, they are trusting, teachable, and meek. They don't have personal agendas or the same levels of sinful pride that adults do. They do not get swept away by power, money, celebrity, and other worldly enticements.

In God's eyes, true greatness is found in humility. It's one of Scripture's beautiful paradoxes. Yet look at the example of Jesus: no one was both greater or humbler than him (Philippians 2:3-11).

Scripture calls us to exhibit childlike faith in God and his salvation for us through Christ. Childlike faith isn't *childish* or immature. Rather, it's a simple, unassuming, yet unwavering belief in the gospel message—that we are sinful people in great need of a Savior who humbled himself for our sake.

True greatness awaits! But it's where the world would least expect it.

Now What?

Prayerfully meditate on these humility verses: Psalm 18:27; Luke 14:11; and James 4:6, 10.

Did You Know?

Humility wasn't an admirable virtue in the ancient Greco-Roman world. To learn more, check out the July 30 devotion.

JULY 19

Shouldn't you have mercy on your fellow
servant, just as I had mercy on you?

MATTHEW 18:33

HAVE YOU EVER WISHED that your forgiveness had a quota limit on it—a fixed threshold you didn't have to exceed before you were allowed to bust out your elite ninja skills on people who continually annoy, insult, or hurt you?

The apostle Peter actually had the same thought (well, maybe minus the ninja stuff).

One day, he asked Jesus, "Lord, how often should I forgive someone who sins against me? Seven times?" (Matthew 18:21). At the time, Jewish leaders taught that forgiving someone three times was sufficient. So Peter probably thought he was being pretty holy.

Jesus' answer must have caught him off guard. "No, not seven times," Jesus replied, "but seventy times seven!" (Matthew 18:22).

The forgiveness quota is not 490. Flying ninja kicks cannot commence at offense number 491. Jesus was using hyperbole to say our hearts should overflow with forgiveness.

To illustrate his point, he told a poignant parable in Matthew 18:23-35 about a servant who owed a powerful king a lifetime's worth of debt. The servant pleaded for more time to pay. In his great mercy, the king absolved the entire amount and let his servant go free.

Later, the man found one of his own servants who owed him a much smaller debt. He treated him harshly and threw him in prison until he could fulfill his obligation. When the king heard about it, he condemned the wicked servant for life. "Shouldn't you have mercy on your fellow servant, just as I had mercy on you?" the king said (today's verse).

What's It Mean?

The meaning of Jesus' parable is clear: God is the king, and we are the servants who owe an unpayable debt of sin. On our own, there is nothing we can ever do to make restitution. But when we trust in Christ's substitutionary atonement on our behalf, God mercifully pardons all our guilt.

Our sins against God are incalculable—far greater than anyone will ever commit against us. Now the choice comes to you: When others wrong you, will you pridefully hold it against them and refuse to forgive? Or will you humbly extend the same love and mercy that God has shown you?

When someone mistreats you, put aside quotas, ninja attacks, and bitterness. Just forgive as your heavenly Father has forgiven you.

Now What?
Is there someone who has wronged you? Extend forgiveness and make it right with them today.

Did You Know?
After denying Jesus, Peter experienced forgiveness in a powerful way in John 21:15-19.

JULY 20

Make me truly happy by agreeing wholeheartedly with each other,
loving one another, and working together with one mind and purpose.

PHILIPPIANS 2:2

TURTLES LIVE A SIMPLE life, don't they?

Sleepy? Scared? Fed up with life? Doesn't matter. Whenever turtles don't like what's happening in the outside world, they just retreat into the safety of their shell.

Oftentimes, when someone sins against us, we act like a turtle, shrinking behind a self-constructed emotional barrier and waiting for the other person to ask for forgiveness. We justify our isolationistic strategy by saying, "Well, he started it," "She should've known better," or "I'll forgive when they ask."

In Matthew 18:15-17, Jesus instructed us to think differently:

If another believer sins against you, go privately and point out the offense. If the other person listens and confesses it, you have won that person back. But if you are unsuccessful, take one or two others with you and go back again, so that everything you say may be confirmed by two or three witnesses. If the person still refuses to listen, take your case to the church. Then if he or she won't accept the church's decision, treat that person as a pagan or a corrupt tax collector.

What's It Mean?

We often think when we've been wronged that it's the other person's responsibility to initiate reconciliation with us. But Scripture teaches an opposite mindset.

If another Christian sins against you, your job is to lovingly, gently approach that person to rectify the matter, not waiting impatiently—with arms crossed and foot tapping—hoping they'll come to you. In other words, the Bible calls you to be proactive in reconciliation.

After all, isn't this what God did for us? He is the supreme example of this. We started life as God's enemies (Romans 5:10), rebelling against him in every way possible, even by our very nature.

Thankfully, he didn't wait for us to "come around" to repentance and faith. We never would have on our own. So he pursued us. Verses such as John 3:17; 2 Corinthians 5:18; Ephesians 2:1-9; and Colossians 2:13-14 are a small sampling of Scripture's overwhelming evidence that God, the aggrieved party, reached out to us first.

When someone sins against you, go and reach out to them. The goal of all this is the underlying message of today's verse: loving fellowship and unity of purpose in the body of Christ.

Now What?

Look carefully at Matthew 18:15-17 again to see Jesus' step-by-step method of reconciliation.

Did You Know?

If *you* have offended someone, it's still your responsibility to approach that person and ask for forgiveness.

JULY 21

You will know the truth, and the truth will set you free.

JOHN 8:32

IN MANY WAYS, AMERICA'S history is one of freedom, promise, and hope. This country has been a place of refuge and liberty for millions of people.

But America's story also includes a terrible legacy of oppression. Until the ratification of the Constitution's thirteenth amendment in 1865, slavery was a legal, thriving industry in many states. Thankfully, the Civil War helped end this abominable practice.

In John 8, Jesus spoke of a different type of slavery as he taught in Jerusalem. "You are truly my disciples if you remain faithful to my teachings," he said. "And you will know the truth, and the truth will set you free" (John 8:31-32).

Jesus' audience vehemently objected to this statement, proudly clinging to their Jewish heritage. "We are descendants of Abraham," they retorted. "We have never been slaves to anyone. What do you mean, 'You will be set free'?" (verse 33).

Apparently, they had forgotten Israel's lengthy captivity in Egypt, and the fact that, by Jesus' time, Palestine had suffered under foreign rule for most of the previous 750 years. (Talk about selective memory!)

Jesus, though, wasn't referring to physical slavery. He was describing spiritual bondage.

"Everyone who sins is a slave of sin," he continued. "A slave is not a permanent member of the family, but a son is part of the family forever. So if the Son sets you free, you are truly free" (verses 34-36).

What's It Mean?

All humans were born into the bondage of sin, obeying the ungodly passions and desires of our fallen nature.

Sin is a master liar. It promises the world to us: *Pleasure! Freedom! Be your own boss!* Yet all the while, it imprisons our hearts in chains of spiritual captivity.

Jesus, however, came to liberate us with "the truth," as today's verse says. This truth is the gospel message—that God sent his Son into the world to break the power of sin (Romans 8:3) and offer eternal life to all who trust in Christ.

Second Peter 2:19 says, "You are a slave to whatever controls you." If that is true, we need to be sure we serve the correct master. Look at Romans 6:22: "Now you are free from the power of sin and have become slaves of God." (See also Ephesians 6:6.)

By becoming a slave to our gracious, loving God, you will be free!

Now What?

Read Romans 6 to learn how to become "dead to the power of sin and alive to God through Christ Jesus" (verse 11).

Did You Know?

- The apostle Paul frequently used slavery analogies since the practice was so widespread in the Roman Empire.

JULY 22

Put on then, as God's chosen ones, holy and beloved, compassionate hearts, kindness, humility, meekness, and patience.

COLOSSIANS 3:12, ESV

HAS ANYONE EVER PESTERED you with lots of questions? Well, Jesus knows the feeling. The Jewish religious leaders were constantly interrogating him and challenging his authority out of fear, jealousy, anger, and disbelief.

One day, a lawyer tested Jesus about how Jews could inherit eternal life. The conversation quickly turned to Deuteronomy 6:5 and Leviticus 19:18: loving God and loving your neighbor. Insincerely, the lawyer responded, "And who is my neighbor?" Clearly, the man cared less about true love and more about putting limits around whom he had to distribute it to.

So Jesus told him the famous parable of the Good Samaritan. (You can read the whole story in Luke 10:25-37.)

In Jesus' parable, bandits robbed a Jewish man and left him badly wounded on the roadside. A priest and a Levite—two men who served in God's Temple—callously walked by their fellow countryman without showing mercy. Finally, a traveling Samaritan approached the man. Moved with compassion, the Samaritan bandaged the man's wounds, took him to the nearest inn, and paid for his care until he was restored to full health.

What's It Mean?

In this parable, Jesus condemned the current religious establishment of his day (represented by the priest and the Levite), which had largely abandoned true worship of God for a man-centered, works-based system. But he also wanted to draw attention to God's definition of "neighbor" and what true biblical love looks like.

By Jesus' day, the Jews and Samaritans had a nearly eight-hundred-year history of hatred toward each other. Yet through this parable and on other occasions (e.g., Matthew 15:21-28; Luke 7:1-10; Luke 17:11-19; John 4:1-45), Jesus showed that God's love extends to—and through—people of all races, nationalities, and skin colors.

Our natural instinct is to gravitate toward those similar to us. But this parable's message is clear: in a lost, hurting world, we must be ready to show God's compassionate love to others, regardless of any differences.

Every person is made in God's image. In God's economy, everyone you meet is your neighbor. Everyone you encounter, especially those in need, should feel God's compassionate care through you.

The Good Samaritan isn't just a character in an ancient parable. By God's grace, he's someone you can be to others today!

Now What?

Read Ephesians 2:11-22 to learn more about our racial and spiritual unity through Christ.

Did You Know?

Samaritans were descendants of interracial marriages between Jews and Gentiles who had been resettled into Samaria after Assyria conquered Israel in 722 BC.

JULY 23

*While he was still a long way off, his father saw him
coming. Filled with love and compassion, he ran
to his son, embraced him, and kissed him.*

LUKE 15:20

DOES A PORK CHOP dinner sound delicious to you? What about a hearty breakfast with a side of sausage or bacon? Do you enjoy vanilla pudding, cheesecake, or chocolate mousse?

Mmmmm!

Do you use soap, shampoo, and toothpaste daily? (Hope so!) Have you painted with a paintbrush or used sandpaper? Have you ever enjoyed listening to a violin?

If so, you should be thankful for pigs. All these products, and many more, come (in whole or in part) from our plump, porcine pals. Pigs might be stinky, but they are quite useful!

In ancient Israel, though, pigs were considered ceremonially unclean. So in Jesus' famous parable of the Prodigal Son in Luke 15, his original audience would've been shocked to hear the story's starving protagonist rolling around in a pigpen, debasing himself by eating from a pig's filthy feeding trough.

How had this man fallen into that wretched state? He was the rebellious, younger son of a wealthy landowner. Wanting to be his own master, he had traveled to a faraway land and squandered his inheritance in reckless living.

Penniless and alone, he resorted to feeding swine. When he finally came to his senses, he realized that returning to his father as a servant was better than wallowing in the muck.

But look above at today's verse. What a beautiful picture of fatherly love and forgiveness!

The Prodigal Son's father threw a party, announcing, "We must celebrate with a feast, for this son of mine was dead and has now returned to life. He was lost, but now he is found" (verses 23-24).

What's It Mean?

Like the Prodigal Son, we have all dishonored our heavenly Father, defiantly choosing the muck of sin over God's love. But in his great mercy, the Lord did not immediately condemn us. Instead, he chose to redeem a people for himself through Jesus (Ephesians 1:4-7). Now, each time a sinner turns to him in repentance and faith, heaven erupts in boisterous celebration (Luke 15:7, 10).

Have you turned from your prodigal beginnings and into your Father's embrace? Renounce sin and run to God. His love and forgiveness are bigger than your sin.

Leave behind the pigpen of rebellion and enjoy the eternal riches of his grace!

Now What?

Read the entire Prodigal Son parable in Luke 15:11-32.

Did You Know?

The Prodigal Son story was one of three parables in Luke 15 that Jesus told condemning hypocritical religious leaders and their disdain for his acceptance of "tax collectors and sinners."

JULY 24

Each person is destined to die once and after that comes judgment.

HEBREWS 9:27

HAVE YOU EVER HEARD the saying, "Let us eat, drink, and be merry, for tomorrow we may die"? It's an age-old phrase dating back into antiquity. King Solomon (Ecclesiastes 8:15), Isaiah (Isaiah 22:13), and the apostle Paul (1 Corinthians 15:32) referenced it in their writings. It speaks to a short-sighted, self-indulgent philosophy of life, eschewing any notion of moral responsibility.

We see this attitude displayed in Jesus' parable of the rich man and Lazarus in Luke 16:19-31. In the story, the rich man lived a secluded, luxurious life. Meanwhile, Lazarus, a destitute and diseased man, waited outside, hoping to feed on the rich man's unwanted table scraps. Yet the rich man never even acknowledged him.

Eventually, both men died. God brought Lazarus to heaven, while the rich man was sentenced to "torment" (verse 23) and "flames" (verse 24). The rich man begged Abraham (as a heavenly representative of God's redeemed people) to allow Lazarus "to dip the tip of his finger in water and cool my tongue" (verse 24). Abraham's response is chilling:

> Son, remember that during your lifetime you had everything you wanted, and Lazarus had nothing. So now he is here being comforted, and you are in anguish. And besides, there is a great chasm separating us. No one can cross over to you from here, and no one can cross over to us from there.
>
> VERSES 25-26

What's It Mean?

There's a stunning finality to death. As today's verse says, every human will physically die because of sin's curse and then experience God's righteous judgment. Those who trust in Christ's atoning sacrifice for their sins (represented by Lazarus in the parable) will enjoy God's heavenly blessings forever.

411

Those who reject God in this life and live only for themselves and worldly pleasures (represented by the rich man) will be condemned to hell eternally.

Life is not a video game. Once we die, there are no do-overs, reset buttons, or round twos. Yet God has made the way of salvation through Christ very clear to us in Scripture (Luke 16:29; 2 Timothy 3:15). Rejection of that message will bring judgment.

Instead of living life self-indulgently, live for the Lord. Trust in his Son. Seek to honor him. Then, one day, he will bring you into his glorious presence forever!

Now What?
Read the entire parable of the rich man and Lazarus in Luke 16:19-31.

Did You Know?
The "Lazarus" in this parable is *not* the same man as Jesus' friend whom he raised from the dead in John 11.

JULY 25

We are unworthy servants who have simply done our duty.

LUKE 17:10

HAVE YOU EVER WATCHED a movie or TV show about the daily lives of British aristocracy? It's always fascinating to watch the decorum that servants had to display around their masters.

Can you imagine if, after serving an elaborate seven-course meal, the chef suddenly burst through the dining room doors and shouted, "*Booyah! I really nailed it tonight, didn't I?*" with hollers and high fives to all his fellow staff before he and the butler capped things off with a celebratory dance routine?

Every jaw in the room would crash to the floor.

Servants aren't supposed to expect special recognition or draw attention to themselves for simply doing their duty. This was Jesus' point in Luke 17:7-10:

> When a servant comes in from plowing or taking care of sheep, does his master say, "Come in and eat with me"? No, he says, "Prepare my meal, put on your apron, and serve me while I eat. Then you can eat later." And does the master thank the servant for doing what he was told to do? Of course not. In the same way, when you obey me you should say, "We are unworthy servants who have simply done our duty."

There is much to learn from this passage.

What's It Mean?

No one likes being called a servant. But if you are a Christian, that's what you are—and an unworthy one, at that! Christ ransomed you from slavery to sin and death with his blood.

History is littered with wicked, oppressive human masters, but every

413

Christian's Master is righteous in all his ways. It's a great privilege to serve the Lord.

God treats believers far differently than the impersonal, businesslike nature of most masters. He is a loving heavenly Father who adopts us as his spiritual children (Galatians 4:5), and "his unfailing love for us is powerful" (Psalm 117:2).

While human masters hire their servants for daily chores (some meaningful, others menial), our heavenly Master lovingly chose all believers "before he made the world" (Ephesians 1:4) and "created us anew in Christ Jesus, so we can do the good things he planned for us long ago" (Ephesians 2:10). Then he empowers us with unique gifts through his Spirit (1 Corinthians 12).

What a privilege to serve the Master of heaven and earth!

Now What?
If you're not currently serving God somewhere, pray about it and ask your parents or another trusted adult where you could minister to others.

Did You Know?
God will reward our faithful service one day with an eternal crown of glory and honor (1 Peter 5:4)!

JULY 26

I tell you, this sinner, not the Pharisee,
returned home justified before God.

LUKE 18:14

OUR LIVES ARE OFTEN built on performance.

In school, if you study and excel on tests, papers, and other projects, you will earn a good grade. In sports, if you perform well, you will likely earn a starting position on the team. If you participate in the Boy Scouts or Girl Scouts of America (or something similar), you must meet certain criteria in various activities to receive merit badges. In your professional career, you will typically earn promotions and pay raises only by performing well.

But when it comes to spiritual righteousness, human performance doesn't matter. This is hard for many people to understand. Maybe it is for you, too. That's why Jesus told the parable found in Luke 18:10-14:

> Two men went to the Temple to pray. One was a Pharisee, and the other was a despised tax collector. The Pharisee stood by himself and prayed this prayer: "I thank you, God, that I am not like other people—cheaters, sinners, adulterers. I'm certainly not like that tax collector! I fast twice a week, and I give you a tenth of my income." But the tax collector stood at a distance and dared not even lift his eyes to heaven as he prayed. Instead, he beat his chest in sorrow, saying, "O God, be merciful to me, for I am a sinner." I tell you, this sinner, not the Pharisee, returned home justified before God.

What's It Mean?

We can't earn our own salvation. There's nothing we can put on a spiritual résumé, so to speak (e.g., Christian upbringing, good works, ethical living, church attendance, etc.), to impress God. We need a righteousness outside ourselves. We need the righteousness that comes "through faith in Christ" (Philippians 3:9).

Your heart's posture must be like that of the tax collector's. He knew he had sinned greatly and had nothing to offer God to merit his own righteousness. So he humbly repented and asked forgiveness. God mercifully justified him—or declared him righteous—by grace through faith (Ephesians 2:8-9).

Are you basing your righteousness on your own merits? Are you trying to earn your salvation like a scouting merit badge or a professional promotion? You can't! Leave pharisaical righteousness behind and take a cue from the humble tax collector!

Now What?
For more on justification, review the August 26 devotion and read Romans 3–5.

Did You Know?
Most first-century Jews looked up to the Pharisees as the elite moral standard, while tax collectors were considered reprehensible sinners. Jesus played on these cultural stereotypes to teach an important lesson about righteousness and justification.

JULY 27

Godly grief produces a repentance that leads to salvation without regret, whereas worldly grief produces death.

2 CORINTHIANS 7:10, ESV

THE DESPISED LITTLE MAN peered through the branches. The teeming throngs below crammed the streets of Jericho, waiting for the Messiah as he made his much-anticipated trip toward Jerusalem for the Passover celebration.

The little man, though, was too short to enjoy the spectacle at street level. So he had climbed a sycamore tree to catch even a fleeting glimpse of Jesus.

In that brief moment, from his leafy perch, he towered above them. On the social ladder, he ranked above most of them, too, thanks to his great wealth. But that's because he was a crook. Jewish by birth and Roman tax collector by trade, he collected what the Romans required and sneaked in an extra percentage for himself. His countrymen considered him a loathsome traitor.

Suddenly, a voice broke through the din of the crowd: "Zacchaeus! Quick, come down! I must be a guest in your home today."

Jesus wasn't just making a social call on Zacchaeus. He was calling Zacchaeus to a new way of life.

At his house, Zacchaeus vowed, "I will give half my wealth to the poor, Lord, and if I have cheated people on their taxes, I will give them back four times as much!"

Zacchaeus had truly repented.

What's It Mean?

Repentance is often misunderstood. In Mark 1:15, Jesus told the crowds, "The Kingdom of God is near! Repent of your sins and believe the Good News!" Both repentance and faith are necessary for salvation.

Repentance is much more than an offhand comment such as, "My bad," or "Sorry about that." True biblical repentance is about heart change.

It's turning from your sins and choosing to follow God—obedience built on saving faith in Christ (see today's verse). This is the radical transformation that Zacchaeus displayed. (You can read his story in Luke 19:1-10.)

Repentance is a vital part of every Christian's conversion. If you've never turned from your sins and trusted in Christ, do so today!

But repentance is also an important part of every Christian's ongoing spiritual life whenever we sin against God or others. When you sin, confess it to the Lord, ask for his forgiveness, and ask the Spirit's help to leave that sin behind. He will faithfully help you (1 John 1:9).

Now What?

Do you have any unconfessed sin toward the Lord or another person? Bring it into the light in true repentance today.

Did You Know?

- Old Testament law required a thief to repay "the full price plus an additional 20 percent" (Leviticus 6:5). Zacchaeus far exceeded these requirements!

JULY 28

Jesus said, "Let the children come to me. Don't
stop them! For the Kingdom of Heaven belongs
to those who are like these children."

MATTHEW 19:14

JESUS WAS A BUSY GUY.

During his earthly ministry, the Son of God was constantly on the move, going from town to town, teaching the people God's Word, healing the sick, and performing other amazing miracles. He endured many sleepless nights and rarely got a break from the huge, spiritually needy crowds who followed him. Even during his downtime, he was usually fellowshipping with his twelve disciples and preparing them for his death, resurrection, and return to heaven.

But Jesus was never too busy for children. We see this in a brief story in Matthew 19:13-15 when some children were brought to Jesus (most likely by their parents) for him to bless them. The disciples, lacking any compassion and heart for God's Kingdom in that moment, sternly rebuked the people and tried to shoo the children off, considering them a nuisance. They thought Jesus was too important for kids.

Jesus "was angry with his disciples" (Mark 10:14).

"Let the children come to me," he said. "Don't stop them! For the Kingdom of Heaven belongs to those who are like these children" (today's verse). Then he blessed the children.

What's It Mean?

Have you ever felt swept aside by society because of your age? Have you ever felt like adults don't notice you? Have you ever felt like *no one cares?*

Take heart. There is a God in heaven who deeply cares about you.

Your generation matters to God. *You* matter to God. In one of his earlier discourses, Jesus issued a stern warning: "Beware that you don't look down on any of these little ones. For I tell you that in heaven their angels are always in the presence of my heavenly Father" (Matthew 18:10). Wow!

If God specifically puts young people under angelic care, it's clear you are special to him.

But there's an even greater indication of God's love for you. It's found in John 3:16: "God so loved the world, that he gave his only Son, that whoever believes in him should not perish but have eternal life" (ESV). God sacrificed his own Son so he could adopt you into his eternal family. This is supreme love.

Age doesn't matter to God. But you do!

Now What?

Now that you know God loves youth, don't use your age as an excuse when it comes to serving the Lord! Read the May 23 devotion on Jeremiah 1:7.

Did You Know?

Psalm 127:3 says, "Children are a gift from the LORD; they are a reward from him."

JULY 29

No one can ever be made right with God by doing what the law commands. The law simply shows us how sinful we are.

ROMANS 3:20

JESUS MET ALL SORTS of interesting people with various questions and needs during his earthly ministry. One day, he met a rich young ruler. The man ran up to him and fell at his feet. Clearly, the man had much on his mind.

"Good Teacher," he said, breathlessly, "what must I do to inherit eternal life?"

Problem alert! The way the man addressed Jesus revealed a deficiency in his knowledge of the Savior's divine nature. Jesus subtly pointed out the man's error.

"Why do you call me good?" Jesus asked. "Only God is truly good. But to answer your question, you know the commandments: 'You must not murder. You must not commit adultery. You must not steal. You must not testify falsely. You must not cheat anyone. Honor your father and mother.'"

"Teacher," the man replied, "I've obeyed all these commandments since I was young." (You've got to wonder if the man's parents would agree with that statement!)

"There is still one thing you haven't done," Jesus said. "Go and sell all your possessions and give the money to the poor, and you will have treasure in heaven. Then come, follow me."

Sadly, the man left for good. He couldn't bear to part with the idols of worldly riches.

What's It Mean?

The rich young ruler had a warped sense of righteousness. "What must *I do*?" he asked. He thought salvation was based on human merit, as if piling up enough good deeds to impress God could somehow atone for his sins.

But deep down, it seems he knew better. When Jesus initially played along by listing the Ten Commandments to reveal his flawed thinking, the ruler replied, "What else must I do?" (Matthew 19:20). The man had a gnawing feeling that merit-based righteousness wasn't sufficient.

It's not. Righteousness isn't about what *we* do; it's about what Christ has already done for us. The Savior who was about to die to provide the rich young ruler eternal life was standing before him. Tragically, the man had no idea.

Today, a choice is before you: God offers you eternal life through his Son. As today's verse says, you can't be made right with God by moral living. You must turn from heart idolatry, receive Christ's righteousness, and follow him.

Will you?

Now What?
Prayerfully ask God where you need his help to root out moralistic or idolatrous tendencies in your heart.

Did You Know?
You can read about this story in all three synoptic gospels: Matthew 19:16-30; Mark 10:17-31; and Luke 18:18-30.

JULY 30

The Son of Man came not to be served but to serve
others and to give his life as a ransom for many.

MARK 10:45

NOT LONG BEFORE HIS death in AD 14, Caesar Augustus, Rome's first emperor, wrote *Res Gestae Divi Augusti*, which recounted the major accomplishments of his forty-year reign. Augustus's effort was an essay in vanity.

Let's start with the title: *Res Gestae Divi Augusti* is Latin for *The Deeds of the Divine Augustus*. You might have an arrogance problem if you call yourself a demigod!

Throughout *The Deeds*, Augustus congratulates himself for his military, governmental, and civic achievements, happily highlighting near the end that "the doors of my Temple were publicly clothed with laurel and a civic crown was fixed over my door and a gold shield placed in the Julian senate-house, and the inscription of that shield testified to the virtue, mercy, justice, and piety, for which the senate and Roman people gave it to me." One wonders if Augustus cramped up from patting himself on the back so much.

Today, we'd say, "Get over yourself, bro!" But remarkably, humility wasn't a virtue in the ancient Greco-Roman world. They prized personal honor and glory above almost everything else.

Then Jesus appeared, preaching a completely different way of living.

What's It Mean?
In Mark 10:42-45, Jesus told his disciples,

> You know that the rulers in this world lord it over their people, and officials flaunt their authority over those under them. . . . Whoever wants to be a leader among you must be your servant, and whoever wants to be first among you must be the slave of everyone else. For even the Son of Man came not to be served but to serve others and to give his life as a ransom for many.

423

Christ's crucifixion was absurdity to the majority of the ancient world (1 Corinthians 1:22-23). But what the world doesn't understand is perfectly in line with God's wisdom: the first must be last, and true spiritual greatness is found in humility, not self-promotion. God's Son, who ransomed his life to purchase our freedom from sin and death, is the example par excellence.

The world says, "Do you want to be great? Then seek honor and glory for yourself and let everyone know who you are!" But Jesus says, "Do you want to truly be great? Then follow my example and serve others."

That is truly divine!

Now What?
Find a way to regularly serve others in your church, neighborhood, or school.

Did You Know?
At Augustus's order, copies of *The Deeds* were distributed throughout his empire and inscribed on bronze tablets for display outside his tomb.

JULY 31

*The crowds that went before him and that followed him were
shouting, "Hosanna to the Son of David! Blessed is he who
comes in the name of the Lord! Hosanna in the highest!"*

MATTHEW 21:9, ESV

JESUS HAD BEEN TO JERUSALEM many times before. But this trip
would be much different. Before the week was over, Jesus would be arrested
and killed.

When Jesus passed through the ancient gates, the whole city was burst-
ing with people (thanks to Passover) and anticipation. In fulfillment of
Zechariah 9:9, Jesus rode into Jerusalem on a donkey's colt—the eternal
King on a humble mount.

The people laid cloaks on the road in deference to Jesus, waved palm
branches, and joyfully danced around him, crying out, "Hosanna to the Son
of David! Blessed is he who comes in the name of the Lord!" (today's verse).

We call this the Triumphal Entry, although that's a bit of a misnomer.
Yes, there was huge excitement surrounding Jesus' entrance into Jerusalem.
Many Jews rightly believed he was the long-awaited Messiah. But their
expectations for his messianic role were greatly skewed. They were antici-
pating a political/military savior who would overthrow Rome and restore
Israel's independence. Once that didn't transpire, they turned on Jesus.

Five days later, the crowd's tone changed drastically. The joyful shouts
of "Hosanna! Hosanna!" turned into bloodthirsty screams of "Crucify him!
Crucify him!"

What's It Mean?

What is your understanding of who Jesus is? Why do you believe he came
to earth? How are you anticipating that he will work in your life? What are
your expectations for being a Christ follower?

Your answers to these questions are vitally important. The crowd in
Jerusalem prior to Jesus' crucifixion answered these questions from their own
assumptions and misguided teaching from wicked leaders (Matthew 27:20).

Don't be like Jerusalem's ancient crowd. Jesus doesn't need to meet your expectations. You need to meet *his*. This means humbly trusting in him as your Savior from sins and following him as the Lord of your life.

Let God's Son instruct you about his identity and purpose. Let God's Spirit turn your heart toward him. Let Scripture build your faith.

Then you will truly be able to say, "Blessed is he who comes in the name of the Lord! Hosanna in the highest!"

Now What?
All four gospels record the Triumphal Entry. Check out the subtle differences in each version (Matthew 21:1-11; Mark 11:1-11; Luke 19:28-40; and John 12:12-19).

Did You Know?
Palm branches were a sign of Jewish patriotism, used in the Feast of Booths (Nehemiah 8:15), and were featured in engravings in Solomon's Temple (1 Kings 6:32).

AUGUST 1

If anyone is ashamed of me and my message,
the Son of Man will be ashamed of that
person when he returns in his glory.

LUKE 9:26

APPROVAL FEELS GOOD, DOESN'T IT? Who doesn't love getting a pat on the back for a job well done?

When Jesus entered Jerusalem on a donkey's colt during his final Passover week, the City of David exploded with *hosanna*-filled approvals at the coming of the Jews' long-awaited Anointed One. But there was still much confusion surrounding the nature of Jesus' messianic mission. So he immediately addressed the multitudes and spoke of his imminent death. This stunned the crowd and weeded out false disciples.

Many who still believed in him kept their newfound faith shrouded in secrecy. Here's how John 12:42-43 evaluates their lukewarm devotion: "Many people did believe in him . . . including some of the Jewish leaders. But they wouldn't admit it for fear that the Pharisees would expel them from the synagogue. For they loved human praise more than the praise of God."

These people loved approval from others too much, at the cost of following Christ in that moment. It's fair to wonder whether they had saving faith at all.

What's It Mean?

True followers of Jesus must be willing to openly declare their allegiance to him. Christianity is not a faith of reticence, privacy, or shame. We are to boldly share the good news of Christ with "all the nations" (Matthew 28:19).

Look at today's verse. If we are ashamed of Jesus on earth, he will be ashamed of us when we stand before God's judgment throne in heaven. That's a frightening thought.

Consider some similar passages of Scripture (emphases added):

- *I am not ashamed of this Good News about Christ.* It is the power of God at work, saving everyone who believes—the Jew first and also the Gentile. (Romans 1:16)
- If you *openly declare* that Jesus is Lord and believe in your heart that God raised him from the dead, you will be saved. (Romans 10:9)
- To that end, keep alert with all perseverance, making supplication for all the saints, and also for me, that words may be given to me in *opening my mouth boldly to proclaim* the mystery of the gospel. (Ephesians 6:18-19, ESV)

Considering what Jesus sacrificed for you on the cross, how can you not joyfully proclaim his name and the gospel message to others?

Now What?
Share the gospel with a friend today!

Did You Know?
To be excommunicated from the local synagogue (John 12:42) was the extreme social and religious disgrace for first-century Jews.

AUGUST 2

No other commandment is greater than these.

MARK 12:31

WE HUMANS HAVE A BAD HABIT of complicating simple things in life.

Take eating vegetables, for instance. When we were younger, our parents said, "Eat your veggies." Simple enough, right? Obey parents, fill body with essential vitamins, and grow up to be a future Olympic star!

But we fussed and let the veggies go cold. Our parents harped on us to finish the cold veggies, we continued to whine, and the problem worsened. Finally, when our parents weren't looking, we dumped the cold veggies in the trash. No veggies and no vitamins. Now, we sit on the sofa and watch the Olympics on TV.

We should've just eaten the veggies.

This, of course, is hyperbole. But the underlying principle remains.

We can complicate simple biblical truths, too. Check out Mark 12:28-34, where "one of the teachers of religious law" asked Jesus which Old Testament commandment was most important. This occurred on Tuesday of Passion Week, three days before Jesus' crucifixion. He replied,

The most important commandment is this: "Listen, O Israel! The LORD our God is the one and only LORD. And you must love the LORD your God with all your heart, all your soul, all your mind, and all your strength." The second is equally important: "Love your neighbor as yourself." No other commandment is greater than these.

VERSES 29-31

What's It Mean?

Oftentimes, we make the Bible out to be a complicated book and Christianity a difficult faith. But they're not! Scripture can be distilled to this simple maxim: love God wholeheartedly and love others. This is what the Christian life is all about.

God graciously gave us a wonderful book of real-life stories to illustrate his love for us and what our love for him and others should look like. When we love God with all our being and love others as ourselves, we fulfill Scripture.

Of course, none of this is possible on our own. To have this godly love, we need a spiritual overhaul, beginning with God's Spirit regenerating our sinful hearts to receive salvation and awakening an outward focus in us.

Loving God wholeheartedly and loving others—it's so simple, it's beautiful! (And it sure beats cold veggies.)

Now What?
Biblical love is sacrificial. Show love to someone today by putting their desires ahead of your own.

Did You Know?
The religious teacher wasn't just referring to the Ten Commandments when he asked Jesus about the "most important" commandment. He was likely referencing the 613 individual commandments—248 positives ("dos") and 365 negatives ("do nots")—that Jewish scribes traditionally count in the Mosaic law (the first five books of the Old Testament).

AUGUST 3

You have neglected the more important matters of the law—justice, mercy and faithfulness. You should have practiced the latter, without neglecting the former.

MATTHEW 23:23, NIV

SOMETIMES, IT'S HARD TO tell if someone is upset with you, especially if they're good at concealing their feelings. But if that person calls you a "hypocrite," "blind guide," "blind fool," "snake," or a "whitewashed tomb," you can be confident they don't think highly of you!

On Tuesday of Passion Week, Jesus let the Pharisees and Jewish scribes know exactly how he felt about them, pronouncing these epithets and seven "woes" on them before the crowd in Jerusalem (Matthew 23). In Scripture, a woe is a warning of divine judgment.

The hypocritical religious leaders were masters of manmade religion. They thought they could earn God's favor by fastidiously keeping hundreds of Old Testament commandments and other manmade laws. They even tithed the smallest herbs from their gardens (verse 23) and strained their beverages before drinking so they wouldn't accidentally swallow a bug—thus becoming ceremonially unclean (verse 24).

Yet as Jesus said in today's verse, they ignored what the law was really trying to teach them—justice, mercy, and faithfulness toward God and others.

They had chosen practice over principle.

What's It Mean?

Practice over principle is not just an ancient problem. We might not struggle with the same specific issues as the first-century Jewish religious leaders did, but we can all get pharisaical about our worship.

Anytime you elevate a specific practice over the biblical principle behind it, you're treading on dangerous ground. The Christian faith is not formulaic.

Elevating any worship practice above the proper heart behind it is a common temptation. As humans, it's easier for us to check things off a list rather than live faithfully by the biblical principle that makes the practice worthwhile. Like the Pharisees two thousand years ago, our sinful hearts can quickly crave God's approval through something other than Christ's finished work on the cross.

Remember, God wants your heart. He's not as concerned about the methods you use as he is your humble devotion to him and the motivation behind your worship. He doesn't care about your obedience if it's not being produced from a heart that loves him and wants to serve others.

So enjoy your garden herbs and drink your soda unstrained! And worship the Lord the way he outlines in Scripture—with "justice, mercy and faithfulness."

Now What?
Test all spiritual "practices" you hear about against the final authority of God's Word.

Did You Know?
Isaiah 1:10-20; Hosea 6:6; and 1 Samuel 15 (especially verses 22-23) are all helpful passages on this topic.

AUGUST 4

God loves a person who gives cheerfully.

2 CORINTHIANS 9:7

PLINK. PLINK...

Plink! Plink!

The coins rattled into the Temple collection boxes, causing quite a racket. The donors didn't mind. They loved hearing the sound of their contributions echoing through the corridors, secretly hoping that others would notice their generosity.

This was all part of the chaotic scene at the Lord's Temple on Tuesday of Passion Week as Jerusalem swarmed with pilgrims shortly before the annual Passover feast. Luke 21:1-4 records Jesus carefully observing this with his disciples.

Then a poor widow came up to one of the collection boxes.

Plink. Plink.

She dropped in two small copper coins. Jesus said to his disciples, "This poor widow has given more than all the rest of them. For they have given a tiny part of their surplus, but she, poor as she is, has given everything she has" (verses 3-4).

What's It Mean?

By today's monetary standards, the affluent Temple visitors that day probably gave hundreds, if not thousands, of dollars. How could Jesus make such a statement?

It's easy: God is the eternal, sovereign Ruler of heaven and earth. He created and owns all things. He doesn't need our money. He wants our hearts.

The rich gave large sums but still had plenty left in savings. The woman, however, gave everything she had to live on. As a widow in a male-dominated society, she likely had no other way to earn money for food, clothing, or shelter. She was completely entrusting her future to God in faith.

Like all blessings in life, our money is ultimately not our own. It's a gift from God that we are to steward well. As today's verse says, God wants us to give joyfully to him, regardless of the amount.

Give your time, talents, and money generously to the Lord. Use what he has given you to bless others and advance his Kingdom. Above all, do it cheerfully, believing that God will provide all you need (Matthew 6:33). Then watch him reach into his heavenly storehouses and bless you in ways you couldn't imagine—not for your financial gain, but for his glory!

Now What?
If you don't already, start tithing (giving 10 percent of what you earn) to your church.

Did You Know?
In the original Greek language of the New Testament, the word for the widow's coins was *lepta*, signifying the smallest copper coin available. It was roughly one centimeter in diameter and worth only a fraction of a laborer's daily wage.

AUGUST 5

Well done, my good and faithful servant. You have been
faithful in handling this small amount, so now I will give
you many more responsibilities. Let's celebrate together!

MATTHEW 25:21

ON TUESDAY OF PASSION WEEK, Jesus sat on the Mount of Olives
outside Jerusalem with his disciples. Using prophecies and parables, he
spoke to them about future events and God's Kingdom.

In the parable of the talents (Matthew 25:14-30), he told of a wealthy
man who entrusted three of his servants with large sums of money before
going on a long journey. The first servant received five talents, the second
received two talents, and the third received one talent. (In ancient times, a
talent was a monetary weight of measurement.)

When the master returned, he found that the first and second servants
had invested his money wisely and doubled their amounts. The master
praised each of the men individually. "Well done, my good and faithful servant," he told them. "You have been faithful in handling this small amount,
so now I will give you many more responsibilities. Let's celebrate together!"
(today's verse).

The third servant, however, had foolishly buried his talent in the
ground. When the master asked for an accounting, the man could only give
back the original talent. The master rebuked the wicked servant and threw
him "into outer darkness" (Matthew 25:30).

What's It Mean?

The master in the parable is Jesus, and the servants represent us. Jesus' long
journey is the current church age between his ascension into heaven and his
future second coming. When he returns, what will he discover that you've
done while he's been away?

God has given you unique spiritual gifts and abilities. These are the
"talents" in the parable. He blessed you with these to glorify him, spread the

gospel, and build his Kingdom. By doing this, you will "multiply your talents" like the good servants in the parable.

Don't be like the wicked, unbelieving servant who wasted his talent by hiding it in the ground and was condemned to eternal punishment. Use your gifts, skills, and abilities to their full potential for God's glory until Jesus returns. Then one day when you enter the Lord's presence in eternity, you will hear those beautiful words: "Well done, my good and faithful servant."

Now What?

Find ways to use your God-given talents to glorify him at church, school, and in your community.

Did You Know?

A talent was worth approximately twenty years' wages for a daily laborer—a huge sum.

AUGUST 6

*Every time you eat this bread and drink this cup, you are
announcing the Lord's death until he comes again.*

1 CORINTHIANS 11:26

IF, SOMEHOW, YOU HAD foreknowledge that you were about to be
betrayed, arrested, abandoned by your closest friends, endure a series of
illegitimate trials, and suffer a torturous death, how would you spend your
last few hours?

Well, Jesus observed the Passover with the same men who would cause
him much pain in his hour of greatest need! Amazingly, he told his disciples,
"I have been very eager to eat this Passover meal with you before my suffering begins" (Luke 22:15).

During the meal, however, he added a twist to this ancient celebration
that literally changed history. Here's how Luke 22:19-20 records it:

> He took some bread and gave thanks to God for it. Then he broke
> it in pieces and gave it to the disciples, saying, "This is my body,
> which is given for you. Do this in remembrance of me." After
> supper he took another cup of wine and said, "This cup is the new
> covenant between God and his people—an agreement confirmed
> with my blood, which is poured out as a sacrifice for you."

We call this the Lord's Supper, and Christians have been observing this
special sacrament ever since.

What's It Mean?

The Lord's Supper (also referred to as Communion) is one of two sacraments that Scripture commands. (The other is baptism; see the June 14
devotion.) A sacrament is a religious ritual that symbolizes a spiritual truth.
Neither the Lord's Supper nor baptism are necessary for salvation, but they
are an important part of every Christian's life.

While baptism is a one-time event, Scripture calls believers to regularly partake in the Lord's Supper. Why? Because as today's verse says, whenever we do, we powerfully proclaim the gospel until Jesus returns—for our sanctification, the edification of the local body of Christ, and a strong witness to any unbelievers present.

The bread we eat represents Christ's body, broken for us on the cross. The juice we drink represents Christ's blood, shed as an atoning sacrifice for our sins. The Lord's Supper is a beautiful reminder of what Jesus did on our behalf to make us right with a holy God. It's also a foretaste of the future "wedding feast of the Lamb" that Christians will enjoy in heaven (Revelation 19:7).

What a joy it is to partake in the Lord's Supper!

Now What?
If you are a follower of Jesus but have never participated in the Lord's Supper, ask your parents about doing so.

Did You Know?
Approaching the Lord's Supper with a worshipful heart is extremely important (1 Corinthians 11:17-34).

AUGUST 7

*Jesus, our High Priest, has been given a ministry that is far
superior to the old priesthood, for he is the one who mediates for
us a far better covenant with God, based on better promises.*

HEBREWS 8:6

NEWER IS OFTEN BETTER. Which would you rather have—a cord-in-the-wall rotary phone or a smartphone? A horseless carriage or a Ford Mustang GT? An outhouse or indoor plumbing?

You get the point!

On Thursday night of Passion Week, Jesus told his disciples that his imminent death and resurrection would replace something old with something newer and much better. As he passed around the wine during the Passover meal, he said, "This cup that is poured out for you is the new covenant in my blood" (Luke 22:20, ESV).

The disciples probably didn't fully grasp the meaning of Jesus' statement at the time, but it was packed with history and promise. The advent of a new covenant naturally means there was an old one. But what was it, and why did it apparently need to be replaced?

What's It Mean?

The old covenant was the Mosaic law that God gave Israel after delivering them from Egypt. God promised to bless his people if they remained faithful to him, but the Israelites transgressed God's laws and broke his covenant. Ultimately, the Old Testament laws and sacrifices were never meant to save the Israelites from their sins but to show them how much they needed a Savior (Hebrews 10:1-4).

In the sixth century BC, as the southern kingdom of Judah was being exiled to Babylon, God said through the prophet Jeremiah, "The day is coming . . . when I will make a new covenant with the people of Israel and Judah" (Jeremiah 31:31). God said he would not write this new covenant on tablets of stone, like the old covenant, but he would "put [his] instructions deep within them, and . . . write them on their hearts" (Jeremiah 31:33).

As today's verse says, Jesus fulfilled Jeremiah's prophecy! Through his death and resurrection, Jesus initiated the new covenant. The new covenant is all about God's forgiveness through Christ's atoning work on the cross. It's all about mercy, grace, and forgiveness. It's all about God changing human hearts by his Spirit.

This is the covenant we get to partake in through faith in Jesus!

Old or new covenant? It's a no-brainer . . . the new covenant through Christ is far better!

Now What?
Read Jeremiah's new covenant prophecy in Jeremiah 31:31-34 and then Hebrews 10:1-18, which expounds on it.

Did You Know?
Ezekiel prophesied something similar to Jeremiah in Ezekiel 36:26.

AUGUST 8

Through love serve one another.

GALATIANS 5:13, ESV

IF YOU KNEW YOU were going to die tomorrow, how would you spend
your last hours? Would you gorge on your favorite foods? Do something
exhilarating such as skydiving or amateur race car driving? Go on a wild
spending spree? Hastily write a last will and testament?

On the night before his death, Jesus washed his disciples' feet. In first-
century Palestine, this was the duty of a house servant, one of the lowest
forms of servitude. Yet during that special Passover meal, the eternal Son of
God took a washbasin and went around the table, humbly kneeling before
each of his friends to scrub the dust and grime from their sandaled feet.

Once he was finished, Jesus asked his disciples, "Do you understand
what I was doing? You call me 'Teacher' and 'Lord,' and you are right,
because that's what I am. And since I, your Lord and Teacher, have washed
your feet, you ought to wash each other's feet. I have given you an example
to follow. Do as I have done to you" (John 13:12-15).

What's It Mean?

Jesus' servanthood that night was stunningly beautiful. But don't worry . . .
this doesn't mean you need to set up a monthly sole-sanitizing schedule
with your friends. Tell them to keep their stinky socks on! Jesus' act was a
symbolic display of the self-sacrificing attitude every believer should have
toward one another.

Here are five reasons why Christians should adopt an others-first
mindset:

- **The Savior commanded us to!** If the Master willingly served his
  servants like Jesus did, the servants have no reason *not* to serve one
  another!
- **God is love (1 John 4:8).** As God's children, we are to embody love,
  which is a joyfully self-sacrificial attitude toward others.

- **It's a powerful witness to nonbelievers.** As Jesus told his disciples after washing their feet, "Your love for one another will prove to the world that you are my disciples" (John 13:35).
- **It sanctifies us.** By nature, we are prideful, selfish, and unkind beings. Serving others helps us put this old nature to death.
- **It builds the church.** Putting others' needs first allows us to practice our God-given spiritual gifts, encourage others, and build up the body of Christ (1 Thessalonians 5:11).

Put your best foot forward, follow the Savior's example, and serve others!

Now What?

Find a consistent way to sacrifice your time and talents for the benefit of other believers in your church or a gospel-centered organization.

Did You Know?

Jesus even washed the feet of Judas Iscariot, his eventual betrayer!

AUGUST 9

*I am the way, the truth, and the life. No one can
come to the Father except through me.*

JOHN 14:6

OH BOY.

The disciples knew something bad—really bad—was about to happen, but they weren't exactly sure what. Jesus had spoken many times about his upcoming departure. Now, as the group made its way to the garden of Gethsemane, Jesus mentioned his looming exit from this world once again.

He told his friends he was leaving to prepare an eternal home for them and eventually return to bring them there. Then, he said something curious: "You know the way to where I am going."

Thomas was confused.

"We have no idea where you are going," he said, "so how can we know the way?"

Jesus replied, "I am the way, the truth, and the life. No one can come to the Father except through me." (You can read the full account of this interaction in John 14:1-14.)

What's It Mean?

Jesus' claim was astounding. In no uncertain terms, he declared that he—and only he—is the exclusive door through which we must pass to get to heaven. There is no other path, no other key, and certainly no shortcut available.

Jesus' bold statement left no room for misinterpretation. Of course, he had to back it up—which he did later that week through his sinless, sacrificial death on the cross and his miraculous resurrection.

For the next four days, we're going to study some important questions related to this topic:

- Is Christianity true while all other religions are false? (Spoiler alert: Yes!)
- If so, how can we be assured that Christianity is the only true faith?

- Why isn't it possible for all religions to lead to heaven?
- If all other beliefs except true Christianity are wrong, how could a loving God send billions of people to hell?
- How should we react when people are offended by our faith and Christianity's claims of exclusive, absolute truth?

These are questions of huge significance, both for this life and for eternity. It's critical to know the truth and be confident in what you believe about God and the salvation he provides only through his Son.

As today's verse tells us, Jesus is the only *way* to heaven, and if you believe this *truth*, you will have eternal *life*!

Now What?
Memorize John 14:6. It will serve you well in life!

Did You Know?
The words of the apostle Peter in Acts 4:12 are very similar to today's verse.

AUGUST 10

Whoever believes in the Son has eternal life; whoever does not obey the Son shall not see life, but the wrath of God remains on him.

JOHN 3:36, ESV

HERE'S AN EYE-POPPING STATISTIC: In 2020, the world's estimated population was 7.8 billion.

That's *a lot* of people.

With that many people comes a glut of different religions. There are the "Big Five"—Christianity, Islam, Hinduism, Buddhism, and Judaism—that most people (almost 5.8 billion) identify with and a multitude of smaller ones. Some experts estimate there are more than four thousand different religions in the world. Another 1.2 billion people classify themselves as "nonreligious." This group includes atheists (those who don't believe in God or the afterlife) and agnostics (those who say they don't know or care if there's a God). The world is a huge melting pot of religious beliefs.

So . . . which is correct? Can one be right while the others are wrong? Or can many religious paths lead to the same eternal happiness?

Jesus answered that in today's verse and John 14:6 (see yesterday's devotion). No one, he said, can experience eternal life with God apart from him.

What's It Mean?

Wow.

In a world overflowing with religious ideas, that's an incredibly bold, polarizing statement. In essence, Jesus declared in John 3:36 and 14:6 that true Christianity—the gospel of Jesus Christ, as declared in the Bible—is true and all other religions are false.

Most people don't like to be told their ideas about religion, morality, and eternity are wrong. Billions of people around the world are committed, to some degree, to specific religious beliefs. Many others take a more relaxed approach, believing that "all roads lead to heaven," as long as you are ethical and remain relatively committed to your cause.

But this is absurd—logically impossible. For instance, Islam and

Judaism reject the doctrines of the Trinity and Christ's deity. Hindus believe in many gods and reincarnation. Buddhists strive to reach enlightenment (a.k.a., "nirvana") through human effort.

All these beliefs directly violate core tenets of Christianity found in God's Word. How can all these viewpoints be correct and lead everyone—somehow, some way—into a righteous standing before God in heaven? The answer: they can't! Would the same God who sent his Son to die to redeem sinners (John 3:16) also accept many other conflicting salvation plans? Absolutely not!

There is only one way to heaven: through the righteousness provided through faith in our Lord Jesus Christ. Amen!

Now What?

Check out tomorrow's devotion to learn how we can be assured that Christianity is the only true faith.

Did You Know?

First John 4:1-6 provides insight in helping us discern truthful spiritual beliefs from error.

AUGUST 11

He commands all people everywhere to repent, because he has
fixed a day on which he will judge the world in righteousness
by a man whom he has appointed; and of this he has
given assurance to all by raising him from the dead.

ACTS 17:30-31, ESV

THE WORLD IS A BIG PLACE, filled with billions of people and thousands of nuanced religious ideas. If you asked ten different people on a busy city street, "How do you get to heaven?" it's quite possible that you'd get ten different answers.

But as we've discussed over the last few days, the Bible clearly proclaims that Christianity is the only true faith. Jesus himself said, "No one can come to the Father except through me" (John 14:6).

Perhaps you are looking for more assurance of this. Maybe you're thinking, *There are so many religions out there. How can I know for sure that Christianity is right and everything else is wrong?*

Let's probe deeper . . .

What's It Mean?

First, you can take the eternal Son of God at his word. If he says he is the only way to God, then it's true because he is perfect, and he defines truth.

That said, let's make a distinction between religion and Christianity. Religion is man's way of trying to impress God. It's a human-centered endeavor to earn eternal life through good works.

Christianity, though, is different. It's the only belief system in the world that acknowledges that salvation is a free gift of God's grace, not to be earned by human merit, but by faith in Christ's finished work of atonement.

Most powerfully, Jesus' resurrection affirms Christianity as the only true faith. As today's verse says, God has "given assurance to all [of Scripture's gospel message] by raising him from the dead." All other gods, prophets, martyrs, or religious pioneers are either myths or dead. But not Jesus. He is alive, risen, and reigning on high!

Of course, forsaking other worldviews and embracing Christ takes faith. You can't please God without trusting him at his word (Hebrews 11:6). But a Christian's faith isn't merely wishful thinking—like blindly throwing a dart at a dartboard of religions and hoping you hit the bull's-eye of truth. No, Christian faith is a confident, expectant hope rooted in the true promises of Scripture.

Trust in the Christian message of God's salvation through Christ!

Now What?

Look up these verses that attest to the doctrine of salvation through Christ alone: John 3:16-18; 3:36; 8:24; 14:6; 17:3; Acts 4:12; 1 Timothy 2:5; and 1 John 4:1-3.

Did You Know?

In an attempt to cover all their religious bases, the first-century Athenians superstitiously worshiped "an Unknown God" (Acts 17:23).

AUGUST 12

There is salvation in no one else! God has given no other
name under heaven by which we must be saved.

ACTS 4:12

OVER THE LAST THREE days, we've been studying how Jesus is the
only way of salvation. For Christians, this is a bedrock truth. But for many
others, the exclusivity of Jesus' claim in John 14:6 (and hence, Christianity's
assertion of being the world's only true faith) is offensive.

"How," they ask, "can Christians say they're right and billions of others
are wrong? How can they be so arrogant?"

Those who take offense at the gospel often ask a second question: "If
Christianity is true, how can a loving God send billions of people who don't
trust in Jesus to hell forever?"

These are both important, but loaded, questions. Each is based on very
misguided presumptions, exalting humanistic reasoning above scriptural
truth.

Let's look at each through a biblical lens.

What's It Mean?

To the first question, we must say this: public opinion is not the judge of
truth. Just because billions of people don't believe in Jesus doesn't mean he
is *not* the way of salvation. Remember, "the highway to hell is broad" but
"the gateway to life is very narrow" (see the July 5 devotion and Matthew
7:13-14).

What's more, it's not a sign of arrogance for Christians to believe they've
found the only way to heaven. If anything, Scripture teaches this is cause for
great rejoicing (Matthew 13:44-46; Luke 15).

Regarding the second question ("How can a loving God send people
to hell?"), this assumes far too much—namely that humans don't deserve
God's righteous judgment. But Scripture is quite clear: "All have sinned and
fall short of the glory of God" (Romans 3:23, ESV).

God doesn't owe us anything. All humanity has egregiously broken his laws. We are guilty as charged, deserving eternal wrath. So the question is not, "How can a loving God send people to hell?" The far better question is, "Why would a holy God save anyone at all?" Thankfully, God is both a righteous Judge who must punish sin *and* a loving Father who is pleased to save.

Yes, Jesus claims to be the only way to God, which is the basis of the Christian faith (see today's verse). Our posture should never be to take offense at this, but to marvel that the Lord God Almighty has offered salvation to those who have greatly offended *him*.

Now What?

Do you know someone who is offended by the gospel? Pray that God's Spirit would soften their heart to the truth.

Did You Know?

According to 1 Peter 2:7-8, Jesus is both the "cornerstone" that Christians build their faith on and "a rock of offense" (ESV) for unbelievers.

AUGUST 13

No longer do I call you servants, for the servant does not know what his master is doing; but I have called you friends, for all that I have heard from my Father I have made known to you.

JOHN 15:15, ESV

HAVE YOU EVER GONE through the process of being picked for a team game at school during gym class, break time, or recess on the playground when you were younger?

Phew! It can be quite an ordeal.

In the highly dramatic world of school social structures, nobody wants to be picked last. You want to be part of the "Chosen Ones"—among those first selected. Of course, the team captains often base their picks entirely on whims and personal preferences:

- *Who are my best friends?*
- *Who's the fastest kid here so I can win?*
- *Whom do I currently have a crush on?*
- *Who traded their candy bar for my applesauce at lunch today?*
- *Who has the coolest hairdo?*
- *Who didn't rat on me when I got Mrs. Sourpuss to sit on the whoopee cushion yesterday?*

As you can see, choosing people for school teams is quite a fair, impartial process.

In John 15, shortly before his arrest, Jesus gave his disciples some stunningly good news: he told them he had *chosen* them to be his friends.

What applied to Jesus' disciples now applies to all followers of Christ. If you are a Christian, Jesus has chosen you to be his friend.

Are you amazed by this incredible reality? You should be!

What's It Mean?

If this news doesn't immediately knock you over, remember our original relationship with God. Apart from Christ, we deserved eternal condemnation in hell (Romans 6:23). But through God's sovereign act of election, he chooses to "befriend" lost sinners. Ultimately, this is an amazing act of God's grace, not our doing. God takes the initiative, and we respond in faith.

Imagine that! Through Christ, you can be a chosen "friend" of the Lord God Almighty—your sins completely washed away. Rather than call you to a life of slavery or servanthood to pay off your sin debts, Jesus gladly calls you "friend." Yes, he's still the Son of God and deserves all of your worship and respect, but this is a huge privilege and a remarkable level of intimacy with the one who created and governs the universe.

Christian, rejoice in your friendship with God and his Son!

Now What?

"Produce lasting fruit." This is what Jesus said he appointed you to do if you are his friend through saving faith (John 15:16).

Did You Know?

Abraham (Isaiah 41:8) and Moses (Exodus 33:11) are specifically mentioned as "friends" of God in Scripture.

AUGUST 14

*I am praying not only for these disciples but also for all
who will ever believe in me through their message.*

JOHN 17:20

HAS ANYONE EVER PRAYED for you? Perhaps this has happened in
a moment of difficulty or grief. Or maybe someone has rejoiced with you
about an answer to prayer. Whatever the scenario, it's a wonderful thing
when someone approaches God's heavenly throne with you in mind.

Shortly before he was arrested in the garden of Gethsemane, Jesus
prayed a beautiful prayer. Found in John 17, we often call it "The High
Priestly Prayer" because of Jesus' unique role as our High Priest who represents us before God the Father (Hebrews 4:14).

During this prayer, Jesus prayed for his disciples. But amazingly, he was
also thinking of you. Imagine that: on the night before his crucifixion, he
had *you* in mind!

What's It Mean?

As he was preparing to die, Jesus knew his disciples would need heavenly
strength for the days ahead. So he prayed for them in John 17:1-19. Then
his mind turned toward "all who will ever believe in me through their message" (today's verse). If you have trusted in Christ, that means you!

Here's what Jesus prayed about for you:

- Our unity as believers would reflect the perfect unity he shares with
  the Father (verses 21-23).
- Our spiritual union with God would result in others coming to faith
  in Christ (verse 21).
- We would eventually see his glory (verse 24).
- God's love would continually be in us (verse 26).

But Jesus' prayer that night wasn't just a one-time petition for us
two thousand years ago. After sacrificing himself on the cross for our

sins—turning God's wrath toward us into favor, known as propitiation (Hebrews 2:17)—Jesus ascended back to heaven, where he now sits at the Father's right hand. In his glorified state, Jesus continually represents us before God as our great High Priest (Hebrews 7:25). In fact, much of the book of Hebrews is dedicated to this wonderful truth.

Jesus doesn't pray for us as a mere human would, asking for things that he doesn't know the outcome to. No! As part of the eternal, omniscient Trinity, the Son of God knows everything. His advocacy for believers is based on his finished, redemptive work on the cross, and the Father is pleased to give the Son what he asks for our spiritual benefit. Amazing!

Now What?
To learn more, read John 17; Romans 8:34; and the November 18 devotion on Jesus as our High Priest.

Did You Know?
In his prayer, Jesus also expressed a desire to be with us in heaven (verse 24). How cool is that?

AUGUST 15

My Father! If it is possible, let this cup of suffering be taken away from me. Yet I want your will to be done, not mine.

MATTHEW 26:39

THE GARDEN OF GETHSEMANE was dark. Unusually dark.

Yes, it was nighttime. But this wasn't simply the lack of sunlight. This was different. This was a spiritual darkness. Shadows fell heavy across the garden. Evil was in the air.

Leaving his disciples behind, Jesus walked farther ahead, fell on his face, and began to pray. His body shook with sorrow.

"My Father!" he cried out. "If it is possible, let this cup of suffering be taken away from me. Yet I want your will to be done, not mine."

Light briefly broke through the gloom as an angel appeared to strengthen him. Jesus prayed more fervently. His sweat fell like great drops of blood, splattering salty red on the ground. The time had almost come (Matthew 26).

Jesus knew the answer to his prayer. He had, in fact, planned it in heavenly councils in eternity past. He would have to drink the cup and all of its bitterness, down to its very dregs.

What's It Mean?

The "cup of suffering" Jesus referred to was a metaphor describing God's just, yet terrifying, wrath toward sin, harkening back to Old Testament prophecies that employed similar imagery (e.g., Isaiah 51:17-23; Jeremiah 25:15-29).

This was God's wrath toward *our* sin, mind you. As the spotless Lamb of God (1 Peter 1:19), Jesus deserved none of it.

Interestingly, Jesus prayed for another way to save mankind. Was he showing ungodly fear or cowardice? Not at all! But he was human. The incarnate Christ was fully God but also fully man, and in those dark moments in Gethsemane, even the divine Son needed angelic encouragement to help overcome the overwhelming anguish associated with "becoming a curse for us" (Galatians 3:13, ESV).

But there was no way other than the Cross. This was the plan that the Father, Son, and Spirit had determined in eternity past. Knowing this, Jesus ultimately prayed for the Father's will, which he always accomplished (John 8:29). Our sins demanded the payment of a life (Romans 6:23). So the Son of God, in perfect human form, would die in our place.

Shortly after he left Gethsemane, Jesus took the cup of God's wrath toward sins—your sins—and drank all of it . . . every last drop.

All because he loves us dearly.

Now What?
Read the garden of Gethsemane accounts in Matthew 26:30-56; Mark 14:26-52; Luke 22:39-54; and John 18:1-12.

Did You Know?
In Luke 22:44, Jesus might have experienced a rare condition called hematidrosis, where capillaries burst under extreme distress, causing a person to literally sweat blood.

AUGUST 16

He was oppressed and treated harshly,
yet he never said a word.

ISAIAH 53:7

THE SPITEFUL SPIT of wicked men dribbled down the innocent man's
face. His cheeks turned red from the insulting slaps. His jaw, smarting from
furious punches, began to bruise and swell.

The trials of Jesus had begun.

From his arrest in Gethsemane until Pontius Pilate sentenced him to
death, Jesus endured a series of bogus legal hearings that were hastily thrown
together to give the pretense of fairness to the murderous agenda of schem-
ing, "lawless men" (Acts 2:23, ESV).

Sometime between the late hours of Thursday night and Friday morning of Passion Week, Jesus experienced the following:

- a brief hearing before Annas, the father-in-law of Caiaphas, the high
  priest (John 18:12-14, 19-24)
- a trial before Caiaphas and the Jewish Sanhedrin, where false witnesses
  made counterfeit claims against him (Matthew 26:57-67; 27:1-2)
- an initial trial before Pilate, the Roman governor of Judea (Matthew
  27:11-14; Luke 23:1-5)
- a hearing before Herod Antipas, a provincial ruler, where Jesus was
  falsely accused and mocked (Luke 23:6-12)
- a second trial before Pilate, where Jesus was ultimately and unjustly
  condemned to die (Luke 23:13-25)

Throughout these judicial proceedings—if you can even call them
that—Jesus was mocked, spat upon, slapped, and punched in the face.
Soldiers stripped off his clothing, forced him to wear a scarlet robe, and jeer-
ingly paraded him around as a captured king. A crown of sharp thorns was
pressed into his scalp. Worse yet, he was scourged, a cruel form of Roman

punishment that went beyond traditional whipping (see tomorrow's devotion for more details).

Then the sinless Son of God was led off to die.

What's It Mean?

The whole, horrible sequence was bitterly ironic. The Lord of Justice received none. The Prince of Peace was attacked. The Holy One endured complete mockery. The Righteous Savior suffered indignity at the hands of wicked men.

Jesus could have defended himself. He could have called innumerable legions of angels to overwhelm the legions of Rome (Matthew 26:50-53). Instead, he chose to remain silent. The Savior who will strike down the nations with only a word from his mouth (Revelation 19:15) held his tongue (see today's verse).

The Son suffered unspeakable injustice because it was the Father's will (Isaiah 53:10). He did this because it was the only way human sins could be atoned for. He did this for you.

Now What?

Read about all of Jesus' trials (in the Bible passages listed above) to see what he endured for your sake.

Did You Know?

One day, Jesus will return as a fearsome warrior to judge the wicked. He is no longer silent! See Revelation 19:11-21.

AUGUST 17

He was pierced for our transgressions; he was crushed for our iniquities;
upon him was the chastisement that brought us
peace, and with his wounds we are healed.

ISAIAH 53:5, ESV

"CRUCIFY HIM! CRUCIFY HIM!"

The bloodthirsty cries filled the morning air in Jerusalem. Pilate, the ineffective Roman governor, realized he wasn't going to convince the frothing mob of Jesus' innocence. So he caved in to their malice.

"I am innocent of this man's blood," Pilate declared, unconvincingly. "The responsibility is yours!" Then he delivered Jesus to be tortured and crucified. Pilate's words couldn't have been hollower.

The Roman soldiers tied Jesus to a post and scourged him. This was a particularly vicious, sometimes fatal, punishment where bareback victims were whipped with leather straps embedded with fragments of bone and metal designed to rip open the flesh to expose organs and bones.

Roman crucifixions, amazingly, were worse. They were excruciatingly painful, lengthy, and public—often held in well-traveled areas. The message was clear: "Don't mess with Rome, or this could be you."

Long nails were driven through the condemned individual's wrists and feet and into a rough wooden cross, which was set upright into the ground. If the victim didn't die of shock, dehydration, or other internal wounds, they would often asphyxiate as their broken body struggled to breathe. Jesus endured this horrific experience for six long hours (Mark 15:25, 34). Then he gave up his spirit.

What's It Mean?

For the next twelve days, we will focus on what God graciously did for us through the death of his Son.

Volumes of books, articles, and sermons have been produced on what Jesus suffered for our sake—and rightfully so. Yet we will never fully understand the pain he endured. It's beyond human comprehension.

And that's okay. A medical dissection of Jesus' sacrifice isn't the end goal. Christ wasn't a martyr. He was God incarnate—the Word made flesh who suffered to pay sin's exceedingly great price and redeem the people God has chosen "before he made the world" (Ephesians 1:4).

As today's verse says, through Jesus' wounds, we are healed. The gospel isn't a clinical report for medical journals. It's a glorious message of substitutionary atonement where a sinless Savior died so that you, a sinner, could have peace with a holy God.

That was the purpose of the suffering. *That* was the mission of the Cross. *That* was what he accomplished for you!

Now What?

Read all four Gospel accounts of the Crucifixion (Matthew 27:32-56; Mark 15:21-41; Luke 23:26-49; and John 19:17-37).

Did You Know?

More than seven hundred years earlier, Isaiah prophesied about Jesus' sufferings in remarkable detail. You can check it out in Isaiah 52:13–53:12.

AUGUST 18

About the ninth hour Jesus cried out with a loud voice,
saying, "Eli, Eli, lema sabachthani?" that is, "My
God, my God, why have you forsaken me?"

MATTHEW 27:46, ESV

RELISHING PERCEIVED VICTORY, wicked men stood in the shadow of the cross and hurled vicious insults. Disappointed onlookers shook their heads, their misplaced hopes for a political messiah dashed.

Soldiers heartlessly gambled for his clothes. Even one of the other criminals hanging on either side of him, condemned and nearly dead, spewed vitriol.

Jesus was dying, yet the wolves kept on attacking.

At noon, darkness covered the land, casting an ominous midday pall over an already bleak scene. The eerie gloom was thick with divine judgment and displeasure.

After hanging on the cross for six excruciating hours, the Son of God uttered an agonizing cry: "Eli, Eli, lema sabachthani?" (Matthew 27).

Those who witnessed the Crucifixion that day wondered aloud what he meant. Even today, Jesus' words continue to provoke questions, spark theological debate, and share beautiful gospel truth.

What's It Mean?

The Savior's exclamation was in Aramaic, the common, first-century dialect of Palestine. Jesus, who perfectly knew the Old Testament, was quoting Psalm 22:1 (ESV), which says, "My God, My God, why have you forsaken me?"

This is one of the most profound statements in Scripture. How could God the Father forsake the Son? And what exactly does that mean?

There is great mystery in the nuances of this phrase, but at some level, the Father had to turn away as the Son became the sin-bearer and "redeemed us from the curse of the law by becoming a curse for us" (Galatians 3:13, ESV). Sin's curse is death and separation from God, but Jesus willingly absorbed all the Father's just, terrifying wrath for our sake.

The beautiful, triune fellowship that the Son had eternally enjoyed with the Father had been temporarily broken.

Jesus cried out for all these reasons. But it wasn't surprise or disbelief. As the Son of God, he shares omniscience with the Father and the Spirit.

Likewise, the Father wasn't being aloof or cruel toward the Son. God's justice and holiness demanded blood payment for sin (Hebrews 9:22). Christ lovingly bore God's righteous anger in your place "because of the joy awaiting him" (Hebrews 12:2).

Trust in Jesus! He was temporarily forsaken by God so you would never have to be.

Now What?
Read Psalm 9:10; 37:28; and 94:14 to see if God ever forsakes those who trust in him.

Did You Know?
Psalm 22, originally a lament by King David, includes many other prophetic allusions to the Crucifixion, including verses 7, 8, 16, and 18.

AUGUST 19

*By his death, Jesus opened a new and life-giving way
through the curtain into the Most Holy Place.*

HEBREWS 10:20

HISTORY'S GREATEST SACRIFICE was nearly complete. Atonement for
sins—something we could never achieve—was at hand. The sinless Son of
God had fulfilled his redemptive purpose. All that remained was for Jesus to
release his final, dying breath.

Six hours into his agonizing crucifixion, Jesus cried out, "Father, into
your hands I commit my spirit!" (Luke 23:46, ESV). Then he declared, "It is
finished," bowed his head, and gave up his spirit (John 19:30).

God's Son, the Savior of the world, was dead.

Suddenly, a chain reaction of supernatural events rocked Jerusalem. A
great earthquake shook the city. Tombs opened, and dead saints returned to
life. (Kind of cool . . . kind of creepy!)

Most significantly, "the curtain in the sanctuary of the Temple was torn
in two" (Matthew 27:51). Maybe that doesn't sound as remarkable as a
bunch of corpses rising from the dead, but it was!

What's It Mean?

The Temple curtain was the veil separating the Holy Place from the Most
Holy Place—the latter being the inner sanctuary that represented God's
unique presence. Only the Jewish high priest could pass through the veil—
and only once a year, on the Day of Atonement—to offer sacrifices for the
nation (see the April 1 devotion).

The massive curtain visually represented the separation between a holy
God and his sinful people. Under the old covenant, sinners' access to God
was heavily restricted and required an approved mediator.

But when Jesus died, God himself supernaturally ripped the Temple
curtain in half, symbolically providing glorious, unfettered entry into his
heavenly throne room for all believers!

Are you overjoyed by this? You should be! The Lord God Almighty has opened up his heavenly throne room to you. He is not aloof. He is a loving heavenly Father who, under the new covenant, now makes the hearts of redeemed sinners his Temple (1 Corinthians 6:19). Amazing! As today's verse says, Jesus, our new and better mediator, "opened a new and life-giving way" to God.

The restrictive curtain is gone. Access to God—all day, every day—is possible for believers in Christ!

Now What?

Come before the Lord daily through prayer and Scripture, asking the Spirit to guide your time with him. This is how we actively access God's presence.

Did You Know?

The Temple curtain was sixty feet high and thirty feet wide, and it was torn top to bottom—not vice versa—at the moment Jesus died. No human could have done this!

AUGUST 20

Without the shedding of blood there is no forgiveness of sins.

HEBREWS 9:22, ESV

HAVE YOU EVER WONDERED why Jesus had to suffer and die? When you think about the horrors of the Crucifixion, have you considered if God could've dealt with humanity's sins another way?

After all, Jesus went to *a lot* of trouble on our behalf—and that's putting it mildly. Christ's incarnation was a miracle of universal proportions that changed the course of human history and continues to stretch the bounds of our comprehension.

But Jesus also suffered greatly to forgive our sins. During his time on earth, he was "a man of sorrows, acquainted with deepest grief" (Isaiah 53:3). His death was indescribably brutal. By the time his lifeless body had been removed from the cross, "his face was so disfigured he seemed hardly human" (Isaiah 52:14).

Why, though, was it "the will of the LORD to crush him" (Isaiah 53:10, ESV) and have him "buried like a criminal" (Isaiah 53:9)? Why was Jesus "pierced for our rebellion" and "crushed for our sins" (Isaiah 53:5)?

After all, can't God do whatever he wants? Why couldn't he just make our sins vanish into thin air like some sort of cosmic magic trick?

In other words, was the Cross really necessary?

What's It Mean?

These are intriguing questions. If you've wondered these things, you're not alone. Many others have asked similar questions over the centuries.

But sin (i.e., breaking God's laws) cannot be taken lightly. Our rebellion against God has subjected his good creation to chaos, corrupted our nature, and threatened to sentence us to an eternity in hell.

God's holiness cannot allow for sin to simply vanish. That would defy his justice. Because he always does what is right, God has to punish disobedience against him.

Thankfully for us, though, God is both perfectly just and loving. In his great love, he provided his Son to bear the punishment and die the death that we deserved.

Yes, the Cross was absolutely necessary because the cost of sin was so high. As today's verse says, forgiveness of sin requires a blood sacrifice. Likewise, Romans 6:23 declares, "For the wages of sin is death, but the free gift of God is eternal life through Christ Jesus our Lord."

God's will to sacrifice his Son was for your salvation. Rejoice and believe!

Now What?
Meditate on the "Suffering Servant" passage of Isaiah 52:13–53:12 to better appreciate the Savior's sacrifice for you.

Did You Know?
More than a thousand years before Christ's death, God taught his people the importance of atoning sin-sacrifices through the Mosaic law, which ultimately pointed ahead to the Cross (e.g., Leviticus 1:4-5 and 17:11).

AUGUST 21

Jesus shouted, "Father, I entrust my spirit into your hands!"

LUKE 23:46

IN **YESTERDAY'S** DEVOTION, WE learned that Jesus' death was necessary because human sin and God's holiness cannot coexist. Atonement was required for our sins to be forgiven and God's justice to be met.

Some people, however, view the Crucifixion as a form of cosmic child abuse. They accuse God of being a coldhearted, manipulative deity who put his Son through the horrors of Roman execution unnecessarily when much less was needed.

Nothing could be further from the truth. But since this heretical theory exists, we must address it—and debunk it—with Scripture.

What's It Mean?

First, these false teachers don't understand the nature of the Trinity. The Father could never abuse the Son because that would cause discord within the Godhead, defying all Scripture. The Father, Son, and Spirit are beautifully One God in three distinct Persons. They are perfectly unified, functioning in complete agreement with each other (2 Corinthians 1:21-22; 13:14). Jesus and the Father are one (John 10:30).

Jesus also went to the Cross willingly. He said, "I sacrifice [my life] voluntarily" (John 10:18). He predicted his death many times and resolutely traveled to Jerusalem, the place of his execution (Mark 10:32; Luke 9:53). He did not go kicking and screaming.

What's more, if the Crucifixion really was an abominable form of divine child abuse, why would Jesus entrust his spirit to God before dying (today's verse)? Jesus' last words don't speak of a distrustful, abusive relationship. They point to a beautiful unity and eternal purpose stretching far beyond human understanding.

God's wrongful accusers also apparently forget what God did to honor his Son after the Resurrection, exalting Jesus above heaven and earth (Philippians 2:9-11). Finally, these people misunderstand the gravity of

467

their own corruption. Human sin required the blood of God incarnate for redemption—nothing less.

The triune God did not owe us anything. Yet he graciously gave up his own Son to purchase our salvation. Don't misjudge his motives in this. He didn't sacrifice Jesus out of callousness or cruelty, but out of abounding love for us (John 3:16; 1 John 3:1), and Christ willingly obeyed—not out of compulsion, but out of his own great love for his people (Ephesians 5:25; 1 John 3:16). Praise the Lord!

Now What?
Check out Psalm 31:5 to see the parallels between David's psalm and today's verse. Jesus was quoting Old Testament Scripture!

Did You Know?
Jesus is not God's child in an earthly way. He is the "Son of God" in the sense of humbly submitting to his "Suffering Servant" role (Isaiah 52:13–53:12), as a human son would obey his father.

AUGUST 22

Jesus came to take away our sins, and there is no sin in him.

1 JOHN 3:5

IN MAJOR LEAGUE BASEBALL history, few players are more legendary than Denton True "Cy" Young.

Young played from 1890 to 1911—long before TV, radio, and Internet coverage—when myths surrounding the players often grew far larger than the men themselves. But Young was a legitimate superstar. In his Hall of Fame career, he won an astounding 511 games and threw 749 complete games—still records.

On May 5, 1904, Young, then thirty-seven years old, pitched what many regard as his greatest performance—the first perfect game under baseball's modern rules. A perfect game in baseball, or a *perfecto*, is when a pitcher retires all 27 batters he faces (three batters per nine innings) without allowing anyone to reach base by any means—a hit, walk, hit batsman, or error.

Young's perfecto came against his nemesis, Rube Waddell, the Philadelphia Athletics ace who had beaten Young and taunted him when Young's Boston Americans faced Philadelphia ten days earlier. When Young retired Waddell for the final out, Young allegedly shouted, "How do you like that, you hayseed?"

Young was perfect on the mound that day, even if he was not a perfect sportsman!

What's It Mean?

Perfection is hard to come by in sports, but it's impossible for humans to achieve moral perfection. The Bible says everyone has fallen far short of God's holy standard (Romans 3:23).

But not Jesus. God's Son lived a completely perfect life. He never sinned in word, deed, or thought (Hebrews 4:15).

This has great bearing on our study of Jesus' sacrifice on the cross. To atone for our sins, we needed someone who had no sin of their own. A sinner can't remove another's sins. Someone who has offended God's laws can't plead another offender's case before God.

To propitiate God's wrath (appease it and turn it to favor), we needed someone who had never sinned. We needed a perfect, spotless Lamb. We needed Jesus!

Thanks to his divine nature (John 1:1), virgin birth (Matthew 1:23), and sinless life (today's verse), Jesus qualified as our "perfect High Priest forever" (Hebrews 7:28) and God gladly accepted his sacrifice on our behalf.

No one but Jesus could die for your sins. Aren't you glad he did?

Now What?

When tempted, Jesus remained sinless by staying true to God's Word (Matthew 4:1-11). Memorize key Scriptures—such as 1 Corinthians 10:12-13; Ephesians 6:10-11; and James 1:13-15—so that you also can stand firm against sin's temptations.

Did You Know?

Major League Baseball's annual award for the top pitchers in each league is called the Cy Young Award.

AUGUST 23

He himself bore our sins in his body on the tree, that we might die to sin and live to righteousness. By his wounds you have been healed.

1 PETER 2:24, ESV

BEING A JEWISH PRIEST in the Old Testament era was a great privilege. That person enjoyed the distinct honor of serving in the Tabernacle or Temple and representing an entire nation as their mediator before the Lord.

But the role wasn't for the faint of heart. A priest's job was gruesome and bloody at times. Priests would slaughter countless animals during their lifetime, according to the strict regulations of the Mosaic law. There were burnt offerings, sin offerings, guilt offerings, peace offerings, the Passover celebration, and the annual Day of Atonement. Death was constantly around them.

Why did the priests have to do this? God was graciously showing his sinful people their great need for substitutionary atonement.

What's It Mean?

Substitutionary atonement, or penal substitution, is a vital doctrine found throughout Scripture. Besides the Old Testament sacrificial system, we see it again vividly in the "Suffering Servant" prophecy of Isaiah 52:13–53:12 and in various passages in the New Testament, such as Romans 3:23-25, 2 Corinthians 5:21, and today's verse.

The Bible says all humans are inherently guilty before God because of sin (Romans 3:23). Left to ourselves, we would die in our rebellious state, forever separated from our Creator in hell.

But God, in his great mercy, did not leave us in this wretched state. He provided substitutionary atonement for us! This is the concept that something—or Someone—must die for the sins of another to cover the guilt of the sin-bearer. As Hebrews 9:22 says, "Without the shedding of blood there is no forgiveness of sins" (ESV).

The Old Testament sacrificial system temporarily achieved this. But God only meant animal sacrifice to point to something infinitely better.

Substitutionary atonement found its true fulfillment in God's Son, Jesus Christ! In his great love for us, "God presented Jesus as the sacrifice for sin" (Romans 3:25).

Jesus is our great substitute! On the cross, he atoned—or made payment for—the egregious sins we committed against a holy God. He fully bore the divine wrath we deserved.

Can anyone say it more beautifully than the prophet Isaiah? "But he was pierced for our transgressions; he was crushed for our iniquities; upon him was the chastisement that brought us peace, and with his wounds we are healed" (53:5, ESV).

Now What?

Now that Jesus has provided substitutionary atonement, we must "die to sin and live to righteousness" to honor our Savior! (See today's verse.)

Did You Know?

Among the five major Old Testament offerings, only the grain offering (Leviticus 2) didn't involve an animal's death.

AUGUST 24

He made peace with everything in heaven and on earth
by means of Christ's blood on the cross. This includes
you who were once far away from God.

COLOSSIANS 1:20-21

THROUGHOUT HISTORY, there have been some famous conflicts
between enemies:

- Moses and Pharaoh
- David and Goliath
- the ancient Greeks and Trojans
- Alexander Hamilton and Aaron Burr
- the Hatfields and the McCoys
- Israelis and Arabs
- Harry Potter and Voldemort

Okay, that last one was fictional—thrown in just for kicks to see if you
were paying attention!

Tragically, many of these bitter struggles resulted in bloodshed and death.
But there's another conflict between enemies that has endured since the world
began that might not immediately come to mind. Can you think of it?

It's between humans and God.

Did you know that you started life as God's enemy? It's true!

What's It Mean?

Perhaps you're thinking, *Wait a minute. How can this be? I've never felt like*
God's enemy. I've always been a pretty good person. I've never committed any
"major" sins like murder, stealing, etc.

Sin is subtle. It tricks us into believing we're not that bad. But our personal feelings or assumptions should never inform our theology. They are
terrible guides!

Scripture is quite clear: because of indwelling sin, every person starts life diametrically opposed to God (Romans 3:23; 5:12; Psalm 51:5). We are fallen not only in nature but also in word, thought, and deed.

But here's the amazing news: Jesus died to radically transform your enmity toward God into peace and friendship. Look at Colossians 1:19-22:

> God in all his fullness was pleased to live in Christ, and through him God reconciled everything to himself. He made peace with everything in heaven and on earth by means of Christ's blood on the cross. This includes you who were once far away from God. You were his enemies, separated from him by your evil thoughts and actions. Yet now he has reconciled you to himself through the death of Christ in his physical body. As a result, he has brought you into his own presence, and you are holy and blameless as you stand before him without a single fault.

God ordained the Cross to bring peace where our sin had once created division. Jesus has already accomplished his atoning work. Your job is to repent and believe in the gospel and grow in its knowledge and grace every day!

Now What?
Memorize Colossians 1:19-22.

Did You Know?
How could God make peace with sinners who have so greatly transgressed his laws? Because he considers our account completely "paid in full" through Jesus' death. That's how powerful the Cross was!

AUGUST 25

For our sake he made him to be sin who knew no sin, so that
in him we might become the righteousness of God.

2 CORINTHIANS 5:21, ESV

IMAGINE IF YOU FLUNKED a year in school, then someone willingly
offered you their valedictorian status while they dealt with the fallout of
your failing grades.

Imagine if you went broke and creditors came to take all you owned.
Then a millionaire kindly offered to pay all your debts.

Imagine if you were caught robbing a bank and convicted by a jury.
Then at your sentencing hearing, someone suddenly walked into the courtroom and asked the judge to take your place in prison.

It's hard to imagine anyone doing anything like that in this life. But if
that happened to you, you'd be both shocked and forever grateful, wouldn't
you?

Spiritually speaking, Jesus has done all this for you through his death
and resurrection—only at an infinitely greater level. It's called the doctrine
of imputation.

What's It Mean?

Imputation is a big theological word, but it's so important for every
Christian to understand this doctrine as we continue to study what Jesus
accomplished for us on the cross.

Imputation reveals a marvelous spiritual transfer that takes place in
every believer's life thanks to Jesus' finished work at Calvary. When Christ
died on the cross, God "made him to be sin" even though he "knew no sin,"
as today's verse says.

This does not mean Jesus became a sinner or God thought of him as
sinful. Jesus lived a holy life and never disobeyed the Father (1 Peter 2:22;
Hebrews 4:15; 1 John 3:5). Rather, today's verse points to Christ's role as
our substitutionary atonement and the glorious reality of imputation.

Through Jesus' sacrifice, God imputed all our sins and guilt on Christ (or thought of it as belonging to him) and imputed Jesus' righteousness to us (or thought of it as belonging to us). In other words, Jesus willingly took God's just punishment for our sins, and we get credit for Jesus' righteousness. We contributed nothing to this great interchange except our sin. Christ gloriously did all the work, and God graciously credits it to our account— all for our salvation. It's the greatest exchange in history!

Why did God initiate this amazing, mysterious process? He did this out of his great love for you, to reconcile you to himself. Praise the Lord!

Now What?
Read 2 Corinthians 5:1-21 to see the context of the apostle Paul's discussion of imputation.

Did You Know?
Imputation is what allows us to be justified before God, or "made right in God's sight by faith . . . because of what Jesus Christ our Lord has done for us" (Romans 5:1).

AUGUST 26

Since, therefore, we have now been justified by his blood, much more shall we be saved by him from the wrath of God.

ROMANS 5:9, ESV

IMAGINE THIS SCENARIO . . .

You are sitting nervously in a courtroom, waiting for a criminal trial to start. You are the defendant. The case? *Heaven vs. You.*

The room is empty, except for one man: your accuser. He sits off to the side, lurking, waiting.

You have no attorney, no one to plead your case. You are alone.

Then the Judge enters the room. Regal in his bearing, he immediately commands respect. He appears wise and just. You know you will get a fair trial.

Immediately, your accuser begins assaulting your character, fiendishly hurling blame and indictments from the shadows of the room. The scroll he's holding of your offenses unfurls from his hand, hits the floor, and rolls down the aisle. He laughs insidiously.

You can't argue with the charges. You are guilty as sin. You are guilty *of* countless sins. You're on trial for your life, and you don't see how you are going to win with all the evidence against you.

Suddenly, another Man enters the courtroom. He bears a humble, compassionate countenance, yet a resolute fire burns in his eyes. As he approaches the bench, your accuser falls silent. The Man speaks quietly to the Judge and, to your surprise, he shows the Judge his wrists, his feet, and his side. It appears the Man is advocating for your freedom. For the first time, you believe there is hope.

The Judge thunders his gavel down and issues the verdict: "Not guilty." This is justification.

What's It Mean?

As today's verse says, Jesus' death on the cross provides all believers justification, which is a vital tenet of the Christian faith. Justification is a legal term. It means "to be declared righteous" or "to be made right with God."

When we trust in Christ, God judges us to be righteous and considers our sins forgiven. He can do this because Jesus' shed blood on the cross provided substitutionary atonement for our sins (1 Peter 2:24; see the August 23 devotion) and allowed for Christ's righteousness to be imputed to us (2 Corinthians 5:21; see the August 25 devotion).

Through justification, heaven's Judge rules us completely blameless—sinners saved by his grace. Our sins no longer condemn us. Satan's accusations ring hollow. The blood of Jesus, our Advocate, covers all believers in his righteousness.

Case closed!

Now What?

Want to do a deep-dive into the topic of justification? Then read Romans 1–11.

Did You Know?

Christians should never use their justification as an excuse to sin (Romans 6).

AUGUST 27

When Jesus had received the sour wine, he said, "It is finished," and he bowed his head and gave up his spirit.

JOHN 19:30, ESV

ON SEPTEMBER 16, 2018, Eliud Kipchoge made history. The Kenyan distance runner won the famed Berlin Marathon in 2 hours, 1 minute, 39 seconds, smashing the previous world record.

Kipchoge's time also topped the reigning Olympic record at the time—fellow Kenyan Samuel Kamau Wanjiru's mark of 2:06:32 at the 2008 Summer Games.

Those times are blisteringly fast compared to the winning mark of Spyridon Louis at the first modern-day Olympics, the 1896 Summer Games in Athens. Louis, a Greek native, won the event in 2:58:50, a sluggish time by current standards.

Finishing first in any marathon is quite an accomplishment. Setting an Olympic or world record is historic.

On Calvary, Jesus crossed his own finish line. But his experience was not a footrace. Rather, it was a marathon of indescribable physical, mental, and spiritual suffering as he bore the weight of God's wrath for humanity's sins. Finally, after six grueling hours on the bloody cross, he let out an anguished cry, "It is finished!"

Then the Son of God gave up his spirit and died.

What's It Mean?

It is finished.

These are three of the most beautiful words in Scripture. They speak to the glorious finality of the Savior's mission. With his death (and imminent resurrection), Jesus had accomplished everything that the Father, Son, and Spirit had planned in eternity past for the salvation of God's chosen people.

Jesus took our sins and gave us his righteousness. He satisfied the Father's holy wrath against humanity's sin. He broke the power of sin, Satan, and the forces of evil. He purchased victory for us over death and eternal punishment.

Hebrews 10:11-12 describes the finished work of Christ beautifully: "Under the old covenant, the priest stands and ministers before the altar day after day, offering the same sacrifices again and again, which can never take away sins. But our High Priest offered himself to God as a single sacrifice for sins, good for all time."

When the Son died, he declared, "It is finished," and the Father accepted his atoning sacrifice by raising him from the dead (Acts 2:24).

It is finished indeed!

Now What?

Prayerfully meditate on the following verses: Hebrews 7:27; 9:12; and 9:26.

Did You Know?

- Marathon races owe their official length, 26.2 miles, to the approximate distance between the Greek cities of Marathon and Athens, which, according to legend, an ancient messenger named Pheidippides ran to herald a Greek victory over the Persians after the Battle of Marathon in 490 BC, then died from exhaustion.

AUGUST 28

The message of the cross is foolish to those who
are headed for destruction! But we who are being
saved know it is the very power of God.

1 CORINTHIANS 1:18

QUIZ TIME! RANK THESE decisions on a scale of 1 to 5—with 1 being
the most foolish and 5 being the least foolish:

- swimming with great white sharks in chum-filled waters
- bringing along your pet elephant during a shopping trip for fine china
- going spelunking in a live volcano
- taking the phrase "I'm so hungry I could eat a horse" literally
- entering a NASCAR race with a moped

Okay, that was a bit of a trick question. They're all ridiculously foolish
choices!

Do you know what else is foolish? The message of the Cross. Don't
believe it? It's true. Just check out today's verse! But we need to put this in
its proper context.

What's It Mean?

As we finish our in-depth study of Jesus' crucifixion, it's important to
understand the truth of 1 Corinthians 1:18.

When the apostle Paul wrote 1 Corinthians in the first century AD,
the Greco-Roman world couldn't fathom the idea of a divine being coming to earth from heaven in human form and willingly submitting to the
indignity and horror of Roman execution for the sins of humanity. For
Gentile unbelievers who were used to reading about superhuman exploits
of mythological gods and goddesses, the idea of a suffering Savior was "all
nonsense" (1 Corinthians 1:23). Jews, meanwhile, who had spent more
than a millennium waiting for their Messiah, were "offended" (verse 23) by
the notion of it all.

Today, it's largely the same. If you are a Christian who professes faith in a crucified and risen Savior, you will meet some people who are indifferent. You will meet other people who might mock you. You might even encounter people who are hostile toward you.

You shouldn't be surprised. Jesus predicted this in John 15:18-27. But take heart! Your job isn't to please the world but to worship and obey God and conform to the image of his Son.

Read today's verse again. The message of the Cross "is the very power of God." In other words, the Cross of Christ reveals God's incomparable power to save us from

- our own human foolishness and depravity,
- Satan's power,
- slavery of sin and death, and
- eternal judgment.

Those who don't believe in the message of the Cross are "headed for destruction." Those who do believe "are being saved."

It's clear which is the foolish choice and which is the wise one!

Now What?
Read John 15:18-27 for encouragement about the world's reaction to Christians.

Did You Know?
Paul wrote a similar message to today's verse in Romans 1:16.

AUGUST 29

God released him from the horrors of death and raised him
back to life, for death could not keep him in its grip.

ACTS 2:24

DESPONDENT AND RESTLESS, THE trio of women couldn't wait any longer.

The Sabbath day between Friday's notorious Crucifixion and the start of a new week felt interminable. They had to see their Lord again, even if his body was shrouded in death. So they left their homes before dawn and hurried to the tomb outside Jerusalem's walls.

After Jesus had died, Joseph of Arimathea and Nicodemus, two God-fearing members of the Sanhedrin, took Jesus' body from the cross and laid it in a tomb Joseph owned. After Saturday's Sabbath, Mary Magdalene, another Mary (the mother of James), and Salome went there early to anoint the body with ointments and fragrances, according to ancient Jewish burial customs.

But when they arrived, they were astonished at what they saw. The large stone blocking the tomb's entrance had been rolled away. The tomb itself was empty. Suddenly, a magnificent angel appeared and pronounced the glorious news: "'Don't be afraid!'" he said. 'I know you are looking for Jesus, who was crucified. He isn't here! He is risen from the dead, just as he said would happen'" (Matthew 28:5-6).

Miraculously, the Son of God was alive!

What's It Mean?

For the next ten days, we're going to study Jesus' resurrection and what it means for us.

The resurrection of Christ is the single greatest event in human history. Of course, his death was undeniably important in God's great salvation plan. But without the Resurrection, Jesus' death would have ultimately been remembered as nothing more than a famous Roman crucifixion—a glorified footnote in the pages of antiquity. The Resurrection gave Jesus' death true meaning.

Jesus actually defeated death! Ponder that. It's staggering. As today's verse says, "God released him from the horrors of death and raised him back to life." *Jesus 1, Death 0. No rematch!*

No matter how often you've heard this life-changing news, don't let your heart grow impervious to it. The Resurrection's spiritual impact for us cannot be overstated.

Without Christ's resurrection, we would only know fear, condemnation, death, and eternal separation from God. But *with* the Resurrection, there is John 3:16. There is forgiveness of sin. There is joy, mercy, and grace. There is eternal life.

Praise God for raising his Son!

Now What?

Read all four gospel accounts of the Resurrection: Matthew 28:1-15; Mark 16:1-8; Luke 24:1-12; and John 20:1-18.

Did You Know?

Scripture affirms that both the Father and Son were actively involved in the Resurrection (see today's verse and John 10:18)—beautiful, divine mystery at work!

AUGUST 30

God raised Jesus from the dead,
and we are all witnesses of this.

ACTS 2:32

BIGFOOT. YETI. THE LOCH NESS MONSTER.

Do you know of anyone who believes in these creatures? Do *you* believe in any of them? There's actually a name for these beasts that lurk in the shadowy corners of human imagination: cryptids. They are beings whose existence remains to be proven by actual observation or science—somewhat similar to ghosts, aliens, and teachers who never assign homework (*ha!*).

These creatures are figments of our fantasy, even if plenty of people defend their existence in varying degrees. The problem is, there have never been any confirmable eyewitness accounts.

Sadly, many people have dismissed the resurrection of Jesus in similar fashion, discounting it as just another unverified fable, such as Sasquatch roaming in the woodlands of the Pacific Northwest. Yet this is where popular mythology and Jesus' resurrection greatly diverge.

The eyewitness testimony for the risen Savior is overwhelming.

What's It Mean?

The Bible affirms that more than *five hundred eyewitnesses* (1 Corinthians 15:6) saw the risen Savior, and it mentions nearly twenty of them by name. That latter group includes the following:

- Mary Magdalene and "the other Mary" (Matthew 28:1, 9)
- Cleopas, one of two travelers on the road to Emmaus (Luke 24:18)
- the eleven original disciples, minus Judas Iscariot (Luke 24:33-49)
- Matthias, who took Judas's place (Acts 1:23)
- Justus, a finalist to take Judas's place (Acts 1:23)
- James, Jesus' brother (1 Corinthians 15:7)
- Paul (Acts 9:1-9)

The eyewitness testimony of Jesus' resurrection was extremely important to the apostles. Shortly after Jesus' ascension, Peter proclaimed to the large Jerusalem crowd at Pentecost that "God raised Jesus from the dead, and we are all witnesses of this" (today's verse). Years later, Paul made it clear to the Corinthian church that the risen Christ had appeared to him—twice mentioning it in his first letter to them (1 Corinthians 9:1; 15:8).

Jesus' resurrection is not speculative, theoretical, or based on flimsy, circumstantial evidence. The eyewitness testimony is overwhelming!

Most importantly, though, Scripture affirms the Resurrection's veracity. If Scripture says it, it's true! The Bible is the authoritative, inspired, inerrant Word of God. Everything God speaks is truth (Proverbs 30:5; John 17:17).

The question isn't whether or not Jesus rose from the dead. That's indisputable. The question is, do you believe?

Now What?

Read these three Old Testament prophecies of Jesus' resurrection: Psalm 16:10; Isaiah 53:10; and Hosea 6:2.

Did You Know?

One of the main requirements of being an apostle in the early church (i.e., the disciples, Matthias, and Paul) was being "a witness of Jesus' resurrection" (Acts 1:22).

AUGUST 31

We know that God, who raised the Lord Jesus, will also raise
us with Jesus and present us to himself together with you.

2 CORINTHIANS 4:14

MANY YEARS AGO, a miracle took place in Lake Placid, New York. This wasn't a supernatural miracle, mind you. But it was a miracle nonetheless: "The Miracle on Ice."

As the 1980 Winter Olympics descended upon Lake Placid, the Cold War was raging between the Soviet Union and the United States. The Soviet Olympic ice hockey team was a powerhouse. Featuring mostly professional players, the Russians had won the previous four Olympic gold medals.

Meanwhile, the US squad, consisting of amateur college players, was seeded seventh. Three days before the Olympics began, the Soviets crushed the US, 10–3, in an exhibition game.

When the teams met in the Olympic semifinals, most onlookers probably thought the outcome had already been determined. But the plucky Americans refused to capitulate, earning a 4–3 win in what is often called the greatest upset in US sports history. As the final seconds ticked away, TV broadcaster Al Michaels yelled his now-classic phrase: "Do you believe in miracles? Yes!" (Two days later, the US beat Finland for the gold medal.)

That's the beauty of sports: the outcome is never determined until the game happens. Jesus' resurrection, though, was different. The result had been predetermined in eternity past.

What's It Mean?

God doesn't deal in contingencies, Plan Bs, or *what ifs*. He is the sovereign Lord of the universe. All things are within his knowledge and control, including the death and resurrection of his Son.

Look at what the apostle Peter said in Acts 2:24: "God released him from the horrors of death and raised him back to life, for death could not keep him in its grip." Jesus' victory was always part of God's plan. Death could never contain the Creator of life!

But there's another wonderful, predetermined outcome at work here. Look again at today's verse.

Thanks to Jesus' resurrection, one day God will raise all true believers from the dead, clothe them with eternal bodies that will never decay (1 Corinthians 15:12-57), and bring them into eternal fellowship with him in the new heavens and new earth (Revelation 21:1-4). That's infinitely greater than any sports upset!

For all Christians, God has already predestined the eternal outcome of their faith. It's a glorious guarantee, sealed by the power and promise of the risen Savior.

Do you believe in miracles? Yes!

Now What?
Read 1 Corinthians 15 to learn more about every believer's future resurrection body.

Did You Know?
In 2004, Disney released a movie called *Miracle* based on the story of the 1980 US Olympic hockey team.

SEPTEMBER 1

They told the soldiers, "You must say, 'Jesus' disciples came during the night while we were sleeping, and they stole his body.'"

MATTHEW 28:13

IMAGINE IF YOU SAW an angel.

Wow! That undoubtedly would be the most memorable experience of your life. Could you even consider *not* telling everyone you know?

Well, the Roman soldiers assigned to guarding Jesus' tomb wanted to keep the news to themselves.

Early on Resurrection Sunday, two angels appeared at Jesus' tomb, causing the terrified soldiers to faint. When they awoke, the large stone at the tomb's entrance was rolled away and Jesus' body was gone.

Uh-oh. For Roman guards, dereliction of duty was a serious offense. So they ran to the Jewish chief priests for help.

The Sanhedrin hastily convened a meeting. Eventually, the wicked council agreed to bribe the soldiers into spreading a lie (see today's verse). You can read about this story in Matthew 28:1-15.

Imagine that: faced with incontrovertible evidence of an angelic visit and the empty tomb, the soldiers and religious leaders decided to stubbornly deny the life-changing truth of Jesus' resurrection.

So sad.

What's It Mean?

Nearly two thousand years have passed since then, and things haven't changed. The world is faced with overwhelming evidence about Jesus' resurrection, yet most people still ignore or outright deny its reality.

But the historicity of Jesus is indisputable. The entire biblical canon, especially the twenty-seven books of the New Testament, attests to the authenticity of Jesus. If that weren't enough—and it *is* because "all Scripture is breathed out by God" (2 Timothy 3:16, ESV)—many extrabiblical sources affirm Jesus' life and death, too, such as Josephus, Tacitus, Pliny the Younger, the Babylonian Talmud, and Lucian of Samosata.

But it's not enough to simply acknowledge the historicity of Jesus. Head knowledge doesn't equal heart change.

To be saved from your sins, you must believe in the atoning work of Jesus' death and resurrection on your behalf. You must submit to God's Son as your Lord and Savior. You must proclaim his name until he returns.

Don't stop at the historical veracity of Jesus' resurrection. Trust in its redemptive power for you!

Now What?
Read Romans 1:18 to see the fate of everyone who suppresses God's truth, including Jesus' resurrection.

Did You Know?
Josephus was an ancient Jewish historian. Tacitus and Pliny were Roman politicians. The Babylonian Talmud is a collection of rabbinical Jewish writings compiled between approximately AD 70 and 500. Lucian of Samosata was an ancient Greek writer/speaker.

SEPTEMBER 2

In fact, Christ has been raised from the dead.

1 CORINTHIANS 15:20

WHY DO SO MANY people debate Jesus' resurrection?

As we discussed in yesterday's devotion, the empty tomb was a sore subject for first-century Jewish religious leaders, who spread lies in a futile attempt to quell the gospel truth. Two thousand years later, the Resurrection continues to be a divisive issue.

Need proof? Just type "Did Jesus rise from the dead?" (or something similar) into an Internet search engine, and you'll get millions of results. Not hundreds. Not thousands.

Literally *millions*.

The question remains: Why do people reject the resurrection of Christ?

What's It Mean?

Nowadays, few serious scholars deny the historicity of Jesus. Yet the Resurrection continues to cause great controversy, even though no one has offered a plausible reason for the empty tomb in two millennia. What gives?

Because the Resurrection changes everything! A dead Jesus is a "safe Jesus" for people. If Jesus is dead, he was nothing more than an impassioned martyr, not someone that anyone has to radically orient their lives around. After all, why would anyone place their eternal hope in a dead man?

But . . .

If Jesus really rose from the dead . . .

- He truly is God incarnate who took on flesh (John 1:14).
- His sinless life and sacrificial death were acceptable to God as the atoning sacrifice for humanity's sins (Hebrews 10:1-18).
- Everything he claimed about himself is true, including this statement: "I am the way, the truth, and the life. No one can come to the Father except through me" (John 14:6).

- All other religions or belief systems are spiritual dead ends, and ultimately apathy or agnosticism is the same as rejection of Christ (Revelation 3:15-16).

If the Resurrection is true, Jesus has a claim on our lives as the all-powerful Son who will one day return to set up his eternal Kingdom, separating the wicked from the righteous. Many people refuse to accept that. They don't want to submit their life to someone else now, and they'd prefer not to think about the repercussions of sin, death, and judgment in the future.

Believing in Jesus' resurrection takes faith. It takes God's Spirit opening spiritually hardened hearts to accept gospel truth.

Jesus is alive! And yes, it changes everything.

Do you believe?

Now What?

Read Luke 24:13-35; Acts 2:14-41; and Acts 10 to see how God opened the hearts of various early Christians to believe in Christ's resurrection.

Did You Know?

Some biblical commentators believe that 1 Corinthians 15:3-5—where the apostle Paul delivers a message of "first importance" (ESV) about Jesus' death, resurrection, and subsequent appearances—was an oral creed in the early church.

SEPTEMBER 3

You believe because you have seen me. Blessed are
those who believe without seeing me.

JOHN 20:29

THE DISCIPLES WERE EXPLODING with excitement. They had seen the risen Lord! On the evening of Jesus' resurrection, he miraculously appeared to them in a locked room in Jerusalem.

But Thomas wasn't with them. Was he out repairing a chariot? Was he dining at Jerusalem's finest fish-and-unleavened bread restaurant? Was he at home watching *Veggie Tales*?

The Bible doesn't say where he was.

But when Thomas later rejoined the disciples, they exclaimed, "We have seen the Lord!"

Thomas wasn't convinced. "I won't believe it unless I see the nail scars in his hands and place my hand in the wound in his side," he said.

Eight days later, Jesus appeared to all the disciples, including Thomas. The risen Lord exhorted his doubting friend, "Don't be faithless any longer. Believe!"

Thomas' disbelief immediately transformed into saving faith. "My Lord and my God!" he exclaimed.

"You believe because you have seen me," Jesus replied. "Blessed are those who believe without seeing me" (John 20:19-29).

What's It Mean?

The last five days, we've discussed many things about Jesus' resurrection. Hopefully, you believe!

But if any doubts still linger, take heart: Thomas struggled to believe too. Then Jesus powerfully confronted him and transformed his skepticism to saving faith.

"Don't be faithless any longer. Believe!" (Check out the account in John 20:19-29.)

Today, the risen Son of God still powerfully confronts lingering doubts about him head-on—not in person, but through the testimony in God's Word. But he doesn't expect any less faith from you just because you can't see him. In fact, it's quite the opposite. You cannot be reconciled to God without faith in the risen Christ (Romans 10:9-10).

Amazingly, though, Jesus promises to bless you for faith without sight! Look at the wonderful promise of today's verse. Believers are blessed beyond the original disciples because we live *after* Jesus' return to heaven. The risen, ascended Savior delights in your faith!

Now consider the words of 1 Peter 1:8-9. The apostle Peter, who was in the room that night to witness Thomas's transformation, wrote this three decades later to encourage persecuted Christians in Asia Minor: "You love him even though you have never seen him. Though you do not see him now, you trust him; and you rejoice with a glorious, inexpressible joy. The reward for trusting him will be the salvation of your souls."

Amen!

Now What?
Today, ask God to strengthen your faith in his Son's resurrection.

Did You Know?
The Bible seems to indicate that Thomas had a twin (John 20:24).

494

SEPTEMBER 4

"My Lord and my God!" Thomas exclaimed.

JOHN 20:28

THOMAS WAS UNDONE.

A week had passed since Jesus' other disciples had reported—incredibly—seeing the risen Savior in a room in Jerusalem. Thomas, though, refused to believe unless he saw Jesus himself.

What a long week for Doubting Thomas!

Now, all the disciples, including Thomas, were gathered together again. Suddenly, Jesus appeared in their midst. Every ounce of Thomas's skepticism, frustrations, and fears vanished in a single, glorious moment.

We can only imagine what the full scene must have been like. Did Thomas burst into tears? Did Thomas and Jesus share a heartfelt embrace? What was the reaction of the other disciples?

Scripture remains poignantly silent on many of the details. But it does record Thomas's reply. Stumbling for words, the disciples' resident cynic blurted out one of Scripture's great confessions:

"My Lord and my God!"

What's It Mean?

Thomas's confession, which sounds quite similar to Peter's great confession in Matthew 16:16 (see the July 15 devotion), was only five words long. But it tells us a great deal about his radical heart change.

By calling Jesus "my Lord and my God," Thomas beautifully crowned Jesus as his heavenly King by acknowledging the Messiah's oneness with God the Father and his sovereignty over Thomas's life. Notice Thomas's words and his posture toward Christ in that moment. It wasn't enough for him to simply express joy that his friend had returned to life, free from the suffering of the Cross. No, Thomas had to come to a place of personal conviction, realizing that Jesus was not just a human messiah, but the incarnate Son of God who was worthy of his total allegiance.

495

What about you? Have you cried out "My Lord and my God" to Jesus? Have you humbly submitted your life to the risen Savior?

If you rightfully acknowledge Jesus as God, everything you read about him in Scripture will make sense. He will hold a proper place of worship in your heart. If you bow before him as Lord, you will gain a loving Master who will provide "rest for your souls" because his yoke is easy and his burden is light (Matthew 11:29-30).

Now What?

Whether for the first time or the one hundredth, confess that Jesus is your Lord and your God today!

Did You Know?

Thomas supposedly evangelized Parthia (modern-day Khorasan) and India before being martyred, but this comes from ancient extrabiblical sources and traditions that cannot be confirmed.

SEPTEMBER 5

All praise to God, the Father of our Lord Jesus Christ.
It is by his great mercy that we have been born again,
because God raised Jesus Christ from the dead.

1 PETER 1:3

AS HUMANS, WE LOVE to accomplish things.

We enjoy celebrating major milestones of human achievement, such as the first man to summit Mount Everest (1953), the first runner to break the four-minute mile (1954), and the first person to land on the moon (1969).

Yet there's one momentous achievement that trumps anything mere mortals have accomplished: the death and resurrection of Jesus Christ. But as we continue to discuss Jesus' resurrection, an important question lingers: What does it actually accomplish for believers today?

More than you could ever imagine.

What's It Mean?

Jesus' resurrection was *the* seminal event of human history. The entire Christian faith stands on the glorious truth that God's Son died for our sins and rose to life again.

Here are a dozen incredible things that the empty tomb means for you:

1. It certifies all of Christ's claims about himself (John 2:18-22).
2. It proves there is no other way to God except through Jesus (John 14:6; Acts 4:12).
3. It allows us to approach God's throne confidently since we have a High Priest who represented us perfectly (Hebrews 4:14-16).
4. It confirms God's acceptance of Jesus' atoning sacrifice for our sins (Isaiah 53:11; 2 Corinthians 13:4; Ephesians 1:19-20).
5. It allows for regeneration, or the ability to be spiritually "born again," for all believers (today's verse).
6. It assures every believer of justification before God (Romans 4:25).

7. It fills every Christian with the same heavenly power that raised Jesus from the dead (Ephesians 1:19-20).
8. It enables sanctification in Christians (Colossians 3:1-4).
9. It encourages godliness and Kingdom building among God's people (John 16:7-8; Acts 1:8).
10. It guarantees believers of eternal salvation in Christ (Romans 8:34-39).
11. It assures Christians of final victory over sin, Satan, and death (Acts 17:31).
12. It assures believers of eternal life in heaven (Romans 8:10-11).

This is by no means an exhaustive list. But are you beginning to see the power, love, and grace that God has lavished on all believers by raising his Son from the dead?

The resurrection of our Lord has accomplished so much for your sake!

Now What?

Prayerfully read and meditate on the Scripture passages mentioned in the list above, praising God for the glories of Christ's resurrection!

Did You Know?

New Zealand's Edmund Hillary and Nepalese Sherpa Tenzing Norgay were the first to top Mount Everest. England's Roger Bannister broke the four-minute mile. American Neil Armstrong was the first man to step foot on the moon.

SEPTEMBER 6

I am the resurrection and the life. The one who believes in
me will live, even though they die; and whoever lives by
believing in me will never die. Do you believe this?"

JOHN 11:25-26, NIV

JESUS WAS A MASTER wordsmith. If crossword puzzles, Taboo, or
Scrabble had existed in first-century Palestine, he would've won every time.
(Of course, being the eternal, omniscient Son of God might give him a
slight advantage over the competition!)

Jesus also loved speaking in paradoxes. A paradox is a statement that
seems false or contradictory but actually contains truth.

Some of Jesus' most well-known paradoxes include the following:

- The last will be first and the first last. (Matthew 20:16, ESV)
- My yoke is easy, and my burden is light. (Matthew 11:30, ESV)
- Whoever would save his life will lose it, but whoever loses his life for
  my sake will save it. (Luke 9:24, ESV)

In John 11, Jesus declared another beautiful paradox before raising
Lazarus from the dead. "I am the resurrection and the life," Jesus said. "The
one who believes in me will live, even though they die; and whoever lives by
believing in me will never die" (today's verses, NIV).

What's It Mean?

As we study the topic of resurrection, this story—which happened prior to
Jesus' death—has much to teach us. Notice that Jesus didn't say, "I *can* res-
urrect people and give them life." He said something far more authoritative:
"I *am* the resurrection and the life" (John 11:25, emphasis added). In other
words, all resurrection power and life—both in this world and the one to
come—originate with him.

Whoa.

You will die one day, and your physical body will be buried. But your soul will immediately go into God's presence or into judgment, depending on your faith in Christ (2 Corinthians 5:8; Luke 16:19-31). Thanks to Jesus' resurrection power, every Christian has the secure hope that their soul eventually will be united after death with a glorified resurrection body—free from all pain and suffering, perfectly immortal, designed to praise God forever in the new heavens and new earth (1 Corinthians 15:35-57).

This is what Jesus is referring to in today's verse. Even though we will all experience physical death (until he returns), believers will never experience spiritual death apart from God in hell. All who trust in Christ have resurrection hope because Jesus has resurrection power!

That's no paradox—it's just glorious truth!

Now What?

The next time you read through the Gospels, look for the paradoxical truths of Jesus.

Did You Know?

Today's verse represents the fifth of Jesus' seven great "I am" statements in the Gospel of John, all of which were references to Exodus 3:14 and clear claims to deity.

SEPTEMBER 7

May he equip you with all you need for doing his will.

HEBREWS 13:21

WHAT'S YOUR FAVORITE SCHOOL subject?

Math? Science? English? Civics? Grammar? Music? Art? A foreign language such as Spanish or French? (Sorry . . . lunch and summer break are
not options!)

What about history? Does it ever feel irrelevant to you, like nothing
more than archaic facts to be memorized for a test? Or does history feel
vibrant and exciting to you, illuminating timeless guideposts for us from
the past?

The Bible is God's revelation of salvation's history, and Jesus' resurrection is the climax. Hebrews 13:20-21 provides a perfect example of how the
empty tomb is both ancient history and perfectly relevant to you today:

Now may the God of peace—who brought up from the dead our
Lord Jesus, the great Shepherd of the sheep, and ratified an eternal
covenant with his blood—may he equip you with all you need for
doing his will. May he produce in you, through the power of Jesus
Christ, every good thing that is pleasing to him. All glory to him
forever and ever! Amen.

What's It Mean?

We've talked a great deal about the glorious spiritual realities that Jesus'
resurrection provides for every believer—and rightfully so! As we discussed
in the September 5 devotion, it affects our regeneration, justification, sanctification, eternal security, and so much more. Lots of big words!

But the Resurrection, although it happened two thousand years ago,
isn't an event confined to dusty history books or stodgy theology volumes. It
affects our daily lives as Christians! Look again at today's Scripture passage.

The same God who raised Jesus wants to "equip you with all you need
for doing his will." He wants to "produce in you, through the [same] power

. . . [that raised] Jesus Christ, every good thing that is pleasing to him" (Hebrews 13:21).

This is amazing news! If you are a believer, the same sovereign authority and might that defeated sin, Satan, and death is now equipping *you* to obey God's will (Ephesians 1:19-20). It's not an overnight process. But it's beautiful, amazing, and life changing.

You are not walking the Christian life alone. God is walking beside you, strengthening you with resurrection power along the way—all for the glory of his name.

Now *that's* one for the history books!

Now What?

Are you unsure about the specifics of "doing his will"? Don't fret! Faithfully read Scripture and pray. God will equip and lead you by his power.

Did You Know?

Today's Scripture passage is a benediction, or a prayer of blessing. Many New Testament Epistles feature them.

SEPTEMBER 8

*Go and make disciples of all the nations, baptizing them in
the name of the Father and the Son and the Holy Spirit.*

MATTHEW 28:19

IF YOU WERE GOING on a long journey and knew you wouldn't see your
loved ones for a long time, your final moments with them would be incredibly important. You'd want your last words to be meaningful and remain
with your friends and family forever.

This was the scene on the Mount of Olives just outside of Jerusalem
about forty days after Jesus' resurrection. The Savior's redemptive mission
on earth was finished. Now, it was time for him to return to the Father in
heaven. But before he did, he had an extremely important message to give
his disciples. Here's what he told them:

> I have been given all authority in heaven and on earth. Therefore,
> go and make disciples of all the nations, baptizing them in the name
> of the Father and the Son and the Holy Spirit. Teach these new
> disciples to obey all the commands I have given you. And be sure of
> this: I am with you always, even to the end of the age.
>
> MATTHEW 28:18-20

Jesus' message wasn't only to his disciples that day two thousand years
ago. It was to us, too. It's called the great commission.

What's It Mean?

Based on Jesus' finished work of redemption, God the Father has given "all
authority in heaven and on earth" to him (Matthew 28:18). Likewise, Jesus
now delegates disciple-making authority to all believers, his representatives
on earth.

If you are a Christian, your mission is to make disciples (Christ followers) of others. Only God can change human hearts, but he graciously works
through us as we proclaim the gospel to others.

How do we do this? Well, did you notice one of the key verbs in the great commission? It's one of the simplest words in the English language: *go*.

The Christian life isn't about inertia. It's about movement and action for God's glory and gospel advancement! Use the spiritual gifts, talents, and interests that the Lord has given you to proclaim the glorious message of salvation in Christ.

You've been commissioned. Now *go* make disciples!

Now What?

Prayerfully consider serving in one of these disciple-making ways: your church's children's ministry, a faith-based summer kids camp, an inner-city mission, or a short-term missions trip.

Did You Know?

After Jesus commissioned his disciples, he ascended into heaven, where he has been ever since. One day, he will return to judge the wicked and inaugurate his eternal Kingdom (Revelation 19–21).

SEPTEMBER 9

Do you not know that you are God's temple
and that God's Spirit dwells in you?

1 CORINTHIANS 3:16, ESV

WIND! FIRE! A SUPERNATURAL visitation! Astonishment!

About ten days after Jesus' Ascension, the disciples and other believers were gathered in a room in Jerusalem, obeying the Savior's earlier command (Acts 1:4-5). Suddenly, the sound of a mighty wind swept through the house, and what looked like flickering flames appeared above their heads. Amazingly, each person began speaking in a foreign language that had previously been unknown to them.

The large crowd of Jewish pilgrims in Jerusalem for the annual "Feast of Weeks" festival (also known as Pentecost) marveled at the sight. They couldn't believe that common, relatively uneducated residents of Galilee could speak in different tongues that spanned the Roman Empire (Acts 2:5-13).

What did it all mean?

God had powerfully poured out his Holy Spirit on the new Christian community!

What's It Mean?

The Holy Spirit plays a vital role in the life of every believer. Over the next three days, we're going to take a closer look at the Spirit's nature and ministry.

The Spirit's outpouring at Pentecost had been long foretold. God had promised a special new Spirit-filled era in believers when he spoke through the prophet Joel (likely around the sixth century BC): "I will pour out my Spirit upon all people. Your sons and daughters will prophesy. Your old men will dream dreams, and your young men will see visions. In those days, I will pour out my Spirit even on servants—men and women alike" (Joel 2:28-29). (Also see Ezekiel 36:26-27.)

The Holy Spirit—a member of the triune God—had always been active

505

throughout the Old Testament, even back to Creation (Genesis 1:2). He had empowered God's people for special purposes (e.g., Judges 14:19; 1 Samuel 11:6; 1 Samuel 16:13; 2 Chronicles 15:1).

Christ's death, resurrection, and the Spirit's indwelling at Pentecost all helped inaugurate the new covenant era between God and his chosen people (Jeremiah 31:31-34), where the Spirit came to dwell permanently in the hearts of God's children (see today's verse). Through his Spirit, God was making his home in his redeemed people. Amazing!

This was the miracle that the first Christians experienced at Pentecost two thousand years ago, and this is what all believers still benefit from today!

Now What?

Do a word search study on the Holy Spirit using an online Bible search engine such as BibleGateway.com to see his amazing ministry to all believers.

Did You Know?

On the day of Pentecost, the apostle Peter preached a sermon in Jerusalem, resulting in three thousand conversions (Acts 2:41) and the start of the early Christian church (verses 42-47).

SEPTEMBER 10

*We know how dearly God loves us, because he has given
us the Holy Spirit to fill our hearts with his love.*

ROMANS 5:5

WHO IS THE HOLY Spirit, and what does he actually do?

If you've ever asked yourself those questions, don't worry—you're not alone. God's Spirit has been active for all eternity, going all the way back to Genesis 1:2 (and beyond) when we read, "The Spirit of God was hovering over the surface of the waters" before Creation. Both Old and New Testaments consistently reference the Holy Spirit, yet he usually takes a backseat to God the Father and the Son (Jesus) in our understanding.

Still, it's vital for every Christian to know who the Holy Spirit is and how he functions in our lives. So let's dive into some wonderful truths about the glorious third person of the Trinity—for God's glory and our spiritual good.

What's It Mean?

While we may overlook or not completely understand the Holy Spirit, he is not in any way neglected or ignored within heaven's holy councils. The Holy Spirit is fully God and shares all the same divine attributes as the other two persons of the Godhead, even if some of his functions may differ from those of the Father and the Son.

The Holy Spirit is far too great to summarize in one day's devotion, but here is a brief overview of some of his primary functions. The Holy Spirit

- directly inspired all the words of Scripture (2 Peter 1:20-21);
- regenerates sinful human hearts to receive the gospel by faith (Titus 3:5);
- permanently indwells all believers at conversion, making them "the temple of God" (1 Corinthians 3:16);
- acts as a "guarantee" of our salvation (Ephesians 1:14);
- brings Scripture to our minds (John 14:26);

507

- helps us in our prayers, especially in our weakness (Romans 8:26-27);
- convicts us of sin (John 16:8) and helps us put it "to death" (Romans 8:13);
- equips us with spiritual gifts to serve God and build the church (1 Corinthians 12:4-11); and
- develops spiritual "fruit" in us as we grow in godliness (Galatians 5:22-23).

As you can see, the Holy Spirit plays an invaluable role in every believer's life, thanks to God's great design! Our salvation and sanctification simply aren't possible without him.

Aren't you glad God the Father has given us his Spirit to help save, sanctify, and strengthen us?

Now What?
Pray for more of God's Spirit in your life!

Did You Know?
The actual term "Holy Spirit" (as rendered by the ESV translation) is only used in three Old Testament verses: Psalm 51:11 and Isaiah 63:10-11. By comparison, it's used nearly one hundred times in the New Testament.

SEPTEMBER 11

*When he comes, he will convict the world of its sin, and
of God's righteousness, and of the coming judgment.*

JOHN 16:8

HAVE YOU EVER SEEN the 1940 Walt Disney classic, *Pinocchio*?

In the movie, a marionette puppet—the title character—comes to life, thanks to the wishes of his creator, Geppetto, and some fairy magic, setting off on an adventure to become a real boy. Before Pinocchio embarks, the fairy christens a sprightly insect, Jiminy Cricket, to be his "Official Conscience." When Pinocchio listens to his conscience, good things happen. When he doesn't . . . well, you'd better just watch the movie.

Of course, in real life, the human conscience is much different than a six-legged insect that hops and chirps. It's a vital part of every person—Christians and non-Christians alike. It's a built-in moral compass that allows us to choose between right and wrong (Romans 2:14-15).

Every follower of Jesus, though, not only has a conscience, but something far greater—the presence of the Holy Spirit in his or her life. This takes us from possessing a general knowledge of right vs. wrong to a true biblical conviction of sin, as today's verse says.

What's It Mean?

Sometimes, people treat their conscience—or even the Holy Spirit—as "that nagging voice inside you," like it's a pesky gnat to be swatted away. That's a completely unbiblical view.

The Holy Spirit is a wonderful gift. His work of conviction in our lives remarkably displays God's grace and mercy toward us. Without him, we wouldn't be aware of our depravity, our need for God, or even many of the daily instances where we transgress God's laws.

But the Holy Spirit brings all of this to light in the hearts of those who are humble before God. He is not a prosecuting attorney, pointing the finger at us. No! John 16:7 says he is our "Advocate" and our "Helper" (ESV). His job is to apply the work of salvation to us and draw us closer to the Lord.

When the Spirit stirs your conscience, don't squash his prodding like a pesky cricket chirping in your house. Allow him to work as he moves you toward repentance, spiritual maturation, and greater faith.

Now What?

How is the Holy Spirit stirring your conscience today? Follow his lead!

Did You Know?

Jesus said it was better that he return to heaven in favor of sending the Holy Spirit (John 16:7) largely because Jesus, in his incarnate form, could only be one place at one time. But the Holy Spirit indwells all believers at all times (1 Corinthians 3:16).

SEPTEMBER 12

*God has put all things under the authority of Christ and has
made him head over all things for the benefit of the church.
And the church is his body; it is made full and complete by
Christ, who fills all things everywhere with himself.*

EPHESIANS 1:22-23

CHURCH.

What comes to mind when you hear that word? Perhaps you think of a small house of worship on a country lane with a weathered steeple and clapboard siding. Maybe you picture a historic downtown building with a large bell tower and adjacent cemetery, or a multisite megachurch, or a "church-in-a-box" that rents space weekly at a local high school.

When you think of church, perhaps your mind wanders to a particular denomination, such as Baptist, Presbyterian, Lutheran, Methodist, Pentecostal, etc. Maybe you think of famous pastors that you see on TV or hear on the radio.

Church can mean many different things to many different people. But biblically defined, the church is not any of these things. It's the worldwide community of true believers in Jesus Christ.

What's It Mean?

All Christians are part of this beautiful global fellowship that encompasses every nation, tribe, and language (Revelation 7:9). In today's Scripture passage, the apostle Paul uses the human body metaphorically to describe the church. Just like the human head acts as the body's nerve center, Christ is the head of his spiritual "body," the church, exercising divine authority over all believers. We must submit our daily lives—not just on Sundays—to our spiritual Head: the Lord Jesus Christ. The Father gave this authority to the Son, based on Christ's finished work of atonement, which glorified God and secured eternal redemption for his chosen people.

As Christ's church, we are to

- gather together regularly to worship God and encourage each other in the faith (Hebrews 10:24-25).
- live in obedience to our Savior (John 14:15), being doers of God's Word, not just hearers (James 1:22-25).
- equip God's people (and be equipped) for gospel ministry (Ephesians 4:12).
- use our God-given spiritual gifts to edify the body (1 Corinthians 12).
- make disciples of the nations (Matthew 28:19-20).
- show compassion to the needy, both inside and outside the church (1 John 3:17; Luke 6:35-36).

The church is way more than a building or a denomination. It's a living, breathing spiritual body of believers—with Christ as the Head, and God receiving all glory. How are you benefitting the body of Christ?

Now What?
Study the biblical passages listed above to see how you can grow in the body of Christ.

Did You Know?
The first Christians began worshiping on Sunday in honor of "the Lord's Day" (Revelation 1:10)—the day of Christ's resurrection.

SEPTEMBER 13

Let us not neglect our meeting together, as some people do, but encourage one another, especially now that the day of his return is drawing near.

HEBREWS 10:25

AFTER THE SPIRIT-FILLED MIRACLE of Pentecost, the apostle Peter preached a powerful sermon in Jerusalem, resulting in about three thousand people coming to faith in Christ and the start of the early church. Ever since then, Christians have been gathering weekly to worship God.

But why? Is attending church just a social gathering for believers, or does Scripture command it?

Today's verse answers that question!

What's It Mean?

God's design is for his people to regularly gather together for corporate worship and encouraging fellowship as we anticipate the return of Christ. The early church provided the model for us in Acts 2, as new believers frequently "devoted themselves to the apostles' teaching, and to fellowship" (verse 42).

Here are seven other reasons why it's important for Christians to gather consistently at a gospel-centered church:

1. **To grow in God's Word.** We need to regularly hear the preaching of Scripture (2 Timothy 4:2-4) to mature spiritually.
2. **To praise God together.** The Bible calls us to exalt the Lord in community (Psalm 149:1).
3. **To uphold gospel truth.** The church is "the pillar and foundation of the truth" (1 Timothy 3:15), protecting the gospel from heresy. Aligning with a gospel-centered church is to join in this important battle.
4. **To build up the body of believers.** Christians should use their God-given spiritual gifts to edify the body of Christ (1 Corinthians 12).
5. **To practice the sacraments.** Corporate worship is where Christians can best obey Jesus' commands to baptize new believers (Matthew

28:19) and observe the Lord's Supper (1 Corinthians 11:23-26) until he returns.

6. **To fulfill the great commission.** The local gathered body of believers is the primary vehicle through which we fulfill Jesus' great commission (Matthew 28:19-20) to "make disciples of all the nations," equipping and sending people to reach the lost both locally and abroad.

7. **To help the needy.** A local church body can pool its resources powerfully to minister to those who are struggling in the community (Acts 2:45).

Don't neglect meeting together at a local gospel-centered church! This is God's design for every Christian who wants to grow in their walk with Christ.

Now What?
If you aren't part of a strong, gospel-centered church, join one! If you are, find ways to deepen your involvement.

Did You Know?
The early Christians of Acts 2:42 "devoted themselves to the apostles' teaching" because there were no New Testament Gospels or Epistles written yet. Until that happened, early believers learned about Jesus through the disciples' oral, eyewitness accounts.

SEPTEMBER 14

He fell to his knees, shouting, "Lord, don't
charge them with this sin!"

ACTS 7:60

IN CHRISTIANITY'S EARLY DAYS, thousands of people were coming to
faith. The church was spreading like a virus—and well, that's how the religious leaders in Jerusalem were treating it.

So when Stephen came along—"a man full of God's grace and power
[who] performed amazing miracles and signs among the people" (Acts
6:8)—the Jewish leaders arrested him and put him on trial before the
Sanhedrin.

When he was allowed to defend himself, Stephen launched into the
longest discourse recorded in Acts—a powerful account of Israel's Old
Testament history, from God's call of Abraham (Genesis 12) to the nation's
rejection of messianic prophecies and the Messiah himself.

"You stubborn people!" Stephen exclaimed. "You are heathen at heart
and deaf to the truth. Must you forever resist the Holy Spirit? That's what
your ancestors did, and so do you!" (Acts 7:51).

You can imagine how well *that* was received. Then when Stephen
reported seeing a heavenly vision of Jesus standing at God's right hand (Acts
7:56), the Sanhedrin's rage exploded into violence. They dragged Stephen
outside the city walls and stoned him to death.

As the rocks were pounding his body, Stephen prayed two prayers:
"Lord Jesus, receive my spirit" (Acts 7:59) and "Lord, don't charge them
with this sin!" (today's verse).

Wow.

What's It Mean?

Stephen's martyrdom, the first in early church history, was a remarkable
display of faith and grace under the most extreme circumstances. Here are
three thoughts to consider from Stephen's inspiring story:

1. He knew Scripture.
2. He unashamedly proclaimed truth amid severe opposition.
3. Despite being rejected, he asked God to show mercy to his listeners.

When you share your faith, some people will receive it with joy. Others won't. But to be an effective witness for the Lord, we should follow Stephen's model.

To faithfully proclaim God's Word, you first have to know it well. Also, like Stephen, we should care more about declaring the truth (our job) than how it is received (the Holy Spirit's realm). Finally, when Stephen was reviled, he didn't revile in return, just like Christ (1 Peter 2:23). Rather, he graciously prayed for his executioners.

May we all be bold, gospel-proclaiming witnesses like Stephen!

Now What?
Read Stephen's story in Acts 6–7.

Did You Know?
Luke wrote both the Gospel of Luke and the book of Acts. What he records of Stephen's final two statements (see above) strongly parallels two of Jesus' last statements on the cross (Luke 23:34, 46).

SEPTEMBER 15

Before I was born, God chose me and called me by his marvelous grace. Then it pleased him to reveal his Son to me so that I would proclaim the Good News about Jesus to the Gentiles.

GALATIANS 1:15-16

SAUL FELL TO THE GROUND—terrified, helpless, and temporarily blinded. He had been traveling on a desert road between Jerusalem and Damascus at midday, with the sun at its zenith, yet a mysterious light had flashed from heaven so brightly, it dwarfed the sun's brilliance and knocked Saul over.

Suddenly, a voice thundered from heaven: "Saul! Saul! Why are you persecuting me?"

"Who are you, lord?" he replied, honestly unaware.

The voice answered, "I am Jesus, the one you are persecuting!" (Acts 22:6-16).

Saul, the great persecutor of the early church, would never be the same.

Rewind to a tragic scene in Jerusalem. With malicious approval, Saul had watched as the Jewish religious leaders stoned Stephen to death (Acts 7:58). He hated Christians. As a devoted Pharisee, he didn't believe in Jesus' deity, and he considered Christianity a threat against Judaism. In Saul's mind, Christianity had to be eradicated.

Then Saul met the risen, glorified Savior, and everything changed.

What's It Mean?

Few conversions, if any, in the history of Christianity are more radical than Saul's. After being stunned by Christ's glory, Saul (who changed his name to Paul) spent the rest of his life proclaiming the gospel and planting churches all over the Roman Empire and writing nearly half (thirteen) of the New Testament's twenty-seven books.

Paul literally changed the world. Two thousand years later, we still benefit daily from his ministry as we read his divinely inspired letters and digest the gospel truths that he so beautifully explained.

But Paul's incredible transformation wasn't his own doing. Look at today's verse: God sovereignly "chose" and "called" Paul, then gave him a job to do ("proclaim the Good News about Jesus to the Gentiles").

Today, God is still calling and equipping all his chosen to "do the good things he planned for us long ago" (Ephesians 2:10). Everyone whom God graciously chooses to save he effectively calls by his Spirit to respond to the gospel. Then he equips them for the ministry that he kindly planned in advance for them.

God has a plan for you! Like Paul, submit to God's will and use your gifts to change the world, one life at a time.

Now What?
Read about Paul's miraculous conversion in Acts 9:1-31.

Did You Know?
- Paul recounts his conversion experience and other interesting autobiographical details in Acts 26:1-20; Galatians 1:11–2:14; Philippians 3:4-6; and 1 Timothy 1:12-16.

SEPTEMBER 16

*Peter replied, "I see very clearly that God shows
no favoritism. In every nation he accepts those
who fear him and do what is right."*

ACTS 10:34-35

WOULD YOU EVER EAT a sautéed iguana with roasted potatoes on the
side? How about a nice, spicy mole rat stew? Would you ever sink your teeth
into a juicy toad burger, with all the fixings?

Ewww. Neither would the apostle Peter.

In Acts 10, Peter received a vision of a large sheet descending to earth,
holding all sorts of creatures—many of which were off-limits under the Old
Testament's strict dietary laws. Yet Peter heard a voice say, "Get up, Peter;
kill and eat them."

"No, Lord," Peter objected. "I have never eaten anything that our
Jewish laws have declared impure and unclean."

Immediately, the voice responded, "Do not call something unclean if
God has made it clean."

Just then, messengers from a Roman centurion named Cornelius
arrived where Peter was staying. They asked him to accompany them to
Cornelius's house. When Peter arrived, Cornelius said God had told him to
send for Peter and listen to his message. Peter connected the dots: God does
not show spiritual favoritism. His marvelous salvation plan is for everyone
(verses 13-29).

What's It Mean?

Like all ancient Israelites, Peter had been raised to believe that the Jews
were God's chosen people thanks to God's provision of the Mosaic law, the
Temple, and the Abrahamic and Davidic covenants. They believed salvation
was exclusively theirs and that any "unclean" Gentile (i.e., a non-Jew) had to
perform various ceremonial rites (such as circumcision) and observe the law
to become spiritually "clean" before the Lord.

But God powerfully showed Peter otherwise. His vision wasn't merely about food laws. It pointed to a greater truth: *anyone* who trusts in Jesus for the forgiveness of sins can be saved.

God created all humans in his image (Genesis 1:26-27); therefore, he values everyone equally. God cares about our hearts, faith, and obedience—not our skin color or nationality.

God is not the God of America or any particular people group or ethnicity. He is the Lord God Almighty, ruler of heaven and earth. His Son's blood "has ransomed people for God from every tribe and language and people and nation" (Revelation 5:9), and one day, the beautifully diverse family of God will worship around his throne forever (Revelation 7:9-10).

Now What?

Do you view others as God views them? Read Ephesians 2:11–3:10 to better understand today's truth.

Did You Know?

God's plan always was to bring Gentiles to salvation (Hosea 1:10; Isaiah 42:6; Isaiah 49:6), but this wasn't fully realized until the church age (Ephesians 3:1-10).

SEPTEMBER 17

Everyone who believes in him is made right in God's
sight—something the law of Moses could never do.

ACTS 13:39

WHEN THE APOSTLE PAUL arrived in Pisidian Antioch (a city in Asia Minor) on his first missionary journey, he first visited the local Jewish synagogue before preaching anywhere else, as was his custom. The synagogue leaders told him, "If you have any word of encouragement for the people, come and give it" (Acts 13:15).

Boy, were they in for a surprise!

Paul gladly stood up before the crowd. Knowing that his audience was Old Testament–savvy, he gave a brief overview of Israel's history before quickly steering the conversation to Jesus, showing how Christ fulfilled Messianic prophecies—such as Psalm 2:7; Psalm 16:10; and Isaiah 55:3—as God's long-awaited Savior who was crucified and resurrected to free the people from their sins.

As he concluded, Paul said,

> Brothers, listen! We are here to proclaim that through this man Jesus there is forgiveness for your sins. Everyone who believes in him is made right in God's sight—something the law of Moses could never do.
> ACTS 13:38-39

Paul didn't mince words. His message was crystal clear: I know you believe in God. But what are you going to do about Jesus?

What's It Mean?

Paul's sermon that day was concurrent with the message of Scripture: a stand-alone belief in God is not enough. Salvation comes through repentance and faith in God's appointed Savior.

From the moment Jesus ascended into heaven, this was the good news that the apostles proclaimed all over the world. Acts 2:22-39; 4:11-12; 8:35;

and 16:31 are just a few examples of this. Jesus himself said that the only way to the Father was through the Son (John 14:6).

Now the question comes to you. If you're reading this devotional, you probably believe in God. But what are you going to do about Jesus? Everything in this life—and eternity—hinges on that.

You cannot shrug at the reality of the Son's incarnation and worship the God who sent him. You cannot spurn the eternal significance of the Savior's crucifixion and adore the God who sacrificed him. You cannot deny Christ's resurrection and love the God who raised him. You cannot reject Jesus and be right with God. "Everyone who believes in him is made right in God's sight."

So the question comes to you again: What are *you* going to do about Jesus?

Now What?
If you have never trusted in Jesus as your Lord and Savior, do so today!

Did You Know?
While some in Pisidian Antioch seemed to believe Paul's message (Acts 13:43), he was ultimately kicked out of the city for his gospel witness (verse 50).

SEPTEMBER 18

My life is worth nothing to me unless I use it for
finishing the work assigned me by the Lord Jesus.

ACTS 20:24

IMAGINE YOU'RE DRIVING HOME after a nice vacation. Suddenly, you see a big, flashing road sign ahead that reads, "WARNING: CONTINUING ONWARD WILL RESULT IN ARREST, IMPRISONMENT, AND MUCH SUFFERING."

Screeeeeeeeech!!!

You'd slam on the brakes, turn around, and make alternate plans, right? Well, guess what? The apostle Paul kept going.

Acts 20 describes how Paul, during his third missionary journey, met with the Ephesian church elders to give them an important, yet harrowing message:

> Now I am bound by the Spirit to go to Jerusalem. I don't know what awaits me, except that the Holy Spirit tells me in city after city that jail and suffering lie ahead. But my life is worth nothing to me unless I use it for finishing the work assigned me by the Lord Jesus—the work of telling others the Good News about the wonderful grace of God. And now I know that none of you to whom I have preached the Kingdom will ever see me again.
> VERSES 22-25

Not exactly a feel-good farewell. But what faith and courage!

What's It Mean?

In Acts 21, we learn that Paul was unjustly arrested in Jerusalem for his faith and spent the next several years imprisoned in Jerusalem, Caesarea, and eventually Rome. But he used his first two imprisonments to preach the gospel to powerful governors and kings (Acts 24 and 26; Matthew 10:18). And in Rome, he wrote Colossians, Ephesians, Philemon, and Philippians, and also "welcomed all who visited him, boldly proclaiming the Kingdom of God and teaching about the Lord Jesus Christ" (Acts 28:30-31).

To be a Christian is to suffer for the name of Jesus (John 15:20; 2 Timothy 3:12). Paul embraced this truth and was willing to sacrifice everything he had for the sake of Christ (today's verse).

This attitude requires a complete overhaul of our natural instincts. Our normal human mindset is to veer toward comfort and selfish desires. But Jesus calls us to something far greater. He calls every true follower of his to "deny himself and take up his cross and follow me. For whoever would save his life will lose it, but whoever loses his life for my sake will find it" (Matthew 16:24-25, ESV).

Paul did that. What about you?

Now What?
Read Acts 21–28 to learn about Paul's arrest, trials, and imprisonments.

Did You Know?
After at least two years in Rome, Paul was released from his Roman confinement (Acts 28:30). Extra-biblical Christian sources say after more ministry, he was eventually rearrested and martyred in Rome.

SEPTEMBER 19

I am not ashamed of the gospel, for it is the power
of God for salvation to everyone who believes,
to the Jew first and also to the Greek.

ROMANS 1:16, ESV

YOU SHOULD FEEL A proper sense of shame if you ever do any of the following things in life:

- taking the Lord's name in vain
- yelling at your parents
- walking past an elderly person in need without lifting a finger to help
- stealing
- lying
- using obscene language
- failing a test because you didn't study

But you should never be ashamed of the gospel of Jesus Christ!

Today, we begin a thirteen-day study of the apostle Paul's letter to the Romans, which contains Scripture's most comprehensive treatment of the gospel. He wrote this letter to Christians living in Rome circa AD 57.

Romans 1:16-17, which acts as Paul's thesis statement for the entire letter, provides the basis for today's devotion:

I am not ashamed of the gospel, for it is the power of God for salvation to everyone who believes, to the Jew first and also to the Greek. For in it the righteousness of God is revealed from faith for faith, as it is written, "The righteous shall live by faith."

ROMANS 1:16-17, ESV

Let's discuss this wonderful passage of Scripture!

What's It Mean?

In Paul's day, the Roman Empire encompassed most of the known ancient world. Christians, though, were often marginalized—or worse—depending on the emperor in power.

Today, despite our religious freedom, there will always be people who look down on you because of your faith. But don't be ashamed!

Some will mock. Some will taunt. Some will say there is no God (Psalm 14:1). Some will say Christians are fools to believe in a resurrected Christ who is returning again (2 Peter 3:4). This has always been the case.

But remember: there is great power in the gospel. It's not earthly power. You can't see it in a bank account, social media followers, or any other human metrics. It's so much better!

It's God's power to save hell-bound souls and bring them into the light of his glorious grace. It's God's power to radically transform broken, rebellious hearts into hearts that want to love him and serve others.

May we never be ashamed of what God has done for us through the great sacrifice of his Son, Jesus Christ!

Now What?

Memorize Romans 1:16-17.

Did You Know?

"To the Jew first and also to the Greek" (Romans 1:16, ESV) means that God's salvation plan extends to all people, regardless of nationality. Praise the Lord!

SEPTEMBER 20

Through everything God made, they can clearly see his
invisible qualities—his eternal power and divine nature.
So they have no excuse for not knowing God.

ROMANS 1:20

THERE'S NO DENYING IT: the people of the ancient world were quite creative. But don't confuse "creative" with "spiritually wise."

As the historic cultures tried to make sense of the world around them, they concocted some wild mythologies. The Mesopotamians and Egyptians, for instance, invented gods and goddesses that were half-human and half-animal. Others, such as the Greeks and Romans, considered themselves "enlightened" by elevating humanity in their divine pantheons (as if worshiping fictitious human entities was enlightened!).

The apostle Paul, writing in Romans 1:18-23, condemned such idolatrous rebellion against God:

God shows his anger from heaven against all sinful, wicked people who suppress the truth by their wickedness. They know the truth about God because he has made it obvious to them. For ever since the world was created, people have seen the earth and sky. Through everything God made, they can clearly see his invisible qualities— his eternal power and divine nature. So they have no excuse for not knowing God. Yes, they knew God, but they wouldn't worship him as God or even give him thanks. And they began to think up foolish ideas of what God was like. As a result, their minds became dark and confused. Claiming to be wise, they instead became utter fools. And instead of worshiping the glorious, ever-living God, they worshiped idols made to look like mere people and birds and animals and reptiles.

This vital passage of Scripture is about human accountability.

What's It Mean?

From the beginning, God has revealed himself to us. He didn't have to. But he chose to out of his great love for us—through general revelation (the universe he created) and special revelation (his spoken and written word). Then, at his appointed time in history, he revealed himself perfectly and sacrificially in human form through the living Word—his Son, Jesus Christ, as a payment for our sins (John 1:14; Galatians 4:4-5). In other words, we have no excuse for not knowing God (today's verse).

Most ancient cultures rebelled against God and chose to worship the creation instead of the Creator. Today, it's largely the same, although we have replaced creature idols with idols of self-absorption, money, and material possessions.

God has adequately revealed himself to you. Have you submitted your heart to him?

Now What?

Pick an ancient culture and study their mythology to see the futility of their religious beliefs in light of Romans 1:18-32.

Did You Know?

The ancient Greeks worshiped many deities, but primarily the twelve residents of Mount Olympus.

528

SEPTEMBER 21

All have sinned and fall short of the glory of God.

ROMANS 3:23, ESV

HOPEFULLY, YOU DON'T WORSHIP the sun, moon, hippopotamuses, or two thousand other false deities like the ancient Egyptians did. Hopefully, you don't believe fanciful tales about twelve fickle demigods on Mount Olympus who bicker, scheme, and toy with humanity just for kicks like the ancient Greeks did.

Remember how we discussed in yesterday's devotion that the apostle Paul condemned humanity's overall rejection of God in spite of God's loving self-revelation? Well, Paul didn't just point the finger at ancient pagans who worshiped weird-looking, make-believe gods. No, he laid the blame of sin at everyone's feet.

In Romans 3:10-18, he quotes a dozen different Old Testament passages of Scripture to show that every human being is guilty before God:

- None is righteous, no, not one. (verse 10, ESV)
- No one understands; no one seeks for God. (verse 11, ESV)
- All have turned aside; together they have become worthless. (verse 12, ESV)

This is all leading up to his famous gospel presentation in verses 23-25 (ESV):

For all have sinned and fall short of the glory of God, and are justified by his grace as a gift, through the redemption that is in Christ Jesus, whom God put forward as a propitiation by his blood, to be received by faith.

These are some of the most beautiful words in the entire Bible!

What's It Mean?

This passage starts with really bad news and ends with really good news. First the bad news: we are all sinners, hopelessly separated from God by our unholy nature and deeds.

Now the good news: God is a loving gift-giver, and he freely wants to justify (or declare righteous in his sight) sinners through his grace. How can God possibly do this and still remain holy and just? Paul answers this in verse 24—"through the redemption that is in Christ Jesus, whom God put forward as a propitiation by his blood, to be received by faith" (ESV).

The word *propitiation* means "a wrath-bearing sacrifice." In other words, Jesus died on the cross to bear all of God's wrath (i.e., righteous anger) toward *our* sin and turn it into favor toward us. Now, when we receive this "redemption that is in Christ . . . by faith," God doesn't count our sins against us any longer. Instead, he sees us clothed in Christ's righteousness (2 Corinthians 5:21).

What an amazing transformation!

Now What?

Memorize Romans 3:23-25.

Did You Know?

The biblical concept of propitiation is also mentioned in Hebrews 2:17; 1 John 2:2; and 1 John 4:10.

SEPTEMBER 22

When Adam sinned, sin entered the world. Adam's sin brought death, so death spread to everyone, for everyone sinned.

ROMANS 5:12

ROMANS 5 is a potential land mine chapter.

The first eleven verses are wonderfully controversy free, filled with beautiful descriptions of justification by faith (verse 1), sanctification through trials (verses 3-5), and reconciliation through Christ (verses 10-11). But in verses 12-21, the apostle Paul brings up an important topic that, if misunderstood, might cause some readers to veer into spiritually dangerous territory. We need to properly understand this critical section of Scripture about our sinful natures.

Today's verse brings us back to that fateful moment in the Garden of Eden when Adam and Eve disobeyed God and ate the forbidden fruit: "When Adam sinned, sin entered the world. Adam's sin brought death, so death spread to everyone, for everyone sinned." In the rest of the chapter, Paul masterfully discusses that while sin and death came through Adam (as humanity's first, fallen covenantal representative), salvation comes through Jesus (humanity's superior "Adam").

What's It Mean?

Romans 5 is an amazing chapter, juxtaposing death in Adam with eternal life in Christ. However, some people read today's verse and get defensive, saying, "That's not fair! Why do I have to pay for Adam's sin?"

If you're asking that question, here are two important considerations:

1. Have you ever sinned in action, thought, or motive? Of course. We all have (Romans 3:23). While Adam was the original sinner, you are responsible for your own transgressions. The Bible states very clearly that God will judge every individual according to their own deeds (Romans 2:6-11) and how they respond to his Son (John 3:18).
2. If you don't think the message of Romans 5:12-21 is fair, consider

the double standard you might be keeping in your heart: you can't gripe that one man's sin (Adam's) brought death to all humanity while praising God that another Man's death and resurrection (Christ's) brings eternal life to all who believe.

But remember, too, the truth of verse 15: "There is a great difference between Adam's sin and God's gracious gift. For the sin of this one man, Adam, brought death to many. But even greater is God's wonderful grace and his gift of forgiveness to many through this other man, Jesus Christ." Adam's sin—despite its terrible effects—cannot compare to the present and eternal blessings that God bestows on all believers through Jesus!

Don't get tripped up on self-made land mines. Glory in what God has done for you in Christ!

Now What?

Read Genesis 3 and Romans 5 to continue your study contrasting Adam and Christ.

Did You Know?

Paul also mentions the Adam/Christ comparison in 1 Corinthians 15:22, 45.

SEPTEMBER 23

*Should we keep on sinning so that God can show us more
and more of his wonderful grace? Of course not! Since we
have died to sin, how can we continue to live in it?*

ROMANS 6:1-2

HAVE YOU EVER PLAYED the board game Monopoly?

If so, you're probably familiar with the well-known "Get out of jail free" card. With this card, you can do just what the card says—get out of jail immediately and without penalty if you get sent there on your turn.

In Romans 6, the apostle Paul anticipated a question he knew was going to arise from his earlier teachings on justification by God's grace through faith in Christ. Being the wise pastor that he was, he knew that some people might think that he was preaching a so-called "Get out of jail free" theology that would give them license to behave in ungodly manners.

He knew some people might misinterpret the first five chapters and erroneously come to the following conclusion—a terribly inaccurate one, at that—in their minds:

- We are all sinners and our sin highlights God's grace, so we should sin more in order to give God more glory for more grace.
- It doesn't really matter how we live since God will just forgive us anyway.

Is this the way we should think and live? Paul emphatically answers this in today's Scripture passage: "Of course not!" Nothing could be further from the truth! Paul rejects this completely fallacious way of thinking in Romans 6.

What's It Mean?

Paul was not preaching a "cheap grace" salvation at all, and nowhere does Scripture ever support any notion of that. Our salvation came at a great cost, and we should always be humbly mindful of that.

To think we can sin anytime we want and tritely ask forgiveness is an insult to God's holiness and to the Lord Jesus Christ, who temporarily "emptied himself, by taking the form of a servant" (Philippians 2:7, ESV) and suffered unspeakably for our sakes so that we could be reconciled with God. That's never to be taken lightly.

What's more, Romans 6:6 says, "Our old sinful selves were crucified with Christ so that sin might lose its power in our lives." Although indwelling sin remains, Christians are not to go on willfully sinning but should seek to live righteously like their Savior (Galatians 5:13).

Leave the "Get out of jail free" card for Monopoly games. Instead die to sin and live for Christ!

Now What?

Next time you play Monopoly (especially when you land in jail!), thank God for his saving grace.

Did You Know?

Parker Brothers began selling Monopoly in 1935.

SEPTEMBER 24

There is no condemnation for those who belong to Christ Jesus.

ROMANS 8:1

YAAARRR, MATEYS! IT'S TIME for dueling cannon fire, clanging swords, and a swashbuckling tale of pirate adventure on the high seas. It's time for the exciting—and ultimately tragic—story of Captain Kidd.

Born in Scotland in 1645, William Kidd eventually became a privateer, which was a different occupation than piracy in the seventeenth century . . . sort of. Nations such as England (which Kidd worked for) would commission (but usually not pay) privateers such as Kidd to attack ships of commerce from countries that they were at war with. The understanding was that the privateers could help themselves to the ship's booty.

Kidd, though, made a fatal choice in 1698 when he attacked the large Armenian ship *Quedagh Merchant*, which was partly owned by a minister in the Indian government who complained to powerful English officials. Kidd was denounced as a pirate, arrested, brought to trial, and condemned to death by hanging on May 23, 1701. To discourage piracy, his corpse was left to rot publicly in a cage along the River Thames.

In the end, William Kidd was a condemned man. Those who had been his friends in the English government turned against him. No one came to his defense, and he died a terrible death, without friends and without hope.

Praise God this is not the reality for anyone who follows Christ!

What's It Mean?

Today's verse proclaims one of the Bible's greatest truths: all true Christians will never face condemnation of any sort from God.

You will go through moments of guilt and shame over sin. You will feel remorse over regrettable actions and words you wish you could take back. Satan, the great "accuser of our brothers and sisters" (Revelation 12:10) will hurl spiritual indictments at you, asking you in sinister whispers, "How can you call yourself a Christian?" But Satan is a liar, and we "have defeated him by the blood of the Lamb" (Revelation 12:11).

Remember, child of God, you will never experience condemnation from your heavenly Father—either in this life or the one to come. That's because Christ stood condemned in your place on the cross. He fully paid the price of your sins so you wouldn't have to. Now you can fully experience God's love, grace, mercy, and forgiveness without fear of wrath or condemnation.

No Kidd-ing!

Now What?

When you do sin, turn to the encouraging truths of 2 Corinthians 7:10 and 1 John 1:9.

Did You Know?

To this day, some people think part of Captain Kidd's treasure is hidden somewhere in the Caribbean.

SEPTEMBER 25

Now we call him, "Abba, Father."

ROMANS 8:15

IN THE APOSTLE PAUL'S day, ancient Roman culture was rife with slavery. Some historians estimate that fifty percent of the Roman Empire's population were slaves of some sort.

So Paul—always on the lookout for a good metaphor—used the slavery motif to illustrate a vital Christian doctrine: God's adoption of believers into his spiritual family. Look at the full text of today's verse, Romans 8:15: "You have not received a spirit that makes you fearful slaves. Instead, you received God's Spirit when he adopted you as his own children. Now we call him, 'Abba, Father.'"

Here's Paul's point: God is both holy (utterly set apart and transcendent from his creation) and personal. When we become part of God's spiritual family through faith in Christ, we don't have to approach him in fear, like a slave cowering before his master. We can approach God like what he truly is: a loving heavenly Father.

What's It Mean?

What comes to mind when you hear the word *father*? A loving dad who showered you with time and affection? A godly patriarch who led your family well in "the discipline and instruction that comes from the Lord" (Ephesians 6:4)? That's certainly the ideal!

But perhaps your family situation isn't that picturesque. Maybe you come from a broken home—or worse, an abusive one. Please understand that divorce and any form of abuse is ultimately the result of sin, which grieves God's heart. That wasn't part of his original family design.

But take heart: regardless of the merits of your earthly father, *God is a perfect heavenly Father*. Because he is holy and just, he will always do what is right. He is completely trustworthy.

God cares for his children with a love that's incomprehensible (Psalm 103:11-12). He knows the most intimate details about you, such as the number of hairs on your head (Matthew 10:30), the unspoken words in your mind (Psalm 139:4), and every detail of your future (Psalm 139:16).

God's love for you far exceeds that of even the most wonderful human father. He counts all your tears (Psalm 56:8), provides for all your physical and spiritual needs (Matthew 6:33; Philippians 4:19), and most importantly, he sacrificed his own Son so that he could adopt you into his spiritual family forever (John 3:16).

What a wonderful Father! What a God! What a Savior!

Now What?
You can pray to your heavenly Father at any time, as Jesus encouraged us to do in Matthew 6:9-13.

Did You Know?
In Aramaic, the word *Abba* means "father." Jesus used this term while praying to God in Gethsemane before his impending crucifixion (Mark 14:36).

SEPTEMBER 26

I am convinced that nothing can ever
separate us from God's love.

ROMANS 8:38

ON OCTOBER 6, 1536, local officials in the Dutch town of Vilvoorde bound William Tyndale to a wooden cross and fastened a rope and an iron chain around his neck. His alleged crime? Heresy against the Holy Roman Empire.

Tyndale, forty-two years old at the time, had already translated the New Testament from Greek to English and had been translating the Old Testament from Hebrew to English when he was arrested in May 1535. Back in 1523, the Catholic bishop in London had forbidden his translation efforts, so he had fled to various other cities in Europe to do his good work.

Tyndale produced his New Testament two years later, smuggled it back into England, and successfully managed to evade the authorities until he was betrayed by a supposed friend. At Vilvoorde, his executioners strangled him first before burning him at the stake.

Of the many tracts Tyndale wrote, one reads as follows (partially paraphrasing Romans 8:31):

> Let it not make thee despair, neither yet discourage thee, O reader, that it is forbidden thee in pain of life and goods, or that it is made breaking of the king's peace, or treason unto his highness, to read the word of thy soul's health . . . for if God be on our side, what matter maketh it who be against us, be they bishops, cardinals, popes, or whatsoever names they will?[1]

Wicked authorities could take Tyndale's life, but they couldn't separate him from the love of God.

---

[1] William Tyndale, Doctrinal Treatises and Introductions to Different Portions of the Holy Scriptures (Cambridge, University Press, 1848), 131, 135.

What's It Mean?

Romans 8 is a slow buildup to the glorious truth of today's verse. In verses 28-30, Paul presents what's commonly referred to as the Golden Chain of Salvation, highlighting God's sovereign, unbreakable plan of salvation for every believer.

With that in mind, he then asks the question that Tyndale posed: "If God is for us, who can ever be against us?" (verse 31).

Clearly, we will face human opposition in this world. Tyndale certainly did, even to the death. But the authorities couldn't separate him from God's love.

If you have trusted in Jesus for the forgiveness of your sins, nothing in heaven or on earth can stand between you and God's love (verses 38-39). Nothing can keep you from seeing your heavenly Father in eternity one day. That's how amazing God's salvation is. That's how powerful his love is for you.

And that's good news!

Now What?

Read some biographies of Christian Reformers such as William Tyndale, Martin Luther, and John Calvin.

Did You Know?

Only one copy of Tyndale's New Testament remains today—at London's British Library.

SEPTEMBER 27

*Do not be conformed to this world, but be
transformed by the renewal of your mind.*

ROMANS 12:2, ESV

ONCE UPON A TIME in America, everyone seemed to live in a nice three-
bedroom home on a nice suburban street with a white picket fence. Dad
went to work, Mom stayed home, and the kids enjoyed peanut-butter-and-
jelly sandwiches while watching *The Howdy Doody Show* on their twenty-
inch manual-knob, black-and-white TV (ask your grandparents). Everything
felt as hunky-dory as a Norman Rockwell painting.

Then came the countercultural revolution in the 1960s.

Tired of conforming to the moral standards of earlier generations, millions of young Americans known as "hippies" embraced all manner of vice,
rebelliousness, and individuality. "Sex, drugs, and rock 'n' roll" became
the motto of a decade. Nonconformity in morality, appearance, clothing,
employment—or anything, really—became, well, hip.

The hippies of the '60s certainly would have benefited from today's
verse! Here it is in its larger context:

> I appeal to you therefore, brothers, by the mercies of God, to
> present your bodies as a living sacrifice, holy and acceptable to God,
> which is your spiritual worship. Do not be conformed to this world,
> but be transformed by the renewal of your mind, that by testing you
> may discern what is the will of God, what is good and acceptable
> and perfect.
>
> ROMANS 12:1-2, ESV

Let's dig deeper into this important exhortation.

What's It Mean?

Using the phrase "living sacrifice," the apostle Paul draws on the imagery
of the Old Testament sacrificial system, with its constant offerings of bulls,

goats, lambs, etc. But thanks to Christ's once-for-all sacrifice, no more animal sacrifices are needed (Hebrews 10:1-18) and all believers have become the Temple of God's Spirit (1 Corinthians 3:16-17).

As such, we *are* to conform—but to a godly standard. Unlike those (including the '60s hippies) who defiantly seek meaning and pleasure in what the world offers, we are to conform to God's righteousness, which is life-giving.

To do this, we must "be transformed by the renewal of your mind" (Romans 12:2, ESV). This includes filling our hearts with Scripture (Psalm 119:11), praying constantly (1 Thessalonians 5:17), following the Spirit's leading (Galatians 5:25), and fellowshipping with other believers (Hebrews 10:24-25).

Being countercultural isn't a bad thing . . . as long as you eschew the tug of the world and are "hip" to God's standards!

Now What?
Memorize Romans 12:1-2.

Did You Know?
One of the seminal moments of the hippie movement was the 1969 Woodstock music festival in New York state, which was attended by an estimated 400,000 to 500,000 people.

SEPTEMBER 28

Abhor what is evil; hold fast to what is good.

ROMANS 12:9, ESV

QUIZ TIME!

Below are three questions with two possible responses to each question. You simply have to guess the politest response to each question. Easy-peasy! Here we go.

> **Question:** Would you care for a helping of brussels sprouts with your dinner?
> **Response No. 1:** No, thank you. I don't particularly care for brussels sprouts.
> **Response No. 2:** Are you joking? I *abhor* brussels sprouts.
> **Question:** Do you like the new polka dot dress I bought?
> **Response No. 1:** It's nice, but I think you look even better in paisley.
> **Response No. 2:** Are you joking? I *abhor* polka dot dresses.
> **Question:** Hey, I really liked that movie. What did you think about it?
> **Response No. 1:** It wasn't my favorite. But I'm glad you liked it.
> **Response No. 2:** Are you joking? Of all the movies I *abhor* in the world, I *abhor* this movie most of all.

Pretty easy quiz, eh? Clearly, the politest response in each instance is number one. But did you notice the common word in the quiz? It's the word *abhor*. It's a very strong word that we don't use much these days.

Abhor was the wrong word to use in our silly quiz above, but according to today's verse, it's absolutely the correct response we should have toward evil and personal sin.

What's It Mean?

In today's verse, the English word *abhor* comes from the Greek term, *apostygeō*, one of the strongest expressions that the apostle Paul could find. It describes a sense of loathing or detesting.

In his holiness, God abhors sin, which, at its essence, is rebellion against him. Our sin brought sadness, pain, and strife into God's perfect creation. It separated us from our Creator. It brought the curse of death upon us, making it necessary for a sinless Savior to suffer divine wrath so that we could be made righteous.

Sin is a really big deal to God.

Therefore, as God's image bearers, we are to treat sin seriously. We must not tolerate it, laugh at it, or brush it under the proverbial carpet. Instead, "hold fast to what is good" (today's verse) and grow in godliness. This is God's will for you!

Now What?

Ask God to reveal areas of your life where you're not taking sin seriously.

Did You Know?

- Remember, when you do sin, you are not condemned (Romans 8:1). Christ suffered condemnation in your place so that you could experience peace with God (Romans 5:1). Confess your sin to the Lord (1 John 1:9) and put that sin to death by the power of his Spirit (Romans 8:13).

SEPTEMBER 29

Do all that you can to live in peace with everyone.

ROMANS 12:18

THE COUNTERCULTURAL REVOLUTIONARIES of the 1960s—those longhaired, casually dressed youth called hippies who often favored mind-altering drugs such as marijuana and LSD—proclaimed to love peace. When the Vietnam War broke out in 1965, many young adults dodged the draft. Countless others protested it—some, ironically, with violence. By the 1960s, the "victory" sign that World War II soldiers had made by forming their middle and index fingers into a V-shape had transformed into a hippie "peace" sign.

Peace, though, is hard to come by. Ironically, the '60s were full of riots. No nation on earth has enjoyed peace for long. Even the famed *Pax Romana* era ("Roman Peace") of the Roman Empire, which historians date from the reign of Augustus (27 BC–AD 14) to Marcus Aurelius (AD 161–180), included some revolts, such as the Jewish War (AD 66–70).

The peace that the apostle Paul describes in today's verse is a very different thing indeed!

What's It Mean?

True, biblical peace isn't simply pacifism—the idea that human war and conflict should be avoided at all costs. Real, abiding peace originates from "the Lord of peace himself" who can "give you his peace at all times and in every situation" (2 Thessalonians 3:16). Peace is a fruit of the Spirit (Galatians 5:22). Therefore, we can truly experience godly peace only when his Spirit has worked salvation in our hearts, reconciling guilty sinners with a holy God as we trust in Jesus, the "Prince of Peace" (Isaiah 9:6).

As recipients of God's peace, the Lord expects us to "live in peace with everyone." We are to freely give what we've been freely given.

Is this always possible? Unfortunately, no. Sometimes, you will encounter difficult individuals in life. Paul certainly did. That's why he worded today's verse like he did: "*Do all that you can* to live in peace with everyone" (emphasis added). But don't be the one to rush to judgment, speak angry words, or stir up trouble. As far as it depends on you, show godly love and be the peacemaker in all situations.

True peace is hard to come by in this broken, messed-up, sinful world. So be a peacemaker through the power of the God of peace!

Now What?

Is there someone you are estranged from right now? Make peace with them today!

Did You Know?

In its truest biblical sense, the word *shalom*, an ancient salutation of greeting or parting meaning "peace" that many Jews still use today, carries the connotation of a right relationship with God.

SEPTEMBER 30

*Everyone must submit to governing authorities. For
all authority comes from God, and those in positions
of authority have been placed there by God.*

ROMANS 13:1

IN AD 54, a seventeen-year-old youth named Lucius Domitius
Ahenobarbus assumed the imperial throne of the Roman Empire. The
young man then took his more infamous throne name: Nero.

Before long, Nero let power utterly corrupt him. He ordered the assassination of his own mother, and he might have also plotted his stepbrother's
mysterious death. Nero committed adultery with a friend's wife and then
killed her with a swift kick to the stomach several years after marrying her.

Some historians accuse Nero of starting a massive nine-day fire in
AD 64 that destroyed three Roman districts simply so he could expand his
palatial complex. Afterward, he blamed Christians and sanctioned horrific
persecutions against them. In AD 68, after years of mounting civil unrest,
Nero committed suicide.

Early on in Nero's terrible reign (c. AD 57), the apostle Paul wrote the
words of today's verse—*to Christians living in Rome, no less!* Was Paul crazy?
Was he oblivious to current events? Was he trying to be ironic or telling a
joke in poor taste?

No.

Paul was writing scriptural truth for first-century Christians—and us—
under the inspiration of the Holy Spirit.

What's It Mean?

We all know it's important to obey our parents (Exodus 20:12; Ephesians
6:1-3; Colossians 3:20). But Paul expands this principle to all governing
authority in our lives, saying "*all* authority comes from God" (emphasis
added). This includes church leaders, teachers, employers, police officers,
and government officials, among others.

God doesn't approve of people who abuse power like Nero. But he has wisely and lovingly instituted authority to govern life on earth. Otherwise, humanity would devolve into chaos because of sin.

God set up human authority—even if it's not always perfect (and it certainly isn't!)—as a blessing to us to teach us to ultimately obey his authority, and to restrain sin (Romans 13:3). For that, we can praise him.

To honor human authority is to honor the Lord!

Now What?
Read Romans 13:1-7 and 1 Peter 2:13-17. Also, pray for your local and national political leaders (1 Timothy 2:1-2).

Did You Know?
Jesus taught this principle, too. In Matthew 22:21, he instructed the people, "Give to Caesar what belongs to Caesar, and give to God what belongs to God." In other words, earthly rulers deserve positional respect, taxes, and obedience within proper parameters of justice and morality. However, God deserves our chief allegiance. If forced to choose between obeying God or man, we must always obey God (Acts 4:19; 5:29).

OCTOBER 1

Decide instead to live in such a way that you will not
cause another believer to stumble and fall.

ROMANS 14:13

WHILE BOTH JEWS AND GENTILES were becoming Christians
throughout the first-century Roman Empire, early church leaders were faced
with a variety of issues as people struggled to break away from old religious
habits. Here's an example:

Group 1: We must honor the Sabbath! We must observe sacred
festivals such as the Passover! We must only eat food that the Torah
declares clean! We would never dare eat meat from an animal
sacrificed to a false idol in a pagan temple!

Group 2: Every day of the week is good for honoring God! You don't
need sacred festivals anymore now that Christ has fulfilled the law!
Food doesn't make us more or less clean before God—even Jesus said
so! As long as we reserve our worship for God and not idols, who cares
if we eat meat taken from pagan temples? It's just a dead animal!

Can you see the conundrum? Group 1 represents the mindset of
many new Jewish converts. Group 2 reflects that of many Gentile converts
(although some former pagan idol worshipers were sensitive to eating meat
sacrificed to an idol because it reminded them of their prior heathenism).

So the apostle Paul wisely addressed this issue in Romans 14:1–15:7.
Rather than quibble over details, he drove his point home with today's verse.

What's It Mean?

Clearly, the specific issues that Paul was addressing in Romans don't apply
to us today, but the principle of today's verse certainly does: don't cause
another believer to stumble.

There are many black-and-white matters in life that the Bible specifically addresses. But there are also a lot of gray areas where godly wisdom is needed. Your job is to obey Scripture in the black-and-white areas and to have a clear conscience before God as you navigate the gray ones (Romans 14:22-23).

When you're walking through either of these with another believer who has a more sensitive conscience, be aware of that. Show gentleness and never judge them for their beliefs. Remember: they answer to God, not you (Romans 14:12).

The paradigm here, of course, is Jesus, who left heaven's glory to die for both of you. Follow his humble example and "accept each other just as Christ has accepted you so that God will be given glory" (Romans 15:7).

Now What?

Read Romans 14:1–15:7 and 1 Corinthians 8 (a similar passage).

Did You Know?

Because of Christ's sacrifice and the advent of the new covenant, Paul took the position represented by Group 2 above (although he said it more tactfully!).

OCTOBER 2

It's not important who does the planting, or who does the
watering. What's important is that God makes the seed grow.

1 CORINTHIANS 3:7

WHEN THE APOSTLE PAUL started the church in Corinth during his
second missionary journey, little did he know what it would take to shepherd those former pagans to godliness. With all their spiritual immaturities,
they certainly gave the great missionary-pastor a run for his money!

In 1 Corinthians 3, we even see that they argued about which Christian
leader of that day was the best to follow—Paul, Peter, or Apollos (who
arrived in Corinth after Paul left to further teach the believers). Here's a
transcript of their debates:

Corinthian No. 1: I follow Apollos! He's all the rage nowadays. The
young, fiery Alexandrian really knows his Old Testament, and he's a
great public speaker. Did you hear how he talked gospel-filled circles
around the Jews in Ephesus? Booyah!

Corinthian No. 2: *Pffft!* That's nothing. Paul's been doing that for
years! He's so old-school. Did Apollos see the risen Savior like Paul
did on the road to Damascus? . . . All I hear are crickets, bro. Case
closed. I follow Paul.

Corinthian No. 3: Puh-lease. This shouldn't even be up for
debate. I've barely heard of Apollos, and Paul seems unimpressive
in person. Besides, were Apollos and Paul part of Jesus' twelve
disciples? Nope. But guess who was? My man, Cephas—'the Rock'!
It's Peter for the win!

Okay, perhaps that's a loose—very loose—paraphrase of the actual conversation the ancient Corinthians had. But you get the point.

Sadly, the church at Corinth had elevated man instead of God.

What's It Mean?

God's church isn't about a small, elite group of super-Christians. The church is the worldwide "bride" (Revelation 19:7), and the focus should be on the "Bridegroom"—Jesus Christ (Matthew 25:1-13). He is the "Cornerstone" on which the entire church is built (Ephesians 2:19-21).

Paul knew this. That's why instead of comparing himself to Apollos or Peter, he admonished the Corinthians with today's verse and 1 Corinthians 3:21: "Don't boast about following a particular human leader."

There are many highly skilled pastors, authors, and other Christian leaders today. Learn from them. Gain godly wisdom from them. However, don't build your hope on them.

Humans are apt to fail. But God never does. Put your hope in the Lord. Exalt him, not his servants. Follow Christ, the Great Shepherd, and he will never fail you.

Now What?

Whenever you hear a sermon, listen to a Christian podcast, read a spiritual book, etc., always test it against Scripture (1 John 4:1-6).

Did You Know?

You can learn more about Apollos in Acts 18:24-28.

OCTOBER 3

*Don't put your trust in mere humans. They are
as frail as breath. What good are they?*

ISAIAH 2:22

AS HUMANS, WE ARE quick to put people on a pedestal—literally. Have
you ever noticed how many marble and bronze statues of famous individuals fill our cities and towns?

We are quick to elevate all sorts of people in life: professional athletes, movie stars, pop singers, etc. We even do this with pastors and other
Christian leaders. That was the problem in the first-century Corinthian
church, as we discussed in yesterday's devotion.

But admiration can quickly become idolization. What happens when
that Christian leader fails? Too often these days, we read about another pastor or well-known Christian figure getting caught in a public scandal.

But the issue goes much deeper than this. Perhaps you *personally* know
someone who is a Christian—or claims to be one—and isn't representing
the Lord well. Or maybe it's a group of people, or even a church. Perhaps
this situation is so disturbing, it has caused you to question the church,
Christianity, or even God himself.

What now?

Let God's Word, which is "alive and powerful" (Hebrews 4:12), give
you wisdom and encouragement today!

What's It Mean?

Isaiah 2:22 cuts to the heart of the matter: even those closest to us and/or
those who are supposed to be our greatest examples—parents, other family
members, teachers, pastors, etc.—will fail us eventually. That's because all
humans—including the godliest ones we know—are still morally corrupt
and as "frail as breath."

But when people—or even an entire religious organization such as a
church—fail you, don't let it skew your view of God. Don't ascribe their
shortcomings to a God who has none.

553

People are sinful, weak, and susceptible to temptation and change. God is not. He is holy—completely transcendent and separate from sin. He is always faithful, and his love is steadfast. He greatly cares for the suffering of his children. "He heals the brokenhearted and bandages their wounds" (Psalm 147:3).

There are many godly people in this world who will be a blessing to you. But our ultimate hope should be God himself! "Blessed are those who trust in the LORD and have made the LORD their hope and confidence" (Jeremiah 17:7).

Now What?

Look up these related passages: Psalm 118:8-9; Psalm 146:3-7; and Jeremiah 17:5-10.

Did You Know?

Today's verse is not promoting skepticism of all people. You'll go crazy if you suspect everyone you meet of hurting you! Isaiah 2:22 is talking about reserving our greatest trust and devotion for God, not humans.

OCTOBER 4

*Don't you realize that in a race everyone runs, but
only one person gets the prize? So run to win!*

1 CORINTHIANS 9:24

EDDIE TOLAN STOOD ONLY 5-foot-7, weighed 145 pounds, and wore round spectacles that he taped to his face while running. Ralph Metcalfe, meanwhile, was tall and lean, looking much more like a prototypical sprinter. Yet these men were neck-and-neck sprinting rivals as the 1932 Summer Olympics in Los Angeles approached.

In the much-anticipated 100-meter dash final, Tolan and Metcalfe appeared to cross the finish line in a dead-heat tie for first place. Initially, the judges, who used handheld stopwatches back then, awarded both runners a 10.38-second time. So they spent several hours looking at black-and-white race film and photographs.

Finally, they declared Tolan the winner, citing that he was the first to cross the finish line with his whole body. It was the first official "photo finish" in Olympic history.

With that in mind, today's Scripture passage couldn't be more appropriate! Here's what the apostle Paul says in 1 Corinthians 9:24-27:

> Don't you realize that in a race everyone runs, but only one person gets the prize? So run to win! All athletes are disciplined in their training. They do it to win a prize that will fade away, but we do it for an eternal prize. So I run with purpose in every step. I am not just shadowboxing. I discipline my body like an athlete, training it to do what it should.

What's It Mean?

Paul's original audience, the Corinthians, were very familiar with sports. Besides being acquainted with the ancient quadrennial Olympic Games in Greece, the Corinthians also hosted the biennial Isthmian Games. Paul knew his audience!

He understood how hard athletes train to achieve glory in their sport. He also knew that earthly glory doesn't last long. Isthmian champions earned "a prize that will fade away"—literally, a wreath of foliage worn on the victor's head. Christians, however, run the race of life for an "eternal prize"—unimaginable heavenly rewards (Romans 8:18) to be enjoyed forever with our Savior.

Until that glorious day, be disciplined in your spiritual training, whether you're an athlete or not. Pray and meditate on God's Word daily, fellowship regularly with other believers, serve others with your spiritual gifts, and spread the gospel. Then at the end of your race, God will award you the heavenly prize that never fades away!

Now What?

Consider ways you can become more disciplined in your daily spiritual training—not to impress God, but to grow in godliness.

Did You Know?

Under today's Olympic standards—in which a runner only needs to cross the finish line with any body part—Metcalfe probably would've won gold in 1932.

OCTOBER 5

*The temptations in your life are no different
from what others experience.*

1 CORINTHIANS 10:13

IN 1704, A SCOTTISH SAILOR named Alexander Selkirk and the rest
of his salty band of privateers—legalized pirates, to put it bluntly—arrived
at a tiny island off the coast of Chile. Selkirk, whose actual surname was
Selcraig, got into an argument with the captain about the seaworthiness of
their ship, the *Cinque Ports*. He decided to stay on the twenty-nine-square-
mile island, probably figuring he'd be picked up by another vessel in a matter of days or weeks.

He figured wrong.

Four years and four months later, he was finally rescued by another British
privateer. Imagine living all that time stranded on an island. What a lonely life!

When you are tempted to sin, have you ever felt like you're alone on an
island? Sometimes, sin tries to isolate us, making us think we're the only ones
on earth enduring the ordeal we're experiencing.

That's when we need the truth of God's Word.

What's It Mean?

If you are struggling with sin, temptation, or even a painful trial that might
tempt you to despair, it's easy to find yourself marooned on Satan's island of
deception, thinking things like this:

- No one else understands.
- No one else has ever gone through this before.
- There is no hope for me.

But Satan is "the father of lies" (John 8:44) and "the accuser of our
brothers and sisters" (Revelation 12:10). He loves to deceive Christians into
thinking that they are cut off from the heavenly blessings and power that are
ours in Christ.

Fill your mind instead with Scripture's truth. Today's verse, in its entirety, says, "The temptations in your life are no different from what others experience. And God is faithful. He will not allow the temptation to be more than you can stand. When you are tempted, he will show you a way out so that you can endure."

What's more, you have a faithful High Priest, Jesus, who has endured every temptation you have, yet without sin (Hebrews 4:15). Therefore, you can "come boldly to the throne of our gracious God. There we will receive his mercy, and we will find grace to help us when we need it most" (Hebrews 4:16).

When tempted, don't be a castaway on the island of fear, doubt, and lies. Jesus defeated sin and Satan at the Cross (1 John 3:8). Trust in Christ for rescue!

Now What?

During temptation, remember God has helped others before you and he will help you, too, if you seek him!

Did You Know?

Many historians believe Selcraig was the inspiration for Daniel Defoe's famous 1719 novel *Robinson Crusoe*.

OCTOBER 6

A spiritual gift is given to each of us so we can help each other.

1 CORINTHIANS 12:7

HAVE YOU EVER NOTICED how virtually every Marvel and DC Comics superhero is gifted with ridiculous superpowers? If they're not slinging webs from their wrists or shooting laser beams from their eyes, they're flying, shapeshifting, teleporting, regenerating, turning invisible, or throwing really, really heavy stuff.

In their quest to save the world, none of them, it seems, is *normal*. Oh sure, there might be a few outliers, such as Batman, who relies on his superior martial arts, stealth tactics, body armor, and gadgetry to beat the bad guys. But overall, most superheroes are blessed with a dazzling array of otherworldly gifts.

When was the last time you watched a superhero movie and saw one of the good guys say to the supervillain, "I just wanted to bless you with an encouraging word of God's love"? That would probably leave poor Thanos, Magneto, and the Joker speechless!

The world has a thoroughly flawed concept of what it means to truly help others. But Scripture—specifically passages such as 1 Corinthians 12–14 and Romans 12:3-8—paints a clear picture of this by revealing how God endows every believer with wonderful spiritual gifts.

What's It Mean?

A spiritual gift is a special Holy Spirit–empowered talent/interest that God gives to every believer for the purpose of building his church (see today's verse) and the advancement of the gospel. We don't earn these by merit. As gifts, God freely gives them to us out of his grace.

Some of the gifts mentioned in the two biblical passages above include prophecy (i.e., words of godly wisdom), tongues (speaking in another language that should be interpreted to edify the church; 1 Corinthians 14), teaching, exhorting, serving, leading, showing generosity, and displaying acts of mercy.

Look at that list above and think about your interests and abilities. Where do you think God has spiritually gifted you? He has uniquely created you! He wants you to enjoy serving him and others. But that's the point—the gifts he has given you aren't for *your* good; they are to glorify God and encourage the body of Christ.

You don't have to save the world with your spiritual gifts! Just start using them faithfully with an outward focus—and rejoice that God lets you share in building his Kingdom.

Now What?
Read 1 Corinthians 12–14 and Romans 12:3-8 and pray that God would reveal your spiritual gift(s) to you if he hasn't already.

Did You Know?
Paul's lists of spiritual gifts in 1 Corinthians 12–14 and Romans 12:3-8 weren't meant to be all-inclusive.

OCTOBER 7

Three things will last forever—faith, hope, and
love—and the greatest of these is love.

1 CORINTHIANS 13:13

LET'S PLAY A GAME.
It's called "Pick the Struggles of the First-Century Corinthian Church."
Which sins and struggles do you think the apostle Paul confronted this
immature group of believers about in his letter known as 1 Corinthians?

1. jealousy and strife
2. arguing about which Christian leader to follow
3. sexual immorality
4. arrogance
5. filing lawsuits against each other
6. causing weaker Christians to stumble in their faith
7. dishonoring the Lord's Supper
8. misunderstanding and misusing spiritual gifts
9. misunderstanding believers' future resurrection
10. all of the above

If you guessed choice number ten, you're correct! They struggled with
all of them. *Phew!* That church needed a lot of help.
In 1 Corinthians 13, Paul addressed number eight—how the church
was struggling in the area of spiritual gifts.

What's It Mean?
Often called "the love chapter," 1 Corinthians 13 is frequently used for
weddings, anniversaries, Valentine's Day cards, etc., because of Paul's beautiful description of true biblical love. But Paul didn't write 1 Corinthians
13 to describe romantic love. He wrote it to explain what love looks like as
Christians exercise their spiritual gifts to edify the body of Christ.
Paul illustrates it vividly in 1 Corinthians 13:1: "If I could speak all the

languages of earth and of angels, but didn't love others, I would only be a noisy gong or a clanging cymbal." To put it another way . . .

- Christians using their spiritual gifts with love = a performance of the London Symphony Orchestra.
- Christians using their spiritual gifts *without* love = a roomful of fussy, hungry toddlers with hand cymbals.

Nobody—and we mean nobody—wants choice number two!

Yesterday, we discussed spiritual gifts. If you're a Christian, God has empowered you with certain abilities to build his Kingdom. But you could be the most talented person in the world, and if you don't exercise your spiritual gifts in a loving way, it's worthless. *That's* the point of 1 Corinthians 13.

"God is love" (1 John 4:8). Therefore, it's imperative for us to live in a way that reflects God's character and accords with the biblical love described in 1 Corinthians 13:4-7.

Even the greatest spiritual gifts will eventually fade away. But as today's verse says, godly love will remain forever!

Now What?

The next time you hear portions of 1 Corinthians 13 being used in a romantic way, remember the proper context of this chapter.

Did You Know?

Jesus said, "Your love for one another will prove to the world that you are my disciples" (John 13:35).

OCTOBER 8

Thank God! He gives us victory over sin and
death through our Lord Jesus Christ.

1 CORINTHIANS 15:57

WHAT IF THIS LIFE was all there was?

What if, after we died, our physical bodies remained six feet underground and our souls also ceased to exist? No heaven. No hell. No afterlife at all. Just an average of seventy years or so on earth and then . . .

Nothingness.

Lots of people believe in this theory. John Lennon, the late superstar of the Beatles, pondered the question in his solo-career song, *Imagine*:

Imagine there's no heaven
It's easy if you try
No hell below us
Above us only sky

Consider that possibility for a moment. It's actually one of the most frightening, depressing, fatalistic thoughts imaginable.

If there were no afterlife, what would life's point be? To eat, drink, be merry, and then die? To do whatever you pleased and then fade to black? Why? For what purpose? That's the essence of hopelessness.

The first-century Corinthian Christians pondered some of these questions. They believed in Jesus' resurrection, but some weren't sure about the future resurrection of believers. The apostle Paul heard of their confusion and addressed it in 1 Corinthians 15. If there's nothing beyond this life, Christians "are more to be pitied than anyone in the world" (verse 19).

But praise God this is not the case! Thanks to Christ, there *is* life after death!

What's It Mean?

When it comes to life after death, everything hinges on Jesus. Because God's Son rose from the dead, so will all who trust in him! As Paul said in 1

Corinthians 15:23, "Christ was raised as the first of the [resurrection] harvest; then all who belong to Christ will be raised when he comes back."

When a follower of Jesus dies, their physical body remains on earth, but their spirit immediately enters the Lord's presence (Luke 23:43; 2 Corinthians 5:8). Then, one day when Christ returns to earth to consummate his eternal Kingdom, he will raise dead saints and give them imperishable heavenly bodies before clothing Christians who are alive with resurrection bodies, as well (1 Corinthians 15:35-58; 1 Thessalonians 4:13-18).

We don't have to only imagine it. This is the great, guaranteed hope of every Christian, thanks to our risen Savior!

Now What?

What do we do with this incredible hope of resurrection in Christ? Paul answers that in 1 Corinthians 15:58. Check it out!

Did You Know?

Most first-century pagans believed a person's soul ceased to exist altogether upon death or continued in some form in the underworld. This is why many Corinthians (who were former idolaters) were confused.

OCTOBER 9

We walk by faith, not by sight.

2 CORINTHIANS 5:7, ESV

IF YOU'VE EVER SUNG a traditional Christian hymn at church, chances are, you've sung a hymn written by Fanny Crosby.

Born in 1820, Crosby tragically went blind at six weeks old when an illegitimate doctor applied hot mustard poultices to her eyes to treat an illness. Her father died while she was young, so she was mostly raised by her Christian grandmother while her mother worked to support the family.

But these great trials didn't dampen young Crosby's spirit. She quickly developed a love for memorizing Scripture and writing poetry. Look at her first poem, written at age eight:

Oh, what a happy soul I am,
Although I cannot see!
I am resolved that in this world
Contented I will be.
How many blessings I enjoy
That other people don't,
To weep and sigh because I'm blind
I cannot, and I won't!

Eventually, Crosby began a prolific songwriting career, composing the lyrics to approximately nine thousand Christian hymns before her death in 1915, at age ninety-four. Her catalogue includes some of the most beloved songs in church history, such as "Blessed Assurance," "To God Be the Glory," and "Jesus Keep Me Near the Cross."

In every sense of the phrase, Crosby lived out today's verse—walking by faith, not by sight.

What's It Mean?

While most of us don't struggle with the physical limitations that Crosby did, all Christians are called to walk by faith, not by sight. This means we are to

- believe in a holy God whom we cannot see;
- believe that he created the world, sovereignly rules over it, and requires worship and obedience from everyone he created;
- believe in God's eternal Son, who came to earth, lived a sinless life, died an atoning death, and gloriously rose again;
- believe that salvation only comes through repentance from sins and faith in this great Savior, Jesus Christ;
- believe that all of God's promises in Scripture are true;
- believe that the Christian life is about faithful obedience to God as he transforms us into his image; and
- believe that one day, Jesus will return to establish his heavenly Kingdom forever.

You can't see any of these things through human sight. But God calls you to walk them out by faith anyway—for your eternal good and his glory. Will you?

Now What?

Where are you struggling for faith? Ask a trusted friend or family member to pray for you in that area.

Did You Know?

Fanny Crosby and her husband (also blind) chose to live in Manhattan's rough-and-tumble Lower East Side so they could minister at a friend's rescue mission.

OCTOBER 10

*If anyone is in Christ, he is a new creation. The old
has passed away; behold, the new has come.*

2 CORINTHIANS 5:17, ESV

WHEN WAS THE LAST time you asked your parents any of the following
questions?

> Mom, Dad, I'm getting a little rusty with my ABCs and 1-2-3s. Can I
> return to kindergarten?
> Solid food is so overrated. Can you start spoon-feeding me strained peas
> and carrots again?
> This whole bathroom thing really isn't working for me. Mind if I go
> back to diapers?

Of course not! That's ridiculous! Those days are long gone. You've
matured and are at a different stage of life now.

Well, take a look at today's verse. The same principle applies to the
Christian life.

What's It Mean?

As 2 Corinthians 5:17 says, being a follower of Christ is about becoming a
"new creation," going from something "old" to something "new." The "old"
is our former, sinful way of living. Here's how Ephesians 2 describes every
human's "old" self, apart from Christ:

- Once you were dead because of your disobedience and your many
  sins. (verse 1)
- You used to live in sin . . . obeying the devil. (verse 2)
- All of us used to live that way, following the passionate desires and
  inclinations of our sinful nature. (verse 3)
- Once you were far away from God. (verse 13)

That's pretty bleak. But thankfully, God steps into every true believer's life and radically transforms them from "lost sinner" into a "new creation." To do so, God's Spirit begins the process with regeneration (a.k.a., "being born again," John 3:3). When you trust in Jesus for the forgiveness of your sins, God reconciles you to himself (2 Corinthians 5:18-19), restoring peace to a broken relationship. Then his Spirit continues to sanctify you throughout your lifetime (2 Corinthians 4:16; 1 Thessalonians 5:23).

In other words, God graciously gives you a new spiritual heart with new spiritual desires to please him that didn't exist before. Sin will always war within you (Romans 7), but Jesus broke its power to rule over you through his death and resurrection (Romans 6:6-11).

As a new creation, don't turn back to the old ways that Christ has redeemed you from. Press forward in your relationship with him. Grow and mature in your new life. "The old has passed away; behold, the new has come!"

Now What?

Do you like to cook, write, draw, paint, or otherwise create new things? Think about today's verse when you do!

Did You Know?

For the Corinthians, being a "new creation" meant giving up all the things listed in passages such as Ephesians 4:22-31 and Colossians 3:5-9.

OCTOBER 11

*Put on your new nature, and be renewed as you learn
to know your Creator and become like him.*

COLOSSIANS 3:10

WHY IS IT THAT, in Disney movies, it always seems so easy to get what
you want or transform into the person you've always wanted to be?

- Want to marry a prince? Just kiss a frog.
- Want your marionette puppet to become a real boy? Just wish upon
  a star.
- Want to go from being a ragamuffin servant to the belle of the ball?
  Just find your fairy godmother, and—*Bibbidi-bobbidi-boo!*—it's done.

Maybe that's why they're called fairy tales. Real life, though, is never
that simple.

Becoming someone new doesn't happen with a kiss, a wish, or the
wave of a magic wand. In fact, becoming a "new creation" in Christ (2
Corinthians 5:17, ESV), as we discussed in yesterday's devotion, doesn't
involve magic at all. It's a wonderful process that God lovingly initiates and
carries through to completion in every Christian's life. And he graciously
calls us to actively be involved.

What's It Mean?

Understanding God's central role in our regeneration and sanctification
process—becoming a "new creation" in Christ—is crucial. Without God's
gracious, saving initiative on our behalf, we'd still be lost in our sins.

However, we do play an important role in our sanctification. God
doesn't "help those who help themselves," as the popular (but mistaken) saying goes, as if he's some sort of heavenly therapist. But he does expect us to
take action, not sit around and wait for him to do all the work.

That's why Scripture uses strong, active verbs in Colossians 3 when it says, "*Put to death* the sinful, earthly things lurking within you" (verse 5) and "*Put on* your new nature, and *be renewed*" (today's verse). Likewise, Ephesians 4 says, "*Throw off* your old sinful nature" (verse 22) and "*put on* your new nature" (verse 24, emphasis added).

Godly character doesn't just magically happen. It transpires over a lifetime, with much prayer, reliance on God's Word, and dependence on his Spirit.

Then—with a far better finale than any Disney movie could offer—God provides a gloriously happy ending: "I am certain that God, who began the good work within you, will continue his work until it is finally finished on the day when Christ Jesus returns" (Philippians 1:6).

Amen!

Now What?
Look up Colossians 3:5-17 and Ephesians 4:17-32 to find out what to "put off" and "put on" as you transition from your sinful nature to being a new creation in Christ.

Did You Know?
Philippians 2:12-13 also talks about the sanctification process.

OCTOBER 12

Do not be unequally yoked with unbelievers.

2 CORINTHIANS 6:14, ESV

BEFORE THE DAYS of advanced machinery, farmers used to plow their fields behind a pair of large animals such as oxen or horses. The animals would do the hard work of pulling the plow, but the farmer would still have to steer the animals.

To do this, the farmer had to make sure the animals were equally yoked. This meant two things:

1. Fastening a yoke to the animals' necks. A yoke is a large wooden crossbeam that joins the animals together and attaches to the plow.
2. Ensuring that two similar animals were yoked together. (A farmer would never want to pair a stronger ox to a weaker ox, or a horse to a milking cow, etc.)

If the animals weren't properly yoked, the plow would always veer toward the stronger animal, and the poor farmer would be left with crooked rows all over his crop fields when it came time for planting seeds.

This was the image that the apostle Paul had in mind when he wrote today's verse.

What's It Mean?

There's much for us to learn about our human relationships from Paul's words, which are part of a larger section on the topic in 2 Corinthians 6:14–7:1. But we must be careful. Paul is not saying you should cut off all unbelieving friends or family members from your life. That's completely unbiblical. We're called to be "salt" and "light" to the world around us (Matthew 5:13-16).

Also, we must guard against ever displaying a haughty attitude toward non-Christians, as if we are better than they are. What a terrible witness that would be! (On the contrary, see Paul's example in 1 Corinthians 9:19-23 and Jesus' example in Mark 2:15-17.)

Here's Paul's point: Christians and non-Christians have different goals, ambitions, and philosophies in life. Ultimately, they are heading in different directions.

A Christian must never be so closely paired with an unbeliever that it distracts from his or her overall mission of personal sanctification and spreading the gospel. You should never associate with a non-Christian to the point where the unbeliever's ungodly values negatively impact your faith. If you're experiencing that now, that might be an unequal yoking.

Rather than yoke yourself unequally to unbelievers, pray for them, show them the love of Christ, and tell them the glorious news of the gospel!

Now What?

Take a few moments to pray for the unbelievers in your life.

Did You Know?

When Paul quotes the Lord in 2 Corinthians 6:16-18, he's actually compiling six separate Old Testament texts: Leviticus 26:11-12; 2 Samuel 7:14; Isaiah 43:6; Isaiah 52:11; Ezekiel 20:34; and Ezekiel 37:27.

OCTOBER 13

Each time he said, "My grace is all you need.
My power works best in weakness."

2 CORINTHIANS 12:9

OKAY, SO THERE'S THIS GUY who went to heaven, came back, and wants to tell you about it.

Hold on! Before you think this is just another modern-day charlatan trying to score a *New York Times* bestseller, it's nothing like that.

We're talking about the apostle Paul!

In 2 Corinthians 12:2-4, Paul reveals one of the most incredible moments of his life. Speaking in the third person, as if reluctant to identify himself as the subject, here's how he described the experience:

> I know a man in Christ who fourteen years ago was caught up
> to the third heaven—whether in the body or out of the body I do
> not know, God knows. And I know that this man was caught up
> into paradise—whether in the body or out of the body I do not
> know, God knows—and he heard things that cannot be told, which
> man may not utter (ESV).

Afterward, God gave Paul a mysterious "thorn in my flesh" to "keep me from becoming proud" (verse 7). Paul pleaded with God to remove the painful trial, but God simply answered, "My grace is all you need. My power works best in weakness" (today's verse).

What's It Mean?

God's words to Paul reveal one of Scripture's most beautiful, yet perplexing paradoxes: God chooses to shine his power brightest through human weakness.

The question is all about glory: who gets it and how. Ultimately, God will be glorified, one way or another. He doesn't *need* us to be glorified.

But he graciously invites us to be part of his plan, looking for those with "humble and contrite hearts, who tremble at my word" (Isaiah 66:2).

When God accomplishes great things in us and through us *despite* our human weaknesses, it highlights his power, majesty, and love that much more. Then he receives glory, which is the whole point.

So we can gladly echo Paul's conclusion: "Now I am glad to boast about my weaknesses, so that the power of Christ can work through me. That's why I take pleasure in my weaknesses, and in the insults, hardships, persecutions, and troubles that I suffer for Christ. For when I am weak, then I am strong" (verses 9-10).

Amen!

Now What?

Do you feel spiritually weak? Fear not! Pray for strength, wisdom, and courage to do great things for God even though the world might disregard you (1 Corinthians 1:26-29).

Did You Know?

Perhaps Paul was thinking about his heavenly vision when he wrote passages such as 2 Corinthians 4:7 and Romans 8:18.

OCTOBER 14

Even if we or an angel from heaven should preach to you a gospel contrary to the one we preached to you, let him be accursed.

GALATIANS 1:8, ESV

IT ALL STARTED with a vision about golden plates.

On September 21, 1823, a young man named Joseph Smith Jr., the fifth child of a hardscrabble and superstitious pair of farming parents, claimed to receive a vision from an angel named Moroni, who told him of supposedly special golden plates buried several miles from the Smiths' home in Palmyra, New York. The plates, according to Smith, contained a description of America's earliest natives and "the fullness of the everlasting gospel."

Smith claimed to dig up the plates and began translating them from their "reformed Egyptian" text thanks to a pair of magical spectacles endowed with seer stones. Finally, in 1829, Smith and an assistant finished the "translation" and called it *The Book of Mormon.*

If this sounds farfetched, well, it is. Yet today, there are fifteen million members of the Church of Jesus Christ of Latter-Day Saints, commonly known as Mormons.

Today's verse couldn't be more appropriate!

What's It Mean?

The letter to the Galatians, written by the apostle Paul, was likely meant for a group of churches that Paul planted during his first missionary journey—probably Pisidian Antioch, Iconium, Lystra, and Derbe (Acts 13:14–14:23). But after he left, a group of false teachers started poisoning the believers' minds. These teachers claimed salvation required faith in Jesus *plus* works—namely keeping certain aspects of the Old Testament law.

Paul was enraged. Using some of the strongest language in any of his New Testament letters, he excoriated the false teachers and admonished the Galatian believers.

But Paul's point is well taken. There is no other true gospel except the biblical gospel of Jesus Christ, and it must be defended.

Any religion that teaches salvation by any other means apart from justification by faith alone in the atoning work of Christ's death and resurrection is a false, "accursed" gospel.

In addition to Mormonism, there are many other cults and belief systems in the world—some of which cloak themselves under "Christianity"—that add or subtract from an orthodox biblical definition of salvation.

Accept no phonies. Hold fast to what is true. Don't submit to a works-based religion. And test everything according to Scripture and whether it honors Jesus as God's eternal Son and the substitutionary atonement for our sins (1 John 4:1-6).

Now What?
See the October 23 devotion on Ephesians 4:14 for more ways to discern spiritual truth from falsehood.

Did You Know?
The Bible never mentions an angel named Moroni.

OCTOBER 15

The fruit of the Spirit is love, joy, peace, patience, kindness,
goodness, faithfulness, gentleness, self-control.

GALATIANS 5:22-23, ESV

WHAT DO THE FOLLOWING have in common?

- Caryopsis
- Feijoa
- Hesperidium
- Jujube
- Kumquat
- Mamoncillo
- Rambutan
- Schizocarp
- Soursop

Why, they're all different types of fruit, of course!

But in today's verses, the apostle Paul talks about nine very different types of fruit that are essential parts of the Christian life. These fruits do not hang from any tree limb or sprout from any vine. But they do grow inside you as your faith matures in the Lord.

These are "the fruit of the Spirit."

What's It Mean?

Why did Paul use the fruit metaphor? Perhaps he was drawing from Jesus' similar teaching about knowing a tree by its fruit in Matthew 7:15-20, where the Savior said, "Just as you can identify a tree by its fruit, so you can identify people by their actions" (verse 20).

Earlier in Galatians 5, Paul gave his readers (and us) the following warning:

When you follow the desires of your sinful nature, the results are very clear: sexual immorality, impurity, lustful pleasures, idolatry, sorcery, hostility, quarreling, jealousy, outbursts of anger, selfish ambition, dissension, division, envy, drunkenness, wild parties, and other sins like these. Let me tell you again, as I have before, that anyone living that sort of life will not inherit the Kingdom of God.

VERSES 19-21

The distinction between "the desires of your sinful nature" and "the fruit of the Spirit" couldn't be any starker. It's literally the difference between night and day, darkness and light, evil and good.

Those who love God should want nothing to do with wicked desires. We should strive "through the power of the Spirit" to "put to death the deeds of your sinful nature" (Romans 8:13).

Rather, we are called to manifest godly spiritual fruit. But this doesn't come naturally from our own morality. That's why it's called the fruit *of the Spirit*. Only when God's Spirit dwells inside us through faith in Jesus Christ—and as we prayerfully, humbly, and obediently walk in step with him—can we truly exhibit these kinds of godly character traits.

Look at those two lists again in Galatians 5. What characterizes your life? May God give you the grace to bear the fruit of the Spirit as you seek to glorify him!

Now What?
Memorize Galatians 5:22-23. (And if you're really feeling adventurous, try one of those exotic fruits mentioned above!)

Did You Know?
There was a reason Paul listed love first in his "fruit of the Spirit" list. See 1 Corinthians 13 for the answer (especially verse 13).

OCTOBER 16

Share each other's burdens, and in this way obey the law of Christ.

GALATIANS 6:2

IN JOHN BUNYAN'S CLASSIC TALE, *The Pilgrim's Progress*, a man named Christian goes on a long journey toward the Celestial City, encountering many hardships and different individuals along the way.

Early on, Christian carries a great burden on his back. But when he climbs a hill with a cross on it, his burden falls off his back and disappears into the empty tomb below. Bunyan's book is a marvelous allegory for the Christian life, and the scene beautifully depicts how God justifies every believer through faith in Christ, removing the guilt of our sins.

Yet as today's verse implies, Christians still carry burdens in our daily lives—some extremely heavy ones. So what's up with that?

What's It Mean?

Today's verse is talking about the effects of living in a fallen world—the daily pain, challenges, sufferings, and sadness that people experience.

All around you, folks are hurting. The people in your circles—family members, friends, neighbors, acquaintances—are all carrying burdens, just like you are. Some are more significant than others. But each of those burdens is challenging to that individual. If you know of someone who is suffering, have you reached out to them in any way?

Here are a few ways you can practically bear someone else's burdens:

- **Pray.** Tell someone you will commit to pray for them—and make sure to keep your promise (James 5:13).
- **Listen.** Sometimes, people just need a listening ear without a lot of advice (Job 2:13; 13:5; 16:1-5).
- **Encourage.** Share where you see God's grace evident in this individual's life and/or share a reassuring Bible verse. But avoid being preachy or patronizing (1 Thessalonians 5:11).

- **Give.** Give your time, money, or other resources if you can help alleviate someone's burden that way (James 2:15-16).

By lifting up others in this way, you will strengthen the body of Christ, be a powerful witness to unbelievers, and honor the Lord!

Now What?
Reach out to someone who is struggling by doing one or more of the suggested steps above.

Did You Know?
When the apostle Paul wrote that we will "obey the law of Christ" by bearing others' burdens, he was probably referring to Jesus' command in Matthew 22:39 to "love your neighbor as yourself," which Jesus cited as second in importance only to loving God wholeheartedly.

OCTOBER 17

Even before he made the world, God loved us and chose us
in Christ to be holy and without fault in his eyes.

EPHESIANS 1:4

WHEN YOU WERE IN elementary school, you learned all sorts of important grammar lessons: noun and verb usage, proper punctuation, capitalization, passive vs. active voice, etc.

You also learned about run-on sentences. This is when two or more independent clauses are joined together without a word or punctuation to separate them.

In Ephesians 1:3-14, the apostle Paul penned one of the Bible's greatest—and longest—descriptions of the triune God's sovereign plan of salvation, using more than *two hundred words* in the original Greek language! One of the highlights of this glorious (and epically long) passage of Scripture is today's verse. Read it again and digest its sacred truth: "Before he made the world, God loved us and chose us in Christ."

What's It Mean?

God's divine choosing—known as the doctrine of election or predestination, because he elected or predestined those whom he will save—is astounding. At some point in eternity past, before creating the universe, God chose everyone whom he would redeem by his grace through his Son, Jesus Christ.

Because God's election occurred before Creation itself, every Christian's salvation is completely a work of divine grace—God's unmerited favor. Salvation cannot be by human effort since we were chosen "in Christ" before we were even born! Yet this doesn't negate our responsibility to respond to the gospel call in repentance and faith (Mark 1:15).

Herein lies the beautiful mystery and tension of election—divine sovereignty and human responsibility wonderfully at work together. Both are biblical. How exactly they perfectly interplay in God's cosmic design falls into the category of "the secret things [that] belong to the LORD our God" (Deuteronomy 29:29, ESV).

Salvation is a work—from start to finish—of God's beautiful, sovereign grace. Every human is a sinner worthy of eternal condemnation (Romans 3:23; 6:23). But God has mercifully chosen to redeem many. Why did he do this? Because it was his sovereign will and good pleasure to pour out his amazing love on his children.

Do you see why Paul needed more than two hundred uninterrupted words to explain it?

Now What?
Prayerfully meditate on these other passages on God's sovereign election: Acts 13:48; Romans 8:28-33; Romans 9; 1 Thessalonians 1:4-5; 2 Thessalonians 2:13; 2 Timothy 1:9; and Revelation 13:7-8.

Did You Know?
Revelation 13:8 and 17:8 speak of a "Book of Life" featuring the name of every true believer "before the world was made." Is this a literal or metaphorical book? Perhaps Christians will find out in heaven!

OCTOBER 18

*Those whom he predestined he also called, and those whom he called
he also justified, and those whom he justified he also glorified.*

ROMANS 8:30, ESV

WHEN YOU THINK of golden chains, what immediately comes to mind?
A hip-hop artist's bling? A little girl's necklace? Your grandmother's jewelry
collection?

God's divinely orchestrated order of salvation is probably *not* the first
thing that pops into your head. But in Romans 8:28-30, the apostle Paul
describes God's sovereign election and its beautiful outworking in every
believer's life. Theologians commonly refer to it as "The Golden Chain of
Salvation." Here's what it says:

> For those who love God all things work together for good, for those
> who are called according to his purpose. For those whom he foreknew
> he also predestined to be conformed to the image of his Son, in order
> that he might be the firstborn among many brothers. And those
> whom he predestined he also called, and those whom he called he
> also justified, and those whom he justified he also glorified (ESV).

Today, we're returning to the doctrine of election to discuss this glorious
process.

What's It Mean?

Unlike man-made chains, God's "Golden Chain of Salvation" cannot be
broken. He will lovingly and powerfully carry each of his chosen people
through to the end, without fail. Who can thwart God's plans? *He's God!*
This is what Paul was driving at with his rhetorical question in Romans
8:35, "Can anything ever separate us from Christ's love?" The answer is an
emphatic, "No!"

Let's take a closer look at the glories of this unbreakable "Golden Chain
of Salvation":

583

1. **God predestines.** This happened before Creation (see yesterday's devotion).
2. **God calls.** He effectively draws to himself all whom he predestines (1 Thessalonians 2:12).
3. **God justifies.** He graciously forgives our sins and declares us righteous based on Christ's character and sacrifice when we receive this gift through faith (Romans 3:24-25).
4. **God sanctifies.** Paul didn't explicitly list this chronologically in Romans 8:28-30, but this refers to the lifelong spiritual maturation process of God conforming us to the image of his Son that all Christians experience (Romans 6:19-23).
5. **God glorifies.** One day, all believers will be fully sanctified and receive perfect, immortal resurrection bodies (1 Corinthians 15:35-58).

This "golden chain" can't be found even in the most upscale jewelry store! It's only found in Christ, through the sovereign elective will of God.

Now What?
Look again at Romans 8:28-30. Do you see how the salvation process is entirely God's initiative from beginning to end?

Did You Know?
In Romans 8:31-39, Paul asks and answers seven questions to further display the eternal security of every believer's salvation, thanks to God's sovereign care.

OCTOBER 19

God chooses to show mercy to some, and he chooses to
harden the hearts of others so they refuse to listen.

ROMANS 9:18

FIND A COIN. Any coin will do.

Wherever it's from, whatever monetary value it represents, it likely has separate images and inscriptions on the front and back. There are two sides to every coin. And if yours doesn't have two sides? Well, sorry . . . you've got a bogus piece of change.

As we continue exploring the doctrine of election, we need to understand both sides of the coin, so to speak, of this beautiful but challenging truth: If God sovereignly elected before Creation to save some people in spite of their sins through Christ, the flip side is that he sovereignly elected in eternity past to pass over others because of their sins for eternal judgment.

This is the doctrine of reprobation. It's as deep, mysterious, and controversial as they come!

What's It Mean?

Let's be honest: election is a lot easier for us to swallow than reprobation. This is often because we fail to grasp—or accept—the depths of human depravity. Nevertheless, the fact remains: apart from Christ, we are all hopelessly lost in our sins (Romans 3).

In electing some to salvation, God showed amazing love and mercy. In passing over others (reprobation), God simply left them to their sinful rebellion and enacted righteous judgment. God never condemns the innocent or judges unjustly.

Perhaps you're wondering, *Why didn't God choose to save everyone?* The apostle Paul addresses this in Romans 9:23: "To make the riches of his glory shine even brighter on those to whom he shows mercy, who were prepared in advance for glory."

This is part of Paul's much larger discussion on election and reprobation in Romans chapter 9. In the end, Paul leaves our questions about election and reprobation with this question to consider: "Who are you, a mere human being, to argue with God?" (Romans 9:20).

God's sovereignty in election and reprobation are inscrutable, and we must accept that. To accuse God of misstep or injustice here is the height of folly and arrogance. Rather than ask, "Why didn't God save everyone?," our question should be, "Why did God choose to graciously save *any*?"

He is God. We are not. We can trust in his sovereignty, goodness, and love, even if we don't always perfectly understand all his ways!

Now What?

Prayerfully read Romans 9 as you seek to grow in your understanding of this challenging but important truth.

Did You Know?

- Besides Romans 9, Matthew 11:25-26; Romans 11:7; 1 Peter 2:8; and Jude 1:4 all speak of reprobation.

OCTOBER 20

*A person's steps are directed by the LORD. How then
can anyone understand their own way?*

PROVERBS 20:24, NIV

CONSIDER THE WONDER OF MACHINES...

Refrigerators preserve our food. Smartphones allow us to communicate,
read the news, and perform other tasks instantly. Cars, boats, trains, and
airplanes quickly transport us places. Egg beaters help us, uh . . . beat eggs.

So let's make today "National Machine Appreciation Day." Take off
school. Take off work. Throw a party. *Hip, hip, hooray for machines!*

Now go hug your toaster.

Today, as we continue studying the doctrine of sovereign election, we
must address a few pressing issues regarding God's sovereignty. Some critics
of divine election say it, in essence, reduces mankind to unfeeling robots
that God has preprogrammed. Yet nothing could be further from the truth.

Yes, it's true that God predestines his elect, and this should constantly
stir our hearts to worship (Ephesians 1:3-14). But if you're wondering if our
daily choices really matter, the answer is a resounding *YES!*

What's It Mean?

Machines are helpful tools in our daily lives. But when God created people,
he didn't create us as machines, androids, or automatons. He created us as
humans—wonderfully, beautifully, and perfectly in his image (Genesis 1:26-
27). We are no more mindless, programmed robots than God himself.

But there *are* biblical complexities to reconcile: while God is completely
sovereign over all his creation, including human hearts (Proverbs 21:1) and
our daily steps (today's verse), our choices *do* matter. We are held morally
accountable for our actions.

Yes, God elects people, but he also calls them to "have faith in God"
(Mark 11:22), "repent and believe the good news" (Mark 1:15, NIV), and
"openly declare that Jesus is Lord" (Romans 10:9). These are actions to
which we are responsible before God.

How does God's sovereignty and our moral accountability coexist? The Bible leaves this question largely unanswered—a fascinating mystery known only in the secret counsels of heaven (Deuteronomy 29:29). Yet God calls us to trust in him, even when we don't fully understand his holy ways.

You are not a robot. You are an image-bearer of the living God. If you've already cried out to the Lord for salvation, praise God! Glorify him through daily faith and obedience. If you're not a Christian, submit today to the sovereign God who graciously shows redeeming love through his Son, Jesus Christ.

The choice is yours.

Now What?

Because our moral choices matter (Ecclesiastes 12:14; Romans 2:6-8; and 2 Corinthians 5:10), seek to display the fruits of the Spirit (Galatians 5:22-23).

Did You Know?

Humans as robots? *Pffft*. No way! God lovingly made each of us unique (Psalm 139:13-16) with different spiritual gifts (Romans 12:3-8).

OCTOBER 21

I pray that your hearts will be flooded with light so that you can understand the confident hope he has given to those he called— his holy people who are his rich and glorious inheritance.

EPHESIANS 1:18

IF YOU ARE FAMILIAR with Christianity, you've probably heard some of the most well-known stories in the Bible: Noah's ark, David and Goliath, Jesus feeding the five thousand, etc. Sometimes, you might even have to ask God's Spirit to amaze you anew at stories you've heard many times, never letting familiarity with Scripture breed complacency in your heart.

Then there are times when God illuminates fresh spiritual truth about wisdom that has always been in his Word—but maybe just hidden from our imperceptive eyes. Perhaps today's verse is one of those previously veiled treasures for you.

Ephesians 1:18 speaks of "glorious inheritance." This is something Christians hear about a lot—all the priceless spiritual blessings that are ours in Christ. And rightfully so! A believer's inheritance is rich beyond measure.

But that's not what Ephesians 1:18 is referring to. Look at it again. It says God's "holy people" are "*his* rich and glorious inheritance" (emphasis added). *WAIT—WHAT???*

We are *God's* inheritance? How can that be?

The answer is as wonderful as it is shocking.

What's It Mean?

Every Christian's inheritance is incredible:

- It's based on his prior election of us, not on our merit (Ephesians 1:11).
- Through Christ, God has pardoned our sins forever (Colossians 1:13-14).
- God has adopted us into his spiritual family with abundant blessings (Galatians 4:4-6).

- God's Spirit lives inside of us, assuring us of salvation and sanctifying us daily (Ephesians 1:13-14; 2 Thessalonians 2:13).
- We have the hope of eternal life in the presence of our Lord (1 Thessalonians 4:17).

And that's just a summary! But to think that God would consider us "his rich and glorious inheritance" is beyond words.

Believer, you are God's treasure. His love for you cannot be measured (Psalm 103:11). He has *written history* with you in mind (Ephesians 1:3–2:10), desiring one day to spend all eternity with you. He's looking forward to redeeming you from this sin-stained world and welcoming you into his holy presence forever. He did this not because of your own innate goodness but because of his amazing grace.

That's what it means to be the Lord's "rich and glorious inheritance."

What a promise! What a God!

Now What?

The predestined nature of God's "holy people" helps explain why he considers believers as such a precious inheritance. To understand more, read Ephesians 1:1-14 and Romans 8:28-30.

Did You Know?

We need godly wisdom and spiritual maturity to understand all these things. That's why Paul prayed for believers' hearts to "be flooded with [God's] light."

OCTOBER 22

By grace you have been saved through faith. And this is not your own doing; it is the gift of God, not a result of works, so that no one may boast.

EPHESIANS 2:8-9, ESV

IN CHARLES DICKENS'S 1843 CLASSIC BOOK, *A Christmas Carol,* the protagonist, Ebenezer Scrooge, receives a chilling visit one night from Jacob Marley, his dead business partner. When Marley's ghost enters Scrooge's bedroom to warn him of three more supernatural visitors that night, here's what Scrooge sees:

> The chain he drew was clasped about his middle. It was long, and wound about him like a tail; and it was made (for Scrooge observed it closely) of cash-boxes, keys, padlocks, ledgers, deeds, and heavy purses wrought in steel. His body was transparent; so that Scrooge, observing him, and looking through his waistcoat, could see the two buttons on his coat behind.[2]

In a spiritual sense, every human being resembles Jacob Marley's character. We all started life, in essence, as the walking dead, tangled in chains of destructive sin and rebellion. Look at how the apostle Paul describes it in Ephesians 2:1: "Once you were dead because of your disobedience and your many sins."

Without God, we were completely void of hope. After all, dead people can't save themselves because, well, *THEY'RE DEAD*!

We needed outside intervention. That's where God's mercy and grace entered the picture.

What's It Mean?

Take a few moments to read Ephesians 2:1-10, which beautifully illustrates the progression of salvation. As you do, pay attention to who initiates

---

[2] Charles Dickens, *A Christmas Carol*, stave 1.

everything in the process. It's God! He powerfully awakens spiritually dead hearts through his Spirit.

Christians are the beneficiaries of God's marvelous mercy and grace. Mercy, simply defined, is not receiving the punishment that you deserve. Grace, meanwhile, is unmerited favor.

In Ephesians 2, Paul describes how God, who is "rich in mercy" (verse 4) "made us alive together with Christ" (verse 5, ESV) and that it is "by grace you have been saved through faith" (verse 8, ESV). Mercy and grace are both spiritual blessings that God lavishes upon all his children even though we didn't deserve them in any way.

Salvation is a beautiful product of divine mercy and grace, initiated by a God who breathes life into those who were once dead. Praise the Lord!

Now What?

Memorize Ephesians 2:8-9. These verses are "must-haves" in the spiritual inventory of any believer.

Did You Know?

Because of God's mercy and grace, there is no room for human boasting (verse 9). We are called to display faith in Jesus (in the salvation process, verse 8) and commit to good works (as a *result* of our salvation, verse 10).

OCTOBER 23

We won't be tossed and blown about by every wind of new teaching. We will not be influenced when people try to trick us with lies so clever they sound like the truth.

EPHESIANS 4:14

WE LIVE IN AN AGE of advancement, where all around us, the message seems to be, "Newer is better!"

NEW VIDEO GAMES!
NEW PHONES!
NEW TABLETS!
NEW COMPUTERS!
NEW CLOTHES!
NEW CARS!

If you don't have the latest-and-greatest gadgets, gizmos, thingamabobs, and doohickeys . . . well, friend, you're on the outside looking in!

At least that's what the world constantly tells us.

Yes, new technology and other material things can be extremely helpful in our daily lives. But "newer is better" doesn't always apply. When it comes to teachings, doctrines, and beliefs about Christianity, newer is certainly *not* better. We must cling to the original truth.

What's It Mean?

Scripture doesn't need any revisions, modernizations, or upgrades. There's no such thing as "The Gospel of Jesus Christ, Version 2.0."

That's because God is completely truthful, eternal, and unchanging. What was perfectly true thousands of years ago when God breathed out his Word through the divine inspiration of his Spirit (2 Timothy 3:16; 2 Peter 1:20-21) is just as true today. Jesus declared this in Matthew 5:18 and 24:35.

Yet false teachings and "new spiritual fads" have been around since the start of the church. Almost every New Testament book contains a warning against false teachers.

593

Look, for instance, at today's verse. The imagery is of a ship on a storm-tossed sea, as gale-force winds threaten to blow it off course or even capsize it. In this metaphor, the ship represents an immature believer, and the winds are "new teaching" that doesn't align with Scripture.

In a world filled with faddish, even demonic, teaching that can scuttle the vessel of young faith, how can you differentiate between what's true and what's false? Here are a few tests you should apply to any spiritual instruction you hear or read:

- Does it align with the rest of Scripture?
- Does it uphold the gospel of Jesus Christ as "most important" (1 Corinthians 15:3)?
- Will the message lead you toward spiritual growth and godly worship or away from them?
- Does the messenger's personal life line up with godly living and the message he or she is preaching?

Remember, newer is not better when it comes to the timeless perfection and sufficiency of Scripture. Set your life's course according to God's Word!

Now What?
Read Jeremiah 6:16 for another reminder of the Bible's eternal truth.

Did You Know?
Scripture reserves harsh words for those who preach a false gospel (Galatians 1:8-9).

OCTOBER 24

Be kind to each other, tenderhearted, forgiving one another,
just as God through Christ has forgiven you.

EPHESIANS 4:32

THE HATFIELDS AND THE MCCOYS are often mentioned in the same breath. But these two nineteenth-century American families hated each other. Sadly, they are infamously known for their long-standing, deadly feud.

The two clans lived across the Tug Fork stream from each other—the McCoys in Kentucky and the Hatfields in West Virginia. The animosity began with the Civil War. Or a stolen pig. It's hard to tell in these matters. But the real fighting started in 1882 when Ellison Hatfield, a brother of the family patriarch, William "Devil Anse" Hatfield, was shot to death by the McCoys. In revenge, the Hatfields kidnapped and executed three McCoy brothers.

That event exploded into several decades' worth of all-out backwoods violence and murder. The lawlessness reached a fever pitch in 1888 when a group of Hatfields attacked the home of the rival leader, Randolph McCoy, resulting in more deaths and injuries. Multiple arrests were made, and years of legal actions ensued. The case even made its way to the US Supreme Court. The feuding slowly abated afterward but didn't fully end until the second decade of the twentieth century.

Boy, the Hatfields and the McCoys certainly could've used Ephesians 4:31-32! Here's what this beautiful passage of Scripture says:

Get rid of all bitterness, rage, anger, harsh words, and slander, as well as all types of evil behavior. Instead, be kind to each other, tenderhearted, forgiving one another, just as God through Christ has forgiven you.

What's It Mean?

These words aren't just for vindictive families! They are vital for all of us.

Bitterness, unforgiveness, and anger create a deceptively destructive spiritual death trap. They don't suddenly overwhelm you. It's a gradual process.

Hebrews 12:15 says, "Watch out that no poisonous root of bitterness grows up to trouble you, corrupting many." That's certainly what happened with the Hatfields and McCoys. But it can also happen to Christians.

Bitterness acts like an aggressive weed. Once it sprouts up, it germinates, multiplies, and corrupts many through the harsh words and angry actions it produces in us.

But you can kill this evil weed at its root! In God, we have a perfect paradigm. He loved us when we were unlovable. Through Christ, he has forgiven us more than we can ever know (Ephesians 4:32). Therefore, choose to reciprocate this heavenly love, kindness, and forgiveness to others!

Now What?
Review the related July 19 devotion about forgiveness and Matthew 18:23-35.

Did You Know?
Ephesians 4:26-27 exhorts us to make amends with others on the same day, if possible, to avoid giving the devil "a foothold."

OCTOBER 25

*Put on every piece of God's armor so you will be
able to resist the enemy in the time of evil.*

EPHESIANS 6:13

WHEN THE APOSTLE PAUL wrote the book of Ephesians, the Roman
Empire was the greatest kingdom the ancient world had ever known.
Thanks largely to its highly trained, well-equipped legionnaires, Rome
expanded and defended its empire for the better part of five centuries.

Paul likely had a Roman soldier in mind when he wrote the well-known
"armor of God" passage in Ephesians 6:10-20. Here's an excerpt:

> Put on every piece of God's armor so you will be able to resist the
> enemy in the time of evil. Then after the battle you will still be
> standing firm. Stand your ground, putting on the belt of truth and
> the body armor of God's righteousness. For shoes, put on the peace
> that comes from the Good News so that you will be fully prepared.
> In addition to all of these, hold up the shield of faith to stop the
> fiery arrows of the devil. Put on salvation as your helmet, and take
> the sword of the Spirit, which is the word of God.
> VERSES 13-17

What's It Mean?

Let's briefly explore the armor listed in this beautiful passage and how it
relates to us today:

- **Belt of truth.** Like a soldier's belt holds clothing and equipment in
  place, the truth of the gospel girds our faith.
- **Body armor of God's righteousness.** Body armor protects a soldier's
  vital organs. Likewise, God's righteousness, which he imputes to
  believers through Christ's atoning sacrifice (2 Corinthians 5:21),
  protects us from divine wrath.

- **Shoes of peace.** Just as a soldier must wear proper footwear into battle, Christians must be prepared to bring the gospel message—peace with God through faith in Christ—into spiritually hostile environments.
- **Shield of faith.** A shield protected ancient soldiers from attack. Likewise, faith in Christ protects Christians from "fiery arrows of the devil" (i.e., temptations and accusations).
- **Helmet of salvation.** A Christian's salvation acts as a "helmet," ultimately protecting the believer's life from all spiritual harm.
- **Sword of the Spirit.** Did you notice this is the only offensive weapon listed? We fight our spiritual battles with the truth of Scripture, cutting and slashing through Satan's attacks, sin's temptations, and worldly deviations.

God's spiritual armor is vital for the life of every soldier in the King's army. By his power, arm yourself with it daily!

Now What?

Beside putting on this armor, don't forget to "pray in the Spirit at all times and on every occasion" (Ephesians 6:18).

Did You Know?

Daniel had a future vision of the Roman Empire in the sixth century BC (Daniel 7:7).

OCTOBER 26

To me to live is Christ, and to die is gain.

PHILIPPIANS 1:21, ESV

THE APOSTLE PAUL led quite a dramatic life.

He was nearly killed by a violent mob; he spoke before powerful kings; he survived a shipwreck, a venomous snakebite, and an assassination plot; and he was incarcerated in three different cities. And this was all within roughly a five-year span, between his arrest in Jerusalem and his appeal for a trial in Rome! In today's world, he could've easily written a *New York Times* bestselling memoir and hit the late-night TV talk-show circuit.

But Paul wasn't interested in self-promotion. Ultimately, his biggest concern wasn't even trying to get out of prison. His chief interest was proclaiming the name of Christ. And he certainly did! Even while in chains, Paul found remarkable ways to spread the gospel (see the "Did You Know?" section below).

Yet Paul didn't know how his house arrest would end. Even though he was innocent, he arrived in Rome around AD 60, during the reign of the infamous Emperor Nero, who viciously persecuted Christians. There was no guarantee Paul would survive the ordeal.

That was a secondary matter to Paul. That's why he could write today's verse to the Philippian church with all sincerity: "To me to live is Christ, and to die is gain."

What's It Mean?

Today's verse is a beautifully concise summary of the Christian life.

If you are a follower of Jesus, your mission should be to glorify God, grow in his grace, and make his name known. This mission should fill your heart and consume your thoughts. Yes, there are many blessings that God gives us in life that occupy our time (family, friends, work, school, sports, hobbies, etc.). But our devotion to Christ should permeate all of these and be preeminent above them.

This is what "to live is Christ" means.

But what about "to die is gain"? Here's what Paul meant: this world is temporary. We are spiritual exiles here. God has given us incredible blessings in this life, but the life to come holds eternal treasures that we can't even begin to fathom (2 Corinthians 4:17-18).

Believer, seek the advancement of God's Kingdom now, knowing that an infinitely greater heavenly Kingdom awaits you one day!

Now What?

Memorize Philippians 1:21. It's a great mantra, and there's no excuse *not* to memorize it since it's only eleven words long!

Did You Know?

While under house arrest in Rome, Paul ensured that "everyone here, including the whole palace guard, knows that I am in chains because of Christ" (Philippians 1:13). Apparently, even some of Caesar's household became Christians through Paul's witness (Philippians 4:22).

OCTOBER 27

*In humility count others more significant than yourselves. Let each of
you look not only to his own interests, but also to the interests of others.*

PHILIPPIANS 2:3-4, ESV

ARE YOU AN EXPERT in anything? Perhaps you excel in music, singing,
acting, writing, photography, math, science, cooking, or sports.

Regardless, you are an expert in at least one subject: loving yourself!
Every human has a PhD in the subject of self-love. As sinful, self-centered
creatures, it comes naturally to us.

But look at today's Bible passage. Scripture calls for us to live differently.
How can we do this? The apostle Paul provides the perfect paradigm in
Philippians 2:5-11 (ESV):

> Have this mind among yourselves, which is yours in Christ
> Jesus, who, though he was in the form of God, did not count
> equality with God a thing to be grasped, but emptied himself,
> by taking the form of a servant, being born in the likeness of
> men. And being found in human form, he humbled himself
> by becoming obedient to the point of death, even death on a cross.
> Therefore God has highly exalted him and bestowed on him the
> name that is above every name, so that at the name of Jesus every
> knee should bow, in heaven and on earth and under the earth,
> and every tongue confess that Jesus Christ is Lord, to the glory of
> God the Father.

What's It Mean?

If anyone in history could consider his own rights, it was Jesus. He is the
eternal, sinless Son of God, for goodness' sake! Yet in an act of supreme
humility, he temporarily set aside many of his divine privileges to become
the substitutionary atonement for our sins.

This is the greatest example of self-sacrifice that the world will ever know.
Jesus had no selfish ambition or conceit. Every inclination of his heart

was to serve those whom he created, who rebelled against him, who sent him to the Cross.

In other words . . . us.

God now calls you to follow Christ's perfect example. By the Spirit's power, cast aside prideful inclinations and vain goals. Prize humility. Elevate others in your life. Serve others first.

By doing so, you will honor the Lord!

Now What?

Consider Philippians 2:10-11 (ESV): you can "confess that Jesus Christ is Lord" now for salvation or when it's too late in eternal judgment. Don't wait!

Did You Know?

When Paul says Jesus "emptied himself" (Philippians 2:7, ESV), he's not saying Christ gave up his "fully God" status in any way. Paul is stressing Jesus' humility in temporarily laying aside his divine rights (not attributes).

OCTOBER 28

*I once thought these things were valuable, but now I
consider them worthless because of what Christ has done.*

PHILIPPIANS 3:7

WHEN ASKED TO GIVE their testimony of faith, many people give at
least one of the following responses:

"I grew up in a Christian family."
"I was raised in church."
"I've always known about God."
"I've never done anything *really* bad."

Before being confronted by the risen Lord Jesus on the road to
Damascus, here's what the apostle Paul based his salvation on, as he mentions in Philippians 3:5-6 (ESV):

- Circumcised on the eighth day.
- Of the people of Israel, of the tribe of Benjamin, a Hebrew of Hebrews.
- As to the law, a Pharisee.
- As to zeal, a persecutor of the church.
- As to righteousness under the law, blameless.

In other words, Paul originally thought God would consider him righteous based on his Jewish heritage and his fastidious observance of the Old
Testament law.

But he was terribly wrong.

Look at his renewed mindset after God changed his heart:

I once thought these things were valuable, but now I consider them
worthless because of what Christ has done. Yes, everything else
is worthless when compared with the infinite value of knowing

Christ Jesus my Lord. For his sake I have discarded everything else, counting it all as garbage, so that I could gain Christ.

PHILIPPIANS 3:7-8

What's It Mean?

Skybalon.

You've almost certainly never used this word before, but it was important to Paul. It's the ancient Greek term he used in Philippians 3:8, rendered in English as "garbage," to describe the worth of human striving when it comes to salvation. But our English translations don't always do justice to original context.

Skybalon can mean rubbish, refuse, or leftovers that you'd throw to dogs. But it also can mean dung or even human excrement. Paul wasn't mincing words! He wanted to be quite clear: salvation comes through God's grace through faith, *not* by human works (see also Ephesians 2:8-9). Without Christ, even our most righteous deeds "are nothing but filthy rags" to God (Isaiah 64:6).

Think about your relationship with God. Have you been basing your salvation on human accomplishments—nothing more than a heaping pile of *skybalon*? Or have you truly placed your faith solely in the merits of Christ's sacrifice on your behalf?

Good works don't impress God. Trust in the Savior who covers your sin with his righteousness!

Now What?

Read Philippians 3 to learn more about the true source of our righteousness.

Did You Know?

Paul mentioned that his family lineage came from the tribe of Benjamin because of its prominence. King Saul, Israel's first king, was a Benjaminite (1 Samuel 9:1-2).

OCTOBER 29

I press on toward the goal for the prize of the
upward call of God in Christ Jesus.

PHILIPPIANS 3:14, ESV

EVERYONE HAS GOALS IN LIFE.

- A teacher's goal is to educate students.
- A police officer's goal is to enforce the law and keep people safe.
- A CEO's goal is to grow his business and make lots of money.
- A gnat's goal is to—well, we're not actually sure about this one. Maybe it's to annoy people before being smashed on the back of someone's sweaty neck?

Like we said, everyone has goals. But what is a Christian's goal? The apostle Paul answers that in today's verse.

What's It Mean?

Philippians 3:14 is an extension of Paul's thoughts from yesterday's devotional topic: counting good deeds as worthless when it comes to our salvation and instead relying solely on the power of Christ.

Paul wanted to experience as much of that spiritual power as he could. But he realized this was a lifelong process, not a one-time experience. So he wrote these words in Philippians 3:12-14:

Not that I have already obtained this or am already perfect, but I press on to make it my own, because Christ Jesus has made me his own. Brothers, I do not consider that I have made it my own. But one thing I do: forgetting what lies behind and straining forward to what lies ahead, I press on toward the goal for the prize of the upward call of God in Christ Jesus (ESV).

As he enjoyed doing, Paul is using athletic imagery here—specifically describing life as a long race. You can almost picture an Olympic runner leaning ahead as he pushes toward the finish line.

But what exactly is the goal Paul is referring to? It's heavenly glory with the Lord—an eternal reward beyond human comprehension (Romans 8:18). Christians should always have an eye on this glorious finish line as we do God's will on earth. This heavenly prize keeps us focused on the task at hand and motivates us when the race gets difficult.

Press on, dear believer. The runner who looks down while racing will lag behind, stumble, or veer off course. But the one who presses forward and keeps their eyes on the beautiful finish line will run a strong, true race.

Now What?

If you're an athlete, post Philippians 3:12-14 somewhere you'll see it often. If you're not, send it to an athlete you know!

Did You Know?

Paul's other athletic metaphors are found in 1 Corinthians 9:24-27; 1 Timothy 4:7-8; 2 Timothy 2:5; and 4:7-8.

OCTOBER 30

Fix your thoughts on what is true, and honorable, and right, and pure, and lovely, and admirable. Think about things that are excellent and worthy of praise.

PHILIPPIANS 4:8

THE HUMAN MIND is truly an amazing thing.

Consider some of the marvels that the human mind has produced: the Pyramids of Giza, the Great Wall of China, *Macbeth*, *Mona Lisa*, Beethoven's "Fifth Symphony," modern vaccines, putting a man on the moon, *War and Peace*, *The Great Gatsby*, *Citizen Kane*, light bulbs, automobiles, telephones, computers, the Internet . . .

And yard gnomes—we can't forget yard gnomes.

But the human mind can also harbor wicked, ungodly thoughts. As today's verse says, we are to fix our minds instead on godly thoughts that are "worthy of praise."

What's It Mean?

It's so important to protect your mind. Since your mind is a central part of your body, you must be careful not to willfully allow anything impure to enter it because "your body is the temple of the Holy Spirit" (1 Corinthians 6:19).

When it comes to our minds, the concept is simple: whatever you put in is what you'll get in return. If you input filth, it will corrupt your mind, heart, and faith. However, if you input God's Word, it will bear righteous, spiritual fruit.

So what are you putting into your mind when it comes to the following?

- movies
- TV shows
- books
- music
- Internet content

Pornography deserves special mention because it is so pervasive, addictive, and spiritually destructive. Pornography is the antithesis of today's verse: it is dishonorable, impure, ugly, and shameful because it degrades what is good (God's gift of sex within marriage) into a "lustful passion" (1 Thessalonians 4:4-5). We are to "put to death the sinful, earthly things lurking within you. Have nothing to do with sexual immorality, impurity, lust, and evil desires" (Colossians 3:5).

Don't believe Satan's lies about your thought life:

I'm mature enough to view this.
I'll turn off this movie/show if it gets too raunchy.
My friends are doing it. I don't want to be the odd one out.
One little look won't hurt.

This is a slippery slope leading down a path of spiritual harm. Instead, God calls his chosen people to choose mental purity. Fill your mind with godly thoughts. Memorize Scripture. Think about how you can honor the Lord and serve others. Then you will please your heavenly Father!

(Even if you don't have a yard gnome.)

Now What?
Besides today's verse, meditate on Colossians 3:2-4.

Did You Know?
God knows our every thought (Psalm 139:2).

OCTOBER 31

I can do all things through him who strengthens me.

PHILIPPIANS 4:13, ESV

BUNNIES AROUND THE WORLD, unite! It's time to stand against the injustice being done to you! No more "lucky rabbit's foot" trinkets!

In general, human beings are a superstitious bunch. Since ancient times, we have created all sorts of myths about luck, chance, and fortune.

Somehow, the notion that keeping a rabbit's foot in your pocket would bring you good luck became popular in America around the beginning of the twentieth century. But the quest for good omens goes far beyond lopping off the hindquarters of poor Flopsy, Mopsy, and Cottontail. Virtually every culture in history has its share of quirky rituals and stories about trying to somehow curry mystical favor on your side.

Take today's verse, for example. Philippians 4:13 is one of the most misused, misquoted verses in the Bible. Sadly, we often apply our superstitious tendencies to it. We must understand it properly, for when we do, we will comprehend both Scripture and God more clearly.

What's It Mean?

These days, Philippians 4:13 has become somewhat of a Christian mantra. We see it everywhere: on T-shirts, posters, placards—even tattoos.

Christian athletes are notorious for twisting this verse out of context for personal achievement: *With God on my side, I can accomplish anything! I can score five touchdowns, net a hat trick, average a double-double for the season, break all the records, and win the championship!*

It's the rabbit's-foot-in-your-pocket mentality.

God doesn't work like that. He isn't a talisman, amulet, or a divine butler here to do your bidding. He is the Lord God Almighty. You are here to worship and glorify *him*!

Any rabbit's-foot reading of Philippians 4:13 is a gross misrepresentation of its true message. The apostle Paul, who was imprisoned in Rome when he authored Philippians, was speaking about true spiritual contentment, regardless of circumstances. Only two verses earlier, he wrote, "Not that I was ever in need, for I have learned how to be content with whatever I have." Paul knew he could be content at all times in life because God would be faithful to sustain him.

Don't read *your* views into Scripture. Let Scripture *inform* your views of life and God. Then you will be able to truly do all things through him who strengthens you by finding your hope and contentment in him. God will be glorified . . . and bunnies everywhere will thank you.

Now What?

Whenever you read Scripture, always consider the context as you seek to understand the meaning of the passage.

Did You Know?

In a world created and governed by a holy, sovereign God, "luck" and "chance" do not exist (Psalm 139:16; Proverbs 16:9; Lamentations 3:37-38).

NOVEMBER 1

*My God will supply every need of yours according
to his riches in glory in Christ Jesus.*

PHILIPPIANS 4:19, ESV

*A HUGE BANK ACCOUNT! Flashy sports cars! Expensive jewelry! Designer
clothing! Annual vacations to exotic islands! A multimillion-dollar mansion!* . . .
*God wants to give you all of this! Your righteousness and earthly wealth go hand
in hand. All you have to do is name it and claim it in faith.*

Does this sound like heresy to you? It should. It's called "the prosperity
gospel"—also known as the "health and wealth" or "name it and claim it"
gospel—and it's an insidious distortion of the true gospel of Jesus Christ.

You need to be on your guard against it.

What's It Mean?

Today's devotion is similar to yesterday's focus on Philippians 4:13. But the
prosperity gospel goes beyond the blatant perversion of one verse. It's an
entire belief system that falls under the biblical category of a "false gospel"
(Galatians 1:6-9).

This message is being spewed by false teachers around the world, leading millions astray. Its proponents lead some of America's biggest churches,
filling huge arenas every weekend with tens of thousands of people hungry
to hear how God—like a magic genie in a bottle—will improve their health
and increase their wealth . . . if they just pray hard enough. These false
teachers write bestselling books, have their own TV shows, and speak at
conferences.

They grossly distort today's verse and other passages—such as
Deuteronomy 8:18; Psalm 112:3; Proverbs 13:22; and 2 Corinthians 8:9—
taking them completely out of context to fit their twisted theology and false
narrative. When they see Philippians 4:19 or 2 Corinthians 8:9—"Though
[Christ] was rich, yet for your sakes he became poor, so that by his poverty
he could make you rich"—they zoom right past the speed limit signs of
proper biblical interpretation and overlay their fleshly desires onto Scripture,

rather than letting Scripture properly inform their thinking. Then they spiritually poison the masses with their worthless rhetoric.

Don't believe their lies.

If you have trusted in Christ, God loves you and absolutely wants to bless you. But he never promises us health or material wealth. What he *does* promise—in today's verse and everywhere else in Scripture—is to lavish believers with every *spiritual* blessing that we need in this life . . . and the life to come.

That's true riches!

Now What?

Check out 1 Timothy 6:6-10. Prosperity gospel proponents seem to skip over this passage.

Did You Know?

- The prosperity gospel movement primarily arose in America in the twentieth century.

NOVEMBER 2

*This same Good News that came to you is going out all over
the world. It is bearing fruit everywhere by changing lives,
just as it changed your lives from the day you first heard and
understood the truth about God's wonderful grace.*

COLOSSIANS 1:6

BEING A CHRISTIAN in the first century AD was *really* hard.

Converting to Christianity often meant being ostracized by family and
friends. Sometimes it meant being persecuted or killed. What's more, first-
century believers didn't have anywhere close to the luxuries that we enjoy
today. They often worshiped each Sunday in people's homes, sometimes to
avoid detection from the authorities. Prior to a formalized New Testament
canon, they had to rely strictly on faith, the apostles' teaching (oral and
written), and the Old Testament. Most orthodox Jews wanted to squash
Christianity, and most Gentiles thought it was a kooky sect of Judaism.

Can you see how first-century Christians might have needed a little
encouragement to persevere in the faith? That's *exactly* why the apostle Paul
wrote today's verse to the young believers in Colossae.

What's It Mean?

If you're a Christian, do you ever feel like you're spiritually alone, like you're
marooned on an island all by yourself?

Satan loves to make us feel isolated and rejected: *Why do you call yourself
a Christian? Why do you follow Jesus? Why do you believe the Bible? Nobody else
does.* Don't fall for his diabolical deception.

Rather, take heart! Today's Scripture was meant for you.

If you're a Christian, you're part of "the church"—the thriving worldwide "body of Christ" (1 Corinthians 12:27, ESV), those who have trusted
in Jesus as their Lord and Savior. There are millions of true believers around
the world whom God has called to be his children.

This should greatly encourage you! You are not alone or part of a dying movement. You are among a powerful, living faith that the Lord God started and sustains by his unassailable power (Matthew 16:18).

Then, one day in heaven, you will lift your voice with every other saint in history to fulfill the apostle John's glorious vision in Revelation 19:6-7:

> I heard again what sounded like the shout of a vast crowd or the roar of mighty ocean waves or the crash of loud thunder: "Praise the LORD! For the Lord our God, the Almighty, reigns. Let us be glad and rejoice, and let us give honor to him."

Now What?

If you don't belong to a local gospel-centered church, make that a priority! You don't have to walk alone.

Did You Know?

- Jesus said the gospel must be preached in every nation before he returns (Matthew 24:14). How can you advance this mission?

NOVEMBER 3

You, who were dead in your trespasses and the uncircumcision of your flesh, God made alive together with him, having forgiven us all our trespasses, by canceling the record of debt that stood against us with its legal demands. This he set aside, nailing it to the cross.

COLOSSIANS 2:13-14, ESV

IN FEBRUARY 2019, the national debt of the United States reached a record-breaking $22 trillion. Yes, that's trillion with a *T*.

That's an absurd amount of money. Remarkably, the government owes a large chunk of that money to itself. Sounds weird, but it's true. (Too hard to explain here.) The remainder is owed to foreign countries, state and local governments, private businesses, and individuals.

Every four years during a new presidential election cycle, we hear promises from candidates vowing to cut the federal deficit. Yet nothing seems to change. It's a massive problem that isn't going away anytime soon.

Did you know the Bible says that each of us owes an immeasurable debt that we can never pay? This liability has nothing to do with money. The overwhelming deficit credited against us is our sins.

What's It Mean?

A debt is something, typically money, that is owed. Carrying financial debt is sometimes necessary in life (a student loan, monthly car payments, a homeowner's mortgage, etc.), but paying off debt is important. You can get into serious trouble if you default on your financial debts.

The problem with sin is that we can't pay God back. The debt is humanly insurmountable (Matthew 18:24-27), and apart from divine intervention, the result is physical and spiritual death (Romans 6:23). There's nothing we can do—good deeds or anything else—to atone for our unrighteousness. Romans 3 makes that abundantly clear.

Because of his justice, God can't magically snap his fingers and make our sin-debt just disappear. It has to be paid for. So what are we to do? Are we without hope?

Not at all! This is where Jesus comes in.

As today's Scripture passage says, God cancels all the sin-debt of everyone who trusts in Christ's substitutionary death and resurrection on our behalf. Jesus paid for our debts so we wouldn't have to. He bore all of our sin and shame on the cross. He shouldered God's terrible, just wrath so you wouldn't have to.

Through faith in Christ, we live debt-free before God!

(Politicians, take note . . .)

Now What?

Read the parable of the unforgiving debtor in Matthew 18:21-35.

Did You Know?

The Second Liberty Bond Act of 1917 created a "debt ceiling" for the nation. But it has been increased dozens of times since then.

NOVEMBER 4

Let your conversation be gracious and attractive so that
you will have the right response for everyone.

COLOSSIANS 4:6

BEFORE ABRAHAM LINCOLN became a great president, he was a great speaker.

In 1858, Lincoln and Stephen Douglas squared off for a series of seven now-famous debates throughout Illinois as they campaigned for a US Senate seat. Lincoln lost that election bid to Douglas, but his oratory skills were well noted. Within three years, he was elected America's sixteenth president, and some of his speeches are regarded among the greatest orations in US history, such as the Gettysburg Address (1863) and both of his inaugural speeches (1861 and 1865).

Christians don't have to be at Lincoln's public speaking level. But speech is a powerful tool, and we are to use it wisely as we seek to spread the gospel. Look at what Colossians 4:5-6 says:

> Live wisely among those who are not believers, and make the
> most of every opportunity. Let your conversation be gracious and
> attractive so that you will have the right response for everyone.

What's It Mean?

If you are a Christian who tries to honor the Lord, that's going to stand out to others. Somewhere, sometime, someone likely will ask you why you're different. What are you going to say?

If you take Jesus' great commission (Matthew 28:18-20) seriously and people have questions about Christianity, what are you going to say?

Do you know how to share your own testimony with others in a gospel-centered way? Do you know how to effectively share the good news of salvation through Christ to the lost, using Scripture (rather than your opinions) to make your points and answer people's questions?

Each of these examples is what Colossians 4:5-6 is talking about.

Evangelism is the responsibility of *every* believer, not just some elite special-ops team of outgoing super-Christians.

Initiate opportunities to share your faith and be ready for those whom God drops into your lap! When they come, share "gracious and attractive" words. Be ready to answer people's tough questions. Don't get defensive or try to win an argument. No one has ever argued an unbeliever into heaven! (See 2 Timothy 2:24-26.)

Follow Jesus' example and offer them words of eternal life. Meet people where they're at in the prayerful hope that they will turn to Christ (1 Corinthians 9:19-23).

But whatever you do, know the gospel well and share it graciously!

Now What?
First Peter 3:15-16 is similar to today's verse. Check it out!

Did You Know?
In each Lincoln-Douglas debate, the first man would open with a sixty-minute speech, the second man would follow for ninety minutes, then the first man would finish with a thirty-minute rebuttal. *Phew!*

NOVEMBER 5

We exhorted each one of you and encouraged you and
charged you to walk in a manner worthy of God, who
calls you into his own kingdom and glory.

1 THESSALONIANS 2:12, ESV

ON JUNE 4, 2002, the Tampa Bay Devil Rays selected Brandon Mann in the twenty-seventh round of Major League Baseball's amateur draft. It was a great day for the eighteen-year-old.

That day, though, was not nearly as historic as May 13, 2018, when Mann (then thirty-three) finally made his major league debut with the Texas Rangers after spending seventeen seasons—*seventeen!*—in the minor leagues and Japan. Talk about perseverance!

For every Brandon Mann success story, there are thousands of other minor league prospects who never get called up to the big leagues. They just aren't good enough.

Have you ever felt like that in your spiritual life? Maybe you have never committed your life to Christ, thinking, *I'm just not good enough for God yet.* Or maybe you are already a Christian, but you feel stuck on the sidelines, thinking, *How can I be of any serious use in God's Kingdom? I'm not good enough yet for him to use me.*

Either way, today's devotion is for you.

What's It Mean?

Today's verse talks about walking "in a manner worthy of God." But perhaps this seems out of reach if you identify with one of the categories described above.

First, remember that you can't become "worthy of God" through your own inherent goodness or efforts. As a sinner deserving God's eternal wrath, you can never be "good enough" to earn God's favor yourself. Praise the Lord that he takes the initiative and "calls you into his own kingdom and glory" through his Son! Jesus was "good enough" for you. His righteousness is yours forever through faith in his substitutionary death on your behalf.

If you are a believer who doesn't feel good enough to be used by God, these are accusatory lies from the devil. Don't believe them!

God "created us anew in Christ Jesus, so we can do the good things he planned for us long ago" (Ephesians 2:10). He will "equip you with all you need for doing his will" (Hebrews 13:21).

No, you're not worthy of God on your own. But he gloriously makes you worthy through Christ!

Now What?

Read Colossians 1:9-14, which talks about walking "in a manner worthy of the Lord, fully pleasing to him" (verse 10, ESV). Pay particular attention to who initiates the action. (Hint: it's not you!)

Did You Know?

Mann pitched in seven games for the 2018 Rangers, struggling to a 5.40 earned-run average. He played in Japan in 2019.

NOVEMBER 6

God's will is for you to be holy, so stay away from all sexual sin.

1 THESSALONIANS 4:3

SEX.

What do you think of when you read that word? Sadly, in our ungodly, overly sexualized culture, *sex* has become a dirty word. God never intended it to be so. When God created the world in perfection, he intended sex to be both a beautiful means of creating new life and an enjoyable gift of intimacy—but always between a married husband and wife. However, sin entered the world and marred God's perfect ideal.

In the centuries that followed, humanity spread across the earth, and pagan religions sprouted up. Sexually speaking, many of these ancient civilizations such as Mesopotamia, Greece, and Rome were grossly perverted. Under the guise of religion, these cultures incorporated all sorts of sinful sexual practices into their worship rituals. They did this to appease the gods and promote a fertile harvest season, among other reasons. Really, it was just an excuse for people to fulfill the lusts of their flesh.

These vile practices were abhorrent to God. Throughout Scripture—in both the Old and New Testaments—the Lord consistently called his people to sexual purity.

He is still doing that today.

What's It Mean?

Today's world is still filled with sexual immorality. Everywhere you turn, the world cheapens sex and offers perverse pleasure to gratify our fleshly desires. Yet God calls his children to "be holy because I am holy" (1 Peter 1:16).

Among all other rebellion against God, sexual sin is unique. Look at 1 Corinthians 6:18-20:

Run from sexual sin! No other sin so clearly affects the body as this one does. For sexual immorality is a sin against your own body. Don't you realize that your body is the temple of the Holy Spirit, who lives in you and was given to you by God? You do not belong to yourself, for God bought you with a high price. So you must honor God with your body.

This means keep your mind pure. Reject pornography. Honor your body and others' as God's temple. And above all, wait until marriage for sexual intimacy.

If you have fallen in this area, remember this: no true child of God will suffer condemnation (Romans 8:1). Christ purchased your forgiveness at the Cross. But God *does* call you to pursue righteousness.

Don't cheapen God's beautiful gift of sex. Enjoy it as he meant you to—at its proper time. You won't regret it.

Now What?
Read these passages about sexual purity: Romans 13:11-14; Ephesians 5:3-14; Colossians 3:5-10; and 1 Thessalonians 4:1-8.

Did You Know?
The apostle Paul denounced sexual immorality in eight of his thirteen New Testament letters.

NOVEMBER 7

The day of the Lord's return will come
unexpectedly, like a thief in the night.

1 THESSALONIANS 5:2

IN THE WEE MORNING hours of September 1, 1861, William Scott drifted off to sleep. This wouldn't have been a problem . . . except Scott was a Union Army private during the Civil War, and he fell asleep during sentry duty at Camp Lyon, which guarded a key bridge linking Virginia to Washington, DC.

OOPS!

Camp Lyon's commanding officer ordered that Scott be executed by firing squad. However, Scott's regiment rallied to his cause, signing a petition for clemency. The appeal reached President Abraham Lincoln, who granted the pardon. "The Sleeping Sentinel," as Scott came to be known, never fell asleep at his post again!

Christians are also sentinels, so to speak. We are called to watch for the return of our Savior. As Jesus said in Matthew 24:42, "So you, too, must keep watch! For you don't know what day your Lord is coming."

What's It Mean?

One day, Christ will return in glorious power to crush all evil, redeem his chosen people, and establish his eternal Kingdom. But as today's verse says, the timing of his return remains a mystery.

When Jesus does come back, he will receive a contrasting reaction: believers will bask in the glory of their much-anticipated Lord (1 Thessalonians 1:10), while unbelievers will come to the sudden, horrific realization that the Savior they rejected their whole life has now become their Judge (2 Thessalonians 1:7-9).

For believers, the mystery surrounding the timing of Jesus' return is a call to action. Don't be idle when the Master is away. (See the "Parable of the Talents" in Matthew 25:14-30, ESV.) As Christ's ambassadors, we must advance his Kingdom, using our God-given talents so that when he returns, we receive his commendation: "Well done, my good and faithful servant" (Matthew 25:21).

But for unbelievers, the suddenness of Jesus' return will feel shockingly different. On that day, all humanity will be brought before God's throne for final judgment (Revelation 20:11-15). The wicked will be sentenced to eternal condemnation in hell, while the righteous will be ushered into God's heavenly presence. There will be no chance for divine clemency at that time.

Don't wait! Don't fall asleep at the sentry post of life! As 2 Corinthians 6:2 says, "Indeed, the 'right time' is now. Today is the day of salvation."

Trust in Christ today!

Now What?
Read the following Bible passages about Jesus' second coming: Matthew 24:27-51; 1 Thessalonians 4:13–5:11; and 2 Thessalonians 1:7-10.

Did You Know?
Seven months after falling asleep at his post, Scott died leading a charge at Lee's Mill (Virginia).

NOVEMBER 8

Never get tired of doing good.

2 THESSALONIANS 3:13

ONE OF THE GREATEST moments in Olympic history involved two female runners who didn't come close to winning the race.

During a qualifying heat for the 5,000-meter finals at the 2016 Olympics in Rio de Janeiro, Brazil, New Zealand's Nikki Hamblin fell down, causing American Abbey D'Agostino to spill over her. The two runners' chance at Olympic glory was instantly in peril. For any chance to reach the finals, they needed to immediately get up and keep running.

But Hamblin was visibly shaken and remained prostrate on the track. Rather than speed off, D'Agostino paused to help Hamblin back onto her feet. Later in the race, D'Agostino crumbled to the track in pain, and Hamblin returned the favor, helping her up so she could finish the race. (Medical tests later revealed that D'Agostino had injured knee ligaments during the fall.)

Both runners finished the race, albeit way behind the pack. But their selflessness will be remembered far more than the competitive results of a qualifying heat.

D'Agostino and Hamblin displayed great kindness in a long race. As Christians, we are called to constantly show this attitude throughout our lives.

What's It Mean?

"Never get tired of doing good."

It sounds so simple and so inspirational. But in reality, we often *do* get tired of doing good. We are sinners who are prone to become selfish, shortsighted, and weary. That's why the apostle Paul gave us this important, divinely inspired reminder.

As the axiom goes, life is a marathon, not a sprint. You will experience highs, lows, and a lot of tedium. Throughout it all, you should always be prepared to do good and show the love of Christ to others.

That's because Christians are God's representatives on earth. Our lives are not our own. We are not here to please ourselves, but to lay down our lives for others. Remember Jesus' sublime example: "The Son of Man came not to be served but to serve others and to give his life as a ransom for many" (Mark 10:45). All this requires much prayer.

You might not ever receive thanks for some of the good things you do. That's okay. You're ultimately working for the Lord, not humans, and your reward will be great in heaven (Colossians 3:23-24)!

Now What?

For inspiration on today's subject, read at least one biography on a historic Christian leader or missionary. Here are some suggestions: John Calvin, Amy Carmichael, Jonathan Edwards, Jim and Elisabeth Elliot, David Livingstone, Martin Luther, Charles Spurgeon, and Hudson Taylor.

Did You Know?

Paul elaborates on today's verse in Galatians 6:9-10.

NOVEMBER 9

Physical training is good, but training for godliness is much better, promising benefits in this life and in the life to come.

1 TIMOTHY 4:8

JOEY CHESTNUT IS A TOTAL HOT DOG—and that's meant as a compliment!

Chestnut is a professional eater. That's right . . . you can make a living at eating. Who knew?

In 2019, Chestnut won his twelfth title in thirteen years at the Nathan's Famous International Hot Dog Eating Contest, an annual July 4th event on Coney Island in New York City. Chestnut earned first place by eating seventy-one hot dogs (buns included) in ten minutes, collecting a $10,000 prize. Not a bad day's work for devouring more than twenty-thousand calories in ten minutes.

Gulp.

Consuming that many hot dogs doesn't come easily. Prior to the contest, Chestnut put in plenty of physical training. We're not talking about weight-room bench presses, bicep curls, and burpees (although there were probably plenty of burps). For two months, Chestnut endured a specific *eating* regimen to transform his body into what he calls a "hot dog-digesting machine."

To be a real wiener—er, winner—in God's Kingdom, Christians must undergo training too. But our training is completely different. It's training of a spiritual nature. Look at 1 Timothy 4:7-10:

Train yourself to be godly. "Physical training is good, but training for godliness is much better, promising benefits in this life and in the life to come." This is a trustworthy saying, and everyone should accept it. This is why we work hard and continue to struggle, for our hope is in the living God, who is the Savior of all people and particularly of all believers.

What's It Mean?

Notice how the Bible *encourages* physical training and staying in shape. But "training for godliness" is even better. That's because the benefits of physical training will fade with age, while the benefits of spiritual training will last forever.

How do we train for godliness? Fortunately, it's not rocket science (or training to mass-consume hot dogs), but it does take discipline, time, and commitment. Like a serious competitor, we must be devoted to God's Word, prayer, fellowship, serving others, and consistent spiritual growth.

Most of all, training for godliness should flow not out of a sense of duty, but from our "hope . . . in the living God" (1 Timothy 4:10). Then we will receive the victor's "crown of righteousness" (2 Timothy 4:8) when our Lord Jesus returns!

Now What?

Make sure the time you spend in physical training is not disproportionate to your "training for godliness."

Did You Know?

The annual Nathan's Famous International Hot Dog Eating Contest is broadcast on TV and online by ESPN.

NOVEMBER 10

True godliness with contentment is itself great wealth.

1 TIMOTHY 6:6

EVERY YEAR, *FORBES* PUBLISHES its much-anticipated "billionaires" list—aka the list of the world's richest people. But have you ever wondered who the richest person in *history* was? Many historians theorize that the honor goes to—drum roll, please—Mansa Musa, a fourteenth-century West African king.

In 1312, Musa began ruling the Mali kingdom, which he expanded into a two-thousand-mile empire covering parts of nine modern-day African nations. All that territory provided Musa with enormous amounts of gold and other natural resources. Allegedly, during his Islamic pilgrimage to Mecca in 1324, his caravan of sixty-thousand people flooded the market in Cairo with so much gold, the city fell into a twelve-year recession. Even his slaves carried golden staffs and wore expensive silk. The man was loaded!

Musa seemed to find contentment in his wealth. This calls to mind the wisdom and warnings of 1 Timothy 6:6-10:

> True godliness with contentment is itself great wealth. After all, we brought nothing with us when we came into the world, and we can't take anything with us when we leave it. So if we have enough food and clothing, let us be content. But people who long to be rich fall into temptation and are trapped by many foolish and harmful desires that plunge them into ruin and destruction. For the love of money is the root of all kinds of evil. And some people, craving money, have wandered from the true faith and pierced themselves with many sorrows.

What's It Mean?

Money is a gift from God. Money itself is not evil, but the love of money is (1 Timothy 6:10) because it elevates something created to a place of worship, and worship is reserved exclusively for God.

The love of money is sinister and spiritually destructive. It doesn't announce itself and say, "Warning! I'm attacking you!" It's much subtler than that, working its way into our hearts through greedy dark alleys and covetous back doors. If left unchecked, the love of money can consume us.

Today's verse reveals how we can conquer this powerful temptation. When we truly find contentment in God and trust him for our daily provision (1 Timothy 6:8; Matthew 6:25-34), we will see money for what it really is—a blessing to be used wisely to meet daily needs and advance his Kingdom, not to hoard and accumulate personal wealth.

Want to be fabulously rich in a spiritual sense? Then be content in the Lord!

Now What?

Look for ways to use your money to bless those less fortunate than you.

Did You Know?

"Mansa" was a kingly title, like "Herod" or "Caesar."

NOVEMBER 11

Fight the good fight of the faith.

1 TIMOTHY 6:12, ESV

AS THE APOSTLE PAUL finished his first letter to Timothy, he gave his good friend some calls to action. One of them is found in today's verse.

At the time, Timothy was leading the church in Ephesus, and Paul wanted to encourage him to remain steadfast in his work. But that short sentence is much more than a throwaway line such as, "Keep it up!" It's a thoughtful, purposefully worded reminder about the realities of the Christian life.

Put it this way: there's a reason Paul didn't write any of the following:

- Enjoy the sun-splashed picnic of the faith.
- Sail the relaxing pleasure cruise of the faith.
- Soak in the breezy Caribbean vacation of the faith.
- Laugh away the carefree amusement park day of the faith.
- Gobble up the delicious hot fudge sundae of the faith.

See the difference?

What's It Mean?

There is nothing wrong with delighting in those pleasures at their proper times. God has given us many blessings to enjoy in this world.

The point is, the Christian life is often a struggle. If you are a follower of Christ, you will face challenges and difficulties because of your faith. Jesus himself said, "Here on earth you will have many trials and sorrows. But take heart, because I have overcome the world" (John 16:33).

This doesn't mean every day is going to be hard. Remember: being a child of God brings spiritual joy, peace, and contentment that are impossible to find anywhere else in life! But we must realize that the Christian life is a life of trials.

This fight is largely a spiritual battle. Here are some of the sources:

- spiritual forces of evil (Ephesians 6:11-12)
- human opposition (John 15:18-20)
- worldly temptations (1 John 2:15-17)
- indwelling sin (Romans 7:7-25)

Also remember: believers have great purpose. As God's ambassadors, we aren't called to kick back and take it easy with vain, self-centered pursuits. No! Before he ascended, our Savior gave us a mission: to reach the lost with his saving gospel. Some will accept this message. Many will reject it. Still, we must fight on!

So never give up. Always keep pushing forward in your faith, powered by God's Spirit inside you. Then one day, like an athlete who fights through the challenges of a long race, you'll receive the victor's crown of blessings in the Lord's presence forever!

Now What?

Meditate on the scriptural references listed above to prepare for the spiritual battles you'll face in life.

Did You Know?

Paul used the same language about "fighting the good fight" near the end of his life in 2 Timothy 4:7-8.

NOVEMBER 12

*Do your best to present yourself to God as one approved, a worker who
has no need to be ashamed, rightly handling the word of truth.*

2 TIMOTHY 2:15, ESV

ONE OF THE MOST important aspects of the American judicial system is
the right to a fair trial—the ability to be judged by a jury of peers.

If the system is working correctly, someone who is accused of a crime
will have the chance to defend himself or herself before an impartial jury.
In fact, both the defending and prosecuting attorneys work hard during the
jury selection process to make sure the trial jury consists of individuals who
are open-minded and not prejudiced in any way against the defendant or
the general subject matter of the case. This impartiality is crucial for truth
and justice to prevail during the trial.

Every time we read God's holy Word or hear it preached, we need to
enter those moments with the same kind of open-mindedness, allowing
God's Spirit and the truth of Scripture to inform our thinking. This was one
of the apostle Paul's main points in today's verse.

What's It Mean?

Paul's purpose in writing 2 Timothy was to encourage Timothy to remain
strong in the faith, spiritually guide the church at Ephesus, and be wary of
false teachers. But all believers, not just pastors like Timothy, must responsi-
bly handle the Word of God. This is absolutely critical to the foundations of
our faith and our spiritual maturation.

Too often, we bring our own preconceived notions and experiences into
our reading of Scripture. We take God's Word out of context to suit our
own personal desires. We make the Bible fit our sometimes faulty presuppo-
sitions about God, Jesus, life, or spiritual matters.

When we do this, it's as if we're treating the Bible like a square peg and
trying to shove its truth into the circular hole of our preexisting beliefs. *It
ain't gonna work.*

Instead of this vain pursuit, we need to be humble and spiritually open-minded to allow God's Word to inform the way we think. This is "rightly handling the word of truth."

Remember, the Bible is completely sufficient for our lives, revealing everything we need to know about God and the gospel. As Psalm 19:7 says, "The decrees of the LORD are trustworthy, making wise the simple."

Rightly handle the word of truth, and your faith will grow tremendously!

Now What?
Look up the following verses, which warn us against adding or detracting from God's Word: Deuteronomy 4:2; 12:32; Proverbs 30:6; and Revelation 22:18-19.

Did You Know?
Paul wrote 2 Timothy from a Roman prison shortly before his execution (1:8; 4:6).

NOVEMBER 13

In the last days there will be very difficult times.

2 TIMOTHY 3:1

THINK ABOUT HOW FAR WE'VE COME as humans in the last century. Here's a small list of modern conveniences—some might say *necessities*—that didn't exist a hundred years ago:

- smartphones
- televisions
- computers
- Internet
- video games
- microwaves
- penicillin
- shopping malls
- mass air travel
- refrigerators
- automobiles
- texting, e-mail, and all forms of social media

How did people in earlier times live without all of this?!

These days, we can communicate with anyone instantaneously. Many diseases that used to ravage entire countries, like polio or measles, are less of a threat. And technology continues to advance at breakneck speed.

From a secular viewpoint, it's easy to see how someone could think humans are evolving and life is getting better all the time. To some extent, that's true. God's common grace allows us to gain and use knowledge about our world.

Yet the Bible also says, "In the last days there will be very difficult times" (today's verse) and things will get progressively worse. Is Scripture contradicting itself?

No, not at all.

What's It Mean?

When the Bible mentions the "last days," it's referring to a period from Jesus' ascension (i.e. the start of "the church age") to his future second coming—a time period of approximately two thousand years and counting.

What's more, today's verse has nothing to do with the marvels of human achievement. It's focusing on the human heart.

As time goes on, human science, medicine, technology, etc. might improve, but our morality won't, according to Scripture. The apostle Paul specifically details the increase of godlessness in the last days in 2 Timothy 3:1-9. People will become more selfish, arrogant, greedy, and hateful. They will scoff at God and mock all that's good.

This is important to know because it affects all Christ followers. We shouldn't be surprised by this. Rather, it should inform how we live.

Remember, dear believer, this world is not your home. Ultimately, there's nothing to cling to here.

But while we're here, we need to be spiritually vigilant. The last days are *now*, not in the distant future. One day, the Lord Jesus will return and destroy all evil and bring us to our eternal home. Until then, our job is to be a salt-and-light preservative (Matthew 5:13-16), helping to keep the darkness at bay with the powerful gospel of Christ!

Now What?

Read 2 Timothy 3, keeping in mind that verses 1-9 present the problem, and 10-17 reveal the solution. (Also see 2 Peter 3.)

Did You Know?

Why are the "last days" so long (by human standards)? Second Peter 3:8-9 gives some clues.

NOVEMBER 14

I have fought the good fight, I have finished the
race, and I have remained faithful.

2 TIMOTHY 4:7

THE OIL LAMP—assuming his captors gave him one—burned dimly. The dank prison cell was cramped and cold. There was so much to say. But now, it seemed, after Paul's incomparably prolific life, his time on earth was suddenly slipping away.

Paul had endured imprisonment for his faith before, but he had always been released. This time, though, he knew would be different. So the aging apostle dipped his quill in the inkwell to finish his letter to his dear friend, Timothy. Here, in 2 Timothy 4:6-8, are some of his final words:

> As for me, my life has already been poured out as an offering to God. The time of my death is near. I have fought the good fight, I have finished the race, and I have remained faithful. And now the prize awaits me—the crown of righteousness, which the Lord, the righteous Judge, will give me on the day of his return. And the prize is not just for me but for all who eagerly look forward to his appearing.

Paul was a titan of the faith. He embodied the word faithful.

What's It Mean?

What's the definition of the word *faithful*? Do you have to evangelize the known world, start churches in pagan cities, joyfully endure multiple beatings and imprisonments, and continue to have an impact on more Christians in the two millennia *after* your death than during your life?

All of this, of course, can be said of Paul. But thank goodness for us, the answer to that question is *NO*!

That's because Christian faithfulness isn't about mimicking or comparing ourselves to any human, regardless of how great he or she is. It's about following our Savior. God isn't going to measure you against anyone else. So why should you do it to yourself?

To be faithful as a Christian, remain steadfast in your commitment to the Lord, using your God-given gifts to serve others and advance his purposes. Seek first his Kingdom and his righteousness (Matthew 6:33). Have the single-minded, heaven-centered focus that Paul alludes to in today's verse.

God is your Judge, and if you faithfully serve him with the talents he's graciously given you, you'll receive the glorious "crown of righteousness" when Christ returns.

Now What?

Are you faithfully using your spiritual gifts at church or elsewhere? If not, find a way to do so.

Did You Know?

- According to Christian tradition, Paul was martyred by the Romans in the late AD 60s.

NOVEMBER 15

He gave his life to free us from every kind of sin,
to cleanse us, and to make us his very own people,
totally committed to doing good deeds.

TITUS 2:14

IN THE FIRST CENTURY AD, the island of Crete was kind of like the
Wild West of the ancient Mediterranean world. There were no saloon
brawls, gunslingers, or showdowns at high noon. But spiritual lawlessness
and idolatry abounded.

"The people of Crete are all liars, cruel animals, and lazy gluttons,"
wrote the apostle Paul in Titus 1:12, likely quoting Epimenides, a Cretan
poet of the sixth century BC. Clearly, Crete needed the saving gospel message of Jesus Christ!

That's why Paul started churches on Crete during one of his missionary
journeys and left Titus, his Christian coworker, behind to help strengthen
the churches. Paul wrote the New Testament letter of "Titus" to encourage
his friend.

The letter of Titus features one of Scripture's most concise, powerful
explanations of the gospel:

The grace of God has been revealed, bringing salvation to all
people. And we are instructed to turn from godless living and
sinful pleasures. We should live in this evil world with wisdom,
righteousness, and devotion to God, while we look forward with
hope to that wonderful day when the glory of our great God and
Savior, Jesus Christ, will be revealed. He gave his life to free us from
every kind of sin, to cleanse us, and to make us his very own people,
totally committed to doing good deeds.

TITUS 2:11-14

What's It Mean?
Let's consider five key points of this wonderful passage in more detail:

- **The grace of God has been revealed, bringing salvation to all people.** Salvation always begins with God's sovereign grace, not human will or merit.
- **We are instructed to turn from godless living and sinful pleasures while we look forward with hope.** Thanks to God's mercy and Christ's sacrifice, Christians can focus on a glorious, eternal future rather than wallowing in their wicked past.
- **He gave his life to cleanse us.** Praise God for the glories of imputed righteousness through Christ!
- **He gave his life to make us his very own people.** Praise God for our heavenly adoption through Christ!
- **He gave his life to make us his very own people, totally committed to doing good deeds.** As God's elect children, Christians are called to reflect the Savior's righteousness through their loving works.

What a beautiful summary of the gospel of Jesus Christ!

Now What?

Memorize Titus 2:11-14.

Did You Know?

Other ancient writers, such as Polybius (Greek) and Cicero (Roman), also cited Crete for its moral decadence.

NOVEMBER 16

Make allowance for each other's faults, and forgive anyone who offends you. Remember, the Lord forgave you, so you must forgive others.

COLOSSIANS 3:13

HAVE YOU EVER PLAYED the middleman in a relationship? This is when you're on friendly terms with two individuals who are at odds with each other, and you're stuck in between them, trying to make peace.

Awkward.

This is the situation the apostle Paul found himself in as he wrote a letter to a good Christian friend named Philemon living in Colossae. At the time, Paul was under house arrest in Rome (Acts 28:16). During his two years there (Acts 28:30) Paul met a fugitive slave named Onesimus, who was on the run after stealing from his master, and led him to faith in Christ (Philemon 1:10).

Guess who Onesimus's master was . . . yep, Philemon! He, too, likely was converted through Paul's ministry (verse 19).

Do you see the remarkable providence of God at work? Paul certainly did! In verse 15, he wrote to Philemon, "It seems you lost Onesimus for a little while so that you could have him back forever."

Wanting reconciliation between the two men, Paul sent his letter (now a New Testament book) before encouraging Onesimus to return to Philemon. Paul graciously offered to pay Philemon for anything that Onesimus owed. Most of all, Paul entreated Philemon to welcome Onesimus back "both as a man and as a brother in the Lord" (verse 16), not as a slave.

What's It Mean?

The gospel of Jesus Christ transforms relationships. First, it miraculously changes our relationship with God from his "enemies" (Romans 5:10) to "dear children" (Ephesians 5:1) through Christ's reconciliatory work on the cross.

As recipients of divine reconciliation, Christians are called to show God's kindness at every opportunity. Having been loved and forgiven so much by God, we should never withhold love and forgiveness from others. That's the message of Paul's letter to Philemon—a powerful word that we still need today.

Has someone wronged you? Is there a damaged relationship in your life that needs reconciliation? Using the gospel as your model, seek out that person in gentleness and love to restore what's broken. As today's verse says, forgive them as God has forgiven you through Jesus.

It's not always easy, but God has called his children to unity, not division. Be quick to reconcile!

Now What?

If someone has offended you, don't wait for them to approach you—graciously start the conversation with them (Matthew 18:15-17).

Did You Know?

- The Bible doesn't say whether Philemon followed Paul's pastoral advice. We can only hope he did!

NOVEMBER 17

*He is the radiance of the glory of God and the exact imprint of his
nature, and he upholds the universe by the word of his power.*

HEBREWS 1:3, ESV

WHEN YOU PICTURE JESUS in your mind, what do you see?

- A baby in a manger?
- A poor carpenter's son?
- A man filled with compassion toward society's outcasts?
- A powerful teacher?
- A great worker of miracles?
- A man unjustly condemned to suffer the horrible death of crucifixion?

During his Incarnation, Jesus was all these things. Each of those
descriptions shed light on just a small part of his earthly experience. But he's
so much more.

Today's verse gives us a fascinating window into the full scope of Jesus'
true nature, helping us form a proper perspective of Christ.

What's It Mean?

From its first verse, the Bible is clear: God created the universe. But today's
verse is critically important because it ascribes to Jesus *the exact same divinity, authority, and ruling power as God the Father*. In other words, it boldly
declares Jesus is the Lord over all creation.

Yes, Jesus is the crucified and risen Savior. But he is also the eternal
Lord of heaven and earth—the divine Agent through whom the Father created and upholds the whole universe!

The apostle Paul elaborates on this in Colossians 1:15-19:

He is the image of the invisible God, the firstborn of all creation.
For by him, all things were created, in heaven and on earth,
visible and invisible, whether thrones or dominions or rulers or

authorities—all things were created through him and for him. And he is before all things, and in him all things hold together. And he is the head of the body, the church. He is the beginning, the firstborn from the dead, that in everything, he might be preeminent. For in him all the fullness of God was pleased to dwell (ESV).

Don't underestimate Jesus. Worship and adore him for who he really is: the Lord of all creation!

Now What?

To get a glimpse of Jesus' full post-resurrection glory, read the following passages: Matthew 17:1-8; Acts 9:3; 26:13; and Revelation 1:12-16.

Did You Know?

The title "firstborn of all creation" (Colossians 1:15, ESV) does not mean Jesus was God's firstborn child physically. That would be heretical and inconsistent with the rest of Scripture. Paul was using metaphor—alluding to ancient inheritance privileges that a monarch would bestow on his son—to show the honor that God the Father gives to the Son. But when every tongue confesses that "Jesus Christ is Lord," Jesus will ensure that all worship ultimately gets directed "to the glory of God the Father" (Philippians 2:11).

NOVEMBER 18

Since we have a great High Priest who has entered heaven,
Jesus the Son of God, let us hold firmly to what we believe.

HEBREWS 4:14

FROM THE TIME OF THE EXODUS from Egypt to the destruction of the
second Temple—approximately 1,300 to 1,500 years (depending on when
you date the Exodus)—the Jewish high priest held a very important position
in ancient Israel. High priests were the nation's spiritual leaders, interceding
for the sins of the people before God.

They had many specific duties, the most important of which was the
annual Day of Atonement ceremony when they made special sacrifices
for the nation and for the Tabernacle itself, making it possible for a holy
God to remain present among unclean people. This was the only day of
the year when the high priest would enter into the Most Holy Place of the
Tabernacle/Temple.

When Jesus came, he became our great High Priest through his once-
for-all sacrifice on the cross and guaranteed a "better covenant with God"
(Hebrews 7:22) than the Old Testament covenant of laws and sacrifices.
Most of the book of Hebrews is dedicated to exploring the glories of Jesus'
eternal high priesthood.

Let's take a look at this marvelous reality.

What's It Mean?

As Hebrews 7:23-25 says,

> There were many priests under the old system, for death prevented
> them from remaining in office. But because Jesus lives forever, his
> priesthood lasts forever. Therefore he is able, once and forever,
> to save those who come to God through him. He lives forever to
> intercede with God on their behalf.

As our eternal High Priest, here's what Jesus has done and continues to do for all believers:

- secured propitiation for us, turning God's wrath toward us into favor through his perfect sacrifice for our sins (Hebrews 2:17; for more on propitiation, see the September 21 devotion)
- helps us in our trials since he has endured indescribable suffering (Hebrews 2:18)
- sympathizes with our weaknesses (Hebrews 4:15)
- allows us to "come boldly to the throne of our gracious God" in prayer (Hebrews 4:16)
- sanctifies us continually so we can grow in godliness (Hebrews 10:14)
- assures us that we are righteous before God based on his sacrifice (Hebrews 10:22)
- motivates us to gather together often with other believers, show Christian love, and do good work until Christ's return (Hebrews 10:24-25)

And that's just a small glimpse of what Jesus does for us. We have an amazing, eternal High Priest who always intercedes for us at the Father's right hand!

Now What?
Read the book of Hebrews.

Did You Know?
While many biblical authors identify themselves, the author of Hebrews is anonymous.

646

NOVEMBER 19

It is impossible to please God without faith.

HEBREWS 11:6

FOR MOST OF ANCIENT HISTORY, the majority of human civilizations believed in a higher power. More often than not, cultures that didn't believe in the one true God of the Bible believed in a deity or pantheon of deities that governed the universe.

But in the seventeenth and eighteenth centuries, a powerful movement swept through Europe. It challenged longstanding views about humanity, nature, science, psychology, ethics, and more. Human reasoning and philosophy came to the forefront.

People began questioning well-established religious beliefs and timeless truths about God. Atheism—the belief that God doesn't exist—became much more popular. This was a very humanistic age, focusing on the accomplishments and potential of mankind.

We now refer to this period as the Age of Enlightenment, which is bitterly ironic since any culture or era that strays from a biblical worldview is anything *but* enlightened. On the contrary, minimizing God's active presence in the universe or outright denying his existence is the epitome of spiritual blindness.

This unenlightened skepticism is thriving today. Spiritual matters seem preposterous to many people because they can't be measured or quantified. If people can't see it, they don't believe in it.

Christians, though, are called to be different. They are called to live by faith.

What's It Mean?

Hebrews 11:1 says, "Faith is the assurance of things hoped for, the conviction of things not seen" (ESV). In other words, faith is believing without seeing.

Atheists say there is no God because there is no empirical evidence—facts that can be verified and observed—to prove his existence. The Bible disputes this. Romans 1:19-20 says that the majesty of creation itself is clear evidence that God exists, and because of it, people "have no excuse for not knowing God" (verse 20).

All the while, we are called to have faith. The Christian life is one of trusting more than what our eyes can see, math can measure, or science can reveal. In the New Testament alone, there are around 250 references to the word "faith." Consider this sampling:

- We are made right with God by placing our *faith* in Jesus Christ. (Romans 3:22)
- You are all children of God through *faith* in Christ Jesus. (Galatians 3:26)
- By grace you have been saved through *faith*. (Ephesians 2:8, ESV)

Want true enlightenment? Have faith in your Creator!

Now What?
For more great verses on faith, check out Romans 1:17; Romans 4:5; and Galatians 2:16.

Did You Know?
Deism, the unscriptural belief that a supreme Being created the universe but has let it run itself according to natural laws ever since, surfaced during the Age of Enlightenment.

NOVEMBER 20

Count it all joy, my brothers, when you meet trials of various kinds.

JAMES 1:2, ESV

HAVE YOU EVER BROKEN your leg and exclaimed, "What fun I'm having!"?

Have you ever endured teasing from others and said, "Wow, this is great! I hope every day is like this!"?

Have you ever survived a tornado, earthquake, avalanche, tsunami, volcanic eruption, wildebeest stampede, and a neighbor's very territorial Chihuahua—all on the same day—and remarked afterward, "Yippee! Let's do it again tomorrow!"?

No, of course not! That would be ridiculous.

This is all hyperbole, of course, but hopefully, you get the point: life's trials aren't pleasant, and nobody wants to go through them. How, then, are we supposed to understand today's verse, which says we are to count trials as "all joy"?

Is that a typo?

What's It Mean?

No, that's not an error. God's Word is perfectly true (Proverbs 30:5). It's really possible to view trials as "all joy." But how? It sounds counterintuitive to our human instincts, which are to avoid hardships and seek comfort and serenity in life at all costs.

The reality is, we live in a fallen world, and trials are a part of life. For the next eight days, we're going to look at what Scripture says about trials and how we should walk through them.

If you are a Christian, you can navigate the challenges of life much differently than the world does. But some context is needed. Look at James 1:2-4:

Count it all joy, my brothers, when you meet trials of various kinds, for you know that the testing of your faith produces steadfastness.

And let steadfastness have its full effect, that you may be perfect and complete, lacking in nothing (ESV).

Christians can count trials as "all joy" because trials are designed—yes, designed—for our spiritual growth. Trials might feel like random and arbitrary events to us, but not to God. He sovereignly ordains our lives (Proverbs 16:9). If you are a believer, he uses everything that happens in your life—both positive and negative—for your ultimate good (Romans 8:28).

We will discuss these things more over the coming days. You probably have more questions about trials and God's sovereignty. But for now, may you trust in the Lord who perfectly rules over all things, including the difficulties of your life.

Now What?

Read these other passages on trials and suffering: Romans 5:3-5; Hebrews 10:32-39; 1 Peter 1:6-7; and 1 Peter 4:12-19.

Did You Know?

We must be careful to differentiate between trials and temptations to sin. God never tempts anyone to sin (James 1:13).

NOVEMBER 21

Count it all joy, my brothers, when you
meet trials of various kinds.

JAMES 1:2, ESV

SO...

You're experiencing a trial in life. Perhaps it's a significant one. Maybe it has dragged on endlessly. You know James 1:2 says to consider it "all joy." But you don't know how to do that. It seems incongruous to be happy about something that causes so much pain. So you're left wondering . . .

Now what?

What's It Mean?

First, take heart! God is not a God of contradictions, but a God of order, sovereignty, power, and love! He cares about you and the challenges you're facing (1 Peter 5:7).

Still, joy in trials sounds so paradoxical, right? But don't miss the beautiful spiritual truth in James 1:2-4 and other related Scriptures: the joy we can experience in trials comes from knowing that God is sanctifying us to be like Jesus.

A Christian's joy is not a fleeting happiness, like the pleasure you get when you eat a candy bar or the thrill of a ninety-second roller-coaster ride. No, biblical joy is a deep, abiding peace and satisfaction rooted in the hope of our eternal union with Christ.

Look also at Romans 5:3-5, which bears similarities to James 1:2-4:

We can rejoice, too, when we run into problems and trials, for we know that they help us develop endurance. And endurance develops strength of character, and character strengthens our confident hope of salvation. And this hope will not lead to disappointment. For we know how dearly God loves us, because he has given us the Holy Spirit to fill our hearts with his love.

Do you see the marvelous progression of sanctification for all believers? God uses life's hardships to develop righteous character traits in us—such as endurance, strength of character, and hope—so that we "will be perfect and complete" (James 1:4).

God's goal for his children is that we would worship him, reflect his image, proclaim his name, and become more like his Son as we prepare for eternity with him. Until that day, he wonderfully uses everything in this life—including trials—to complete our spiritual refining process.

Therefore, we can consider it "all joy" when suffering comes. The trial itself isn't fun. But we can rejoice that God is lovingly shaping us into his image, all for our good!

Now What?

Are you currently experiencing a trial? Prayer is one of your greatest tools—use it often!

Did You Know?

God never promises to explain why trials happen, but he is "close to the brokenhearted" and "rescues those whose spirits are crushed" (Psalm 34:18).

NOVEMBER 22

We know that God causes everything to work together for the good of those who love God and are called according to his purpose for them.

ROMANS 8:28

HARDSHIPS ARE INEVITABLE in a fallen world. If you aren't going through any now, you will one day. That's not cynicism. It's just reality in a sinful world.

But there's a thorny question that lingers. It's one that every human has asked since the dawn of time . . . and no, it's not, "That small caramel frappé costs *how much*?"

The question is, "How can a loving God allow bad things to happen to good people?" In fact, a slightly rephrased version of the question—"Why do bad things happen to good people?"—entered into an Internet search engine will produce nearly two billion results.

Clearly, it's a popular and fascinating question. But there are erroneous assumptions we must address to reach a biblically based conclusion.

So grab your overpriced flavored coffee, and let's dive in!

What's It Mean?

First, we must dispel the notion of "good people" in that question. What's the definition of "good," and who is the arbiter of that? Jesus told the rich young ruler in Luke 18:19, "No one is good except God alone" (ESV). Don't assume God is somehow wrongfully burdening exceptionally upstanding citizens with undue trouble. That's a deeply flawed misunderstanding of God's character and human nature.

Our rebellion against God plunged his perfect creation into its current state—a world of great beauty that also bears sin's terrible scars, which manifest into hardships and adversities (Genesis 3:1-19; Romans 8:18-23). Ultimately, we have no one to blame but ourselves for the trials of life.

Scripture, in fact, consistently bears witness to a far more magnificent viewpoint. Yes, bad things happen to people—even terrible, unexplainably awful tragedies. But in his divine sovereignty, mercy, and love, our loving

Creator takes the wretched consequences of sin and "causes everything to work together for the good of those who love God and are called according to his purpose for them," as today's verse says.

In his mysterious wisdom, God allows us to endure trials. But Christians can consider them "all joy" because we know they are ultimately for our spiritual good. The Lord flips the script on sin's curse out of his great love for us!

Now What?

Prayerfully thank God that he sovereignly ordains a good purpose in the trials of all believers.

Did You Know?

James 1:12 tells us that "God blesses those who patiently endure testing" by blessing them with "the crown of life" in eternity.

NOVEMBER 23

*The Lord hears the cries of the needy; he does
not despise his imprisoned people.*

PSALM 69:33

ALL SEEMED LOST.

David felt like he was going to die. Israel's great king sensed the darkness closing in on all sides. So he expressed his anguish with vivid imagery in Psalm 69:

> Save me, O God, for the floodwaters are up to my neck. Deeper
> and deeper I sink into the mire; I can't find a foothold. I am in deep
> water, and the floods overwhelm me. I am exhausted from crying
> for help; my throat is parched. My eyes are swollen with weeping,
> waiting for my God to help me.
>
> VERSES 1-3

Over the last three days, we've been discussing trials. But there are varying degrees of trials. What David was describing in Psalm 69 is not garden-variety adversity. His experiences touched the depths of his soul.

Have you ever experienced a trial of this intensity? Here are some examples:

- a lengthy battle with poor health
- terminal illness in a friend
- prolonged, physical persecution for one's faith
- the challenges of extended poverty
- a fire or natural disaster that destroys a home
- the death of a family member
- a broken home
- the horrors of abuse

What's It Mean?

There are no easy answers for these kinds of devastating hardships, or others like them. If we're not careful, our hearts can quickly turn from cries of

"How long, O Lord?" to "Why are you doing this to me, God?" Do you see the subtle, yet sinister, shift from a prayer for help to an accusation against God's righteous character? That's why, in moments of despair, we must always turn to God's Word to inform our thoughts.

Sadly, the aftereffects of the Fall—sin, sickness, suffering, and death—will eventually touch us all. But these things don't alter God's unchanging character. In fact, if we have eyes of faith, we'll see how they reveal God's holiness more powerfully.

In the midst of your darkest trials, never doubt God's goodness, sovereignty, or his love for you. He loves his children immeasurably (Psalm 103:11). He "heals the brokenhearted and bandages their wounds" (Psalm 147:3).

Remember David? Despite his dire circumstances, all was not lost! He knew God would be faithful. That's why David wrote today's verse: "The Lord hears the cries of the needy; he does not despise his imprisoned people."

He will do the same for you.

Now What?
Cry out to the Lord in your time of need. He wants to hear from you.

Did You Know?
The Psalms are filled with cries of distress to God (e.g., Psalms 6, 7, 13, 18, 42, 77, 102, and 142).

NOVEMBER 24

Who is this that questions my wisdom with such ignorant words?

JOB 38:2

REMEMBER OUR BUDDY JOB?

As we continue our study of life's trials, it's only natural to turn our attention to this remarkable man of faith and perseverance. No other person in Scripture is more associated with extreme adversity than he is.

As you recall from the April 30 devotion, Job was "a man of complete integrity" (Job 1:1), but God allowed Satan to inflict terrible hardships upon him, including the loss of his exceeding wealth, his ten children, and his health. As Job wrestled with his plight, he asked God why he was even born (10:18) and accused God of wronging him (19:6).

Finally, God answered Job from a mighty whirlwind. He asked Job a series of pointed rhetorical questions, such as today's verse: "Who is this that questions my wisdom with such ignorant words?" The implication was that Job—as a small, created being—had no right to question the Creator's governance of the universe. The fact that God also never provides any reasons for Job's trials is significant.

What's It Mean?

God never wishes evil on his children. He is not sadistic or capricious in his dealings with mankind. He does not delight in our hardships.

But God sometimes allows us to endure evil. Why? God usually doesn't reveal this to us. There is great mystery here that exceeds our finite human comprehension.

When discussing human trials, we need to remember the difference between God's "revealed will" and his "hidden will." (See the May 13 devotion.) There are many things in life—including our trials—that God has chosen to keep hidden (Deuteronomy 29:29).

As in Job's case, God doesn't owe us any answers. In fact, God doesn't owe us anything. Whatever God reveals to us—especially his love for us through Christ—is a gift of his grace. When you acknowledge that, your trials won't magically disappear or become weirdly fun, but you will find them easier to deal with as you rest in God's providence.

What's more, you can always trust in God's love, righteousness, and wisdom. He always does what's best for you (Romans 8:28), and he uses trials to strengthen your faith (James 1:2-4).

Knowing that, you can echo Job's words in Job 42:3: "You asked, 'Who is this that questions my wisdom with such ignorance?' It is I—and I was talking about things I knew nothing about, things far too wonderful for me."

Now What?
When you endure a trial, ask God for wisdom, strength, and endurance, but never question his goodness.

Did You Know?
Ezekiel (14:14) and James (5:11) wrote about Job, showing that he was a real person, not an allegorical figure.

NOVEMBER 25

O Lord, I am calling to you. Please hurry!
Listen when I cry to you for help!

PSALM 141:1

WHAT DO YOU DO when the trials of life overwhelm you?

Do you roll up your sleeves and try to meet the trials head-on? Do you seek a distraction or a way to anesthetize the pain? Do you give into anxiety or fear? Do you isolate yourself from others?

Do you ever cry out to God?

What's It Mean?

As we continue our eight-day study on biblically handling life's trials, it's imperative to understand this truth: God *wants* you to cry out to him in your suffering. First Peter 5:7 says, "Give all your worries and cares to God, for he cares about you." This is a step of obedience, faith, and spiritual growth.

Scripture is filled with anguished cries to God. Besides today's verse, here are a few examples from the book of Psalms:

- O Lord, how long will you forget me? Forever? How long will you look the other way? How long must I struggle with anguish in my soul, with sorrow in my heart every day? (13:1-2)
- O God, listen to my cry! Hear my prayer! From the ends of the earth, I cry to you for help when my heart is overwhelmed. (61:1-2)
- From the depths of despair, O Lord, I call for your help. Hear my cry, O Lord. Pay attention to my prayer. (130:1-2)

God doesn't expect you to enjoy your trial. You don't have to put on a plastic smile and pretend to love suffering. That's disingenuous. Some of the Bible's godliest examples of faith amid sorrow—such as Job, Hannah, David, and Paul—beseeched God to remove their hardships. Even Jesus cried out to the Father in the garden of Gethsemane (Luke 22:44).

When you call out to God, you're not telling him anything he doesn't already know. He has ordained everything in your life. Your prayers are for your benefit, not his. He's omniscient! Rather, your prayers build *your* faith. They help you trust God in the dark times. They help you rely on someone other than yourself.

So cry out to your heavenly Father. Call for help to the one who created you, loves you, and sent his Son to die for you. He will answer!

Now What?

Remember: when you cry out to God during hardship, never point an accusatory finger at him, as if he is somehow wronging you.

Did You Know?

Need more proof that you can cry out to God during trials? The twenty-fifth book of the Bible is called Lamentations!

NOVEMBER 26

This High Priest of ours understands our weaknesses, for he
faced all of the same testings we do, yet he did not sin.

HEBREWS 4:15

WHEN LIFE'S TRIALS FEEL like a blistering desert, with no relief in
sight, is it best to search for an oasis alone? When you navigate turbulent
waters, should you row the boat by yourself? When you enter gloomy forests
that seem to obscure all light, is it best to travel without a companion?

No, of course not. Humans were meant to live in community with each
other, not isolation. This is especially true as we endure hardships.

As we continue our series on life's trials, we turn our attention to someone who can truly empathize with all our weaknesses—in a way that no
mere human can. He is your best ally. He is your greatest hope.

His name is Jesus.

What's It Mean?

Hebrews, more than any other book in Scripture, provides great insight
into why God's Son is so uniquely qualified to help us endure trials. Look at
Hebrews 4:14-16:

Since we have a great High Priest who has entered heaven, Jesus
the Son of God, let us hold firmly to what we believe. This High
Priest of ours understands our weaknesses, for he faced all of the
same testings we do, yet he did not sin. So let us come boldly to the
throne of our gracious God. There we will receive his mercy, and we
will find grace to help us when we need it most.

During his time on earth, Jesus endured physical deprivation, sleepless
nights, emotional burdens, and severe rejection. Adversity was his shadow,
and struggle was his companion. In every way, God's Son perfectly comes
alongside us during our distress. (See today's verse and Hebrews 2:17.)

But Jesus' love and compassion for us goes far beyond familiarity with our daily challenges. Hebrews refers to Jesus as our "High Priest" because, through the Cross, he perfectly fulfilled the Old Testament high priestly role of representing God's people and atoning for their sins. He endured indescribable suffering for our salvation.

Our trials don't compare with what Jesus went through for our sake—not even close. Yet he doesn't minimize our sufferings; he empathizes with us. He wants to bear our burdens (Matthew 11:28-30).

Praise God that, in his Son, we have a great High Priest who understands all our weaknesses and perfectly represents us before the Father through his atoning sacrifice!

Now What?

Read Isaiah 42:3 to see how gently Jesus treats those who are suffering.

Did You Know?

· Hebrews 12:2 is a great example of persevering through adversity while focusing on future hope.

NOVEMBER 27

He comforts us in all our troubles so that we can comfort others.

2 CORINTHIANS 1:4

IF YOU'VE LEARNED HOW to drive a car, your driving instructor (hopefully!) taught you an important rule: don't just focus on what's immediately ahead of you; look farther down the road.

Young motorists are often guilty of nearsighted driving—not looking much farther than their car's hood ornament. This is dangerous: nearsighted drivers won't see the road hazard in the distance . . . until it's too late. Being aware of your surroundings makes you a better driver.

A similar principle applies to us as we navigate the trials of life. We've spent a great deal of time focusing on how to walk through adversity in a God-glorifying manner—and rightfully so. Hardships affect us all.

But there's an aspect of enduring trials that we often neglect: thinking of others. Look at the fascinating words of 2 Corinthians 1:3-4:

> God is our merciful Father and the source of all comfort. He comforts us in all our troubles so that we can comfort others. When they are troubled, we will be able to give them the same comfort God has given us.

Using the adversity we experience to bless others? For many of us, that's a spiritual U-turn.

What's It Mean?

By nature, we are self-centered people. We can get so wrapped up in our own lives. It's especially easy to do when we are suffering. However, our trials are not all about us. In his divine wisdom, God has designed them both for our spiritual good and for the benefit of others.

The Lord wants us to use everything we learn from our hardships—the spiritual comfort we receive, the wisdom we attain, the faith that is built up—to encourage others. Today's verse exhorts us to shed a nearsighted view of our trials and embrace a more expansive, outward-focused mentality.

Has God worked mightily in your trials? Has he shone his marvelous light into the darkness you've experienced? Tell others about the comfort you've received from him. Be a beacon of gospel-centered hope.

In this way, you will be like a seasoned driver, aware not only of what is immediately ahead of you, but also of your greater surroundings—like those hurting around you.

Now What?

Read Romans 12:15; Galatians 6:2; and Proverbs 17:17 to learn more about how to put today's principle into practice.

Did You Know?

Maybe your trial is so dark that you can't give encouragement to others right now. That's okay. Just remember that God wants to bring you to a place where you eventually can testify about his gracious comfort.

NOVEMBER 28

*Don't just listen to God's word. You must do what it
says. Otherwise, you are only fooling yourselves.*

JAMES 1:22

ADMIT IT . . .

When you wake up, you've got plenty of work to do on yourself from
the neck up. Hey, it happens to the best of us. Sleep takes a heavy toll.

First, you've got to rub Mr. Sandman out of your sagging eyes. A tissue
or two might help your nose. Even if your mouth *looks* okay, it tastes like
death. Then, you've got to deal with the facial creases from your pillow that
make it seem as though you barely survived a back alley knife fight. And oh,
the bed head!

Looking in the mirror after waking up can be a real comedy show. You
would never walk away from it without improving yourself, right?

This is exactly the point of James 1:22-25.

What's It Mean?

As a New Testament author, the apostle James wrote in a beautifully
straightforward manner, providing practical insight to live out one's faith on
a daily basis. Take James 1:22-25 for example:

> Don't just listen to God's word. You must do what it says.
> Otherwise, you are only fooling yourselves. For if you listen to the
> word and don't obey, it is like glancing at your face in a mirror. You
> see yourself, walk away, and forget what you look like. But if you
> look carefully into the perfect law that sets you free, and if you do
> what it says and don't forget what you heard, then God will bless
> you for doing it.

God's Word acts like a mirror for our hearts. It shows who we truly
are—our spiritual strengths and weaknesses. It also reveals who God is, what
we truly believe about him, and where we need to grow in our theology.

Just like you don't walk away from your bathroom mirror unchanged in the morning (at least hopefully not!), don't walk away from the mirror of God's Word unchanged. Consider these questions:

- Do you go to Sunday worship services just to mark off a spiritual checklist or to worship God?
- Do you attend weekday Bible study gatherings because it's "what you're supposed to do," or because you want to grow in your faith?
- Do you prayerfully enter your devotional times with God seeking to hear from him, or are you simply going through the motions?
- Don't merely be a hearer of God's Word—be a doer!

Now What?

Whenever you read God's Word, pray for God's Spirit to speak to your heart.

Did You Know?

James was the earthly brother of Jesus. He also led the early church in Jerusalem before being martyred in AD 62.

NOVEMBER 29

If you claim to be religious but don't control your tongue,
you are fooling yourself, and your religion is worthless.

JAMES 1:26

WITH ITS HOT, DRY CLIMATE spanning the summer/fall months and large forested areas, much of California is a prime target for devastating wildfires. Worst of all, the deadliest infernos can start from the smallest sparks.

On July 23, 2018, a recreational trailer's tire blew out as it was traveling on State Route 299 near Redding in Northern California. A few sparks flew over the guardrails and into some dry brush, igniting what quickly became a full-fledged blaze. The Carr Fire, as it was named, eventually killed eight people, consumed more than 229,000 acres, and destroyed nearly 1,100 homes over the span of thirty-nine days.

Tragically, that was just the beginning of California's catastrophic 2018. Over the next four months, four other major wildfires ravaged various parts of America's most populous state, burning hundreds of thousands of acres, destroying thousands of homes, and killing at least one hundred people.

A few fiery sparks can cause incomprehensible damage, both literally and metaphorically. This was the apostle James's message in James 3:1-12. Look at verses 5-6:

> A tiny spark can set a great forest on fire. And among all the parts of the body, the tongue is a flame of fire. It is a whole world of wickedness, corrupting your entire body. It can set your whole life on fire, for it is set on fire by hell itself.

We must take this powerful portion of Scripture to heart.

What's It Mean?

When it comes to human relationships, our words hold enormous power. They can praise, encourage, equip, and restore. Yet they can also cause untold amounts of destruction, like a wildfire indiscriminately scorching everything in its path. As James says, too often we praise God one minute, then slander people made in God's image the next. This is hypocritically wicked (James 3:9-10).

How can such evil come from a Christian's mouth? Jesus gets to the heart of the matter—literally—in Matthew 12:34: "Whatever is in your heart determines what you say." If your heart is filled with anger and bitterness, your speech will reflect it. If your heart is controlled by God's love, joy, and peace, your speech will reflect that instead.

Your mouth can be a destructive inferno or a wellspring of encouragement. Which will yours be?

Now What?
Be on the lookout daily for ways to encourage others with your words.

Did You Know?
Jesus also said everyone "must give an account on judgment day for every idle word you speak" (Matthew 12:36). Sobering words!

NOVEMBER 30

Faith by itself isn't enough. Unless it produces
good deeds, it is dead and useless.

JAMES 2:17

WHEN YOU GET A WILD NEW HAIRCUT, start working out at the
gym, lose weight, or do something else to drastically change your appearance, people typically comment on your new look, right?

It's easy to recognize external change because everyone can see it. But
what about *internal* change? That's harder to detect unless there's outward
evidence of your inner transformation.

This was the crux of the apostle James's important—and often
misunderstood—passage in James 2:14-26. Here is a portion of it (verses
14-17):

> What good is it, dear brothers and sisters, if you say you have
> faith but don't show it by your actions? Can that kind of faith save
> anyone? Suppose you see a brother or sister who has no food or
> clothing, and you say, "Good-bye and have a good day; stay warm
> and eat well"—but then you don't give that person any food or
> clothing. What good does that do? So you see, faith by itself isn't
> enough. Unless it produces good deeds, it is dead and useless.

Let's take a closer look at this wonderfully practical passage.

What's It Mean?

Over the centuries, many people have mistakenly believed James to be advocating a doctrine of "salvation by works," or "faith plus works"—both of
which would contradict the rest of Scripture. Nothing could be further from
the truth. James is merely saying that a Christian's good deeds are external
evidence of an inner transformation.

Good works are not needed for salvation in any way. The Bible is explicit
about this. Romans 3:23-25 says, "All have sinned and fall short of the glory

of God, *and are justified by his grace as a gift*, through the redemption that is in Christ Jesus, whom God put forward as a propitiation by his blood, to be received by faith" (ESV, emphasis added). Our good works are not a *means to* salvation, but rather a *product of* it. (See also Ephesians 2:8-10.)

James's point was simple: if your Christianity is real, it should be evident in the way you live. Your good works should prove your faith, joyfully flowing from a heart that loves the Lord and wants to serve him.

(As for that wild new haircut . . . well, you'd better talk to your parents.)

Now What?
Read James 2:14-26. Also see Matthew 7:15-20 and John 14:15.

Did You Know?
Martin Luther, the great Protestant Reformation leader, denounced James's letter, calling it a "right strawy epistle compared to these others" in the preface to his New Testament translation. (We're going to respectfully disagree with the great theologian on that one!)

DECEMBER 1

What is causing the quarrels and fights among you? Don't
they come from the evil desires at war within you?

JAMES 4:1

WAR IS A TERRIBLY BRUTAL BUSINESS.

World War I, fought between 1914 and 1918, was history's first truly
global war. It officially involved nations from three continents (Europe,
Asia, and North America) and left approximately 8.5 million soldiers dead.
It was called "the war to end all wars."

That moniker lasted a whopping twenty-one years. In September 1939,
Nazi Germany invaded Poland and began World War II, which dwarfed
the previous world war in scope and carnage. Approximations vary, but
the National World War II Museum estimates the battle deaths at 15 million, the battle wounded at 25 million, and civilian deaths at 45 million
worldwide.

Wars wreak havoc on nations and on individual lives. So does sin.
That's why the apostle James combined the two for a powerful metaphor in
today's verse to describe what happens inside our hearts when we allow "evil
desires" to consume our relationships with others.

Just like war, the results can be devastating.

What's It Mean?

The human heart is a spiritual battleground. Sin, our powerful enemy,
has been entrenched in our hearts since the day we were born. It has built
a huge base—barbed-wire fences, booby traps, foxholes, bunkers, supply depots, airstrips, etc.—all with the goal of launching offensives. Don't
believe it? Read Romans 7.

When we quarrel and fight with others, it's easy to shift blame and
accuse others. But as today's verse says, the source of all this is the warring
nature of our sinful hearts. The animosity we experience in our relationships
is typically our selfishness, pride, anger, greed, unforgiveness, and lust bub-
bling to the surface.

But fear not! Every follower of Christ can win this war. Through his death and resurrection, God's Son broke the power of sin in every Christian's life. The enemy has not been destroyed yet. Dying pockets of sinful resistance still remain in your heart, tempting you to lob grenades of unkindness and fire missiles of hostility at others in your anger. But you can achieve victory over these dying vestiges as you pray, walk by the Spirit, and humble yourself.

Don't be a relational warmonger. Be a peacemaker!

Now What?
"Humble yourselves before God. Resist the devil, and he will flee from you. Come close to God, and God will come close to you" (James 4:7-8).

Did You Know?
The Civil War remains the deadliest conflict in US history, claiming the lives of nearly 498,332 military personnel. In comparison, US mortality figures reached 405,399 in WWII.

DECEMBER 2

We live with great expectation, and we have a priceless
inheritance—an inheritance that is kept in heaven for you,
pure and undefiled, beyond the reach of change and decay.

1 PETER 1:3-4

BILL GATES IS ROLLING IN DOUGH—and we're not talking about the stuff you bake bread with.

Gates, the cofounder and former chairman and CEO of computer software giant Microsoft, is one of the world's richest individuals, with an estimated net worth of $93.9 billion in 2018, according to *Forbes Magazine*. In 2016, he announced most of his vast fortune would be going to charity when he died, rather than to his three children—Jennifer, Rory, and Phoebe.

The inheritance of Gates's children will certainly be nothing to laugh at, but it probably won't compare to, say, what the Walton children—Jim, Alice, and Rob—inherited from their father, Sam, who bequeathed them control of the Walmart retail empire upon his death. In 2018, *Forbes* estimated each of Sam's children was worth an estimated $45 billion or so. Then there's billionaire investor Warren Buffett, who announced in 2014 that he would give his three children $2 billion each when he dies.

What's It Mean?

What would you do if you inherited billions of dollars? Your mind is probably spinning with ideas. But money fades quickly and never truly satisfies. Once you die, what good is it?

There is a far greater inheritance awaiting every true follower of Christ. As spiritually adopted sons and daughters of the living God, believers await an eternal, "priceless inheritance," as today's verse says—one that is infinitely beyond monetary value. This everlasting treasure doesn't change like the fluctuating stock market, cannot be stolen by thieves, and can't decay (Matthew 6:19-20).

An inheritance is material possessions that are passed down from one generation to another, typically upon death. It's something that is bequeathed because of familial relations.

Similarly, God will give the priceless inheritance of eternity only to those who are in his heavenly family, who have received the gift of salvation through faith in Christ. This inheritance won't be fully realized until we pass from this life to the next, ready to spend eternity with the Lord in the new heavens and new earth.

Are you living in "great expectation" of this inheritance? You should! Nothing in this world compares to it.

Now What?

Prayerfully meditate on the glorious eternal inheritance awaiting you in Christ Jesus using today's passage; 2 Timothy 4:8; 1 Peter 5:4; and Revelation 22:1–22:5.

Did You Know?

Good works cannot merit our "priceless inheritance." But Scripture frequently speaks about heavenly rewards that believers can store up through righteous deeds (Matthew 5:12; Matthew 6:1-6; 1 Corinthians 3:14; 2 Corinthians 5:10; 2 John 1:8).

DECEMBER 3

You are a chosen people. You are royal priests, a
holy nation, God's very own possession.

1 PETER 2:9

ABOUT EIGHT WEEKS after escaping Egyptian bondage, the Israelites
arrived at Mount Sinai. God summoned Moses up Mount Sinai and gave
him an incredible message for the people:

> You have seen what I did to the Egyptians. You know how I carried
> you on eagles' wings and brought you to myself. Now if you will obey
> me and keep my covenant, you will be my own special treasure from
> among all the peoples on earth; for all the earth belongs to me. And
> you will be my kingdom of priests, my holy nation.
>
> EXODUS 19:4-6

Wow!

This was sovereign, elective grace in action. After all, the Israelites were
nobody special. They were a ragtag collection of former slaves who had to be
rescued from four hundred years of captivity. They were weak and helpless—
homeless wanderers with no true purpose or identity.

God powerfully changed that with his gracious elective decree.

Some 1,300 to 1,500 years later (depending on when you date the
Exodus), the apostle Peter recalled Exodus 19:4-6 as he wrote a letter to a
network of churches in the Roman Empire:

> You are a chosen people. You are royal priests, a holy nation, God's
> very own possession. As a result, you can show others the goodness of
> God, for he called you out of the darkness into his wonderful light.
> "Once you had no identity as a people; now you are God's people.
> Once you received no mercy; now you have received God's mercy."
>
> I PETER 2:9-10

This good word is also for us today!

What's It Mean?

If you have placed your faith in Christ, you are part of God's "chosen people." You are one of his "royal priests, a holy nation, God's very own possession." There is no greater honor!

Like the Israelites, God has elected you, not *because* of anything special you've done, but *despite* your many faults. Now, he has empowered you through his Spirit to become part of a "holy nation"—his worldwide church.

Why?

Peter also answered that: so "you can show others the goodness of God, for he called you out of the darkness into his wonderful light." God wants you to testify about his life-changing power to others.

What are you waiting for?

Now What?

Do you know someone in spiritual darkness? Lovingly encourage them to come into God's "wonderful light"!

Did You Know?

To be God's "holy nation" means to be set apart from the world for the Lord's Kingdom purposes.

DECEMBER 4

While you are waiting for these things to happen, make every effort to be found living peaceful lives that are pure and blameless in his sight.

2 PETER 3:14

HAVE YOU EVER WON a championship in any sport? Finishing a season on top is exhilarating! Even as a fan, it's exciting to experience the thrill of victory through your favorite team.

Conversely, have you ever rooted for or played on a team that perpetually stinks? What a drag.

Nobody likes to lose. Everybody wants to be a winner.

In many ways, the letter of 2 Peter is like a contrast of two teams—one that follows God and receives an eternal reward (the winner) and one that chaotically rebels against him and receives eternal punishment (the loser).

Let's look at this fascinating letter.

What's It Mean?

The apostle Peter wrote his letter to first-century Christians who were surrounded by religious charlatans and destructive spiritual lies. Here's how Peter describes these dangerous false teachers:

- They teach heresy, including falsehoods about salvation. (2:1)
- They greedily exploit people for monetary gain. (2:3)
- They proudly scoff at the thought of supernatural creatures. (2:10)
- They love to indulge in evil pleasures in broad daylight. (2:13)
- Their desire for sin is never satisfied. (2:14)
- They are expert boasters. (2:18)
- They promise people freedom from the "rules" of Christianity, but actually enslave people to sin. (2:19)
- They mock the veracity of Jesus' second coming, living only for today. (3:4)

From this summary of 2 Peter 2:1–3:7, do you see a theme? In describing these wicked individuals, Peter portrays total spiritual chaos. In many ways, it sounds like the world we live in today.

What is the end for these rebels? Sadly, "they are being kept for the day of judgment, when ungodly people will be destroyed" (2 Peter 3:7).

Christians, on the other hand, are to live differently in light of our godly calling and Jesus' return. Peter says we are to do the following:

- be on our guard against false teachers (3:17)
- live "pure and blameless" lives (today's verse)
- pursue spiritual growth in Christ (3:18)
- joyfully anticipate our heavenly home (3:13)

Wow! Do you see the utter distinction between the two teams? In the Christian life, there's no chaos or disorder. There's only a patient, holy manner of living as we faithfully obey God and await the return of our Savior.

The choice of teams is before you. But let's be honest: there's no question which one you should pick. Choose the winning team!

Now What?
Read 2 Peter to learn more about how to live "pure and blameless" before God.

Did You Know?
Peter probably wrote this letter shortly before he was martyred (2 Peter 1:14; John 21:18-19).

DECEMBER 5

If we confess our sins to him, he is faithful and just to forgive
us our sins and to cleanse us from all wickedness.

1 JOHN 1:9

IMAGINE IF YOU WENT to visit some family members for a week and during the course of your visit, one of your cousins did the following to you:

- decided to nickname you "Captain Stinkypants"
- put worms in your cereal bowl
- kicked you in the shins ten times a day
- gave you a wet willy at the top of every hour
- asked you questions such as, "So what's life like on Mars?" or "Is it true that the leaders of your planet are planning to attack Earth next summer?"
- put rocks in your pillow
- sang "Rock-a-bye Baby" to you—very loudly—each night at bedtime

This, of course, is a bit ridiculous. But can you imagine if all this happened and your cousin never apologized or showed any remorse? That person would always remain your family member, but the relationship would be hindered, to say the least!

Confession and repentance are so important for the restoration of fellowship after we have sinned, both with other people and with God. That's what today's verse is driving at.

What's It Mean?

Scripture is quite clear: initial salvation from our sins requires confession/repentance and faith in Jesus (Mark 1:15). But the ongoing life of a Christian should be marked by confession, as well. This doesn't mean a believer can lose their salvation and needs to confess to "re-earn" it. Not at all. A Christian's sins don't alter his or her eternal position before God because of Christ's finished work on the cross (Romans 8:28-39).

But sin can still temporarily strain fellowship. That's why the principles of today's verse are crucial. When you sin, truly confess it to the Lord—not with a perfunctory exclamation of, "Sorry," but by naming your transgression, expressing genuine sorrow (2 Corinthians 7:10), and asking God to help you grow in righteousness.

When you do this, a wonderful promise awaits: "He is faithful and just to forgive us our sins and to cleanse us from all wickedness." For believers who have already experienced the justification from sin through Christ, this cleansing refers to the beautiful renewal of temporarily hindered fellowship that sin sometimes causes in our spiritual lives.

Aren't you glad God is a God who faithfully forgives, cleanses, and deeply desires unhindered fellowship with his children?

Now What?
Don't let unconfessed sin impede your relationships with God or others. Humble yourself and confess your sin today!

Did You Know?
Great examples of confession include Job 42:1-16; Psalm 51; Nehemiah 1; and Daniel 9:1-9.

DECEMBER 6

*Do not love this world nor the things it offers you, for when you
love the world, you do not have the love of the Father in you.*

1 JOHN 2:15

DO YOU LIKE LONG days at the beach, splashing in the surf, relaxing
in the sand, and soaking up the sun? Do you love camping, fishing, or
hiking—immersing yourself in the great outdoors where stress quickly fades
into the stillness of the woods and the hypnotic rhythms of a forest stream?
Do you relish sunrises, sunsets, thunderstorms, rainbows, or waterfalls? Do
you like to kayak, canoe, stargaze, explore new cities, walk in the park, visit
museums, or go to the zoo?

These are all ways we can enjoy God's marvelous creation.

But wait!

Hold the phone!

Stop the presses!

Red alert!

Switch to DEFCON 5!

Today's verse says, "Do not love this world nor the things it offers you."
If we enjoy these worldly things, are we in terrible spiritual mutiny?

No, not at all. We need to understand the difference between loving the
goodness of God's creation in a positive way and loving the world in a negative sense.

What's It Mean?

In 1 John 2:15-17, the apostle John writes the following:

Do not love this world nor the things it offers you, for when you
love the world, you do not have the love of the Father in you. For
the world offers only a craving for physical pleasure, a craving for
everything we see, and pride in our achievements and possessions.
These are not from the Father, but are from this world. And this

world is fading away, along with everything that people crave. But anyone who does what pleases God will live forever.

When John speaks of the "world," he's referring to the rebellious system of human and satanic powers that are opposed to God. We see this in government, entertainment, fashion, media, schools, and more. When ungodly people or institutions promote unbiblical ideas, values, and goals, this is "the world." John defines what the world offers in verse 16:

- a craving for physical pleasure
- a craving for everything we see
- pride in our achievements and possessions

These things might seem appealing at first, but in actuality, they are hollow and temporary—spiritually fatal dead ends. We would be wise to avoid them. Instead, "anyone who does what pleases God will live forever" (verse 17).

Now What?
We are all susceptible to worldly desires. Ask God to reveal your fleshly cravings, overcome them, and give you a heart for what pleases him.

Did You Know?
How do we know what pleases God? Meditating on Romans 12:2 is a good place to start!

DECEMBER 7

Don't be surprised, dear brothers and sisters, if the world hates you.

1 JOHN 3:13

ON FEBRUARY 7, 1964, Pan Am flight 101 from London landed at New York's John F. Kennedy Airport. Out stepped four young British musicians wearing mod suits and mop-top haircuts, instantly launching a pop-culture phenomenon that the world has never experienced since.

An estimated three thousand screaming fans were there to welcome the Beatles. Two days later, the band members—John Lennon, Paul McCartney, George Harrison, and Ringo Starr—performed on the *Ed Sullivan Show* before an estimated 73 million US television viewers, roughly 40 percent of the US population at the time.

"Beatlemania" had been born. The group would ultimately record a dozen-plus top-selling studio albums and a record twenty-one number-one singles on the "Billboard Hot 100" list before breaking up in 1970.

What's It Mean?

Popularity is a funny thing. For every wildly successful band like the Beatles, there are thousands that we never hear about.

Popularity isn't inherently a bad thing, but as Christians, it should never be our ultimate goal. Our main priority should be worshiping God and becoming more like Jesus.

What is popularity anyway? It's being liked or supported by others. It's the approval of man. If you are popular, you need to ask yourself, "Who am I popular with?" and "What am I popular for?" The answers might reveal a lot.

As today's verse says, followers of Christ should actually *expect* to be unpopular and hated by "the world"—sinful humanity that rejects God. If you fit in perfectly with the world, something is wrong. It likely means your faith isn't evident and you are undistinguishable from unbelievers.

When the apostle John wrote today's verse (likely around AD 85), he must have remembered Jesus' words shortly before his arrest in Gethsemane: "If the world hates you, remember that it hated me first. The world would love you as one of its own if you belonged to it, but you are no longer part of the world. I chose you to come out of the world, so it hates you." Those words affected John so deeply, he recorded them in his gospel fifty years later (John 15:18-19).

Jesus' words should also affect us. Don't run after worldly popularity. Be different from the world and follow Christ. And if you experience rejection for your faith, just remember, your Savior did too.

Now What?

Prayerfully evaluate if you are popular with the world or following Christ. Also consider asking a trusted adult or friend if you're chasing worldly popularity.

Did You Know?

After finishing his prearrest discourse, Jesus prayed for his disciples—and you! (See John 17:20-21.)

DECEMBER 8

If we don't love people we can see, how can we love God, whom we cannot see?

1 JOHN 4:20

HAVE YOU EVER SEEN a Chihuahua feeding worms to baby birds in a nest? Have you ever seen a tractor trailer taking flight as it rushes down an airport runway? Have you ever seen a newborn baby playing quarterback in the NFL?

No, of course not. That's absurd. All these things are completely incompatible with each other.

So is the idea of a Christian who hates someone else. Listen to the strong words of the apostle John in his first epistle:

If anyone claims, "I am living in the light," but hates a fellow believer, that person is still living in darkness.

1 JOHN 2:9

Anyone who hates another brother or sister is really a murderer at heart. And you know that murderers don't have eternal life within them.

1 JOHN 3:15

If someone says, "I love God," but hates a fellow believer, that person is a liar; for if we don't love people we can see, how can we love God, whom we cannot see? And he has given us this command: Those who love God must also love their fellow believers.

1 JOHN 4:20-21

John certainly didn't mince words!

What's It Mean?

In his first epistle, John spends a great deal of time talking about love. He uses the word "love" nearly fifty times. He talks about how "God is love" (1 John 4:8) and how we must love others.

The opposite of love, obviously, is hate, and John says those who claim to love God but hate others are "liars," "murderers at heart," and "living in darkness." There is simply no place for both in a believer's life.

It's one thing to get frustrated at someone else. That's natural in life. But we must be quick to extend forgiveness, never letting seeds of bitterness take root in our heart and blossom into full-blown jungles of hatred against others.

Examine your heart. As a Christian, loving God often comes easily, given all that he has done for us through his Son, Jesus Christ. But loving others isn't always as simple. It involves humility, patience, self-control, and sacrifice. To say "I love God" one moment but then in another moment spit venomous hatred (or even think it) toward someone made in his image is hypocritical.

May God help us to love him *and* love others!

Now What?

Read James 3:1-12 for a reminder on how to use our speech to show love, not hatred, toward others.

Did You Know?

God doesn't want us only to love "fellow believers." Our love should extend to everyone.

DECEMBER 9

I rejoiced greatly to find some of your children walking in the truth, just as we were commanded by the Father.

2 JOHN 1:4, ESV

HAVE YOU EVER TAKEN a walk on the beach at sunset? Few things in life are as relaxing. Have you ever walked in the park on a sunny afternoon? That's good, too! Have you ever taken a walk in the woods? Not a bad idea either—unless, of course, you're Little Red Riding Hood. (*Just stay on that path, Red.*)

Today's verse, from the letter known as 2 John, gives all Christians unique walking instructions. As Christ followers, we must be "walking in the truth, just as we were commanded by the Father." This is what the apostle John's entire letter is about.

Naturally, this leads to two questions: What is the truth, and how do we walk in it?

What's It Mean?

In a world filled with endless religions, ideologies, and opinions, it's crucial to understand that absolute truth exists—and Someone defines it for us. Jesus said, "I am the way, *the truth*, and the life. No one can come to the Father except through me" (John 14:6, emphasis added; see also the August 9–12 devotions). Likewise, in his "High Priestly Prayer," Jesus prayed the following to the Father for all believers: "Sanctify them in the truth; your word is truth" (John 17:17, ESV).

Truth, ultimately, comes from God, and he graciously reveals it to us through Jesus and Scripture. To walk in the truth is to obey God by trusting in Jesus and living in obedience to the Lord through his Word.

How do we do this on a daily basis? Here are three thoughts based on John's second epistle:

- **Love one another (verse 6).** This speaks to our relationship with others. When we joyfully sacrifice our needs for the good of others, we reflect God's character.

- **Be diligent so that you receive your full reward (verse 8).** This speaks to a lifetime of faithful obedience to God, as we seek his glory and the promise of eternal blessings in heaven.
- **Be someone who remains in the teaching of Christ (verse 9).** This speaks to a lifetime of faithful doctrine, exhorting us never to fall into disbelief, heresy, or rebellion.

Don't walk in darkness, lies, sin—or in the woods with big, bad wolves! Walk in the truth, just as God commanded us.

Now What?

Read Romans 1:18-32 to see a description of those who have "traded the truth of God for a lie" (verse 25).

Did You Know?

- John addressed his second epistle to "the chosen lady and to her children" (verse 1), likely code language for a church.

DECEMBER 10

*Do not imitate evil but imitate good. Whoever does good
is from God; whoever does evil has not seen God.*

3 JOHN 1:11, ESV

"Stop doing everything I do!"

"Why are you always imitating me?"

"Mom, tell him to stop being a copycat!"

When you were younger, did you ever say any of those things? Or did someone else say any of those things to you?

Of course. Every child experiences the copycat stage. On the annoying scale, copycatting generally falls somewhere between noogies and wet willies.

But doesn't the old axiom tell us that imitation is the sincerest form of flattery? Well, yes. But imitation has its limits. Take, for instance, our Christian lives. Imitation must be limited to what pleases God.

This is the main point of 3 John, the letter that the apostle John wrote to a friend named Gaius, who was part of a church (perhaps in ancient Asia Minor) that included a wicked man named Diotrephes. In 3 John 1:9-10, John warned Gaius that Diotrephes

loved to be the leader;

refused to have anything to do with them;

made evil accusations against them; and

refused to welcome the traveling teachers, told others not to help them, and when others did help, he put them out of the church.

John's message was clear: Diotrephes was bad news. Don't copycat Diotrephes!

What's It Mean?

John's third epistle was a specific letter to a specific church about a specific situation. But the message of today's verse found within his letter applies broadly to all Christians.

There are plenty of people like Diotrephes these days, both inside and outside the church. We are not to imitate them. Rather, we are to imitate what is good—in other words, exhibit godly characteristics.

This seems so simple, yet oftentimes it isn't. Bad influences can be beguiling. Diotrephes certainly didn't achieve his position of church authority by acting like a blatant jerk. More likely, he weaseled his way to power through cunning, manipulation, and self-serving friendships. And it seems like he tricked some people along the way.

This calls for wisdom on our part. Remember the words of Jesus in Matthew 7:20: "Just as you can identify a tree by its fruit, so you can identify people by their actions." Once you identify these individuals, steer clear. Imitation of those folks isn't flattery; it will only leave you spiritually flat!

Now What?

Prayerfully evaluate your friendships and the influences in your life. Also, ask a parent or trusted adult if you're imitating the wrong people.

Did You Know?

Many biblical scholars believe that John wrote all of his New Testament books between approximately AD 85–95.

DECEMBER 11

They told you that in the last times there would be scoffers whose purpose in life is to satisfy their ungodly desires. These people are the ones who are creating divisions among you.

JUDE 1:18-19

CAN YOU IMAGINE BEING an earthly sibling of the Lord Jesus Christ? Wow! Think of the stories you'd be able to tell.

This was the experience of Jude, the writer of the New Testament letter named after him. Interestingly, though, Jude didn't immediately believe in his older brother's divinity or messianic mission (Mark 3:21). Only later in life did he have faith that the man he grew up with in Mary and Joseph's household was actually the incarnate Son of God. What a revelation that must have been!

Eventually, Jude became a leader in the early church. By the time he wrote his New Testament letter, false teachers had started infiltrating the church. His letter is a powerful exhortation for believers to stay strong in the faith—advice that we would be wise to heed.

What's It Mean?

In many ways, today is no different than Jude's day. The "scoffers" with their "ungodly desires" and false teachings that he described in today's Scripture passage still abound. We must be careful to "defend the faith that God has entrusted once for all time to his holy people" (Jude 1:3).

How do we do this in the midst of so much devious, often subtle heresy that swirls around us? Jude lists three ways in verses 20-21:

- **Build each other up in your most holy faith.** We fight false teachers and destructive teaching by staying deeply rooted in a strong biblical church community with other believers (Hebrews 10:23-25).
- **Pray in the power of the Holy Spirit.** Through prayer, believers can approach the throne of God with confidence (Hebrews 4:16) as "we

use God's mighty weapons, not worldly weapons, to knock down the strongholds of human reasoning and to destroy false arguments" (2 Corinthians 10:4).

- **Await the mercy of our Lord Jesus Christ, who will bring you eternal life.** This is a call for perseverance as we anticipate the promised second coming of our Savior. Remaining confident in the hope of Christ's return and future glory helps us stay true to our earthly mission.

"In this way," Jude says in verse 21, "you will keep yourselves safe in God's love." Amen!

Now What?
Read the letter of Jude. (The doxology at the end is particularly awesome!)

Did You Know?
- Some popular belief systems, including Jehovah's Witnesses, Mormonism, Seventh Day Adventists, Universalism, and the "prosperity gospel," add to or subtract from the complete sufficiency of Christ's atoning work on the cross for our sins. Be aware of such false doctrine.

DECEMBER 12

While they were there, the time came for her to give birth.
And she gave birth to her firstborn son and wrapped
him in swaddling cloths and laid him in a manger,
because there was no place for them in the inn.

LUKE 2:6-7, ESV

THE BIG DAY IS COMING! The weekend roads are as full as your family's calendar, the local stores are buzzing, and radio stations are playing songs about reindeer, snowmen, and silver bells.

Christmas is almost here!

For the next two weeks, we're going to pause in our study of New Testament letters and focus on the birth of God's Son, Jesus Christ, and the wonderful spiritual truths found within his incarnation.

Look at today's Scripture passage. Maybe this is the first time you've read these verses. Maybe you've read them a hundred times. Either way, don't let the spiritual significance found within the manger pass you by. It can change your life!

What's It Mean?

During this time of the year, we are inundated with Christmas-themed messages. Retailers now start their holiday-themed songs and advertisements shortly after Halloween. Everywhere you go, it's Christmas, Christmas, Christmas!

If you have a church background, you've probably heard the story of Jesus' birth many times. But it should never grow old. It's too amazing! It's too important! It's too life-changing!

Why? Perhaps the angel who visited the shepherds outside Bethlehem that beautiful night said it best: because Jesus' birth was "good news that will bring great joy to all people. The Savior—yes, the Messiah, the Lord—has been born today in Bethlehem, the city of David!" (Luke 2:10-11).

In sending his Son into the world, God's love for us burst forth from the heavens and spilled to earth. "The armies of heaven" (Luke

2:13) erupted into song over this glorious news. God actually became man—incredible!

Why did he do this? Because we were lost in our sins. Because we desperately needed a Savior. Because God didn't want us to spend eternity without him.

That's why Mary marveled. That's why the shepherds celebrated. That's why the angels rejoiced.

That's why we should worship anew.

Jesus' birth is the greatest miracle in history. No matter how many times you've heard about it, let the wonder, majesty, and life-changing power of the Savior's birth amaze you again this Christmas!

Now What?

Read the first two chapters of Matthew and Luke at least once before Christmas Day.

Did You Know?

Mark and John's Gospels immediately jump into Jesus' adult ministry, skipping his birth account.

DECEMBER 13

The people who walk in darkness will see a great light. For those
who live in a land of deep darkness, a light will shine.

ISAIAH 9:2

WE ALL KNOW ABOUT nocturnal animals that become more active
at night. But did you know there are animals who exist in total darkness?
Creepy creatures such as the snipe eel, phantom anglerfish, and something
aptly called the black sea devil all live in environments completely void of
light. How depressing!

In the late eighth century BC, Isaiah spoke of *humans* living in this
wretched condition. This was all part of a larger prophecy of God's coming
judgment through Assyria against Israel, which had abandoned the Lord
and chosen to walk in spiritual darkness.

Amid Isaiah's gloomy message of imminent destruction, however, he
pronounced a message of hope—a message of light piercing through the
darkness.

What's It Mean?

The darkness Isaiah spoke about in today's verse, of course, was metaphorical. It's the darkness of spiritual blindness. It refers to someone who is in
willful rebellion against God, stumbling around in the morass of sin.

While some weird-looking deep-sea creatures are suited to live in total
darkness, humans are not. In darkness, we stagger, fall, take wrong paths,
incur injuries, and even die.

God's image-bearers were made to walk in the light. Yet sadly, many
people choose to live in the darkness. Sin blinds us to God's truth. Millions
choose to lurk in sin's shadows rather than bask in the life-changing glory
and transformative grace of the one who created them. John 3:19 says,
"God's light came into the world, but people loved the darkness more than
the light, for their actions were evil."

All this begs the question: How would people walking in spiritual darkness see the "great light," as Isaiah predicted? The prophet famously provides

the answer a few verses later: "A child is born to us, a son is given to us" (verse 6). The "great light" that pierces sin's darkness is the child who was born in Bethlehem—Jesus! Matthew confirmed this in his gospel (Matthew 4:12-17). Jesus testified of himself, "I am the light of the world. If you follow me, you won't have to walk in darkness, because you will have the light that leads to life" (John 8:12).

This is why God sent Jesus into the world—to break the power of darkness and bring us into the light of salvation. This Christmas, worship in the light of the Son!

Now What?

Read Isaiah 9:1-7 and Matthew 4:12-17 to see Isaiah's powerful messianic prophecy and how Jesus fulfilled it.

Did You Know?

· Light and darkness is a common biblical motif, extending back to Genesis 1.

DECEMBER 14

In the beginning the Word already existed. The Word
was with God, and the Word was God.

JOHN 1:1

WORDS ARE CRITICAL TO OUR LIVES. We communicate with them thousands of times a day. We speak with them, write with them, read them, and listen to them.

God is a God of words. He *spoke* the universe into being. He personally relates and communicates to us primarily through the written words of Scripture.

However, one Word (notice the capital *W*) reigns supreme above all. This Word isn't merely a grouping of letters that forms an element of speech. This Word is a Person. This Word is whom the apostle John praised to begin his Gospel:

> In the beginning the Word already existed. The Word was with God, and the Word was God. He existed in the beginning with God. God created everything through him, and nothing was created except through him. The Word gave life to everything that was created, and his life brought light to everyone. The light shines in the darkness, and the darkness can never extinguish it.
>
> JOHN 1:1-5

As Christmas approaches, let's consider the glorious Incarnate Word.

What's It Mean?

With the first three words of his Gospel, "In the beginning," John beautifully links the Word to Genesis 1:1. And who is this Word? It's none other than Jesus Christ, the immortal Son of God who existed in eternal triune glory with the Father and the Spirit before time began.

Two thousand years ago, the Son left heaven's holiness and majesty to shine his light into the oppressive darkness of a sin-stained world. He came to offer hope to the downcast and set the captives free. He came to save lost sinners like you and me. "The Word became human and made his home among us" (John 1:14).

Jesus fulfilled every word written in Scripture and obeyed every word the Father spoke (2 Corinthians 1:20). As the Incarnate Word, Jesus revealed everything the Father wanted to convey about himself. "Don't you believe that I am in the Father and the Father is in me?" Jesus said in John 14:10. "The words I speak are not my own, but my Father who lives in me does his work through me."

The Word entered our world—this is the glorious message of Christmas—and spoke words of life to us. Do you believe?

Now What?

Use your words to tell someone about *the* Word today!

Did You Know?

The Bible also refers to Jesus' existence before Creation in Hebrews 1 and Colossians 1.

DECEMBER 15

The Word became human and made his home among us.

JOHN 1:14

THROUGHOUT HISTORY, God has performed some astounding miracles:

- the creation of the universe
- the worldwide Flood
- the parting of the Red Sea
- the walls of Jericho falling
- Jonah surviving in the belly of the great fish

But the greatest miracle in history is captured in today's verse: "The Word became human and made his home among us." We call this the Incarnation. It literally changed the course of human history.

What's It Mean?

Throughout the Old Testament, God appeared to his people in many ways. He appeared to Moses in the burning bush; to the Israelites at Mount Sinai in thunder, lightning, and smoke; and to Ezekiel in a vision of a heavenly throne room so magnificent that it stretched the prophet's ability to describe it with human language.

But the Incarnation was completely different.

In the Bethlehem manger, God took on human flesh. This wasn't just a brief manifestation. The eternal Second Person of the Trinity became one of us and lived among us for more than thirty years. The Lord walked like us, talked like us, and looked like us. He got thirsty, hungry, and tired. He felt joy and pain. The human experience was his, excluding sin (Hebrews 4:15).

He was—wonderfully, miraculously, inscrutably—fully God and fully man. This is why Matthew declares in his Gospel that Jesus was "Immanuel, which means 'God is with us'" (1:23). There is beautiful mystery to Jesus' incarnate nature that we were never meant to fully understand this side of heaven.

Why on earth would God *come* to earth? Why would the Father send his Son to a world ravaged by sin, where his own image bearers—in the most fiendish of ironies—would reject, torture, and kill him?

That's exactly why. The answer lies within the question. He came because we needed him desperately. Because there was no other way for our sins to be atoned for. Because only the Father's love and the Son's sacrifice could restore the relationship sin had severed. He came to save us from ourselves.

Christ left heaven's glory and took on human flesh for you. What is there left to do but worship and adore the incarnated-now-glorified Savior? Praise his name!

Now What?

Read the apostle Paul's beautiful treatment of Jesus' incarnation, sacrifice, and glorification in Philippians 2:5-11.

Did You Know?

The Bible clearly states that anyone who denies that Jesus came in the flesh is a liar and a false prophet (1 John 4:2; 2 John 1:7).

DECEMBER 16

They grabbed him, dragged him out of the vineyard, and murdered him.

MATTHEW 21:39

IN MATTHEW 21, Jesus told an interesting parable at the Temple in Jerusalem. Here's what he said:

> A certain landowner planted a vineyard, built a wall around it, dug a pit for pressing out the grape juice, and built a lookout tower. Then he leased the vineyard to tenant farmers and moved to another country. At the time of the grape harvest, he sent his servants to collect his share of the crop. But the farmers grabbed his servants, beat one, killed one, and stoned another. So the landowner sent a larger group of his servants to collect for him, but the results were the same. Finally, the owner sent his son, thinking, "Surely they will respect my son." But when the tenant farmers saw his son coming, they said to one another, "Here comes the heir to this estate. Come on, let's kill him and get the estate for ourselves!" So they grabbed him, dragged him out of the vineyard, and murdered him.
> VERSES 33-39

What does this have to do with Christmas? Glad you asked! In its immediate context, Jesus spoke this parable against the hard-hearted religious leaders of first-century Palestine. But the Savior's words can help us appreciate the wonderful Christmas message even more.

What's It Mean?

The triune God—Father, Son, and Spirit—graciously determined a perfect plan for sinful humanity in eternity past. Then, "when the fullness of time had come, God sent forth his Son . . . to redeem those who were under the law, so that we might receive adoption as sons" (Galatians 4:4-5, ESV).

While Jesus' incarnation and earthly life unfolded in wondrous, mysterious real time for everyone else, nothing that happened shocked the Father or Son. When the Father (the landowner in Jesus' parable) sent his Son into the world, they knew how the story would unfold. They had written the script! (Notice also how Jesus used this parable to predict his death.)

That's what makes Jesus' incarnation so amazing. The Father willingly sent his Son to earth knowing what would happen because he had designed the plan. The Son willingly obeyed the Father knowing that the plan called for him to endure indignity, suffering, and death at the hands of wicked men.

Want to know the best part? Everything about this glorious, eternal plan was for *your* benefit.

Now What?
When you make plans this holiday season, remember your plans can change—unlike God's glorious, eternal plan of salvation in Christ.

Did You Know?
- Jesus told this parable two days before his arrest.

DECEMBER 17

The Lord himself will give you the sign. Look! The virgin
will conceive a child! She will give birth to a son and will
call him Immanuel (which means "God is with us").

ISAIAH 7:14

CHRISTMAS OFTEN BRINGS TO MIND dazzling trees, delicious treats, gift-wrapped goodies, festive carols, and a sacred manger scene. We certainly don't associate the holidays with rampant idolatry, divination, and the horrors of child sacrifice. Yet did you know these terrible pagan evils helped birth one of our most beloved "Christmas verses"?

This begs for an explanation!

In the late eighth century BC, King Ahaz of Judah made an alliance with Assyria, the most powerful empire in the world at the time, to help stave off attacks from Syria and Israel, rather than trusting in the Lord. Ahaz was a wicked ruler, leading Judah into all the horrible sins mentioned above. Through the prophet Isaiah, the Lord challenged Ahaz to put his trust in him: "Ask the LORD your God for a sign of confirmation, Ahaz. Make it as difficult as you want—as high as heaven or as deep as the place of the dead" (Isaiah 7:10-11).

When hard-hearted Ahaz refused, God responded through Isaiah in today's verse: "All right then, the Lord himself will give you the sign. Look! The virgin will conceive a child! She will give birth to a son and will call him Immanuel (which means 'God is with us')." Isaiah then predicted that before the child grew up, Assyria would destroy Syria and Israel and turn on Judah.

What's It Mean?

Some Bible interpreters believe that Isaiah's words were a "single fulfillment" prophecy, meaning it was fulfilled exclusively in Jesus. Other interpreters believe it was a "double fulfillment" prophecy, meaning it was fulfilled partially in Isaiah's day and completely in Christ. Either way, Jesus provided the ultimate fulfillment of Isaiah's prophecy, and Matthew pointed to this in his Gospel (Matthew 1:18-25).

Jesus' incarnation and virgin birth was the greatest miracle in history. Because he was not born by normal human procreation, Jesus did not inherit a sinful nature like the rest of us. He was "God with us"—fully God, fully man—and therefore could represent us perfectly as our sinless Savior.

Who could have conceived this? Who could have injected messianic hope into the corrupt reign of a depraved king? Who could have performed such wonders?

Only the God who loves you.

Now What?

Read about King Ahaz in 2 Kings 16 and 2 Chronicles 28, and the context of Isaiah's related messianic prophecies in Isaiah chapters 7–11.

Did You Know?

Ahaz's son, Hezekiah, was faithful to the Lord and one of Judah's greatest kings.

DECEMBER 18

The passionate commitment of the LORD of
Heaven's Armies will make this happen!

ISAIAH 9:7

IN THE EIGHTH CENTURY BC, the prophet Isaiah was a busy man. The
northern kingdom of Israel was mired in idolatry and utterly corrupt. The
looming Assyrian Empire would soon destroy it.

Isaiah constantly warned the nation of coming judgment if they did
not repent. But in Isaiah 9, the prophet inserted a glorious message of hope,
promising a coming Savior in one of the most beloved messianic prophecies
in Scripture:

> A child is born to us, a son is given to us. The government will
> rest on his shoulders. And he will be called: Wonderful Counselor,
> Mighty God, Everlasting Father, Prince of Peace. His government
> and its peace will never end. He will rule with fairness and justice
> from the throne of his ancestor David for all eternity. The passionate
> commitment of the LORD of Heaven's Armies will make this happen.
>
> ISAIAH 9:6-7

What's It Mean?

When Isaiah wrote this prophecy, Israel's rulers were exceedingly wicked,
leading the nation toward destruction. But the prophecy looked forward
to a time when God's anointed one would usher in an eternal Kingdom of
peace and prosperity.

How will all this be accomplished? By "the passionate commitment of
the LORD of Heaven's Armies" (today's verse). Who are "Heaven's Armies"?
They are the angelic warriors who filled a mountainside, vastly outnum-
bering the Aramean army in 2 Kings 6. They are the seraphim in Isaiah's
Temple throne room vision in Isaiah 6. They are the cherubim of Ezekiel's
Babylonian exile vision in Ezekiel 1. They are the mighty princes whose
cosmic battles against demonic forces are briefly described in Daniel 10:13.

They are the "thousands and millions of angels" who surround God's heavenly throne in Revelation 5:11. They are the "vast host" (Luke 2:13) who serenaded the Savior's birth and lit up the nighttime sky above Bethlehem.

"Heaven's Armies" are awesome indeed. Yet they *all* bow their knee to the Lord God Almighty.

This is the God who created you, not angels, in his image. This is the God who answered your sins with mercy and grace instead of just wrath and fiery retribution. This is the God who sent his Son to be your Prince of Peace.

The Lord of Heaven's Armies, who owns all authority and power, is passionately committed to your salvation!

Now What?

The next time you read a Bible story or sing a Christmas carol involving angels, remember who they worship.

Did You Know?

Anytime someone tried to worship an angel in Scripture, these celestial beings quickly redirected that adoration to God (Revelation 19:10; 22:8-9).

DECEMBER 19

Mary responded, "I am the Lord's
servant. May everything you have
said about me come true."

LUKE 1:38

TODAY'S DEVOTION is about one angel, two special birth announcements, and two completely different reactions.

One day, about two thousand years ago, the angel Gabriel appeared to Zechariah while he was performing his Jewish priestly duties and announced that he and his wife, Elizabeth, would soon have a special baby boy. This child, John the Baptist, would eventually herald the coming of the long-awaited Messiah.

Zechariah couldn't believe it.

"How can I be sure this will happen?" he asked. "I'm an old man now, and my wife is also well along in years" (Luke 1:18).

For his faithless response, Zechariah's speech was removed until shortly after John was born.

Six months after visiting Zechariah, Gabriel appeared to a young, unmarried girl named Mary to deliver another birth announcement—this one even more miraculous. When Gabriel told Mary that she would give birth to the Savior of the world, she, too, had questions. Unlike Zechariah's questions, though, hers seemed to stem from curiosity and wonder rather than disbelief.

"But how can this happen?" she said. "I am a virgin" (Luke 1:34).

"The angel replied, 'The Holy Spirit will come upon you, and the power of the Most High will overshadow you. So the baby to be born will be holy, and he will be called the Son of God'" (verse 35).

That was good enough for Mary!

"I am the Lord's servant," she replied. "May everything you have said about me come true" (verse 38).

What's It Mean?

Two incredible announcements. Two different responses. One sprung from a heart of skepticism. The other sprung from a heart of faith and willing submission to God's purposes.

This Christmas season, as you consider that the Most High sent his Son into the world to be the Savior of mankind through a Holy Spirit-empowered Virgin Birth that defies all human reason, what is your response? Is it skepticism? Like Zechariah, are you asking, "How can I be sure?" Or like Mary, are you displaying a faith and submission to God's purposes that will be rewarded?

Mary and Elizabeth were relatives, and when Mary visited Elizabeth after her angelic visit, Elizabeth joyfully prophesied, "You are blessed because you believed that the Lord would do what he said" (Luke 1:45).

May the same be said of you this Christmas season.

Now What?

If skepticism about Jesus has ruled your life until now, believe on his name in repentance and faith today! (See Mark 1:15; Acts 4:12; and Romans 10:9-10.)

Did You Know?

Zechariah regained his speech when he obediently named his son John (Luke 1:57-66).

DECEMBER 20

*At the name of Jesus every knee should bow, in heaven and
on earth and under the earth, and every tongue confess that
Jesus Christ is Lord, to the glory of God the Father.*

PHILIPPIANS 2:10-11, ESV

HAVE YOU EVER NOTICED how much emphasis we put on baby Jesus
during this time of year? With our carols, greeting cards, church plays, and
other seasonal hallmarks, we sometimes fawn over him as if he were still a
cute, chubby newborn cooing in his mother's arms.

There's nothing wrong with these Christmas traditions, as long as they
are a worshipful means to an end, not the end itself. Too often, however,
we tend to leave Jesus in the manger. But the eternal, incarnate Son of God
didn't stay in a Bethlehem feeding trough any more than he remained nailed
to a Roman cross or entombed in a Jewish grave.

In Philippians 2:6-11, the apostle Paul details Christ's progression of
glory:

> Though he was in the form of God, did not count equality with
> God a thing to be grasped, but emptied himself, by taking the form
> of a servant, being born in the likeness of men. And being found
> in human form, he humbled himself by becoming obedient to the
> point of death, even death on a cross. Therefore God has highly
> exalted him and bestowed on him the name that is above every
> name, so that at the name of Jesus every knee should bow, in heaven
> and on earth and under the earth, and every tongue confess that
> Jesus Christ is Lord, to the glory of God the Father (ESV).

What's It Mean?

In these verses, Paul masterfully takes us from Jesus' preexistent state, to his
incarnation, his humiliation, and his glorification. The Savior is certainly
not still wrapped in swaddling cloths, trapped in perpetual infancy!

At the height of Jesus' messianic exaltation, there's a handoff. Did you notice it? It's glory of God the Father!

Having achieved supreme victory, Jesus willingly gives all glory back to God. What an example of humble submission!

The Christmas story is about so much more than a cuddly baby in a manger. It's about the sinless Son of God becoming an atoning sacrifice for human sins—something no one else in history could or *would* do—then returning all his fame, honor, and praise back to the Father.

Now *that* is something to sing about!

Now What?

When you sing carols about Jesus' birth, remember the full purpose of his incarnation!

Did You Know?

- "Silent Night" is the most popular Christmas carol ever, with 733 copyrighted recordings from 1978 through 2014, according to *Time*.

DECEMBER 21

*After seeing him, the shepherds told everyone what had happened
and what the angel had said to them about this child.*

LUKE 2:17

HAVE YOU EVER WONDERED what would've happened if Jesus' birth
was a little more grandiose—something more befitting the King of kings
and Lord of lords?

For instance, what if Joseph and Mary were a regal couple and Jesus'
birthplace was an ornate palace nursery? What if the shepherds were a company of royal courtiers trumpeting the news from the castle ramparts and
official couriers on white steeds delivering the news through neighboring
towns and villages with great fanfare? What if the wise men were visiting
monarchs from allied nations coming to pay their respects?

Just imagine if Jesus' birth had played out this way!

But of course, it didn't. That's not the way God works, and it's certainly
not how the eternally ordained incarnation of his Son transpired. Not at all.

What's It Mean?

God sovereignly chose people and places who were much less ostentatious—
a poor carpenter as Jesus' earthly father; a nondescript girl as his mother;
and a dirty manger as his crib.

And what about the two groups who visited the Christ-child? One was
a grubby group of Jewish field workers. The other was a cohort of pagan
Gentile astrologers, likely from Persia. Neither group was whom you might
expect Scripture to highlight as the long-awaited Messiah's first worshipers.
Don't think the biblical spotlight on the shepherds and wise men is coin-
cidental. God loves flipping the traditional human script (1 Corinthians
1:27-28).

Meanwhile, Israel's leaders were largely oblivious to the Savior's arrival.
It's telling that God didn't send his angels to announce Jesus' birth to the
Jewish priests, Pharisees, or other members of the Sanhedrin. God's people

had been waiting, literally, millennia for the Messiah, and when he came, the religious establishment was too blinded by its religiosity to notice.

Look around you. In many ways, today's world is no different. Some people are ignorant to the Messiah. Elsewhere, religiosity abounds as people desperately try to earn God's favor while ignoring his Son. Ironic, eh?

Neither apathy nor religiosity pleases God. Rather, take a cue from the people whom Scripture highlights: those who rushed to worship the Savior, then hurried to tell others the good news. This Christmas, may we be like the shepherds and the wise men, who bore no pretense of piety, yet humbly worshiped the Messiah and joyfully told others.

Now What?
Tell an unbelieving friend or family member about the Savior who came to save them today!

Did You Know?
Israel's leaders identified Bethlehem as the Messiah's birthplace (Matthew 2:1-6) but apparently didn't connect it to Jesus!

DECEMBER 22

*Glory to God in highest heaven, and peace on
earth to those with whom God is pleased.*

LUKE 2:14

THINK OF THE BIGGEST, brightest Fourth of July spectacle you've ever
seen. Well, that was nothing compared to what the shepherds witnessed outside Bethlehem on the night of Jesus' birth.

The sky was still black and quiet, just like every night. Being a shepherd
had to be pretty boring, honestly, unless a thief or a predator was prowling
nearby.

Suddenly, an angel appeared to the shepherds, piercing the dark tran-
quility with heaven's brilliance and sending them cowering in fear. After the
angel announced the Savior's birth, the sky exploded into a dazzling display
of God's glory as a countless angelic army appeared, singing, "Glory to God
in highest heaven, and peace on earth to those with whom God is pleased!"

The angels' song was a beautiful chorus of praise to God. But it also
poses a fascinating question: How do you please God?

What's It Mean?

It doesn't take much to please us. Look what happens every Christmas
morning: we get *stuff* and we are pleased—very pleased!

That doesn't work with God. What can we give God that he doesn't
already own? As the apostle Paul said in Acts 17:24-25, "He is the God
who made the world and everything in it. Since he is Lord of heaven and
earth, he doesn't live in man-made temples, and human hands can't serve his
needs—for he has no needs."

Besides, God is holy—highly exalted above his creation, completely set
apart from sin, and perfectly righteous in all his ways. Left to ourselves, sinners like us cannot please him.

Yet today's verse says there are people who have peace with God because
he is pleased with them. How is that possible?

Because of Jesus!

He didn't stay "a baby . . . lying in a manger" (Luke 2:12). He lived a sinless life and died an atoning sacrifice on our behalf. His death made propitiation for us, turning God's wrath toward us into favor. "Therefore, since we have been made right in God's sight by faith, we have peace with God because of what Jesus Christ our Lord has done for us" (Romans 5:1).

We can't please God on our own. But Jesus pleased God on our behalf through his finished work on the cross. When we submit to Christ in repentance and faith, we please God and experience the peace the angels sang about more than two thousand years ago!

Now What?
Memorize Romans 5:1.

Did You Know?
The angels' song connects Jesus to Isaiah's prophecy about the "Prince of Peace" (Isaiah 9:6).

DECEMBER 23

Wise men from eastern lands arrived in Jerusalem, asking,
"Where is the newborn king of the Jews? We saw his star
as it rose, and we have come to worship him."

MATTHEW 2:1-2

DO YOU LOVE MYSTERIES? If so, you'll love today's devotion! It's all about a famous group of individuals whose brief but fascinating appearance in Matthew 2 has captivated our imaginations and spawned a whole cottage industry of Christmas-related songs and paraphernalia.

Yep, we're talking about the wise men.

The Bible doesn't give us many specifics about these mysterious travelers, but we can make some educated guesses based on a couple of scriptural clues. Today's passage describes them as "wise men from eastern lands." They were probably from Persia (modern-day Iraq or Iran). Our English phrase "wise men" comes from *magoi* in the New Testament's original Greek language. *Magoi*, or *Magi*, refer to magicians and astrologers—experts in ancient pagan religious rituals of sorcery, spells, incantations, astrology, etc. The wise men were stargazers, looking for cosmic signs to interpret the times. This was a big part of ancient near-Eastern religion (Daniel 2:2; 4:7; 5:5-8).

How did these faraway magicians know about a promised "king of the Jews" and connect him to "his star as it rose" (Matthew 2:2)? It's a mystery! Perhaps they knew about messianic prophecies, such as Numbers 24:17, from Old Testament scrolls that exiled Jews brought with them to Babylon after they were conquered and deported by King Nebuchadnezzar six hundred years earlier.

Did the wise men truly have saving faith in the Christ-child, or did they travel hundreds of miles to only satisfy mystic curiosities and superstitious fascinations?

Another mystery!

What's It Mean?

While so many questions surround the wise men, there is no mystery about God's love for you. He sent his Son to a dark, fallen world to redeem sinners like you to himself. Amazing love and mercy!

There's also no mystery about the child that the wise men worshiped. Jesus is God's promised Savior who came to save us.

Where is your faith right now? It's no mystery to God. He knows your heart. Bow down in humble adoration before the Savior. Present to him the gifts of your time and God-given talents.

Mysteries are for novels and movies. Your love for the Lord should be unmistakable!

Now What?

Read about the wise men in Matthew 2:1-12.

Did You Know?

The wise men didn't visit Jesus at the manger. That's a man-made tradition. Their trip likely took weeks after Jesus' birth.

DECEMBER 24

Thank God for this gift too wonderful for words!

2 CORINTHIANS 9:15

WHAT'S THE WORST CHRISTMAS present you've ever received? A fruitcake? An ugly sweater with a hideous pattern that *may* have been hip in 1982? A shiny glass tree ornament shaped like a toilet bowl plunger? (Yep, they make them—google it.)

Or has anyone ever played the trick on you where they give you a huge gift-wrapped box, but you open it only to find it's filled with progressively smaller, empty boxes, until you get to a really small box with the gift inside? And who doesn't have a well-meaning relative who always gives you something crazy each year?!

Half of the fun of giving and receiving presents is the anticipation of not knowing what's to come. Christmas gifts are not always what they seem, and they are not always what we expect.

In many ways, God's Son, Jesus Christ, was the same way. But he was infinitely greater than anyone could have ever anticipated.

What's It Mean?

It sounds cliché, but make no mistake: Jesus is the greatest gift the world has ever known. Through his Son, God has done something for sinful humanity that—apart from the regenerating work of his Spirit—we neither wanted, expected, nor knew we needed (Ephesians 2:1-9).

Ever since the Fall, God had promised a coming Savior (Genesis 3:15) and continued proclaiming this message of messianic hope through the Old Testament prophets. But when Jesus was born, the world barely noticed. When Jesus started his public ministry, the world largely rejected him. Jesus was a Messiah whom the world wasn't expecting. As the apostle Paul wrote in 1 Corinthians 1:23, "When we preach that Christ was crucified, the Jews are offended and the Gentiles say it's all nonsense."

It's no different today. Everywhere, people are hurting, looking for answers, and desperately drowning in their sins. God holds out the same gift of salvation to all who would believe in his Son.

Most people disregard God's gift completely. Some people curiously begin to unpeel the wrapping, take a peek inside, but ultimately leave the gift alone—nothing more than a fleeting interest. A few receive the gift with faith and thanksgiving, overwhelmed at God's mercy and grace toward them through Christ, and live a life in joyful obedience to him.

Which one of these describes you?

Now What?
Give a gift to someone in need this week, just like God gave you the gift of his Son.

Did You Know?
Ultimately, every good gift you receive in this life—both spiritual and material—is from the Lord (James 1:17).

DECEMBER 25

*Unto you is born this day in the city of David a
Savior, who is Christ the Lord.*

LUKE 2:11, ESV

MERRY CHRISTMAS!

Today is the big day—the day that everyone has been waiting for
all year! No matter who you are, how old you are, or where you're from,
Christmas is special.

There is no other annual holiday when so many people across the earth
gather together to celebrate with family and friends. Some celebrations are
sacred; others are secular. Regardless, Christmas brings people together and
creates traditions in ways that few other things can.

Speaking of traditions, have you dashed down to see what's under the
tree and yanked your stocking off the mantle yet? If we're completely honest, one thing we love most about Christmas is the gifts! Who *doesn't* love
getting stuff?

A gift is a wonderful thing. It's something willingly given to someone
without expectation of payment. This, of course, is a beautiful description
of God's love toward us.

What's It Mean?

God's love toward us is hard to describe because it's so big. You can't wrap it
up and put a holiday bow on it. But it's real, it's amazing . . . and it's completely free.

You did nothing to earn God's love. You can't work for it like a pay-
check, merit it like a Boy Scouts badge, or qualify for it like a sports championship. God gives it to you as a free gift of his grace through faith in his
Son, Jesus Christ.

God doesn't expect you to pay for the gift of his love. You *can't!* That's
why Jesus came. You were utterly helpless to earn righteousness before God
on your own. So Jesus did it for you through the Cross.

When you trust in Jesus, God lovingly showers you with gifts from his storehouse of heavenly riches:

- unending supplies of his mercy and grace (Hebrews 4:16)
- the indwelling of his Holy Spirit (1 Corinthians 3:16)
- freedom from sin's bondage (Romans 6:6)
- access to spiritual peace that "exceeds anything we can understand" (Philippians 4:7)
- eternal life in his presence (John 3:16)
- and so much more!

God's love is like opening a gift of spiritual treasures that never ends. It's truly the gift that keeps on giving!

On this very special day, as you give and receive gifts, remember the supreme demonstration of God's love toward you, expressed through "a Savior, who is Christ the Lord" (today's verse). He is our greatest gift!

Now What?

Prayerfully meditate on the verses listed above about God's gifts to us.

Did You Know?

God's love for us is so great, biblical writers strained to adequately describe it. See Psalm 103:11 for an example.

DECEMBER 26

This is a revelation from Jesus Christ, which God gave him to show his servants the events that must soon take place.

REVELATION 1:1

JOHN NEARLY FAINTED.

You would've, too, if you had seen what he saw.

The old apostle, possibly in his nineties by then, was exiled on the small Aegean island of Patmos for his faith. One Sunday, the risen Christ appeared to him in overwhelming glory, causing John to fall "at his feet as if I were dead" (Revelation 1:17).

Jesus gently strengthened his disciple and gave him a marvelous vision, telling John to "write in a book everything you see" (verse 11) as a witness to a network of churches in Asia Minor. John's vision is what we now call the book of Revelation—perhaps the most mysterious, debated book of the Bible.

Mystery? Debate? Sounds like the perfect topic for a five-day series of devotions!

What's It Mean?

Revelation is a book of both prophecy (predicting future events) and apocalypse, which stems from the Greek term *apokálypsis*, meaning "unveiling," "disclosure" or (drum roll, please) "revelation"!

In other words, through the book of Revelation, God not only reveals future events that will one day take place (prophecy), but he also has unveiled remarkable events that are occurring (and will continue to occur) in the unseen spiritual realm until Jesus returns.

The biggest question about Revelation is how to interpret it. Jesus gave John visions of cataclysmic disasters, mysterious creatures, wicked beasts, talking eagles, bowls of wrath, rivers of blood, and much more.

Phew!

What is literal and what is symbolic imagery? Have any of Revelation's prophecies already been fulfilled? If so, which ones? How do we make sense of it all? It's enough to drive a seminary student nutty!

While Bible scholars debate those questions, the following points are refreshingly clear:

- God will direct the end times perfectly according to his sovereign plan (Revelation 1:1; 5:1-14; 10:5-7; 11:16-18; 22:6).
- Through faith, obedience, and patient endurance, believers will achieve victory over evil (Revelation 2:26; 14:12; 21:7).
- One day, Jesus will return to destroy all evil and condemn the wicked to eternal punishment (Revelation 19:11-21; 20:7-15) while bringing the righteous to their eternal reward (1 Thessalonians 4:16-17).
- God will replace the current, corrupted universe with a new heaven and new earth, free of all sin and death (Revelation 21:1–22:5).
- God will reign forever in his perfect Kingdom, as believers worship him and enjoy his new creation always (Revelation 22:1-5).

Praise God for the book of Revelation!

Now What?
Read the book of Revelation.

Did You Know?
Apocalyptic literature such as Revelation, Daniel, and Ezekiel were particularly helpful to God's people during intense tribulation because it strengthened their faith with future hope.

DECEMBER 27

*Those who are victorious will sit with me on my throne, just
as I was victorious and sat with my Father on his throne.*

REVELATION 3:21

FROM 1965 TO 1973, the United States engaged in perhaps the most
unpopular conflict in the nation's history, the Vietnam War.

With the Cold War against the Soviet Union simmering, the United
States and its ally, South Vietnam, fought a long, grueling war against
North Vietnam in the jungles of Southeast Asia, costing nearly three mil-
lion lives, including more than fifty-eight thousand American soldiers. The
war was ultimately unsuccessful. America withdrew its troops in 1973, and
Communist forces took control of South Vietnam in 1975.

If the overall failure of the war had been known from the start, would
America have gotten involved in the first place? Probably not. Of course, no
nation can ever know the full outcome of a conflict before it gets involved.
Humans don't possess that kind of knowledge.

But God does. In the book of Revelation, he reveals some incredible
details about an age-old conflict that has been raging since Creation. It's a
cosmic battle of good vs. evil, and yet the great Champion was determined
in eternity past.

We are talking, of course, about God's marvelous salvation plan for his
chosen people through his Son, Jesus Christ.

What's It Mean?

Mankind has been in rebellion against its Creator since Creation. Satan and
his spiritual forces of evil have been trying to subvert God's plan longer than
that. Yet the sovereign Lord God Almighty has always been in control, and
his plan is culminating perfectly according to his will, as Revelation attests.

In his fury, Satan has tried everything to thwart God's plan, but Jesus
dealt him a fatal blow through his death and resurrection (Genesis 3:15; 1
John 3:8). He continues to wreak plenty of havoc, but only within the bounds
of divine allowance as a creature in its death throes (Revelation 12:12).

One day, the sky will break open and the King of kings and Lord of lords will crush all evil with nothing more than words from his mouth (Revelation 19:11-16). Then, as today's verse indicates, Jesus will share the eternal glory of his triumph with all his followers. Amazing!

This should encourage you when you are feeling weary or discouraged. Don't lose heart! As a believer, your victory in this great spiritual battle has been assured—purchased by the powerful blood of Christ.

Stand strong, have faith, and rejoice!

Now What?

Check out what Colossians 2:15 and Hebrews 2:14 have to say about this subject.

Did You Know?

Satan will be thrown into hell (Revelation 20:10), along with all other evil-doers (verse 15).

DECEMBER 28

*I saw a new heaven and a new earth, for the old
heaven and the old earth had disappeared.*

REVELATION 21:1

WHAT WILL HEAVEN BE LIKE?

It's a question that intrigues us, sells books, generates movies, and
sparks debate. With great fascination, we read the apostle Paul's account in
2 Corinthians 12:4 when he "was caught up to paradise and heard things
so astounding that they cannot be expressed in words, things no human is
allowed to tell."

As Christians, we realize that this world is not our home. We yearn to
know what our eternal dwelling place will be. Yet there is great mystery surrounding it. But God *has* given us clues. He has told us just enough to make
our hearts dance with anticipation!

Let's discuss this fascinating topic.

What's It Mean?

First, we must dispel a few false ideas about heaven:

- We will not get bored after we've been there awhile. If you think that,
  you think too lowly of God's holiness and his eternal plans for us!
- We will not be little winged cherubs floating around the clouds
  strumming harps all day. (Now that *would* get boring!)

Those ideas are found nowhere in the Bible. But here are some glorious
truths about heaven:

- The place believers go now when they die (sometimes called "paradise"
  or the "intermediate state") is different from our final eternal dwelling.
  Their soul immediately goes to be with the Lord (Luke 23:43;
  2 Corinthians 5:8). Then when Christ returns, they will receive a
  perfect, imperishable resurrected body (1 Corinthians 15:50-53).

- Our eternal dwelling place will be the new heaven and new earth (today's verse). God's plan is not to annihilate the current universe, but to *purify* it from sin's curse and *renew* it (Romans 8:19-22; 2 Peter 3:10-13).
- There will be no more sin, sorrow, or death in the new creation (Revelation 21:4).
- We will reign over God's renewed creation, delighting in its perfect goodness (Revelation 22:5).
- Best of all, God will dwell once more among his people, allowing us to see him face-to-face and worship him perfectly, as we were originally created to do (Revelation 22:3-4).

If heaven were an ocean, we have just examined a few drops of water. The amount of spiritual riches and blessings that await us is unfathomable!

Now What?
Don't try to fill any voids of information about heaven with conjecture. Instead, search God's Word for answers, be content with divine mystery, and joyfully await the Savior's return!

Did You Know?
There will be no sun in the new creation. God's glory will fully illuminate it (Revelation 22:5)!

DECEMBER 29

They will see his face.

REVELATION 22:4

WHEN SIN ENTERED THE WORLD in Genesis 3 and Paradise was lost, our relationship with God changed drastically. Sin brings shame, judgment, and death. Sin separates us from perfect, intimate fellowship with our Creator.

We see this over and over again in Scripture. Moses asked to see God's full glory, and God refused—for Moses' own protection. "You may not look directly at my face," God told him, "for no one may see me and live" (Exodus 33:20). Jacob (Genesis 32:30), Gideon (Judges 6:22-23), Manoah (Judges 13:21-22), and Isaiah (Isaiah 6:5) all saw various forms of God and marveled that they lived through it.

God instructed the Jewish high priest to burn incense when he entered the Tabernacle/Temple's Most Holy Place on the Day of Atonement to purposefully obscure the priest's view of God's holy presence above the Ark of the Covenant so he "[would] not die" (Leviticus 16:13).

In all these instances, the message was unmistakable: sinful humanity cannot see the Lord God Almighty in his full, unrestrained glory and live. His sheer majesty, power, and holiness would overwhelm us.

But one day, all that will change.

What's It Mean?

When God renews all things in the new heaven and new earth, he will completely destroy sin and its curse (Revelation 22:3). No more fear, anger, or shame! No more separation, judgment, or death! Everything that is currently broken in the world will be made right.

Most beautifully, God will restore perfect fellowship with his chosen people. Paradise lost will become paradise restored! Look again at today's Scripture passage: we will see God's face. Let that sink in: *WE WILL SEE GOD'S FACE!*

What was once off-limits to us because of our rebellion will be

727

wonderfully ours to behold. We will be fully sanctified, clothed in glorified, resurrected bodies thanks to the Lord Jesus Christ—completely free of any encumbering sin for all eternity.

No longer will we faint or cower in fear in God's presence. Instead, we will flock to him (Revelation 21:24), joyfully delighting in the full, overwhelming radiance of God's glory for all eternity.

What a promise!

Now What?

Read the Old Testament stories referenced above of God's limited accessibility. Then compare them to our heavenly reality of Revelation 21:1-4 and 22:1-4!

Did You Know?

God is a spirit (John 4:24), so he doesn't have a human face like ours. When the apostle John says we "will see his face," he was probably attempting to describe the indescribable with personification—attributing human characteristics to something nonhuman. God's glory and magnificence are far beyond human description!

728

DECEMBER 30

He who is the faithful witness to all these things says, "Yes,
I am coming soon!" Amen! Come, Lord Jesus!

REVELATION 22:20

WAIT, WAIT, WAIT.

Sometimes, it seems like all we do in life is wait. What's more, whatever it is we're waiting for is often pretty mundane.

We wait in line at the grocery store. We wait at the doctor's office. We wait to board our plane at the airport. In traffic, we wait . . . and wait . . . and wait.

Phew! That's a lot of waiting.

For two thousand years, Christians have been waiting for something infinitely more glorious—the return of the Lord Jesus Christ. Yet one day, the Bible says, all our waiting will be over.

After Jesus had given the apostle John all the visions in the book of Revelation, he declared, "Yes, I am coming soon!" (today's verse).

What's It Mean?

Is there a greater promise found in Scripture? As Titus 2:13 says, all believers "look forward with hope to that wonderful day when the glory of our great God and Savior, Jesus Christ, will be revealed."

Our minds race with excitement as we consider Jesus' second coming and everything that God has revealed to us about heaven. Yet we know we've only been given a fleeting peek behind the curtain of eternity—and this makes our imaginations soar.

So we joyfully echo the words of John and say, "Amen! Come, Lord Jesus!"

Come, Lord Jesus, and transform this sin-stained world.

Come and wipe away all our tears.

Come and rid the world of loneliness.

Come and wipe out doubt, fear, and suffering.

Come and abolish bigotry, slavery, and all oppression.

Come and eradicate hatred and murder.

Come, Prince of Peace, and establish your eternal reign of harmony.

Come and bring us into the joy of the Father.

Come and make us shine perfectly beside you.

Come and let us see your nail scars and touch where the spear pierced your side.

Come, Crucified and Risen One, and show us your full glory.

Come so that we may fall down and worship you.

Come and take us before the throne of God that we may behold his face.

Come and let us worship you and the Father alongside a chorus of angels forever.

Come and reveal heavenly pleasures that our earthbound minds cannot fathom.

Yes, Son of God, you are worth the wait. But we long to see you. We long to be home—truly home.

Come, Lord Jesus!

Now What?
Read 2 Timothy 4:8 for Christian encouragement in the waiting.

Did You Know?
When Jesus returns, he will reward people according to their faithfulness toward him or rejection of him (Revelation 22:12).

DECEMBER 31

He causes us to remember his wonderful works.
How gracious and merciful is our Lord!

PSALM 111:4

YOU MADE IT!

Another year is in the books. Most likely, it had plenty of highs
and lows. That's the way life goes. But now, the year is over, and a new
one is about to begin. You've also made it to the end of this devotional.
Congratulations—and Happy New Year's Eve!

Since ancient times, humans have celebrated the turning of the annual
calendar. In America, we fill New Year's Eve with college football games,
parties, the famous ball drop in New York City, and many other festivities.
No matter what kind of celebrations you have planned for today, New Year's
Eve is a perfect time for reflection. And what better to reflect on and celebrate than God's blessings to you over the last twelve months?

What's It Mean?

Whether you've had a great year or a tough one, there is so much to be
thankful for. God's goodness is always abundant. Philippians 4:4 says,
"Rejoice in the Lord always; again I will say, rejoice" (ESV). And psalms such
as Psalm 30:4 are continually exhorting us to "Sing to the LORD, all you
godly ones! Praise his holy name" for all his mercy and grace toward us.

In the Old Testament, God's people frequently set up memorial stones
and other markers to commemorate God's mighty deeds. Today, we don't
need to erect altars or earthen pillars, but we should set aside time to reflect
on God's "wonderful works" (today's verse). People who drift from the
Lord are those whose hearts grow cold and thankless toward him. But those
whose faith is vibrant have a joyful, grateful spirit.

New Year's is also a traditional time for resolutions. How do you want
to grow spiritually this year? Spending more time in prayer? Growing in
your knowledge of God's Word? Maturing in a particular fruit of the Spirit
(Galatians 5:22-23)? Finding a way to serve others inside or outside the

church? Whatever it is, commit it to prayer and do it out of a worshipful heart toward your Creator.

As this year—and this book—draws to a close, the hope is that you've received even a small glimpse of God's holiness, his indescribable majesty, and his overwhelming love for you through his Son, Jesus Christ.

May this new year be your best one yet for God's glory as you remember his goodness toward you!

Now What?

Start a journal of God's "wonderful works" so that you can gratefully reflect on them a year from now!

Did You Know?

NYC's Times Square ball made its inaugural drop in 1907.

About the Author

Joshua Cooley is a *New York Times* bestselling author and a full-time children's minister. He has authored or contributed to eleven books, including *The One Year Devotions with Jesus, Heroes of the Bible Devotional,* and *The Biggest Win: Pro Football Players Tackle Faith.* In 2018, he teamed with Super Bowl LII MVP Nick Foles to coauthor the star quarterback's bestselling memoir, *Believe It: My Journey of Success, Failure, and Overcoming the Odds.* He lives with his wife and four children in Durham, NC. You can visit his website at joshuacooleyauthor.com.

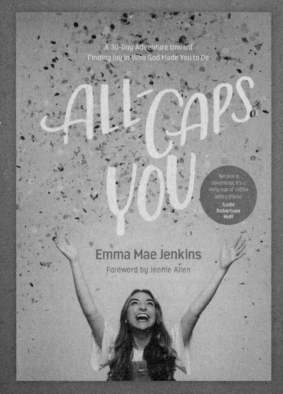

GOD'S STORY
FROM EDEN TO ETERNITY

ILLUSTRATED BY DC AND MARVEL ARTISTS

wander
An imprint of
Tyndale House
Publishers

CP1634